Collection Management Basics

Recent Titles in
Library and Information Science Text Series

Collection Management Basics

Sixth Edition

Previous editions entitled
Developing Library and Information Center Collections

G. Edward Evans and Margaret Zarnosky Saponaro

Library and Information Science Text Series

 LIBRARIES UNLIMITED

AN IMPRINT OF ABC-CLIO, LLC
Santa Barbara, California • Denver, Colorado • Oxford, England

Library of Congress Cataloging-in-Publication Data

Evans, G. Edward, 1937–
  [Developing library and information center collections]
  Collection management basics / G. Edward Evans and Margaret Zarnosky Saponaro. — Sixth edition.
        pages cm. — (Library and information science text series)
  Includes bibliographical references and index.
  ISBN 978-1-59884-863-2 (hardback) — ISBN 978-1-59884-864-9 (paperback) — ISBN 978-1-61069-259-5 (ebook)
  1. Collection development (Libraries) 2. Libraries—Special collections—Electronic information resources. I. Saponaro, Margaret Zarnosky. II. Title.
  Z687.E918 2012
    025.2'1—dc23   2012008872

ISBN: 978-1-59884-863-2 (case)
       978-1-59884-864-9 (pbk.)
EISBN: 978-1-61069-259-5

16 15 14 13 12   1 2 3 4 5

This book is also available on the World Wide Web as an eBook.
Visit www.abc-clio.com for details.

Libraries Unlimited
An Imprint of ABC-CLIO, LLC

ABC-CLIO, LLC
130 Cremona Drive, P.O. Box 1911
Santa Barbara, California 93116-1911

This book is printed on acid-free paper ∞
Manufactured in the United States of America

We wish to dedicate this edition
to all the students,
who will begin developing the collections of the future,
and their instructors who will assist them in their learning.

As a personal dedication:
to the young reader Katie Saponaro

Contents

Illustrations

Preface

Developing Library and Information Center Collections, the precursor to this text, first appeared in 1979. Since that time, the world of librarianship has changed dramatically as did the successive editions of the title. However, after 30-plus years and incremental changes, we believed that the text required radical revision in order to represent the current face of collection management. Although technology and an up and down economy have been the primary drivers of the changing face of librarianship, most of the basic functions remain constant. Nevertheless, the manner in which those functions are carried out are very different from those of the early 1980s. Thus we believe a total restructuring of the work was required and that restructure warrants a new title: *Collection Management Basics*.

The chapters in this text are grouped into three broad categories: background, process, and special issues in collection management. The first two chapters provide the reader with the background or context on collection management, its history, and its philosophy. The next chapters cover assessing user needs, selecting and acquiring materials to meet those needs, and assessing the collection itself. The remainder of the text focuses on special issues of concern for collection management practitioners, including collaborative collection development, digital materials, preservation, legal issues, and ethics. Each chapter includes sidebars with suggested resources, issues to watch, "points to ponder," and the like.

This work would not have been possible without the contributions of a great number of individuals. We are especially grateful for the comments, suggestions, and insight of our three advisory board members, all of whom have brought a unique perspective and insight to the work: Dr. Sandra Hughes-Hassell, Professor, University of North Carolina School of Library and Information Science; Dr. Carol Sinwell, Dean of Learning and Technology Resources, Northern Virginia Community College; and Dr. Virginia Walter, Professor and Chair, Department of Information Studies, University of California, Los Angeles Graduate School of Education and Information Studies. You will see some of their many contributions to this work appearing throughout the text as "From the Advisory Board" sidebars. We would also like to extend a very special thanks to Karen E. Patterson, Education and Information Studies Librarian, University of Maryland Libraries, for her assistance. The input of each of these individuals greatly improved the manuscript. However, they are not responsible for errors in content.

G. Edward Evans
Flagstaff, AZ

Margaret Zarnosky Saponaro
Rockville, MD

1
Introduction

When someone confidently projects the disappearance of the
physical library *and* a bright future for librarians, I suspect a
background in special libraries—where that might make sense.
                                              —Walt Crawford, 2009

Despite the persistence of print, large-scale digitization is
transforming the library world.
                                              —Dan Hazen, 2010

Although both of our opening quotations might appear pessimistic, both of
the above authors were confident about the future of libraries, as are we.
Optimists are in agreement that the world of librarianship is in a state of
transformation. The first edition of this book appeared in 1979. Each edition
since that point reflected the ever-changing environment in which libraries
were operating. Two of the major driving forces causing the changes were,
and still are, technology and an up and down economic environment. This
edition may well be the last edition in a paper-based format, as technological
changes are also changing the face of the publishing industry.

In the article from which the opening quotation above was taken, Walt
Crawford noted that "We will continue to see revolutionary predictions
based on oversimplification, bad economics, infatuation with technology,
and failure to appreciate people. Librarians and library supporters must be
ready to challenge unlikely projections, analyze faulty economics, and assert
the need for choice and the importance of both history and the present" (p.
59). We believe that a major reason for optimism regarding the future of
libraries lies in their history. Not because libraries are inherently "good," but
rather because they have been in existence for thousands of years and have
a track record of adapting to technological changes.

Longevity of Libraries

Given the fact that the earliest known libraries, over 4,000 years ago, were dealing with clay tablets and today's libraries are handling both paper-based and digital formats suggests technology will not cause the death of libraries. There are a host of examples where devotees of this or that technology have predicted the demise of this or that activity because of the new technology. Certainly there are cases of where the technology did in fact displace an activity, at least in terms of the activity's original purpose. One such example is the internal combustion engine. In developed countries, the horse has been displaced as a primary mode of transportation; nevertheless, people still ride horses for pleasure, enjoy horse races, and even still refer to the power of a vehicle as horsepower.

Unlike the horse, libraries have become a valued part of the social fabric. When a society has valued and supported an institution for thousands of years, it is very difficult to displace that institution. Throughout time, complex societies around the world have had several constant values or beliefs about libraries:

- It is a physical place.
- It is a collection of what is deemed to be important information.
- It encourages reading and reading promotion.
- It organizes those materials and provides assistance in their use.
- It preserves the information for future users.

This last point is important; libraries are the only institutions to have long-term preservation of important societal information as part of its expected function. Libraries connect people to the world of information and knowledge. People use that information or knowledge to improve their lives and society, and, in the process, they create new knowledge that requires preservation. Whether that information was contained on a clay tablet or in a digital file, libraries perform the above functions and, we believe, will continue to do so well into the future.

In today's environment, the talk is about technology and electronic information. Although "information" is what libraries have always been about, for many people, libraries are linked to and equated with paper-based books. That image has not been valid for a great many years. Library collections are and have been a mix of information formats for almost 100 years. (Public libraries in the United States started collections of recorded music in the very early 20th century. Photographs have also been part of collections for almost as long.)

Throughout history, libraries have added or adapted many technologies in order to carry out their societal role of collecting, organizing, and preserving information. Early Middle Eastern societies stored their information on clay tablets and created "libraries" to house the collection. At some point in history, there was probably concern when a new technology—the scroll—came on the scene, in that it did not seem very permanent. That concern was obviously overcome, as Egyptian libraries' collections were papyrus scrolls, while Roman libraries' collections were vellum scrolls. When the codex or book appeared, another transition was necessary.

During the Middle Ages, the vellum manuscript books were so costly to produce and preserve that books were literally chained down—the ultimate in a noncirculating collection. The development of paper-based books and the printing press presented another new technological challenge for libraries. It is likely that just like the times of the scroll versus clay tablets, there was more than a little skepticism about the impact of books on the need for libraries. Some people may have gone so far as to suggest there would be no need for libraries as anyone could afford to own many books and create their own personal library. Although personal libraries did arise, libraries became even more important as the volume of information increased. Just as for those of us who enjoy reading and owning paper-based books, in time we run out of space to store them and money to purchase everything we would like to read. It is then that we turn to libraries to fill in the gaps. Even e-readers have a finite amount of storage space, and libraries are offering the chance to gain access to digital titles we'd like to read but not keep.

The turmoil in today's publishing industry is almost the same as it was in the 15th century. Just as the printing press shifted access to information from a few to many people in the mid-17th century, we are seeing a similar shift today. That shift is from libraries to end users. Libraries are becoming intermediaries, rather than short-term storehouses, of information. Joseph Janes (2010), in his technology column for *American Libraries*, wrote about various formats and the library's role in making information available to users. He noted "that, in an ever-more locked-down, rights-managed, pay-five-times-for-the-same-thing world, we're the only ones really invested or even interested in maintaining the concept of the 'public book'" (p. 37).

The 20th century brought with it an expansion in the formats libraries collected—microforms, sound recordings, CD-ROMs, video recordings, and so forth. By the end of the century, electronic resources had become important components in library collections, while other formats continued to be collected. Thus, libraries have changed and adapted over time, but their basic functions have remained constant. As Dan Hazen (2010) noted: "'Content'—a category that encompasses everything to which a library enjoys ready physical or digital access regardless of ownership—is central to all that we do" (p. 119). There is and will continue to be a major role for libraries in the digital age who engage in digital curation or preservation. As we will discuss later in this text, preservation is not going to go away; in fact the issues related to long-term digital information preservation today are even greater than those of paper-based materials.

Check These Out

Perhaps one of the most comprehensive recent histories of libraries is the three-volume set titled *The Cambridge History of Libraries in Britain and Ireland*, edited by Peter Hoare (Cambridge: Cambridge University Press, 2008). Volume 1 covers up until 1640, volume 2 covers 1640 to 1850, and volume 3 covers 1850 to 2000.

Michael Harris's *History of Libraries in the Western World*, 4th edition (Lanham, MD: Scarecrow Press, 1999) is an excellent summary of library history.

A recent and easy to read title about publishing, the book, and society is Ted Striphas's *The Late Age of Print: Everyday Book Culture from Consumerism to Control* (New York: Columbia University Press, 2009).

Is Reading Dying or Already Dead?

Public libraries have historically been a major resource for people interested in reading and learning for personal enjoyment. Educational libraries (academic and school) had some sense of an ongoing mission as class assignments would require some library usage. However, just as some pundits have been predicting the demise of libraries, there have also been suggestions that reading, other than work or school related, is a dying activity. That decline, coupled with advances in technology, would surely doom libraries to the "ash heap" of history. At least in terms of reading, pre-2009 National Endowment for the Arts (NEA) survey data showed a downward trend in "recreational" reading. On the other hand, some data reported in 2010 (Varvel 2010) suggest that perhaps the level of reading by the general population was not as low as the NEA surveys reported.

Varvel (2010) reported the results of 2009 Public Library Data Service (PLDS) survey. In addition to reviewing the basic survey data, he provided some analysis of data from 403 public libraries that had completed every PLDS survey between 2002 and 2008. There are two particularly interesting sets of data in that analysis that relate to reading. One set indicated that during that timeframe, circulation in those libraries increased from 8.87 to 10.19 circulations per year per capita. The other statistic indicated that collection turnover (circulations per items in the collection) rose from 2.83 to 3.25.

As has been true of the predictions that advances in technology will cause libraries to disappear, reading for pleasure apparently is neither dying nor dead. A 2009 survey by the NEA suggests the doomsayers were wrong, or at least premature. Dana Gioia, chairman of the NEA stated in the preface to the report: "[This] new report, documents a significant turning point in recent American cultural history. For the first time in over a quarter-century, our survey shows that literary reading has risen among adult Americans. . . . Best of all, the most significant growth has been among young adults, the group that had shown the largest declines in earlier surveys" (p. 1). Certainly two surveys alone do not constitute a trend, especially in a time of a major economic downturn. However, the fact that young people indicated a sharp rise in their recreational reading is highly encouraging for the future.

The NEA survey defined literary reading as a person having read a novel or short story, poetry, or play during the preceding 12 months (p. 3). The survey included one question about "literary" reading and one about reading in general (results for both showed increases). Wording for the general question was, "With the exception of books required for work or school, did you read any books during the last 12 months?" (p. 11). Neither question made reference to the format (paper or digital) of the material read.

What were some of the survey results?

- The absolute number of literary readers has grown significantly.

- Literary reading has increased most rapidly among young adults.

- Literary reading has risen among whites, African Americans, and Hispanics.

- For the first time in the survey's history, literary reading has risen among both men and women.

From the Authors' Experience

Many years ago, while in high school, Evans worked as a page in his local branch public library. The branch manager had strong views as to what type of reading a person should engage in: fiction or nonfiction. Each Friday afternoon, the manager calculated the weekly number of circulated fiction and nonfiction titles. She would be rather grumpy if fiction came out ahead, both in terms of staff and users' preferences. The staff began to keep a running total so that if fiction was leading the way, they could find something else to do on Friday afternoons, away from the circulation desk, where the tally was taking place. For Evans, the always available task was shelf reading the picture books; he spent many hours in that activity during his two-year tenure as a page.

Clearly, at least one librarian did not place a high premium on literary reading.

- Greater reading of fiction is responsible for the new growth among adult literary readers.

- *Most individuals who read online materials also reported reading books.* (Italics added.)

Libraries' Societal Value Beyond Preserving Information

During times of economic distress, serious budget shortfalls for individuals and organizations, and an ever-growing demand for organizations to demonstrate effectiveness and accountability, libraries must be ready to demonstrate their "worth" to parent organizations. In the not too distant past, about the only libraries that were called on to prove their value were those in a business or corporate environment. Today, all types of libraries can and do benefit from having data available regarding the fact that their benefits to the overall organization—city, county, state, school district, society—far outweigh their costs to maintain and operate.

Historically libraries have been viewed as a public good, rather like motherhood and apple pie. Most people probably still hold that view from a theoretical point of view. However, when the reality of financial hard times hits, practicality displaces most theoretical values. Difficult economic times almost always lead to leaner library budgets and, as Jill Grogg (2009) noted, "Budgets are shrinking and, often, one of the first cuts libraries make is to their collections budgets" (p. 127). Collection management personnel should always be concerned with stretching collection funds as far as possible, but in bad times, it becomes imperative to do so.

Libraries receive the vast majority of their funding indirectly from taxpayers and student fees. Further, the taxes and fees apply to everyone, not just those who make use of the library. Carol Tenopir (2009) made the point that "When perceptions of the importance of a product or service decrease, but the price of the product or service increases, a gap is formed. . . . That gap puts pressure on libraries to justify their budget in the future or to decrease their expenditures" (p. 20). For those who make little or no use of libraries, the gap that had existed in the best of times grows wider when the economy goes bad. This is when hard facts rather than anecdotal data become very important. Roxanne Missingham (2005) made the following points regarding the need to solid data. She noted that "Over the past two decades research and activity on library value has adopted new approaches and increased in its scope and implementation—harnessing increasingly sophisticated methods developed in metrics" (p. 142). She later went on to remark, "If these can be developed they have the potential to enable objective measurement of the match between funding and service models and targets for return on investment" (p. 156).

In the past, and to a much greater extent today, libraries have used output measures to demonstrate they were making effective use of the funds provided. Some examples of such measures were and are gate counts (people entering the facility), total circulation, cost per item circulated, titles purchased, cost per title purchased, reference questions answered, and user surveys. Although useful and perhaps interesting to some people, such measures do not truly address the value to the user or the people providing the funding. Did we get more back in value than we put into the service? That is the question libraries must answer today. It is the ultimate assessment and accountability question.

Why does the demonstration of library value matter to those involved in collection management beyond the obvious desire to have one's place of employment continue to be operational? There are at least two very important reasons. First, the two primary elements in a library's operational budget are salaries and funds for the collections/access to content. Between them, they represent 70 to 80 percent of the total budget. Of the two, salaries are largest and have been representing a growing percentage, while collection funds have shrunk as a percentage and often in total dollars. Nevertheless, collections/access funding is still very significant.

Second, and perhaps most important, is that collection content plays a key role in determining a library's benefit, value, and return on investment for the parent to the parent organization. One of the most obvious benefits, from a public library point of view, is the information or data it makes available to businesses. In addition, community leaders are seeing and learning that libraries can provide significant benefits that go beyond dollars and cents and what most people think of as library services. Beth Pollard (2008) noted, "Local government managers are finding that libraries are able to bridge economic, educational and social divides that have continued to challenge their communities" (p. 18). Pollard noted four activities or services that related to her point, to which we have expanded with further examples: public libraries are often the only free source for gaining access to the Internet (or information in general), a place where school-age children can come to learn to read (or establish a love for reading) or for assistance with their homework and adults can get assistance in language and other learning activities (GED), a civic and economic "anchor" for people and businesses, and a place where the city, county, and state services can inform and interact with people (pp. 18–19).

One of the most frequently employed and "more sophisticated" methods of demonstrating organizational value with hard data is return on investment (ROI). ROI is a methodology for assessing whether an organization/department/activity produces more value/income/profit than it expends on the outcome/product/service. Libraries have taken to using this approach to help bolster their contention that they provide a tangible value for their parent organization. Public libraries have been engaged in ROI efforts for some time now. Reported ROI data show that the average return from a

---

Check This Out

A good Website that lists a growing number of state and community public library ROI surveys and reports is the "Economic Impact of Libraries" site from the Wisconsin Department of Public Instruction: http://dpi.wi.gov/pld/econimpact.html. We also included several such studies in the Suggested Readings section at the end of this chapter.

---

public library to a community is $4 or more for every dollar the community expends on the library. Stephanie Zurinski's (2007) article about public libraries' impact on small communities (populations of fewer than 10,000 people) provides some surprising ROI results. She noted that "Small libraries operate with minimum staff and small budgets. Yet, the average ROI for the small libraries in west Texas is $12. The communities served by these small libraries receive an average value of $407,322 in return for the dollars they can afford to invest" (p. 127).

Libraries supporting educational activities have been less quick to see the need for such data; however, a few have undertaken ROI studies of one or two of their activities. One such study in terms of academic libraries is that of Paula Kaufman and Sarah Barbara Watstein (2008). Their study of public services showed that there was a four to one return to the University of Illinois Urbana-Champaign on its expenditures related to public service activities (p. 227).

Another of the "sophisticated" methods, if somewhat less fiscally based in its final data than ROI, is contingent valuation (CV). CV is an economics-based technique for estimating the value of a good or service based on alternate prices. Essentially, it is a method of assessing a person's preference for a good or service at different prices.

Perhaps the most detailed CV study published in the open literature is Philip Hider's (2008) article. The project goal in this case was to assess what dollar value citizens of Wagga Wagga (Australia) placed on their public library. Heads of households were asked a series of six questions related to how much they would pay in an annual fee for library service. The basic question was the same, except the dollar amount increased from a low of $2 to a high of $20. The mean dollar (Australian) figure was $8.27 (p. 258)—converted into 2010 U.S. dollars that would be $6.99. This amount comes rather close to the $4 or $5 figure previous public library ROI studies have found.

Content vs. the Package

As we noted earlier, content is what libraries are about. One hundred years ago, or even only 50 years ago, people did not think about the content of a book or journal article as being "information." It is only relatively recently that people began thinking about and treating (pricing) information as an economic good or product. People in general, and even librarians on occasion, do not differentiate between the content of a "package" (a book for example) and the packaging itself when thinking about the price. "Why does this cost so much" comes out rather often without any real regard for anything other than the package.

There are two economic aspects to the sale of information: (1) the cost of packaging the information, and (2) the cost or value of the information contained in the package. When the package is a book, newspaper, magazine, DVD, or CD, for example, people tend to think of the package as the information. An individual confronted with an online system where one pays for information by the "screen" and yet cannot retain a hard copy or one who is considering paying $50,000 for a quarterly newsletter subscription quickly begins to appreciate the differences between information and package value.

The net effect of the shift in thinking creates challenges for libraries and society. Many problems relate to handling the economic aspects of information and access to that information (often written about in terms of ownership versus access). Although a detailed discussion of these challenges is far beyond the scope of this book, we do mention them where they have an influence on collection management.

Information is a difficult "product" to price. It is almost unique in overall character in comparison to other products and services that economic pricing models were designed to address. Perhaps the most special, if not unique, characteristic is that unlike other economic commodities, the buyer shares information with the seller even after the sale. Sellers always retain the information in some form, if only in a person's memory. When I sell you my car, I have your money and you have the car. I no longer have access to or use of the vehicle. When you purchased this book you gained access, in a physical form, to the information we put into the text. We, the publisher, and probably one or two others have a share of the price you paid. However, unlike the car, we and the publisher have access and legal use rights to the material in the book you acquired. We all share the information. That fact creates some challenging pricing issues. It also creates challenges for decision making when it comes to collection building.

Another characteristic that is unlike most other products is that information is not scarce. In fact, often there is too much available and sorting through the good, the best, and the useless is time consuming and frustrating for people. Collection management personnel in a very real sense assist people by doing some of that sorting by deciding what and what not to add to the library collection. Alternatively, most conventional pricing models are based, to some extent, on the concept of scarcity or at least the ability to control the amount of a product that is available at one time.

Some of the other special characteristics of information that can impact pricing and people's perception of its value are that it is expandable, contractible, and can be manipulated (such as combined or reinterpreted). An industry has existed for some time based on one or more of these characteristics—abstracting and indexing services and now services that provide full-text articles from a variety of journals in proprietary databases. Each of the firms engaged in these activities employ a variety of pricing structures. We explore such pricing models in more depth in Chapter 5.

Libraries' Bright Future

Libraries have a very long track record of serving society while adjusting to changing circumstances. We believe the future is positive for libraries *if*. There is a very big if, or set of challenges, at present confronting the field. These challenges are surmountable, if the best minds of our professions commit to thinking about all of the challenges and the means to overcome them. Based on our experience, reading the professional literature, and many conversations with colleagues, we suggest the following are necessary for libraries to achieve a bright future.

The greatest challenge is to effectively do what libraries have always done—change. What is different this time around is the pace and nature of adaption to changes must be far faster than at any time in the past. Incremental change will not do; the adjustments libraries make must be radical in nature and extend across all the activities libraries now perform. Anything less dramatic is unlikely to lead to long-term success. The broad nature of library functions will very likely remain, such as managing collections. However, the how, where, when, and who carries out the associated activities are probably going to look rather different in 20 years. What follows are 15 areas where we believe the changes are most likely to take place. As noted above, the elements that follow are drawn from our experiences, from reading the literature, and most importantly by far from talking with our many colleagues in the field.

First and foremost, in order to engage in significant, if not radical, change the field must reconsider its basic assumptions, concepts, and purposes. We need to think long and hard about what we currently do in this digital and technological world that is no longer necessary or effective. A starting point for such thinking for many libraries would be their mission statements and long-range planning documents (strategic plans). Lee Price (2010) made the following observation about strategic plans and change: "The strategic plan should be flexible enough to deal with change. Furthermore, the multiyear strategic plan should be converted each year into a new document with tasks and goals specific to the year" (p. 26). Sound strategic planning is a time-consuming activity and, all too often, there is a tendency once the task is done to set it aside until there is again pressure to develop a plan. This urge to "shelve" the plan until it needs to be reviewed again should be resisted.

Because almost all libraries are a small part of a larger organization, their mission statements as well as strategic and long-range planning documents are expected to be in "harmony" with the parent body. It is not all that uncommon for the parent organization to mandate such plans with the caveat that the library plans reflect the larger picture. Whatever the motivation for such library planning materials, there is a tendency for them to reflect what is currently being done rather than thinking along new and innovative lines. What we need now is new thinking and innovation.

Our basic business models also require scrutiny. We have certainly witnessed a shift in thinking about our collections over the past 15 to 20 years—there are probably other business areas that may well benefit from a careful examination. In the past, most libraries thought in terms of purchasing or owning the vast majority of resources their service communities were thought to need. Today, it is less and less about ownership and more and more about providing access to information regardless of who owns it. That trend will likely increase well into the future. Although the shift has not saved libraries money, it has led to great increases in what the library's end users have available to them. We explore shifts in other business functions in terms of collection management in Chapter 5.

Technological adjustments are obvious to almost everyone. Although not a new change in a broad sense, the fact that the digital world has become so pervasive makes this the field's most pressing challenge. Not only has technology become completely intertwined in people's lives, but the speed at which new developments arise seems to increase daily. From a library point of view, new technologies come on the scene faster than the staff can effectively assess the last development, much less realistically test what it can do in the real world. Technology is part of all young people's lives; Linda

From the Advisory Board

Two examples of joint service efforts noted by Advisory Board member Carol Sinwell are those in San Jose (California) and Virginia Beach (Virginia). In California, San Jose State University partnered with the city public library to build a shared facility for both collections. George M. Eberhart detailed this venture in his 2003 *American Libraries* piece titled "San Jose's New Joint-Use Library Sets a Record" (34, no. 8: 16). A similar joint-use project between the City of Virginia Beach and Tidewater Community College was under way at the time this volume was being prepared. For more information on this project, see: http://tinyurl.com/2fkkvw2.

Advisory Board member Sandra Hughes-Hassell and her colleague Jacqueline C. Mancall wrote a chapter on the subject of collaborative efforts as reflected in the school library setting. Their work is titled "Developing a Collaborative Access Environment: Meeting the Resource Needs of the Learning Community," found in *Student Learning in an Information Age: Principles and Practice*, edited by Barbara K. Stripling (pp. 21–359, Englewood, CO: Libraries Unlimited, 1999).

Uhler and Becky O'Neil (2010), in writing about service to young adults noted, "Ask teens how they'd feel about removing technology from their daily lives, and you'd probably hear a comparison to losing a body part" (p. 472). These are the people who will soon be making judgments about how or even whether to fund library services. It behooves the profession to stay on top of technological developments and to intelligently implement those that are appropriate.

Libraries have been among the most proactive organizations in seeing the potential benefit of computer technologies and integrating technology into daily activities. Today, the majority of libraries have at least some computer capability. For example, a small library today can purchase a small, but surprisingly capable, ILS (Integrated Library System) for about $1,000 (in the United States). Although it took more than 60 years for the integration of just this one technology into library daily operations, today the integration is so complete that for many libraries, should the system "crash," work comes to almost a complete stop. Many current ILS systems are capable of quickly generating useful reports for collection management purposes such as assessment (more about this in Chapter 6).

It seems as if almost daily one reads about this or that new application or technology that will "revolutionize" the digital world. The reality is that only a few live up to more than half the early claims; and even fewer come close to revolutionizing anything. The professional literature has examples of libraries making an early jump on the "bandwagon" for a new technology (for example, e-readers of the late 1990s and early 2000s) only to painfully learn the move was much too soon. This may be an area where being at the top of a technological curve is much more prudent than being on the cutting or bleeding edge.

Digitization and technology are so closely related that a person well might conclude there is no distinction between the two terms. However, digitization is a narrower concept. Technology, broadly thinking, is the application of "tools" to an activity. (An example is using a computer to assist in accessing information for a library user.) Digitization is the process of converting analog information into a digital format (an example is the Google Books Project, discussed in Chapter 9). Currently, there is little clarity as to

---

From the Authors' Experience

One of Evans' consulting projects took place in 1998 at a private university with a very extensive distance education program. The institution's Academic Vice President (AVP) contracted with Evans to look into student complaints regarding the on-campus library.

Based on the complaints submitted to the AVP as well those the library received, it was clear that the number one issue was the quality of the library collections. Using the library's ILS, a report was generated that represented 60 percent of the database records with the information arranged by the copyright date in the record. That report took less than one hour to generate. Trying to generate such a report manually would have taken weeks, and probably never would have been undertaken.

The report showed that the newest copyright date in the sample was 1984. Essentially no new titles had been added to the collection in over 13 years. Collection funds had been diverted to providing document delivery services to the distance learners.

The outcome of the project was the library received a substantial increase in funding that was earmarked for use in meeting on-campus student needs.

---

who should digitize what and even less clarity regarding who will be responsible for the long-term preservation of the digitized material. We will be returning to this issue and challenge throughout this book.

Lampert and Vaughan (2009) commented, "With digitization becoming the norm in many institutions, the time is right to consider what factors contribute to the success and rapid growth of some library digitization programs while other institutions find digitization challenging to sustain" (p. 116). Certainly digitization is more often than not an academic library activity; however, some larger public libraries have engaged in such projects. We suspect as the methods and "challenging" aspects of the endeavor are worked out, more and more public libraries will engage in creating "community repositories" similar to what their academic counterparts are now doing. We look at repositories in more detail in Chapter 8.

Another issue that today's libraries are facing is the perception that while there may be a future for the virtual library, the library as "place" is dead or dying. Carnegie and Abell (2009) made the point that "Spaces and interfaces intersect with modern and postmodern narratives as the library vies to establish its identity as a legitimizer and purveyor of knowledge in the information age. Through architecture, the library comes to speak the language of hybridity to reassert its relevance and reposition itself" (p. 242). In writing about the changes implemented over time at the Seattle Public Library, the authors ended their essay by stating, "The library has not simply adapted and survived; it has altered the rules and changed the game, positioning itself not on the periphery but at the center of the information age" (p. 257).

Public libraries are unlikely to disappear as a physical facility in the foreseeable future. As noted earlier, at the very least they have become the primary place where individuals who are unable to afford Internet access find free access and assistance. Libraries of all types are offering more services that bring people together. For some neighboring academic libraries, there is a possibility in hard economic times that "collaboration" may lead to the closure of one of the facilities. One example of such a move took place in 2010 when the Coconino County Community College merged its library with that of neighboring Northern Arizona University. It was a merger due to economic conditions, not a function of the institution thinking its students did not need access to a physical library. The challenge is for libraries to do as the Seattle Public Library has done and reposition themselves as one of the "key players" in the information game. One way some libraries are changing their approach to service and through those changes the public perception of what a library is, is by creating new or redesigning existing spaces to be "gathering" places for social, cultural, technological, and other activities and where people have access to staff trained in the use of information and technology.

Related to the concept of library as place is the fact that almost every library, but particularly academic libraries, have substantial collections of what some individuals refer to as "legacy collections"; legacy at least in the sense of print-based materials. In our opening section of this chapter, we noted that one of the significant roles of libraries is the long-term preservation of what is deemed important societal information and records. Even if all such information is digitized at some long distant time, the material will still require some type of physical facility. Harloe and Williams (2009), in writing about the college library, commented that "One transition that college libraries face in the 21st century involves creating access to high-quality collections in both digital and print forms while reconfiguring existing space to allow for active learning and engagement, as well as study and research" (p. 514).

Service to the entire user population is a fundamental value underlying all library activities and programs. For a rather long time the heterogeneous composition of that population has been an issue. How much service do we provide a single component of the population? Do we do this at the expense of another component, especially if one of the two is not a heavy user of library services? How do we reach an underserved group? Such questions and many more have grown in importance as the population mix has become increasingly diverse. (We look at the issues of assessing information needs and diverse populations in more detail in Chapter 3.)

There is another form of diversity that will, in the short term, present a difficult challenge for libraries. That diversity relates to technology and the very real divide that exists within service populations: digital natives and digital immigrants. Digital natives (20 years old and younger) grew up in a digital world in which technology was ever present. They have very different expectations regarding technology; essentially, it will be there when they want it, it will work, and it will be almost instantaneous in response to their needs. The balance of people are individuals who have had to make an effort to learn to use technology and are not always quick to accept the need for or value of a new technology, much less take the time to learn some of the basics of that technology. The library challenge is twofold: how to provide meaningful services to both groups given very limited funding and how to create and maintain effective staff working relationships on a staff consisting of the two groups who have such different views about the nature and role of technology in daily life.

In order to hold existing users and attract new users, libraries will have to find ways to enhance the users' experiences within the analog and digital arenas. Just meeting the basic user expectations will be a challenge in a period of low funding. Going beyond that level will take some very serious innovative thinking. Aaron Schmidt (2010) noted that "Every touchpoint, or place that someone can come into contact with your library or its services, is fair game for evaluating how it fits into the experience you're giving your users" (p. 28).

Related to enhancing users' experiences is another user-focused issue—improving their information literacy skills. By doing this, libraries can also help people become more effective in "researching" issues in their daily lives in today's information world, not just in academic or scholarly activities. Although the American Association of School Librarians (2008) *Learning4Life* document was prepared in terms of the school library context, it applies to all libraries and users. The document states in part: "The future compels us. We know that the future belongs to those who can adapt quickly to the ever-changing landscape that has moved from a need for industrial workers to information and knowledge workers to conceptual workers. Students live in a global community and will compete in a global marketplace" (p. 5). Libraries who choose to engage in activities that do assist people in becoming effective members of a global community and able to compete in a global economy will provide a valued service to their communities. Certainly academic and school libraries have a reasonably long history of instruction programs for their users. For decades, most of that instruction focused on the effective use of local resources and some instruction in how to do research for school-related projects. The current trend is on acquiring lifelong information skills.

A specific collection management issue that requires attention is how to best balance the needs of print-based and digital resources (blended collections). No one doubts that the shift to digital is permanent; however, it also appears likely that print is going to continue to be an element in collection decisions for at least the foreseeable future. Jankowska and Marcum (2010) provided a concise summary of the challenges for libraries when it comes to handling the need for blended collections. They noted:

> Developing a blended model of print and digital resources supported by social networking services has raised a major concern that sustainable progress of academic libraries is threatened by a variety of factors such as: developing and preserving print and digital collections, supplying and supporting rapidly changing technological and networking infrastructure, providing free services to the public, maintaining growing costs of library buildings and lowering libraries 'ecological footprint.' (pp. 160–161)

Collaboration, something libraries have engaged in to some extent for more than 70 years, is likely to become ever more important. One could claim that the Library of Congress's practice of sharing cataloging data was an early cooperative venture that would push the starting point of collaboration back to the turn of the 20th century. This increase in importance will take place if for no other reason than collaborative activities can allow institutions to share costs; however, it must be remembered such activities rarely reduce overall cost. Without much doubt, consortia are a fact of life for many libraries, at least for acquiring access to electronic databases. (We explore cooperative collection-building activities in Chapter 7.)

In the future, we will likely see an increase in collaborative efforts at the individual level as well as institutionally. Academic and school librarians who have collection management responsibilities have a history of at least attempting to work closely with instructors regarding resource needs. Often, for those of us who have done this, we get the feeling it is a one-way street—our reaching out only to find little in the way of useful feedback. The authors do not believe it is due to a lack of interest on the part of most instructors, rather it is just one of the realities of teaching—so much to do, so little time, while still maintaining a semblance of a personal life. Kristi Jensen (2009) noted that "Liaisons and selectors are continually challenged to identify new opportunities to engage faculty in order to gain information about their research and teaching that will help libraries provide better collections and services" (p. 117). Her points apply to more than academic libraries, as even public libraries have influential community "gatekeepers" who, if one can engage them, are invaluable in developing high community interest collections. Again, we explore the issues of creating meaningful and useful collections in more detail in Chapters 3 and 4.

Thinking about and developing new ways of carrying out library services and activities is one thing. Getting those ideas funded and implemented is another. We believe that if librarians take a leadership role as "change agent" both in their library and parent institutions and work hard at being an effective advocate of change, they will be successful in getting the necessary funding and implementation support. Library leaders in the 21st century must be able to present compelling visions of the future in nonconfrontational terms—as advocates. As Kramer and Diekman (2010) noted, "Advocacy is about educating stakeholders using the best available evidence and it is an ongoing process" (p. 27).

Without much debate, one of the largest challenges facing libraries in 2011 and over the near term is financial in nature. Addressing all of the above issues will require additional funding. Where that funding will come from is hard to predict. Norman Oder (2010), in writing the *Library Journal* report about its budget survey, commented that "The economic crisis, coupled with continued demands on libraries for traditional services such as books and programming, portends significant, perhaps permanent, realignment regarding library spending" (p. 44). Compounding the funding challenge is that as the profession starts assessing its "sacred cows," engages in innovative thinking about how to reposition libraries, and takes part in ever more complex collaborative efforts, simply relocating existing funds will not do the job. Libraries must be seen as a core value.

Assuming the field achieves some, if not most, of the above, the future will indeed be bright. It will also mean those of us working in libraries will need more and new skills in order to be effective. Libraries will have to find a method of providing training in the new skills as well as greater depth in existing ones. Professional schools will need to rethink their curriculums and offer a variety of new subjects. For individuals in collection management, one can see a hint of what is to come in Sarah Pomerantz's (2010) comments, "In recent years, there has been a proliferation of new library positions, such as electronic resources (ER) librarian, licensing librarian, and digital collections librarian which include responsibilities related to acquiring electronic resources and maintaining, troubleshooting, and training users of these collections" (p. 40). We cover the issues related to such positions in various chapters throughout this book.

Points to Keep in Mind

- Libraries have had a very long history as part of society's institutional fabric.
- Libraries have also had a solid track record of being able to adapt to changing societal conditions as well as to technological developments.

- While long-term preservation has been, and is likely to continue to be, an important component of libraries' worth to society, they also have other immediate tangible values as well.

- Data suggest that reading for enjoyment is rising in the United States. That bodes well for the future of libraries who provide access to both print and digital books.

- Another factor that suggests that public libraries have a long-term future is there is a growing body of data that demonstrates society receives an excellent return on its investment in public library operations, as much as $12 for every $1 spent.

- What everyone, the general public and the profession alike, must keep in mind is that it is the content rather that the package that is of greatest importance. The idea of content rather than the package sometimes is overlooked with the image of libraries as a "book place." This occurs when the general public and the profession's focus is on technology at the expense of content.

Works Cited

American Association of School Librarians. 2008. *Learning4Life*. Chicago: American Association of School Librarians. http://www.ala.org/ala/mgrps/divs/aasl/guidelinesandstandards/learning4life/document/l4lplan.pdf.

Carnegie, Teena A.M., and John Abell. 2009. "Information, Architecture, and Hybridity: The Changing Discourse of the Public Library." *Technical Communication Quarterly* 18, no. 3: 242–258.

Crawford, Walt. 2009. "Futurism and Libraries." *Online* 33, no. 3: 58–60.

Grogg. Jill E. 2009. "Economic Hard Times and Electronic Resources." *Journal of Electronic Resources Librarianship* 21, no. 2: 127–130.

Harloe, Bart, and Helene Williams. 2009. "The College Library in the 21st Century." *College & Research Library News* 70, no. 9: 514–516.

Hazen, Dan. 2010. "Rethinking Research Library Collections: A Policy Framework for Straitened Times, and Beyond." *Library Resources and Technical Services* 54, no. 2: 115–121.

Hider, Philip. 2008. "How Much Are Technical Services Worth? Using the Contingent Valuation Method to Estimate the Added Value of Collection Management and Access." *Library Resources and Technical Services* 52, no. 4: 254–262.

Janes, Joseph. 2010. "The Public Book." *American Libraries* 41, nos. 6/7: 37.

Jankowska, Maria Anna, and James W. Marcum. 2010. "Sustainability Challenge for Academic Libraries: Planning for the Future." *College & Research Libraries* 71, no. 2: 160–170.

Jensen, Kristi. 2009. "Engaging Faculty in Collection Development Through Utilizing Online Survey Tools." *Collection Building* 28, no. 3: 117–121.

Kaufman, Paula, and Sarah Barbara Watstien. 2008. "Library Value (Return on Investment, ROI) and the Challenge of Placing a Value on Public Services." *Reference Services Review* 36, no. 3: 226–231.

Kramer, Pamela K., and Linda Diekman. 2010. "Evidence = Assessment = Advocacy." *Teacher Librarian* 37, no. 3: 27–30.

Lampert, Cory, and Jason Vaughan. 2009. "Success Factors and Strategic Planning: Rebuilding an Academic Library Digitization Program." *Information Technology and Libraries* 28, no. 3: 116–136.

Missingham, Roxanne. 2005. "Libraries and Economic Value: A Review of Recent Studies." *Performance Measurement and Metrics* 6, no. 3: 142–158.

National Endowment for the Arts. 2009. *Reading on the Rise: A New Chapter in American Literacy.* Washington, DC: National Endowment for the Arts. http://www.arts.gov/research/readingonrise.pdf.

Oder, Norman. 2010. "Permanent Shift?" *Library Journal* 135, no. 1: 44–46.

Pollard, Beth. 2008. "Libraries: Partners in Sustaining Communities." *Public Management* 90, no. 2: 18–22.

Pomerantz, Sarah. 2010. "The Role of the Acquisition Librarian in Electronic Resources Management." *Journal of Electronic Resources Librarianship* 22: 40–48.

Price, Lee. 2010. "On the Vital Importance of Strategic Planning." *Public Libraries* 49, no. 2: 25–27.

Schmidt, Aaron. 2010. "The User Experience." *Library Journal* 135, no. 1: 28–29.

Tenopir, Carol. 2009. "The Value Gap." *Library Journal* 134, no. 12: 20.

Uhler, Linda, and Becky O'Neil. 2010. "Technology Isn't Just for the Experts." *Voice of Youth Advocates* 32, no. 6: 472.

Varvel, Virgil E. 2010. "Characteristics and Trends in the Public Library Data Service Report." *Public Libraries* 49, no. 3: 36–44.

Zurinski, Stephanie. 2007. "The Impact of Small Community Libraries." *Texas Library Journal* 83, no. 3: 126–127.

Suggested Readings

Association of College and Research Libraries. 2010. *Value of Academic Libraries: A Comprehensive Research Review and Report.* Researched by Megan Oakleaf. Chicago: Association of College and Research Libraries. http://www.acrl.ala.org/value/.

Chowdhury, Gobinda. 2010. "From Digital Libraries to Digital Preservation Research." *Journal of Documentation* 66, no. 2: 207–223.

Digital Curation Centre. http://www.dcc.ac.uk.

Funk, Carla J. 2008. "Using Standards to Make Your Case: Examples from the Medical Library Community." *New Library World* 109, nos. 5/6: 251–257.

Genoni, Paul. 2007. "Libraries, the Long Tail and the Future of Legacy Print Collections." *Libres* 17, no. 1: 1–10.

Horava, Tony. 2010/2011. "Collection Management and Sustainability in the Digital Age: Chasing the Holy Grail." *Against the Grain* 22, no. 6: 22–26.

Indiana Business Research Center. 2007. *The Economic Impact of Libraries in Indiana.* Bloomington, IN: Indiana University. http://www.ibrc.indiana.edu/studies/EconomicImpactOfLibraries_2007.pdf.

Linn, Mott. 2010. "Cost-Benefit Analysis: A Primer." *Bottom Line* 23, no. 1: 31–36.

List, Cara, and Faye Chadwell. 2011. "What's Next for Collection Management and Managers?" *Collection Management* 36, no. 2: 79–88.

McMenemy, David. 2007. "What Is the True Value of a Public Library?" *Library Review* 56, no. 4: 273–277.

Mezick, Elizabeth M. 2007. "Return on Investment: Libraries and Student Retention." *Journal of Academic Librarianship* 33, no. 5: 561–566.

Pabērza, Kristine. 2010. "Towards an Assessment of Public Library Value: Statistics on the Policy Makers' Agenda." *Performance Measurement and Metrics* 11, no. 1: 83–92.

Priestly, Beatrice. 2008. "An Argument on Why the City Should Contribute to the Library Budget in a Means Similar to Corporate Funding of R&D." *Library Administration and Management* 22, no. 3: 125–129.

Steffen, Nicolle, Zeith Lietzau, Keith Curry Lance, Amada Rybin, and Carla Molliconi. 2009. *Public Libraries, A Wise Investment*. Denver, CO: Library Research Service. http://www.lrs.org/public/roi/.

2
From Selection to Collection Management

Book selection is the first task of librarianship.
—Lionel R. McColvin, 1925

In this book I have tried to describe the best way to manage
library collections. Providing a good and appropriate collection
is, I believe, the library's primary mission, and to fulfill this
mission librarians must devise and carry out a comprehensive
collection management program based on a sound understanding of library materials.
—William Wortman, 1989

Training collection development librarians, whether they are
new to the profession or to the institution, is a critical and
complex process that has far-reaching effects on libraries and
their communities.
—Allison Cowgill, 2008

How libraries approach the creation and preservation of their collections
has evolved over time. Our opening quotations provide a hint as to how
much collection creation has changed in the past 90-plus years. Two major
trends in collection building have occurred over the past 125-plus years. One
is how the process takes place and the tasks involved. The second is what
the underlying goal for collection content should be.

In terms of the first trend, the process has become increasingly complex
and the people involved in decision making have been changing. Collections
have become ever-more expansive and inclusive in terms of appropriate content as well as formats. The shift in how the process takes place has moved

from accepting gifts of books to assessing a wide variety of formats (print, media, and digital), acquiring physical ownership or access rights, and (at times) determining the proper equipment needed to access the information (microfilm readers, computers, etc.). There has also been a shift to librarians being the primary decision makers regarding what to place in the collection and how long to retain it.

The second trend, in the United States, has been a shift from "gate keeping" (controlling what people could read) to open access. In 1908, American Library Association (ALA) President Arthur Bostwick gave a speech titled "Librarian as a Censor" that reflected the early view of librarians' role in creating a collection. In it, he noted, "The collection for the free use of the general public and especially collections intended for circulation. . . . It is to these [books] that the censorship to which I have alluded may properly apply and upon these it is generally exercised. . . . We may thus reject it on one of three following grounds: badness—that is undesirable moral teaching or effect; falsity—that is, mistakes, errors or misstatement of fact; and ugliness—matter or manner offensive to our sense of beauty, fitness, or decency" (p. 114). That view is in sharp contrast to today's professional position, seen in the ALA "Freedom to Read Statement" (2004) that states, "We believe that every American community must jealously guard the freedom to publish and to circulate, in order to preserve its own freedom to read. We believe that publishers and librarians have a profound responsibility to give validity to that freedom to read by making it possible for the readers to choose freely from a variety of offerings" (http://www.ala.org/ala/aboutala/offices/oif/statementspols/ftrstatement/freedomtoreadstatement.pdf). (We explore intellectual freedom and censorship in more detail in Chapters 4 and 12.)

Concepts and Terms

There are a variety of terms commonly used to refer to the concept of creating information collections for organizations and the transfer of that information. The common denominator is the notion that information must be controlled as well as organized in some manner. From a strictly library perspective, terms such as collection building, collection development, and collection management are all used to describe this process. The authors prefer the term *collection management* because it reflects all the aspects of what is required for the effective creation and maintenance of today's library collections from beginning to end. We get into the specifics of what is entailed in collection management later in this chapter.

Other types of organizations also have information management or transfer issues; some of the terms used in these environments are: information resource management, knowledge management, content management, and records management. The terms cover similar activities and differ primarily in organizational context. *Information resource management*, as used today, relates to any organizational context, often without any centralized collection of materials, in which the information resource manager is responsible for identifying and making available to appropriate staff members both internal and external sources of information. Practitioners in computer science and information systems often define *knowledge management* as the "management of objects that can be identified and handled in information systems" (Brogan, Hingston, and Wilson, 2002, p. 2). Martin White (2002) defined *content management* as software that "provides a platform for managing the creation, review, filing, updating, distribution, and storage of structured and

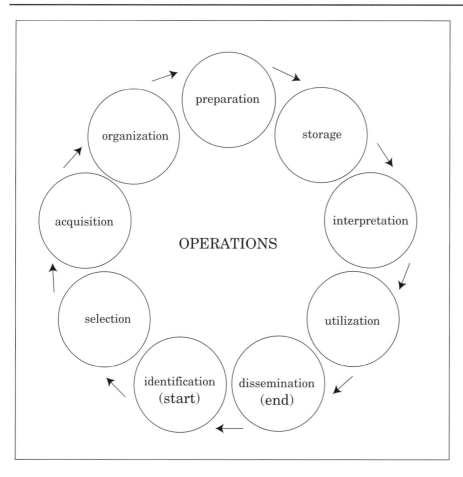

ADMINISTRATION

Figure 2.1. Information Transfer Process

unstructured content" (p. 20). *Records management* is the process of handling the working records of an organization with an emphasis on retention, retrieval, and access issues. No matter which term is most familiar to you, the resulting goal of each is to provide accurate information in a timely and cost-effective manner to all members of the service community.

Regardless of type, one of the primary purposes of libraries is to assist people in locating and accessing useful information. Figure 2.1 illustrates the process involved in accomplishing that purpose. The basic elements are the same regardless of organizational context.

There is the *identification* stage, during which designated personnel sort through available information resources to identify appropriate from inappropriate resources. In most instances, there is vastly more appropriate information available than the library can acquire much less house. Thus, there is a need to *select* the most useful information to *acquire*. After acquisition, the library adds value to that information by *organizing* it in some manner. That process is followed by some form of the physical or digital *preparation* of the resource for *storage* and access; the goal of organizing and preparation activities is to ensure the easiest possible access for the end users. Users often need assistance in identifying and accessing desired information from staff members (*interpretation*). Finally, users draw on the accessed material to assist them in their activities or work (*utilization*), and on occasion *disseminating* the outcome of their work to the internal or external environment, or both. If the transfer process is to function properly, there must be procedures, policies, and people in place to carry out the necessary *operational* steps. As always, there must be coordination and money for the staff to operate as effectively as possible; this is the administrative/managerial aspect of information work.

As in prior editions of this book, we define *collection development* as "the process of identifying the strengths and weaknesses of a library's materials collection in terms of patron needs and community resources, and attempting to correct existing weaknesses, if any." Our view is that the term *collection management* is broader in scope, and while retaining the goals of meeting the information needs of the people (a service population) in a timely and economical manner using library resources, it adds elements such as long-term preservation, legal aspects of user access to materials, and collaborative efforts with others to provide the most cost-effective access as possible. This new definition is broader and places emphasis on thoughtful (timely and economical) long-term collection building and on seeking both internal and external information resources.

Collection management (CM) is a universal process for libraries. Figure 2.2 illustrates the major components of the process. One can see a relationship between Figures 2.1 and 2.2, in that CM involves three of the nine information transfer elements (identification, selection, acquisition). As implied by the circle, CM is a constant cycle that continues as long as the library exists. All of the elements in the cycle are discussed in subsequent chapters.

Because of our philosophy of CM, which has a focus on meeting the information needs of the service community, we begin our discussion with the needs assessment element. The terms *needs assessment, community analysis*, or *user/service community*, as used throughout this text, mean the group of persons that the library exists to serve. They do *not* refer only to the active users, but include everyone within the library's defined service parameters. Thus, a community might be an entire political unit (i.e., a nation, region, state, province, county, city, or town). Alternatively, a community may be a more specialized grouping or association (i.e., a university, college, school, government agency, or private organization). Also, the number of people that the library serves may range from very few to millions. Data for the analysis come from a variety of sources and are not limited to staff-generated material. For CM personnel, the assessment process provides data on what information the clientele needs. It also establishes a valuable mechanism for user input into the process of collection development. (Note the size of the arrow in Figure 2.2 from the community to collection development; the size indicates the level of "community" input appropriate for each element.)

One use for the data collected in needs assessment is in the preparation of a collection policy (or policies). Clearly delineated policies on both collection development and selection (covered in Chapter 4) provide the CM staff with guidelines for deciding which resources are most appropriate for the collection. Some libraries call the document an *acquisitions* policy, some a *selection* policy, some a *collection management* policy, and others simply a *statement*. Whatever the local label, the intent is the same: to define the library's goals for its collection(s), and to help staff members select and acquire the most appropriate materials.

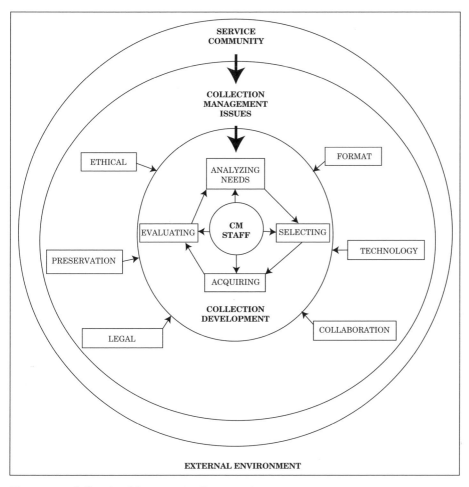

Figure 2.2. Collection Management Process

For many people, selection is the most interesting element in the CM process. One constant factor is that there is never enough money available to buy everything that might be of value to the service community. Naturally, this means that someone, usually one or more professional staff members, must decide which items to buy. It may involve deciding among items that provide information about the same subject; deciding whether the information contained in an item is worth the price; deciding on a format for the information; or determining whether an item could stand up to its projected use. In essence, it is a matter of systematically determining quality and value. Most of the time it is not just a matter of identifying appropriate materials, but of deciding among items that are essential, important, needed, marginal, nice, or luxurious. Where to place any item in the sequence from essential to luxurious depends, of course, on the individual selector's point of view. Its placement on such a continuum is a matter of perception and is an area where differing views regarding that placement can be problematic for the library (see Chapter 12 for more on this issue).

An individual buying an item for him- or herself normally does not have to justify the expenditure to anyone. However, when it is a question of spending the community's money, whether derived from taxes or an organization's

---

From the Authors' Experience

While selection can be the most interesting element in the CM process, Saponaro knows from experience that it is much more challenging to manage a small amount of funds for a subject area than a larger amount. When responsible for managing the fund lines for subjects amounting to less than $500 a year, she had to very carefully weigh selection choices, to make sure those funds she spent had the most impact or "bang for the buck."

---

budget, the decision may be debatable. The question of whose perception of value to employ is one of the challenges. Needs assessments and policies help determine the answer, but there is a long-standing question in the field: How much emphasis should selectors place on clientele demand and how much on content quality?

Acquisition work is the process of securing materials for the library's collection, whether by purchase, as gifts, or through exchange programs. This is the only point in the collection development process that involves little or no community input; it is a fairly straightforward business operation. Often the individuals who have selection duties are not directly involved in the work of acquiring the selected material. In those cases, once the CM staff decides to purchase or lease an item, the acquisition department staff proceeds with the preparation of an order, the selection of a vendor, eventually recording the receipt of the item, and finally paying the bill (invoice). (In school library/media centers, for example, these duties are often performed by the same person who selects the items.) Although details vary, the basic routines remain the same around the world, just as they do in either a manual or automated work environment. We address acquisitions work in Chapter 5.

Evaluating (see Chapter 6) is the last element in the collection management process. Evaluation of a collection can serve many different purposes, both inside and outside the library. For example, it may help to increase funding for the library. Certainly it will be an element in any library accreditation process. Occasionally, it may help in assessing the quality of the work done by CM staff. For effective evaluation to occur, the service community's needs must be considered, which leads back to community analysis.

The most common internal reason for evaluation of items or resources in a collection is the fact that all resources have a finite period of high use, or even useful, lifespan. Frequently the driving force behind such assessments relates to the fact that libraries have limited shelf or storage space. Eventually the library will have to address the evitable situation of having to secure additional collection space, stop acquiring new material, or withdraw items occupying existing space. Most libraries will engage in the latter activity. Public, school, and special libraries rarely, if ever, have the opportunity to select either of the first two options. Larger academic and some very large public libraries may have additional options available—by storing low-use items in compact shelving units installed within the facility or sending items to a remote (lower cost) facility and providing delayed access. The withdrawal process has several labels, the oldest being *weeding*. Another term for this process is *deselection* or *deaccessioning*. In the United Kingdom, the term used for the process is *stock relegation*. Regardless of the label, the end result is the same; when a library decides to withdraw an item, it will dispose of the item (by selling it, giving it away, or even discarding it).

Check This Out

Some public library "Friends of the Library" groups are able to sell "weeded" and donated items as a way to support library operations. One Website that helps identify such sales is Book Sale Finder (http://www.booksalefinder.com/). Sales are listed there by state, city, and date.

Beyond the four core CM activities (covered in Chapters 3–6), there are a host of issues that impact those activities in some manner. We have grouped those issues into six very broad categories (addressed in Chapters 7–12):

- Collaboration
- Formats
- Technology
- Preservation
- Legal
- Ethical/intellectual freedom

Collection Management and Library Types

In Figure 2.2, the all encompassing outer area has the label "external environment." It is that external environment/service community that determines library type. The concepts discussed above are generic in character regardless of type. How the concepts are translated into the real world of library operations arises from the library's external milieu.

One important fact to understand about libraries is that there are very few standalone operations. Libraries are almost always a component of a larger parent organization. That organization is also surrounded by external events, pressures, expectations, values, and so on. Those external elements eventually become factors for the library. A clear example of how this impacts a library's operations was touched on in Chapter 1—the world economic problems that began in 2007–2008. Every person and organization, at least in the United States, has felt some of the effects of the economic downturn. Also, as we noted in Chapter 1, those economic waves washed over CM activities primarily in the form of a substantial loss in purchasing power for collection resources.

We should also mention three other "generic" aspects of CM. The size of a library's service community has a definite bearing on collection development. Three facts of collection development are universal:

1. As the size of the service community increases, the degree of divergence in individual information needs increases.

2. As the degree of divergence in individual information needs increases, the need for resource sharing increases.

3. It will never be possible to satisfy *all* of the information needs of any individual or class of clientele in the service community from locally held or leased resources.

Institutional Libraries

Institutional libraries, as most people in the United States think of them today, came into existence in the mid-19th century. (Certainly there were libraries earlier in the United States; however, they had little resemblance to today's libraries.) They also shared many similar startup experiences, such as their early collections consisted of donated books from well-to-do individuals. One of the first, if not the first, U.S. institutional library resulted from a gift of several hundred books and a small endowment to an as yet unnamed college in Cambridge, Massachusetts, from one John Harvard (1636).

There were a surprisingly large number of well-educated individuals with rather substantial personal libraries from the early colonial period up to the present. Those early personal libraries were the sources for the beginning college library collections and "social libraries." (Social libraries were the forerunners of today's public libraries.) Clearly, the notion of giving personal books and magazines to nearby libraries has a very long tradition in the United States (more about gifts and CM in Chapter 5).

The notion of purchasing books (in the early days it was just books, other formats came later) for the academic library was not widespread until near the middle of the 19th century. The concept of actively developing, much less managing, a collection did not come about until the early 20th century. College library collections were small and narrow in scope and depth until well into the 19th century. (Note: universities did not come about in the United States until the late 19th century.) Because most of the early colleges were affiliated with a religious denomination with a primary purpose of turning out pastors for the church, the curriculum was restricted to learning or memorizing a few select texts. Naturally, students had little or no need for library material to support their studies. A highly trusted faculty member had authority to decide what books should be in the library collection as well as who might read them. Some colleges provided some student library access for a few hours a week, but only under the watchful eyes of one or more trusted faculty members.

By the mid-19th century, students began establishing local literary or debating societies off campus and creating their own libraries with books, journals, and newspapers of interest to their members. Often these collections had far greater depth and scope than did their college library; certainly hours of access were far greater and one could explore any topic of interest without faculty approval and oversight.

It was only in the later 20th century that academic librarians began playing a major role in how campus libraries created and maintained their collections. The shift from faculty to librarian control came about for several reasons that were indirect outcomes of World War II. Because thousands of war veterans took advantage of a federal government program for higher education enrollment, colleges and universities were swamped with students. Increased enrollments meant there were more sections of more courses offered as well as students requiring advisement or assistance. This created a strain on faculty members' time to attend to what had been traditional faculty responsibilities. A further factor and time commitment for faculty was research. The success scientists had had in helping to solve wartime problems lead to the U.S. government offering a host of research grant opportunities. Since the institution received a share of each grant in the form of "overhead," there was institutional pressure on faculty to apply for such grants. The end result was that faculty slowly gave up their collection development responsibilities to librarians.

Public Libraries

Deciding when "public libraries" originated is very much a matter of definition and of course debate. We know that some Greek and Roman communities had places where people might read scrolls. For example, in some Roman public baths there were "dry rooms" filled with scrolls that people could read. However, there is no indication that such rooms were government supported but rather were a service that some baths offered.

In 1731, Benjamin Franklin organized what he called a subscription (social) library (e.g., individuals had to pay a fee to have access). (Franklin's library still exists today as the Library Company of Philadelphia, see http://www.librarycompany.org/.) Franklin's idea was that people would greatly benefit from pooling their money and could purchase a greater quantity and variety of material than they could on their own. The concept spread rather quickly; it was this idea that college students drew upon when they started their literary or debating libraries.

So, which elements might constitute a definition of what we now call a public library? There are at least four attributes of modern public libraries. One attribute that categorizes a public library is that it is supported by a government body—usually a municipality or county—with tax revenues. In many cases, there is a specific item or levy in a local tax bill for the library. Another attribute is that the library is freely available to all residents within the taxing jurisdiction. Many public libraries now have reciprocal agreements between neighboring community libraries that allow registered borrowers access to all the collections of the collaborating libraries. A third attribute is that the collection is wide ranging in scope, catering to interests of the community from children's picture books to scholarly monographs. Our final attribute is that registered borrowers may check out a majority of the items in the collection for a period of time.

Thinking about the above attributes, is it any wonder that there are debates about which library was the first public library—first to have tax support or free access, for example, while lacking one or more of the other attributes? Who was first is really not all that important beyond illustrating the relatively long and varied history and origin of today's public libraries.

The Boston (BPL) and New York City (NYPL) public libraries can serve as examples of the varied beginnings and why the "first" is so difficult to pin down with certainty. What follows was drawn from the Websites of the two institutions (http://www.bpl.org/general/history.htm and http://www.nypl.org/help/about-nypl/history). In the mid-1800s, both cities had a community library open to their citizens. Boston officially established such a library in 1848; however, it did not open to the public until 1854. New York City had a library open to the public in 1849; however, it was financially supported by a bequest ($400,000) from one person—John Jacob Astor.

When it opened, BPL allowed people to borrow items, while materials in the Astor Library were intended for reference only. There was another library in New York at the same time that was open to anyone who secured an admission ticket—Lennox Library. This was a collection of the personal library of James Lennox who was a bibliophile and scholar of early printing; thus it was a specialized research library. It was only in 1895 that the Astor and Lennox libraries merged, with the financial backing of the Tilden Foundation, and formed the nucleus of today's NYPL system.

BPL was also dependent at the start on individual philanthropists to become operational. Joshua Bates pledged $50,000 for the purchase of books in 1852, if the city would provide a free public reading room. Boston Mayor

---

Check This Out

For a review of the history of the Carnegie Libraries, visit "Carnegie Libraries: The Future Made Bright" from the National Park Service: http://www.nps.gov/history/nr/twhp/wwwlps/lessons/50carnegie/50carnegie.htm.

Josiah Quincy provided the requisite funding, and the facility opened to the public two years later. Additionally, BPL claims to have opened the first children's room in 1895 and was the first public library to offer storytelling in 1902.

The above illustrates how difficult it is to really identify the "first" U.S. public library. Few other public libraries had such distinguished benefactors as BPL and NYPL; however, almost all originated through some outside party's philanthropic efforts. One example of such an outside influence was Andrew Carnegie's program of funding a public library building for a community, if that community agreed to fund its operations. There are still hundreds of "Carnegie Libraries" across the country in communities that might never otherwise have decided there was a need for such a library in their town. Most of the social libraries became part of the community free libraries once they were formed. Student literary libraries were also absorbed into the campus libraries by the 1870s.

Unlike other library types, public library collection building has always been in the hands of the library staff. Initially selection was the director's responsibility, but as the collections and staffing patterns grew, librarians at lower administrative levels took over the work. The early textbooks about creating a library collection arose from the need in public libraries for people trained in book selection. One of the very first such books is the McColvin title we quoted from at beginning of this chapter. Two other early texts on book selection, both focusing on the public library environment, were Arthur Bostwick's *The American Public Library* (4th edition; New York: Appleton, 1929) and Francis Drury's *Book Selection* (Chicago: American Library Association, 1930). Over time, many large public library systems have centralized their collection and selection activities.

School Libraries

School libraries also have their origins in the 19th century; however, their development has been considerably choppier than other library types. Even today, as communities struggle to address the economic conditions, school libraries are often categorized as one of the "nice," but not essential,

---

From the Advisory Board

Advisory Board member Virginia Walter notes that an interesting trend in young adult services is to involve the teens directly in evaluating and selecting materials. It started with popular music but has moved beyond that to include manga, graphic novels, and reading materials of all kinds. Almost all libraries with a designated young adult librarian rely on a youth advisory committee of some kind to assist with this task.

elements of elementary and secondary education (along with school nurses, counselors, art, and music instruction).

Unlike academic and public libraries, school libraries have some basis in state legislation as well as occasional regulations. New York State Governor DeWitt Clinton recommended the creation of school libraries in 1827. Over the next 50 or so years 21 other states passed legislation, often as part of an omnibus education bill, that included authorization of school libraries. Unfortunately, recommending and authorizing do not always translate into something happening. Certainly that was, and still is, the case for school libraries.

An interesting government document was published in 1876 by the Department of Interior, Bureau of Education. Its title was *Public Libraries in the United States of America: History, Condition, and Management*. The "public libraries" in the title referred to any library that was open to the public and/or funded in part by tax monies. The usual label at that time, for what we think of as public libraries, was free library. (There are chapters on college, law, medical, and many other library types in the 39 chapter and 1,200-plus-page document.)

Chapter 2 of the report had a title that many people today might view as ironic and sad—"School and Asylum Libraries." That chapter may well create a sense of déjà vu or "back to the future" for today's reader. An early statement in the chapter is, "Although the history of school libraries in the United States is marked by many changes and mishaps, it would be untrue to say that these libraries have entirely failed to accomplish the good expected of them. From first to last, their shelves have held millions of good books, affording amusement and instruction, and cultivating a taste for reading in millions of readers, young and old" (p. 38). A statement about Massachusetts's various stalled school library projects has implications for thinking about today's school library: "The school libraries have been superseded by free town libraries" (p. 42). Perhaps at the time of the report, communities had yet to see an advantage of combining public and school library operations into a single system. Certainly many had done this by the mid-20th century. Later, during good economic times, some communities dismantled their combined systems. Perhaps today (given tight economic conditions) would be a good time to revisit the idea and address the issues that led to dismantling these systems. Some jurisdictions have done just that. The Carrboro Branch Library (Orange County, North Carolina) is a current example of such combined systems—where the public library (http://www.co .orange.nc.us/library/carrboro.asp) is housed within a middle school facility

From the Authors' Experience

In Chapter 1, we noted that Evans's first experience as a user and library employee took place in his local branch library. That branch was located in his neighborhood elementary school, because at that time the city had a combined public and school library system. One result of that combination was that the juvenile nonfiction section very much reflected the curriculum of the school district. Based on his experience one can identify one of the issues of having joint public/school physical facilities—during school hours very few adults tried to use the library. Adult usage was very high during nonschool hours. From a student's point of view, having access to a curriculum-oriented nonfiction collection during evenings and weekends made doing homework a little easier.

(http://www2.chccs.k12.nc.us/education/dept/dept.php?sectiondetailid= 4874&). In addition to sharing a facility, both institutions share an online catalog.

With nominal state oversight, funding of school libraries lay in the hands of local school districts or even the state superintendent of education (sometimes the sole book selector for the state's school libraries). Very often, the funds for libraries were diverted to other usages. The New York section of the aforementioned 1876 *Public Libraries in the United States* report indicated, "The diversion of the library fund to other purposes continues, and all the official reports indicate that, in the majority of the districts, the people have come to accept the diversion as a matter of course, and that in some the very existence of the library at any time is rather a matter of tradition than of knowledge" (p. 41).

Aside from funding issues, the issue of what is appropriate for children and young adults to read has probably been with us for as long as printed books have existed. Certainly there was a general thought in the profession at the time that libraries had a moral obligation to control access to some books regardless of the reader's age. However, the concern regarding children's reading matter is perhaps as strong today as it ever was. George Hardy's (1889) comment would still resonate with many people today. He noted, "In your collection of books remember that it is important to guard against not only those books that mislead the conscience and studiously present ideas that are fundamentally false, but also against those that merely interest and consume time, but neither elevate the taste nor brighten life" (p. 347). Without question, one of the most challenging CM tasks is creating collections for children and young adults regardless of library type.

To summarize, today's selection process is most varied among and within library types. We explore the issues involved in the selection phase of collection management in Chapter 4. Because of those many variations, it is difficult to make many generalizations. However, with that in mind, the following are some general statements about the variations:

1. Public libraries emphasize title-by-title selection, and librarians have traditionally done the selecting. (The concept of patron-initiated selection will be covered in Chapter 4.)

2. School libraries select based on subject areas or topics for educational purposes as well as recreational reading. Although the media specialist may make the final decision, a committee composed of librarians, teachers, administrators, and parents may have a strong voice in the process.

3. Special and corporate libraries select materials in rather narrow subject fields for specific research and business purposes. Often the client is the primary selector.

Check This Out

A good article that explores the push-pull of freedom to read in the school environment is Rebecca P. Butler's 1999 piece, "Contending Voices: Intellectual Freedom in American Public School Libraries: 1827–1940," in *School Libraries Worldwide* vol. 5, no. 1: 30–39.

Check These Out

The American Association of School Librarians (AASL) has produced an extensive list of guidelines well worth reviewing: *Empowering Learners: Guidelines for School Library Programs* (Chicago: American Association of School Librarians, 2009).

Patricia Boehm (2009) provides an overview of the guidelines in her article "The New AASL Program Guidelines for School Library Programs," in *School Library Monthly* (26, no. 1: 50–52).

---

4. Academic libraries select materials in subject areas for educational and research purposes, with selection done by several different methods: faculty only, joint faculty/library committees, librarians, or subject specialists.

Collection management is a dynamic process that should involve both the professional staff and the service community. Few information professionals question the need or value of client input; the question is how much there should be. The best answer is, as much as the organization can handle and still carry out its basic functions, and as much as the community is willing to provide.

Selection also varies by the role the library has in the "parent" organization of which it is part. The academic libraries' role is in the dissemination and creation of knowledge. School media centers focus on dissemination and the development and utilization of knowledge, while public and special libraries' roles are the dissemination and utilization of knowledge.

Standards and Guidelines

This is as reasonable a place as any to briefly discuss guidelines and standards in terms of collection management. There are a number of professional organizations, both within the field of librarianship and beyond, that have guidelines or standards that may influence CM work. A few of the standards are focused just on CM issues such as those found on the ALA "Standards and Guidelines" Webpage (http://www.ala.org/ala/professionalresources/guidelines/standardsguidelines/index.cfm). This page lists 35 broad categories of standards and guidelines, with the number of standards and guidelines appearing under each of the categories being many times greater. Certainly not all of those categories apply in any direct way to CM work; however, 16 of the categories are applicable. The most obvious category is "Collection Development and Management," which lists 11 separate standards and guidelines.

Collection-related guidelines cover almost every area of CM activities. Knowing the standards and guidelines pertinent to one's library environment is obviously important; however, they are not the driving force behind daily CM work. They most often come into play during assessment activities or accountability projects. They can, however, be helpful in efforts to address budgetary issues and occasionally staffing concerns. The majority of today's standards and guidelines are qualitative rather than quantitative in character, which generally requires more time and effort when making a case for more resources. Nevertheless, they can be useful.

Library organizations are not the only ones to have created standards that relate to libraries and their collections. Perhaps the most important group of organizations are those that accredit educational institutions or some component within such institutions. There are literally hundreds of such agencies whose scope of interest may be national, regional, or state-wide in nature. One very important group of agencies is the six regional accrediting agencies. These agencies look at educational institutions (kindergarten through postsecondary) to essentially give a "stamp of approval" that an institution is meeting established quality criteria. Going through the accreditation process is voluntary; however, most institutions do so for two major reasons. The first reason is "accredited status" is very often essential when seeking federal funds; lacking such status generally means there is no reason to even attempt to request such funds. The second reason is, in the minds of the general public, being accredited means the institution is of high quality, even if people have no idea of what criteria were employed to determine such status.

We will use the Western Association of Schools and Colleges (WASC) as a brief example of the role of accrediting agencies on library collections. (WASC covers the states of California, Hawaii, and the U.S. Pacific islands such as Soma and Guam.) WASC's statement of purpose and criteria for assessing institutions reads, "The criteria are research-based guidelines of systematic school improvement that address accreditation's central tenet: a school operates with a clear understanding of its purpose" (http://www .acswasc.org/about_criteria.htm). In accreditation "speak," that statement translates into institutional purpose equals mission, which equals appropriate support resources for that mission. At least as far as WASC is concerned, "support resources" include libraries and their collections. WASC's position

---

From the Authors' Experience

Although the above discussion of accreditation agencies' interest in library collections did not mention public libraries, there are times, however, when there is an impact. During his time in California, Evans served on a number of WASC accreditation visiting teams. One such visit highlights how a college accreditation visit can impact a public library's collection building activities.

The site visit was to a college with a modest distance education program. WASC did and does take long hard looks at such programs especially in terms of the types and quality of services distant students receive in comparison to on-campus students. As part of the college's efforts to provide library services to such students, it indicated that at two locations there was an agreement with the public library to provide services to any student enrolled in the distant "ed" program. Needless to say, the visiting team was concerned about how a public library collection and services would meet the needs of a college program. While there was a formal agreement between the academic and public libraries, there was no indication the college had or would provide the public libraries with funds to supply access to the appropriate journals or books. In looking at the public library holdings, it was also clear their existing collections were very inadequate for the proposed purpose.

Certainly there were other issues that led to the visiting team's recommendation that the college be put on probationary status; however, the issue of poor library support played a role in the decision. Had the college provided funding to the public libraries to enhance their collections for the school's programs the libraries supported, that would have removed the issue from the team's list of concerns.

on "Resource Management and Development" is, "The resources available to the school are sufficient to sustain the school program and are used to carry out the school's purpose and student achievement of the school-wide learning results" (ibid.). Failure to meet those criteria will have a negative impact on the institution's accredited status. Regional accreditation agencies have a variety of categories for institutions they review, ranging from fully accredited to nonaccreditation.

Taking on Collection Management Responsibilities

Our opening quotation for this chapter from Allison Cowgill regarding the importance of CM for today's library environment is not overstated. Collections, whether physical or virtual, are the very cornerstones of any library's service program. While much of the current professional literature regarding CM tends to focus on the digital information world, print is not yet dead. Thus, CM personnel must understand both worlds, at least for the present. One way to develop excellent collections, both print and digital, is to always keep in mind that content is the most important concern, after which comes such issues as format and cost.

Given the importance of CM, it is rather disappointing to read articles, such as those by Joanne Oud (2008) and James Tucker and Matt Torrence (2004), describing the challenges recent graduates face and the stress they feel when asked to engage in CM activities. Joanne Oud was interested in factors related to a beginning librarian's job satisfaction, as evidenced by comparing expectations with on-the-job experience. One area where there was a large gap between expectations and reality was in collection management. She wrote that, "New librarians in their first professional position reported relatively low pre-existing knowledge in a number of aspects of their jobs. They reported especially low pre-existing knowledge in two areas: dealing with workplace politics and selecting resources for the library collections" (pp. 258, 260). Tucker and Torrence's focus was solely on CM responsibilities. They noted that, "The transition from graduate school to a professional academic library position is a challenging one, especially when facing the initial journey into collection development. Many librarians experience the stress of this move because in most instances recent graduates do not have the necessary skills, simply due to lack of applied experience and education" (pp. 397–398).

What is it about CM that creates such concerns and stress, particularly for new practitioners? Broadly thinking, there are fourteen areas that CM personnel must master. The list reflects our real-world experience in CM:

- Differentiating between the responsibilities of CM librarians from other interested parties (faculty, parents, or governing boards, for example).

- Determining/assessing the service community's information needs.

- Understanding local collection development policy issues.

- Knowing the locally used selection sources (reviews, publishers, etc.).

- Comprehending how the library balances its collections between print, other media, and digital resources.

- Ascertaining how collection development fiscal issues and allocations are addressed.

- Gaining an awareness of the local acquisitions system(s), existing approval plans, and standing or blanket order plans.

- Discerning and understanding local CM collaborative initiatives.

- Learning local standards for assessing the collections and CM in accreditation projects.

- Knowing local storage and deselection issues, concerns, and practices.

- Understanding how the library handles preservation issues.

- Participating in discussions regarding legal issues related to collection access and use.

- Investigating and understanding how the library handles intellectual freedom issues and any library policies regarding ethical interaction with vendors.

- Developing skills to function as an effective liaison or advocate for the library and its collections.

The truth is that graduate library and information science courses are excellent at providing the basics of the areas a graduate may find her- or himself working in; however, they cannot provide anything but a few examples of how a library makes local adjustments in those basics. It is highly unlikely that any two or more libraries are identical in all respects; if for no other reason than their external environments are different, which in turn requires adjustments in practices. Thus, this book will provide a good exposure to the basics, and the Authors' Experience and Advisory Board boxes illustrate some real-world examples. Nevertheless, there will, of necessity, be much to learn. This learning can certainly begin in any field studies or practicum opportunities that are available or required during the library program, and will continue well into the formal job setting.

Some libraries, recognizing the critical importance of CM, provide incoming librarians who will have some CM responsibility with an in-depth orientation to local practices. Such orientation is very valuable for all new individuals—recent graduate or longtime professional—as the local variations must be mastered before one's performance is as effective as possible. Table 2.1 provides an example of what one academic library expects CM staff to understand.

Clearly, as seen in both the list of 14 points previously outlined, as well as from topics listed in Table 2.1, Allison Cowgill's statement is true: "Learning how to be a good collection development librarian takes serious effort on everyone's part" (p. 25).

Points to Keep in Mind

- Collection management should be geared primarily to identified needs rather than to abstract standards of quality; however, an identified need can be a long-term need (more than five years into the future), not just an immediate need.

Table 2.1.   Collection Management Activities

Acquisitions
University purchasing and fiscal policy
Materials budget cycle/dates; reports; structure of fund codes
Electronic/print
Collection development policies
Preparing orders
Monographs/approvals
Firm orders
Sets/continuations
Rush orders
Serials selection—electronic/print
Licenses/policies
User suggestions (faculty, staff, students)
Ordering
Who does what; unit organization chart
Assigning vendors, funds, inputting and receiving
Cancellations
Purchase plans
Ordering monographs online
Monitoring individual funds
Gifts
Reviewing/accepting materials; appraisal and tax guidelines
Special Projects
Shared purchase plans/collaborative selection
Purchase on demand
Order records—finding and understanding them
Serials records
Creating reports

Collection Assessment
Assignment tables/specific subject areas and their call number ranges
Usage/interlibrary loan statistics
Trial database
Storage/weeding/transfers/withdrawals
Reports; creating lists; fund balances
Wants list
New faculty list
Book/resource reviews
Replacing lost materials
Assessment methods/evaluation of outcomes

Thank you to Colorado State University staff members Sandy Brug, Donnice Cocherar, Jessie Council, Teresa Negrucci, Mary Seaman, and Patricia Smith for sharing their orientation plan.

- Collection management, to be effective, must be responsive to the *total* community's needs, not just to those of the current or the most active users.

- Collection management should be carried out with knowledge of and participation in cooperative programs at the local, regional, state, national, and international levels.

- Collection management should consider all information formats for inclusion in the collection; however, it is the content that matters more than the format.

- Collection management was, is, and always will be subjective, biased work. A periodic review of the selector's personal biases and their effects on the selection process is the best check against developing a collection that reflects personal interests rather than customer interests. Selection policies in place can help offset any personal biases that may arise (these will be further discussed in Chapter 4).

- Collection management is not learned entirely in the classroom or from reading. Only through practice, taking risks, and learning from mistakes will a person become proficient in the process of developing a collection.

Works Cited

Bostwick, Arthur E. 1908. "Address of the President: The Librarian as a Censor." *Bulletin of the American Library Association* 2, no. 5: 113–121.

Brogan, Mark, Philip Hingston, and Vicky Wilson. 2002. "A Rich Storehouse for the Relief of Man's Estate." In *Advances in Library Administration and Organization*, ed. Edward Garten and Delmus Williams, vol. 19, 1–26. Greenwich, CT: JAI Press.

Cowgill, Allison. 2008. "Training Collection Development Librarians." *Colorado Libraries* 34, no. 2: 34–37.

Hardy, George E. 1889. "The School Library a Factor in Education." *Library Journal* 14, no. 8: 342–347.

McColvin, Lionel Roy. 1925. *The Theory of Book Selection for Public Libraries*. London: Grafton.

Oud, Joanne. 2008. "Adjusting to the Workplace: Transitions Faced by New Academic Librarians." *College & Research Libraries* 69, no. 3: 252–266.

Tucker, James Cory, and Matt Torrence. 2004. "Collection Development for New Librarians: Advice From the Trenches." *Library Collections, Acquisitions, and Technical Services* 28, no. 4: 397–409.

United States Department of Interior, Bureau of Education. 1876. *Public Libraries in the United States of America: Their History, Condition, and Management*. Washington, DC: Government Printing Office.

White, Martin. 2002. "Content Management." *Online* 26, no. 6: 20–22, 24.

Wortman, William A. 1989. *Collection Management: Background and Principles*. Chicago: American Library Association.

Suggested Readings

Buck, Tina Herman, Stephen Headley, and Abby Schor. 2010. "Collection Development in Public Libraries." *Serials Librarian* 50, nos. 2/4: 253–257.

Chadwell, Faye A. 2009. "What's Next for Collection Management and Managers?" *Collection Management* 34, no. 4: 254–259.

Genco, Barbara. 2007. "20 Maxims for Collection Building." *Library Journal* 132, no. 15: 32–35.

"Guidelines for Liaison Work in Managing Collections and Services." 2010. *Reference and User Services Quarterly* 50, no. 1: 97–98.

Jackson, Carleton L. 2006. "The Soul Inside the Center: One Librarian's Perspective on Media Guidelines and Their Assumptions." *Media Review* 12, no. 2: 61–71.

Kusik, James P., and Mark Vargas. 2009. "Implementing a 'Holistic' Approach to Collection Development." *Library Leadership and Management* 23, no. 4: 186–192.

Loertscher, David. 2009. "Practical Advocacy: The Collection." *Library Media Connection* 28, no. 3: 7.

Lyons, Lucy Eleonore. 2007. "The Dilemma for Academic Librarians with Collection Development Responsibilities: A Comparison of the Value of Attending Library Conferences Versus Academic Conferences." *Journal of Academic Librarianship* 33, no. 2: 180–189.

McElfresh, Laura Kane. 2009. "Good Things Come in Small Libraries: 21st Century Collection Management in the Small College Library." *Technicalities* 29, no. 5: 1, 3–5.

Midland, Susan. 2008. "From Stereopticon to Google: Technology and School Library Standards." *Teacher Librarian* 35, no. 4: 30–33.

Munro, Bruce, and Peter Philps. 2008. "A Collection of Importance: The Role of Selection in Academic Libraries." *Australian Academic and Research Libraries* 39, no. 3: 149–170.

Pymm, Bob. 2006. "Building Collections for All Time: The Issue of Significance." *Australian Academic and Research Libraries* 37, no. 1: 61–73.

Teel, Linda M. 2008. "Applying the Basics to Improve the Collection." *Collection Building* 27, no. 3: 96–103.

Wessels, Nicoline, and Hannalie Knoetze. 2008. "Collection Development in High-Poverty School Libraries in Multilingual Environments." *Mousaion* 26, no. 2: 290–303.

White, Jackie. 2003. "Ebb and Flow: The History of the School Library in the Commonwealth of Kentucky." *Kentucky Library Association* 67, no. 2: 8–10.

3
Assessing User Needs

We are providing that essential service for our users, the materials and information they need, read, and, our hope, profit from.
—William A. Wortman, 1989

We as collection managers like to think that we administer our collections in ways that always keep our users in mind. But let's be honest. What we had in mind was often what we *thought* our users wanted.
—Faye A. Chadwell, 2009

All successful organizations (for- and not-for-profit) understand what their "target" populations need, want, demand, and expect in the way of service or products. They commit substantial resources to monitoring that population in order to understand what areas they are doing well in and those areas that require improvement. There are two general techniques that are useful in engaging in learning about and monitoring potential users of a service or product: environmental scanning and market research.

Relatively recently, libraries began referring to what they do in this area as environmental scanning or market research. In the past other labels were more common. Public libraries may still employ the older term *community analysis* for the process; business libraries sometimes refer to it as an *information audit*. Another commonly used term, regardless of library type, is *needs assessment*. School library media centers often use terms such as *curriculum mapping* and *collection mapping* for the activity. Today, more and more academic libraries have positions with the word *liaison* in the title—one responsibility of the position is to monitor faculty and student needs and interests. Regardless of the label used, however, the goal was, and remains, similar—attempting to understand potential and actual users of their services and collections. Sometimes people forget that, in order to be effective, the monitoring should be continuous. Faye Chadwell (2009), author of one of this chapter's opening quotations, highlighted the importance of understanding the service community when she wrote: "It is also going to be imperative that we keep our users' developmental, education, and entertainment needs in mind—more than we ever did in the print realm" (pp. 76–77).

Today, more and more libraries are engaging in long-term and strategic planning and employ both environmental scanning and market research as part of that process. Although the purpose of such data gathering is far broader than CM work, the results generally prove useful to CM personnel. A major advantage of conducting one broad-based analysis is that it will actually save time and effort in the long run. Any effort to examine a service population, whatever its label, is time consuming and often the staff goes over much of the same ground with slight variations when doing single focus projects. Also, people get less and less responsive when approached repeatedly by the library seemingly asking the same questions.

While community analysis and market research share some basic characteristics, an environmental scan can also produce the following information:

- Why a person does or does not use a particular product or service.

- How a person uses a product or service.

- Where a person gains access to a product or service (a library example would be in the library or via remote access).

- What a person's attitude is about the service or product.

- What, if any, new services or products are desired.

- How much a person is willing to "pay" (time, effort, money for example) for a service or product.

One can see how each of the above might translate into CM work as well as other aspects of library programs and planning activities.

There are hundreds of reports and articles that contain information about users' information needs and their use of information. However, there is little that is specific enough in these materials to be very useful to both library A and also library B. As a result, other than for very broad generalities such as "women tend to read more fiction than men," or "young people do not read anymore," each library must conduct its own study. Some in the profession have raised questions about the value of such studies given the time and effort involved. As noted above, studies of library users and non-users require the investment of considerable time and effort. Mick, Lindsey, and Callahan (1980) suggested that user studies "provide little information which can be applied to problems involving either the management of information work or the design of information products or services" (p. 348). In their conclusions, they suggest a major factor that causes the lack of practicability or transferability to other libraries is that "Information travels through diffuse, complex paths. Individual information behaviors are the product of complex interactions involving personal attitudes, backgrounds, role, function, specific task situation, environment, etc. It is highly unlikely that any two individuals would display the same information behaviors" (p. 354).

Although the article is over 30 years old, as its title suggests ("Toward Usable User Studies"), it contains valuable insights into how to create and conduct studies that produce practical information for collection management work. It seems rather likely the authors would be in agreement with

Faye Chadwell that to some extent "user information needs" is a library construct rather than a user perception. Librarians must keep this in mind. Asking a person, "Tell me about your information needs" will more often than not cause the person to stare blankly while attempting to understand just what you are asking.

Douglas Zweizig (1980) raised valid questions about the utility of many community studies and suggested ways in which a library can get practical data for CM purposes. He noted that, "The use of community analysis data is a creative act, and one who expects findings to clearly suggest action will be disappointed" (p. 41). For all of his concerns regarding the challenges for translating data into decisions or plans, Zweizig ends his essay with a quotation from a Dylan Thomas poem in which a sheep herder is asked why he danced in a fairy ring to protect his sheep and who responded with, "I'd be a damn fool if I didn't" (p. 45). Libraries likewise would be foolish if they did not engage in community assessments. Understanding the limitations of such studies is one key to knowing how to construct useful studies. Like the Mick article, Zweizig's chapter is well worth reading as the basic issues of assessing the service community's interests and concerns remain unchanged. Further, he provides excellent advice on how to develop an effective instrument for data collecting.

Even individuals who raise concerns about the time, effort, and money that goes into such studies acknowledge that when they are carefully developed, carried out, and thoughtfully analyzed they do provide valuable data for CM work. Those who have some doubts regarding value for time and effort rightly contend that there must be a clear goal(s) for the study and not stretch results beyond the original goal(s) after the data are collected.

Concepts and Terms

It is far beyond the scope of this chapter to address all the concepts that are employed in needs assessment studies. However, there are three we must define: needs, wants, and demands. We employ them not only in this chapter but several others as well:

- *Needs* are issues for the community, institution, or person that require one or more solutions; it does not always follow that a need is something the community, organization, or person wants.

- *Wants*, on the other hand, are things that the group or person is willing to expend time, effort, or money to acquire; it does not necessarily follow that the want is good for those wanting it.

- *Demands* are wants that a group or person is willing to take action to achieve (such as, paying for it, writing letters requesting it, making telephone calls, testifying, or demonstrating). From a library perspective, the ideal outcome of a study is identification of needs that are wanted and demanded.

The above terms are generic in character. Because the literature of librarianship, including this book, makes frequent use of the term *need*, the following breaks down that term into more discrete meanings. Jonathan Bradshaw (1972) discussed four types of social needs—normative, felt, expressed, and comparative—that have had wide acceptance within the social sciences.

Normative needs often are based on expert opinion. One commonly cited normative need is the need to increase the literacy level. Teachers, librarians, and others, in their professional roles, express this normative need. To some degree, the general public accepts this need; however, finding adequate funding to address the need is often a challenge. This is due to the fact that the community or society does not perceive the importance of the normative need.

Felt needs (wants) come from the community based on its belief about a problem or issue. How appropriate or realistic felt needs may be is often debatable; nevertheless such needs are a reflection of a community's perception of a situation. Just as normative needs are not always what the community thinks is important, felt needs do not always reflect what is good for the community.

Expressed needs (demands) reflect behavior. Individuals often say they want or need something, but their behavior shows they really want or need something else. Libraries tend to respond well to expressed needs. That is, libraries are more likely to meet a greater percentage of the active customers expressed needs than they are to the needs of infrequent users. A needs assessment project can reveal whether the library is overresponding to active users' needs.

Comparative needs are the result of comparing the service population to other like populations. From the library perspective, one such comparison might be the number of items circulated per capita. When making such comparisons, the service level or collection relevance for the two groups must be the same. One advantage of focusing on comparative needs is that they usually result in some quantitative measures that can be useful in setting goals for new services or programs according to the results of the assessment project.

Another term that more accurately reflects the service community's view of what librarians are seeking when doing a community assessment is *interest*. That word is something that is easy to understand and reflects how a person thinks about what information they are looking for; a person rarely thinks "I have an information need for a recipe for chicken supreme." They might think "need" but not "information need."

It is useful to remember, both during the processes of data collecting and analysis, that as the importance of the information wants increases, so too do the amounts of money, time, and other resources organizations or people are willing to expend to secure accurate information. From the individual to the largest organization, all information seekers place a value on each type of information used, often without being fully aware they are doing so.

Several factors influence the information's value; one factor is its importance for pending decisions. The type and format of information wanted may also play a role in the valuation process. Another factor is accessibility and the effort required to gain access to information, sometimes labeled the "law of least effort."

According to the law of least effort, people and organizations expend as few resources as possible (time, money, or effort) to secure information. Frequently when a person is preparing a document, there is a need for more or updated information. A typical reaction is to turn first to materials at hand. Most people try this even when they know where they can secure the appropriate information, just because the known source is less convenient. Today, the process follows some variation of:

- Check existing files/materials at hand (both physical and computer hard drive/storage device).

- Check the Internet.

- Ask a friend or work colleague (the "invisible college").

- Check with the local library and its databases for resources available on-site or electronically.

- When all else fails and the need is great enough, request the library to secure the material from some other source (document delivery or, when available, purchase on demand).

Experienced CM personnel are well aware of a sequence such as the above. They factor that knowledge into their thinking and decision making regarding what resources to acquire or lease.

Why Spend the Time and Effort on Service Community Studies?

One reason to engage in service community studies for CM purposes is the fact that the information world contains hundreds of millions of information sources. Only a tiny fraction of the universe is likely to be relevant to one's service community. Even that small fraction is a rather large number of potentially relevant items; it is far greater than any one library can hope to acquire or provide access to. Data from user studies can narrow the focus to a more manageable pool to consider.

Earlier in the chapter, we noted that the data collected from a properly constructed study can meet a variety of library needs. Certainly the inclusion of each additional purpose adds to the time, effort, and cost of conducting the project; however, there will be substantial savings over undertaking a series of single focus projects. A sampling of potential uses for service community studies are:

- Developing collections (assessing demographics changes or topics of high and low interest, for example).

- Planning new services (e.g., exploring the level of interest in some types of new services, or responding to rapidly changing platforms for accessing information).

- Locating service points (such as expanding or contracting service locations including mobile service locations).

- Assessing physical facility requirements (such as complying with legal physical access as required in the Americans with Disabilities Act [ADA] of 1990, creating group or quiet study areas, etc.).

- Adjusting staffing patterns (assessing the need for additional staff at service points, staff with different skill sets, or using staff at lower skill levels).

- Assessing collections and services (one typical example is addressing accreditation requirements).

- Planning budgets (for example, adjusting fund allocations).

Each of the above uses or goals does have some importance for those involved in CM work. One issue that you might not think had any implications

---

Check This Out

One example of a user study is described by Ian Rowlands and David Nicholas in their 2008 article "Understanding Information Behaviour: How Do Students and Faculty Find Books?" in the *Journal of Academic Librarianship* 34, no. 1: 3–15. The authors undertook a study of user information seeking behavior in a U.K. university. (The issue of interest to them applies to any library providing access to e-books regardless of type or country.) Rowlands and Nicholas provide an example of a focused study and its practical value for CM, the purpose being "to develop an initial baseline understanding of people's levels of awareness and previous experience of using e-books so that the impact of different kinds of interventions (e.g., including or not including e-books in the library catalogue) could be systematically explored" (p. 3).

---

is the example of ADA compliance. Although the ADA does primarily focus on physical facilities, it does address other access issues that people with disabilities may face. A small example of the physical facility aspect is that when a library has an open stack collection, the aisles must be wide enough to accommodate wheelchairs, or the library must provide someone to assist the person who uses a wheelchair in accessing the collection. (Collection growth and available space is a major challenge in academic libraries, and one of the first methods to gain more stack space is to look at narrowing aisle width to perhaps be able to add a few more stack ranges. ADA requirements limit that option.)

On the nonphysical side, one ADA issue to consider is access for those with vision limitations. Public libraries have for many years purchased "large print" editions of titles that are also in standard print form. Educational libraries often do not have the option of enlarged print versions of their titles; however, they must provide access to that material for anyone requiring assistance. Again, that assistance may be mechanical (for example, reading machines) or human, but the assistance must be provided. Digital materials and even library Websites raise similar access issues. Knowing what percentage of the service community might call for such assistance helps plan fund allocations.

What follows are some examples of assessment projects that demonstrate why conducting studies are essential for effective collection management. One clear example of why it is imperative for libraries, especially public libraries, to have a regular community monitoring process in place is in the following. The example draws on the authors' and a member of our advisory board's experience in Los Angeles. Everyone knows communities change over time. How fast or dramatic such changes are is less well known in the absence of regular monitoring. What follows shows how the western part of Los Angeles changed over a 50 year period—1950 to 1990 (Figures 3.1–3.5).

The maps drew on the U.S. Census tract data for the years covered and the terms used are those of the Census Bureau. Shading of tracts on the maps represent those with or without 51 percent of the population in that tract being one of racial/ethnic categories the Bureau employed at the time. Unshaded tracts indicate that at least 51 percent were "white." "Transitional" tracts are those in which there was no 51 percent majority.

The data represent *very* broad stokes of what the tract populations may have been at the time. Even in the 2010 Census there was concern that some ethnic groups would be vastly underrepresented in the count for a variety of reasons. Certainly those reasons were much stronger in earlier periods. Also, for CM purposes, labels such as Asian, black, and Spanish mask huge differences. The categories lump together various cultural groups—Asian includes Japanese, Chinese Korean, and Vietnamese, for example—and, from a collection building point of view, very likely mask huge differences in interests. Despite these and other shortcomings, the data do help illustrate the need to monitor service population demographics.

In 1950 (Figure 3.1), the data show that all but a few of the tracts were white with the exception of tracts along the 405 Freeway between Santa Monica and Pico boulevards. A librarian working at the Santa Monica Branch of the Los Angeles Public Library (LAPL) at the time probably was well aware that the "transitional" areas had a large Japanese American population and that area had the potential to become "Asian" by the next census. Figure 3.2 (1960) illustrates that did in fact happen; it also shows a large number of other tracts had become transitional, both west of the now Asian tracts and farther south along the 405 Freeway.

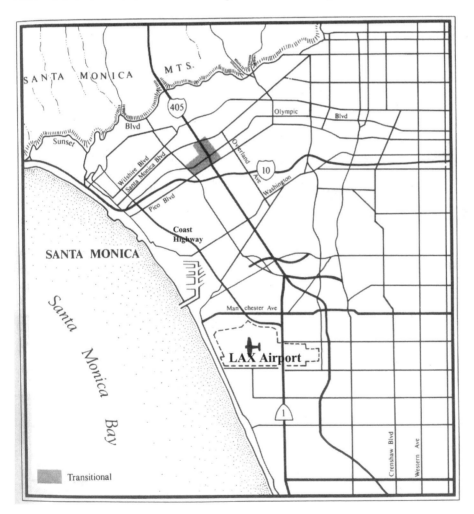

Figure 3.1.   Western Los Angeles Demographics—1950

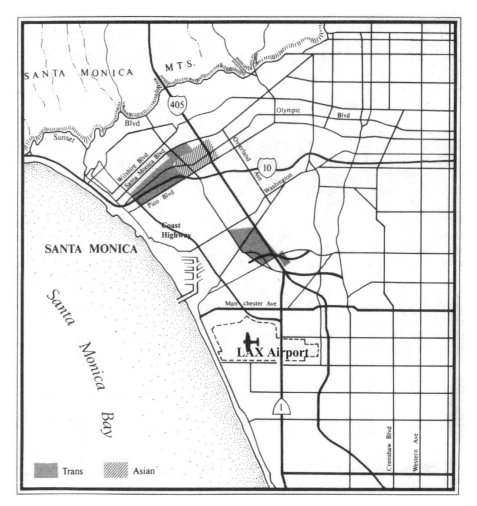

Figure 3.2. Western Los Angeles Demographics—1960

Figure 3.3 (1970) demonstrates that change had overtaken more and more tracts. Tracts that were transitional in the Pico area still existed, but some had become "black." The area south along the 405 Freeway had more transitional tracts with an Asian area tucked in between. Along the Coast Highway, there were now tracts of "Spanish" and blacks. Libraries serving these areas faced the challenge of adjusting collections to better address current users' interests and dealing with items that already existed in their collections that reflected the interests of a different population.

The 1980 and 1990 maps (Figures 3.4 and 3.5) provide a sense of the dramatic shift in population patterns in just 10 years. It also highlights the necessity of continuous monitoring on a yearly basis. The area along Pico that was black at the time of the 1970 census shifted to being 51 percent Spanish in 1980 and then to being transitional in 1990, as had the tracts along the Coast Highway. When libraries must continually address major shifts in population such as the foregoing, this creates some serious funding challenges, especially when attempting to meet new needs. Such funding challenges will be discussed further later in this section.

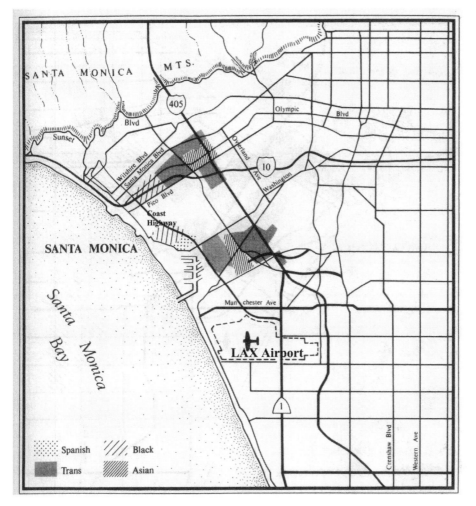

Figure 3.3.   Western Los Angeles Demographics—1970

It is certain that data from the 2000 and 2010 censuses would show a similar state of constantly shifting population patterns. From a CM point of view, one of the best ways to avoid some surprises like the above is to take some time on a monthly or more regular basis to either walk or drive through the service area with the objective of noting differences in people on the street, store sign language, and perhaps going into stores that might be selling reading material. Using new census data to confirm observations is a plus.

The LAPL system as a whole faced the challenge of addressing these population shifts; it was not just a western LA phenomenon. During the 1960s and 1970s, economic conditions were not strong, so funding was limited for most of the city's cultural and recreational services. LAPL has a long history of providing quality service to residents as well as following the current best practices for public libraries. However, even with the best of intentions and service record a library can face simultaneous challenges over a practical and political issue.

In the mid-1970s, the Los Angeles City Attorney's office issued a document that raised questions about marked differences in branch services

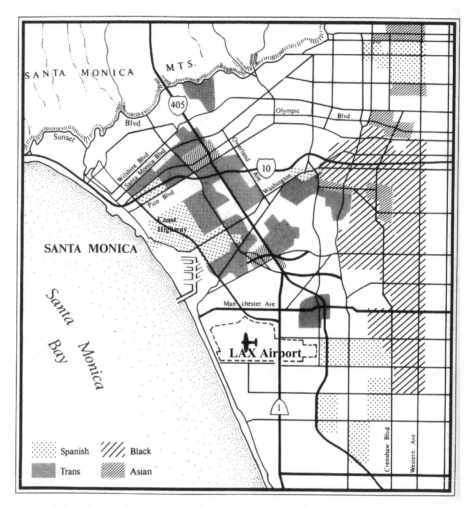

Figure 3.4.　Western Los Angeles Demographics—1980

(McDermott, 1975). That document raised the issue of the legality of funding for some branch libraries:

> Based on information available to our office, disparities in library resources among the City's branch libraries appear to impact adversely on minority communities and raise serious questions under federal and state constitutional and statutory, including the following: (1) the equal protection provisions of the United States Constitution; (2) the federal Civil Rights Act of 1964; (3) the Federal Revenue Sharing Act; and (4) the equal protection provisions of the California Constitution. . . . We hasten to mention, however, that we have seen no evidence indicating that the existing disparities in allocation of library resources have in any way resulted from willful action or bad faith of any City official. (pp. 1–2)

The city attorney's report had a number of tables illustrating the disparities, such as those shown in Table 3.1.

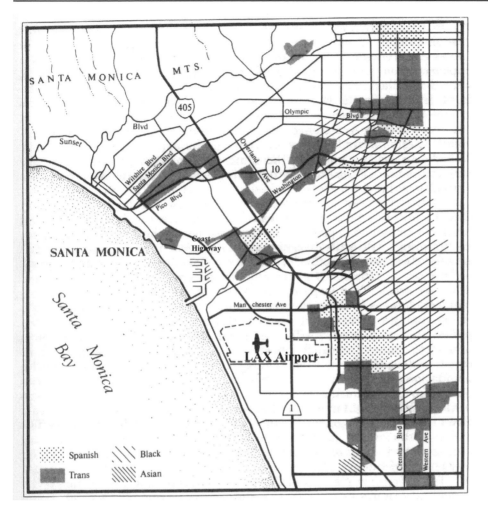

Figure 3.5. Western Los Angeles Demographics—1990

Table 3.1. Excerpt from Los Angeles City Attorney Report

Region	Percent Minority	Total Books	Total Periodicals	Total A-V Materials
Western	16.8	308,448	1,282	9,617
West Valley	9.0	390,398	1,274	8.397
East Valley	19.0	468,527	1,691	10,923
Hollywood	33.6	331,363	1,451	4,476
Northeast	64.8	230,255	1,180	7,723
Central	88.9	203,801	997	2,091
Southern	72.5	170,454	589	4,991
Average	39.4	302,241	1,202	6,888

Source: McDermott, 1975, p. 8.

Table 3.2.   Excerpt from LAPL Response
Total Branch Book Circulation—Regional Totals, 1974–75

Region	Total Book Circulation	Average Circ. Per Branch	Circ. Per Capita	Rate of Book Turnover
Central (9)*	431,212	47,912	1.23	1.8
East Valley (10)*	2,362,630	236,263	4.19	4.8
Hollywood (11)*	1,732,668	157,505	3.90	4.8
Northeast (9)*	829,451	92,161	3.07	3.3
Southern (6)*	515,183	85,864	1.50	2.8
West Valley (7)*	2,581,463	368,780	6.42	6.3
Western (9)*	1,980,939	220,104	5.14	6.1
Total	10,433,436	171,040	3.66	4.6

* Number of branches in region.
Source: Jones, 1978, p. 188.

At the time (1970s), the LAPL system consisted of 54 small "community branches" that emphasized circulating material of high interest to its surrounding community, seven large regional branches that provided both community branch service and reference/research services for the branches in its region, and a central library located in downtown Los Angeles. The city attorney's report focused on the community branches.

LAPL responded with a detailed assessment (Jones, 1978) emphasizing that the problems that existed were real, but due to serious budgetary shortfalls. The response document contained dozens of charts showing the disparities (see examples in Tables 3.2–3.4). The good news from the two

---

From the Advisory Board

Virginia Walter worked at the LAPL when the aforementioned "subbranches" were upgraded to full branch status. She provides the following account of what transpired from an employee's perspective during the time when the McDermott report was an issue for the library system:

Councilman Art Snyder initiated this, and it was a political issue. All of the sub-branches were located in inner city—i.e., non-white—areas. They were open fewer hours and had a smaller staff than "full" branches. The rationale for this was complicated. Usage—i.e., circulation—was certainly a factor as well as the fact that these libraries were built much closer together than the larger suburban branches. At any rate, Councilman Snyder had a number of these in his district and was able to get additional funding for all of the sub-branches in the city. I took the opportunity to transfer from Encino-Tarzana to Malabar in Boyle Heights because I wanted the challenge of creating a more viable and vibrant library in that Boyle Heights community. The result was an increase in the book budget as well as staffing, and we were able for many years to actually get special funding to purchase books in Spanish. While the perception persisted that book funds were allocated on the basis of circulation, the formula was more complicated after this and did in fact take into account the needs for books in multiple languages, replacing outdated collections, etc.

While I was branch manager at Malabar, we had one very elderly Jewish resident who had never moved away, and we continued to subscribe to their Yiddish newspaper just for him.

Table 3.3.   Excerpt from LAPL Response
Input Data on Twenty Branches with Highest Total Book Circulation, 1974–75

Branch	Rank in Salaries	Rank in Book Funds	Rank in Total Exp.	Rank in Exp. Per Capita
1. West Valley *	1	1	1	3
2. Woodland Hills	6	8	6	1
3. W. Los Angeles*	4	2	4	15
4. N. Hollywood	7	3	7	11
5. Granada Hills	5	10	5	9
6. Sherman Oaks	13.5	7	14	6
7. San Pedro*	8	6	8	14
8. Northridge	15	16	15	10
9. Van Nuys	3	9	3	29
10. Hollywood*	2	4	2	4
11. Canoga Park	12	14	12	27
12. Panorama City	10	15	10	31
13. Encino Tarzana	18	17	18	17
14. Studio City	28.5	18	28	5
15. Arroyo Seco*	9	5	9	12
16. Palms Rancho	13.5	20	13	18
17. Fairfax	21	23	21	16
18. Westchester	11	22	11	7
19. Palisades	20	33	20	2
20. Brentwood	32	32	32	8

* Regional branch.
Source: Jones, 1978, p. 215.

Table 3.4.   Excerpt from LAPL Response
Input Data on Twenty Branches with Lowest Total Book Circulation, 1974–75

Branch	Total Book Circulation	Rank in Age of Building	Rank in Bldg. Area in Sq. Ft.	Rank in Total Books
1. Junipero Serra	17,326	52	53	56
2. Watts	23,990	15	56	53
3. Ascot	29,770	36	27	50
4. Vernon	30,800	0	9	48
5. John Muir	31,965	45	39	47
6. Jefferson	32,972	52	59	43
7. Angeles Mesa	33,958	47	41	44
8. Mark Twain	37,288	15	47	38
9. Ben Franklin	41,408	0	7.5	34
10. Wash. Irving	43,010	49	40	32
11. Expo. Park	44,453	0	7.5	49
12. Wilmington	50,171	48	55	46
13. Hyde Park	50,784	15	45	60
14. R. L. Stevenson	52,714	48	44	51
15. Vermont Square	59,191	62	18	12
16. Cypress Park	61,666	48	58	54
17. Malabar	66,023	48	51	58
18. Lincoln Heights	71,253	59	13	40
19. Memorial	71,893	45	15	37
20. Atwater	77,061	22	60	59

Source: Jones, 1978, p. 116.

From the Advisory Board

Carol Sinwell provided the following about the current need to understand one's service community:

Fairfax County Public Library (FCPL) is "market-driven and customer-driven" (i.e., how can and does the library system best serve its customers' needs in the community where they reside?). Those needs and interests determine how the individual branches of the library respond to their respective communities. Convenience for the patrons and providing what best serves the customer are the primary goals of FCPL—that the libraries "add value to and are valued by" the community.

One of the greatest challenges currently facing FCPL is the changing demographics and increasing numbers of languages used in Fairfax County. Although uncertain at this time as to the best way to encourage new Americans to use the system, the library intends to be proactive, not reactive, to the situation and the future. For instance, in order to assess how well the library has responded to patrons' needs, FCPL has conducted telephone surveys, in-branch user surveys, and online surveys. The telephone survey included questions that specifically related to how FCPL has responded to demographic changes such as cultural, lingual, and age-related.

---

reports was the library system was given additional funds to help address the issues exposed. The above, while most atypical, does illustrate the point that the library must be vigilant in its monitoring of its service community and attempt to address concerns as quickly as possible.

As the comments from one of our advisory board members suggest, there was a political aspect to the situation. There was also a practical aspect. The maps presented earlier illustrate the fact that branch library service communities were, and probably still remain, in a state of rather rapid transformation. Developing a fund allocation model that will adequately address shifts in demographics in which an area's population goes from 51 percent of one ethnicity, to another, and then to still another cultural group all within a relatively short timeframe is a significant challenge. It is a big challenge for collection management staff.

Practical Aspects

Regardless of its name (community analysis, needs assessment, collection mapping, information audit, market research, environmental scanning, as well as other labels for such studies), all assessment projects draw on some of the following data collecting techniques covered below. When considering an assessment project, careful planning is a must. A sample of the planning issues to consider includes the following:

1. What is/are your target population(s)?

2. What is the goal or purposed use of the data you hope to collect?

3. Is the target population knowledgeable, interested, or willing enough to respond to questions? Might there be a language problem that would require translations?

4. Is there staff available, with the requisite skills, to carry out the project?

5. Is a consultant necessary? Where would the funding come from to pay for such services?

6. How will you ensure the data collected accurately reflect the respondents' true thoughts rather than responding with what they think the library wants?

7. What methods for data analysis are most appropriate?

8. Will the data collecting/questions asked raise unrealistic expectations for both respondents and staff?

Assessment projects are most easily accomplished and useful when they have a relatively narrow focus. As noted above, the first step in a project is to identify the target population(s). *Target populations* or *market segments*, to use terms from the business world, are essentially the same thing. That is identifying a distinctive set of characteristics in the overall population to study, to communicate with, to provide service to, and so forth. Lea Bailey's (2009) article "Does Your Library Reflect the Hispanic Culture?" is an example of a target population. Armstrong, Lord, and Zelter's (2000) article "Information Needs of Low-Income Residents in South King County" is an example of another target group.

Sometimes there are preexisting sources of data related to the proposed project, occasionally in sources that may appear to be unrelated to libraries. For example, marketing firms often collect "lifestyle" data and occasionally have a question or two about library usage such as, "How frequently did you use the library in the last year?" Because the organization asking the question is not a library, more people will answer honestly than they would have had a library ask the question. (Respondents often attempt to please or not give a negative impression of themselves. Thus, they provide responses they think will give the questioner what is wanted rather than the truth.) Locating such studies can save time and effort and perhaps provide more reliable data. Another example of a library-based project, but for a non-CM purpose, that may generate useful CM information is Sherri Jones and Jessica Kayongo's (2008) article "Identifying Student and Faculty Needs through LibQUAL+™: An Analysis of Qualitative Survey Comments."

Developing a set of questions to ask is not as simple as it might seem. Several resources exist that can assist in formulating project questions. Almost any basic textbook on research methods outline the fundamental techniques of survey research, as do many marketing books. Beyond the fundamental research methodology level, there are some practical guides available. Currency is less an issue than having guides with sound track records. Some useful titles include:

Henczel, Susan. 2001. *The Information Audit: A Practical Guide.* Munchen: K.G. Saur.
    (While the information audit is most often associated with the special library, this book has useful ideas for any type of library; it also contains three case studies.)

Hughes-Hassell, Sandra, and Anne Wheelock, eds. 2001. *The Information-Powered School.* Chicago: American Library Association.

(This practical book provides tools and templates for conducting collection analysis and curriculum mapping in school libraries.)

Kaufman, Roger, and Fenwick English. 1979. *Needs Assessment.* Englewood Cliffs, NJ: Educational Technology Publications.
>(A useful book that provides an excellent overview of the process.)

Lamb, Annette, and Larry Johnson. *The School Library Media Specialist: Collection Mapping.* http://eduscapes.com/sms/program/mapping.html.
>(An online resource that provides a sound overview of collection mapping for the school library environment.)

Lauffer, Armand. *Assessment Tools for Practitioners, Managers, and Trainers.* Newbury Park, CA: Sage, 1982.
>(A practical guide to assessment methods.)

Nicholas, David. *Assessing Information Needs: Tools and Techniques.* 2nd ed. London: Aslib, 2000.
>(This is a concise guide to assessing information needs; covering how to frame a project, methods of data collecting, and how to set realistic goals and outcomes.)

Nickens, John M., Adelbert J. Purga, and Penny P. Noriega. 1980. *Research Methods for Needs Assessment.* Washington, DC: University Press of America.
>(A sound work for developing a needs assessment project.)

Rossman, Marlene L. 1997. *Multicultural Marketing.* New York: American Management Association.
>(Written for businesses wishing to become more effective in marketing products to a wider base, this book provides excellent insights that apply to library needs assessments. Particularly good for public libraries.)

Warren, Roland L. 1955. *Studying Your Community.* New York: Russell Sage Foundation.
>(This is a classic for anyone planning a public library assessment project.)

Common Types of Data Collected

There are a host of data categories that may be useful for a library's assessment project, and they vary from library type to library type. We can only touch on a few of the many variations here. The resources provided above explore many more of the options that exist.

Historical data are useful in several ways. Understanding a community's historical development may lead to a better, and sometimes quicker, understanding of the current environment. Historical background information also provides clues about areas of the collection to weed or areas in which it is no longer necessary to acquire material.

Geographic information answers questions such as: In which physical direction is the community growing? (This is an issue for large academic campuses as well as for public libraries.) What is the distribution of population over the geographic area? (One example of where such information is useful is in schools where there is a busing program.) This type of information helps the library staff determine service points or other access points, which, in turn, may influence the number of duplicate titles they acquire or provide access to. Even in today's digital information world, geography matters. A good article regarding current geographic issues and libraries is by Julia Todd (2008).

A good source for public library related geographic and mapping data is GeoLib (http://www.geolib.org/PLGDB.cfm), which is affiliated with Florida State University's College of Information. As of mid-2011, the database contained information on 16,000 U.S. public libraries. It also has the Census data that are most often associated with library use and provides access to library statistics from the National Center for Educational Statistics.

Transportation availability data, combined with geographic factors, are important in the library's decision-making process regarding how many service points to establish and where to locate them. The aforementioned "law of least effort" is a factor to keep in mind when thinking about "transportation." What service exists? What does it cost? What are its service hours? Who uses the service? Answers to such questions play a role in planning service points, which can in turn impact CM decision making.

Legal issues will not be too difficult to determine, nor will the amount of data accumulated be large. Nevertheless, there may be legal implications for collection development. In some academic institutions, the teaching faculty has the legal right to expend all book funds. We explore legal issues and CM in more detail in Chapter 11.

Political information, both formal and informal, has a relationship with legal data, much like the link between geographic and transportation information. Our earlier example of the LAPL challenges in the mid-1970s illustrates the point that politics can be an issue for CM work. Some questions are: To what extent is the library a political issue? How do the politics of the community work? Who influences fiscal decisions? Answers to most of these questions will not have a direct bearing on which titles go into the collection, but they may influence the way in which the library secures and allocates funds.

Demographic data are essential in formulating an effective collection development program, regardless of library type. Academic and school libraries experience changes in student demographics just as public libraries must adjust to community changes. Waiting until change takes place creates an image of an institution that is slow to adapt.

Today, census data are easier to access through services such as the American Community Survey (ACS, http://www.census.gov/acs). Data from the U.S. Census long form (SF3, STF3, and STF3A) are the most commonly used data sets for library projects. ACS is an *annual* survey that produces SF3-like data for the noninstitutionalized population. The sample methodology employed is the same as that used on the SF3. In 2010, the site included data for "places" with populations of 20,000 or greater. The plan is that eventually ACS will report data at the tract level nationwide.

Economic data may help the library better plan its collection development activities. That is, anticipating increases or decreases in funding can lead to a more even collection. An economy based on semiskilled or unskilled workers calls for one type of collection, a skill-based economy calls for another, and an economy based on knowledge workers calls for still another.

Communities with a seasonal economy or a predominantly migrant population face several problems. What type of service and which formats would best serve the seasonal population?

Social and educational organizations reflect community values. Although social patterns are slower to change than individual attitudes, the library must consider such pattern shifts in planning an integrated collection building program. Social clubs, volunteer groups, and service organizations, for example, affect and reflect community interests. The most important group of organizations is educational. Academic institutions no longer offer only two-year, four-year, and postgraduate degree programs. Evening adult education classes, day and night degree programs, off-campus or electronic-only classes, and even some remedial high school–level courses create complex instructional programs, each facet having different collection needs. A public library's concern must be broader than public and private primary and secondary schools; it should also consider adult vocational programs and higher education.

Cultural and recreational organizations also reflect community interests. As with social organizations, these formal groups provide useful clues to highly specialized interest areas with enough community interest to sustain a formal group. Many of these groups, when given library service, join the library's most solid and influential supporters.

Other *community information services* are, in some respects, the most important CM issue. If the library identifies several community information sources, and if the various sources can develop a working cooperative agreement, everyone will benefit. All too often public, school, and academic libraries in the same political jurisdiction operate as if they existed in isolation. When a group of publicly supported libraries in a local area fails to develop cooperative programs, considerable resources and services go to waste. We explore collaborative issues in Chapter 7.

Data Collecting and Analysis Techniques

A number of options exist for data collecting activities. As part of the planning process, the methodology (or methodologies) to employ should be decided upon as well as how the data are intended to be analyzed/used. In this section, we cover a few of the options available, ranging from the very common survey method to focus groups to the less widely employed techniques such as the information audit.

Key informants and community forums primarily use some form of interview or focus group techniques. Social indicator and field survey projects, using the interview method, often rely on questionnaire data and results of behavior observations. Occasionally in educational situations, the diary method can be employed. Large-scale projects almost always use a combination of methods as each has certain strengths and weaknesses. Multicampus or multibranch sites need to be sure there is "buy-in" to use the same methodology at the same time in order to enhance validity and credibility. (However, this does not mean that individual sites cannot conduct their own supplemental user studies.)

Regardless of the method chosen, a challenge for gathering data is gaining community buy-in to the process. Often it is advisable to start with some small-scale data collecting activities that will assist in formulating larger-scale efforts. One place to commence and begin to gain some understanding of interests is with one or two people—key informants, gatekeepers, or community opinion makers.

Key Informants—Gatekeepers

Key informants are individuals who are in a position to be aware of community interests such as public officials, senior administrators, department chairs, community organization officers, or business leaders who are influential and whom other people view as knowledgeable about community affairs. Through interviewing such individuals, insights are gained into areas of interest and concern that ought to be explored in more depth. Another term that is sometimes used for key informant is *gatekeeper*.

One shortcoming of the key informant approach is the person does not fully represent the community. They are selected because of the presumed knowledge rather than a statistical random sample. Therefore, you cannot assume the person's views necessarily reflect a broad spectrum of the community. The opinions of key informants will reflect personal biases, and that is why several such individuals should be interviewed. In essence, these types of data supply subjective but useful information about how people of influence perceive the community information needs.

Focus Groups and Community Forums

A *focus group* is a small-sized group drawn from the general community; however, having a number of sessions with different memberships will provide some broad insights. The *community forum*, on the other hand, is a form of "town meeting." Focus group members are recruited or selected, whereas anyone is welcome at a community forum.

Two advantages of the community forum are that it is easy to arrange and relatively inexpensive, and a broad range of topics may arise. Focus groups are more complicated to organize but, as the name implies, they are focused on topics of the library's choice rather than open forums. A major disadvantage of both methods is that the data obtained are impressionistic and subjective. These data may be extremely difficult to categorize and are not readily amenable to statistical analysis. Although these disadvantages are serious, both formats are useful as a "grassroots democratic process" for soliciting opinions, ideas, and criticism from the service community. When exploring options for starting a service to an underserved cultural or ethnic group, both options can be effective in securing otherwise difficult to secure data.

Check This Out

A comprehensive treatment of creating, implementing, and running focus groups is Richard A. Krueger and Mary Anne Casey's *Focus Groups: A Practical Guide for Applied Research*, 4th ed. (Los Angeles: Sage, 2009).

Social Indicators

Social scientists have developed a method (natural area) that makes use of *social indicators* to determine the needs of various segments of a community. A "natural area" is a unit within the community that can be set apart from other units or areas by certain characteristics. Those characteristics, or social indicators, may be geographic features, such as rivers or transportation patterns; sociodemographic characteristics, such as age, gender, income, education, and ethnicity; population factors, including distribution, density, mobility, and migration; the spatial arrangements of institutions; and health and social well-being characteristics, such as conditions of housing or suicide rates.

By selecting factors that researchers think are highly correlated with those groups in need of information, the library may be able to extrapolate the information needs of the whole community. What these social indicators (also called factors, variables, or characteristics) may be is a point of much disagreement among researchers in library and information science. Some social indicators are age, health, gender, employment, education, marital status, income, and location of domicile or worksite.

What are the implications of those indicators for the library? The following are some broad generalizations based on library research:

- Use of libraries tends to decrease with age, especially among adults over the age of 55. (One reason for decreased use is deteriorating vision and other health problems.)

- Senior faculty, researchers, and organization officials tend to use libraries less as they increase in status and age. (They still use information; however, the actual gathering is usually done by junior or support staff, who tend to be younger.)

- Women make greater use of libraries than men, regardless of the library's institutional environment (public, academic, or corporate).

- As the number of years of education increases, so does use of libraries, up to about 16 years of formal education. After earning a bachelor's degree, a person's library use curves downward. (Apparently, graduate and postgraduate education moves the person into the invisible college network, so there is less need to use formal information systems.)

- Income level and use of formal information systems also show a J-shaped curve. That is, low income usually translates into low use; use rises through middle and upper-middle income levels; and use sharply decreases at high income. (Apparently, those with high incomes can purchase a large percentage of the information they require.)

- Generally, as health declines, there is a decrease in the use of formal information systems. (However, with proper equipment and special services, libraries can reverse this tendency.)

- Persons employed in manual labor tend not to use formal information systems. Information use tends to increase in direct relationship to increased levels of skills required to perform the work.

- The so-called librarian's axiom—that economic downturns result in an increased use of libraries and library materials.

- The "law of least effort" is clearly evident in the finding that as the distance of the residence or workstation from the information center increases, there is a corresponding drop in use.

- Single people and married couples with no children tend to use formal information systems less than couples with children, and as the number of children rises, so too does use.

Field Surveys

The field survey approach depends on the collection of data either from a sample or the entire service population. It is rare to attempt to survey every member of a service community, if for no other reason than the high cost in time and effort to do so. Thus, sampling and sample size become the keys to collecting valid and reliable data—books on statistical methods will provide details about sampling techniques.

A goal of some field surveys is to contact nonusers as well as users. The most common means of collecting data is through interview schedules or questionnaires. The methods most frequently used are telephone interviews, person-to-person interviews, and mailed questionnaires. Some libraries have research offices available to them in order to help develop, execute, and analyze surveys. If such an office is not available, other resources, such as library associations, may provide suggestions for where to turn for assistance.

To be effective, the library must pretest survey questions, whether they are to be used by interviewers or as a form from which a respondent works. The library tests the proposed questions with individuals who have backgrounds or positions similar to the target population. The purpose of pretesting is to learn what responses the library might expect to receive and whether the answers will in fact address the project issues. People are often surprised to see just how many interpretations an apparently simple question can generate. The goal of pretesting is to reduce that variation to the smallest possible size. It is not at all uncommon for there to be several rounds of testing before achieving consistent results. Consistency in this case means having questions that respondents will interpret and understand in the same way.

One choice the library must make is between structured or unstructured questions for the survey. Open-ended questions (unstructured) take more time to answer than fixed-alternative, or closed, questions (structured). The type of question asked can affect both the response rate and data analysis. Open-ended questions are more difficult to code and analyze, and there are fewer methods of statistical analysis that one can apply to them. With the structured format, data are homogeneous and are more easily coded and analyzed.

If some of the target population does not speak English, it is necessary to translate the questions into the language(s) of the target population, if one wants to understand all the information needs. Respondents should be offered both versions of the questionnaire; offering only the translated version may be interpreted as an insult. A local native speaker should do the translation; slang or local usage may not follow formal speech patterns that nonnative speakers tend to use.

The next step in the field survey is to select a sample. Cost is an important issue when selecting a sample size. A large sample may call for complex selection methods, which in turn add to the time and costs of a survey. An important element for gathering useful data is to have a statistically random sample of the proper size to ensure the data are both valid and reliable.

One survey method is *interviewing*. This approach allows face-to-face contact, may stimulate a free exchange of ideas, and usually has a high

---

Check This Out

Robert V. Krejcie and Daryle W. Morgan (1970) outlined a method for determining sample size that is frequently referred to in the literature in their article "Determining Sample Size for Research Activities," in *Educational and Psychological Measurement* (30, no. 3: 607–610).

---

response rate. The drawback to this method is that for any large sample size, it becomes labor intensive. It also requires some thorough training in interviewing techniques for those conducting the interviews. The training is necessary to reduce the real risk that interviewers may not be absolutely consistent in how they ask the questions or respond to the interviewee's nonverbal behavior. Both of these actions will lead to less reliable data. Telephone interviewing may save some staff time, but it has the disadvantage of how long a respondent is willing to give to such calls. Preplanned telephone interviews will work, but they also take more time to schedule.

Mailed, E-mailed, or online surveys require less staffing and training than surveys that depend on in-person or telephone interviews. These two advantages can significantly reduce the cost, in both time and money, of conducting a survey. However, there are some significant disadvantages to such surveys. First, most mailed or E-mailed surveys have a low response rate. Often the rate is less than 20 percent, and such low response rates can seriously affect the validity and reliability of the collected data. Even with repeated mailings, the response rate is frequently low, and the cost of keeping track of who has or has not responded is high. Additionally, unless extra steps are taken to limit access or being able to track Internet provider addresses, online surveys have the added disadvantage of the possibility of a few people with an "agenda" repeatedly filling out the survey.

Another issue is language(s), both in terms of literacy level and not being a native English language speaker. With an interview, a trained interviewer can detect, from the respondent's verbal and nonverbal signals, when there is something not quite right about a question.

Because of these disadvantages, libraries using the mail or E-mail survey method must carefully design the questionnaire and use the simplest and most succinct language possible while still meeting the established objectives. Libraries should also attempt to determine what an acceptable response rate will be before expending the time and money for a survey that could be of questionable value.

Some other data collecting techniques are observation, diaries, transaction logs, and citation analysis. *Observation* of user behavior can serve as a cross-check on what users report as their behavior in an interview, questionnaire, or through a diary. A concern about observation data is how

---

Check This Out

A good article about the process of using an online survey for collection building is Kristi Jensen's (2009) article "Engaging Faculty Through Collection Development Utilizing Online Survey Tools," in *Collection Building* 28, no. 3: 117–121, which describes its use with students and faculty in an academic setting.

much the observer's presence affects the observed behavior. *Diaries* can be excellent sources of detailed information about what, when, where, and how information was sought and used. Getting participant cooperation is an issue, as recording activities can be viewed as unnecessary extra work. In educational situations where the diary is linked to a classroom activity, it works well. One can also get satisfactory results in a corporate setting where only a few individuals participate. There is concern that since the data are self-reported they would be biased toward making the reporter "look good" rather than reflecting actual behavior. This is where the observation method can come into play as a cross-check.

Electronic databases do or should provide "management reports" or *transaction logs* that can supply very important information about when and what was accessed. With the cost of the resources being so high, checking such reports or logs should be a regularly scheduled activity. In most cases, one will not be able to determine who (type of user) accessed the database, but there should be data on when, how (on- or offsite), and how often.

Citation analysis is a helpful tool for collection development. It can assist in identifying "core" collections weakness as well as strengths. We explore this method in Chapter 6. Below is a small sample of the ways in which libraries have employed some of the techniques we have covered.

Check This Out

One title that covers a number of assessment models is Denise Troll Covey's 2002 title *Usage and Usability Assessment: Library Practices and Concerns* (Washington, DC: Digital Library Federation, Council on Library and Information Resources, http://www.clir.org/pubs/reports/pub105/contents.html). Each method covered (such as focus groups, user protocols, etc.) includes a discussion of how assessment results can be applied, as well as challenges associated with using that particular assessment methodology.

Academic Libraries

One university library that engaged in studying its service population is the University of Michigan (Crist, Daub, and MacAdam, 1994). They employed the focus group as their data collecting method. At the University of Michigan, the focus group information led to the formulation of a telephone survey. With the assistance of a marketing firm, the library designed a study to ensure there would be statistically reliable and valid data. They used open-ended questions related to coursework and library use. In today's digital information world, academic libraries might specifically focus on aspects such as:

- What electronic databases do you use more than once a month?

- When preparing the results of your research, do you prefer print or electronic "notes" and resources?

- What are the major or critical problems you encounter when using digital resources?

- What type(s) of assistance would you like to have available when using electronic resources?

Public Libraries

King County Library System (KCLS) in Washington, with a service area of more than 2,000 square miles, has engaged in studying its service areas for some time. Between 1991 and 1997, 24 of 40 service areas had in-depth studies done (Thorsen, 1998). KCLS used a variation of a method Dr. Evans employed when consulting on needs assessment—a visualization of the service area. In their case, they drove the team through the area, making stops at various points. (Dr. Evans would also drive the area, then return to photograph "typical" areas. In working with the branch staff, he would mix the photographs with some from other service areas and determine just how well the staff knew their service area.) KCLS used its data for more than collection development purposes, as suggested earlier in this chapter. They planned services, collections, hours, programs, and so forth around, at least in part, the data gathered during the survey and assessment activities.

School Library Media Centers

In the school environment, a popular assessment tool is collection mapping. As with other methods covered in this chapter, the technique can be useful in a variety of planning activities, not just collection management. The technique assumes a person has also utilized a curriculum map. This mapping can help answer questions such as:

- How well does the collection support the curriculum and meet the academic and recreational needs of the students?

- To what degree does it assist teachers in their class preparation activities?

- What is the right balance between print and media, and has it been achieved?

- How much of the budget can/should go toward e-resources?

- To what extent must students depend on the public library collections and free Web resources to complete class assignments?

Jo Ann Everett (2003) provides an entertaining and informative essay about collection mapping. In the same volume, Charlotte C. Vlasis (2003) covers the techniques and issues in curriculum mapping. When combined with demographic data about students such as gender, socioeconomic level, learning differences, native language, and ethnic, racial, and cultural background, curriculum mapping and collection mapping enable school librarians to develop collections that address the information needs of the broader school community and fit the teaching-learning context.

Special Libraries/Information Centers

Special libraries tend to focus on small groups and individuals within an organization. Thus, the assessment techniques used by large libraries are seldom appropriate. Corporations, research institutes, professional organizations, and the like seldom have a sound knowledge of the basic issues related to acquisition and use of information within themselves, unless there are regular information audits. Some of the key issues are:

- What information resources are currently in use?

- How are these resources used?

- What are the outcomes, if any, of their use?

- What equipment is required to use the information, and who uses that information?

- What is the cost of the information and its associated equipment?

- What is the "value" of the results? That is, what is the cost/benefit of information acquisition and use within the organization?

Information audits are one assessment technique available for special or corporate libraries. Such audits can help ensure maximum value is realized from the organization's expenditures on information resources. They are usually company- or division-wide in scope and take into consideration all information resources, not just the resources housed or made available through the library. DiMattia and Blumenstein (2000) reported on a survey they conducted about the value of information audits. They noted that the audits "often detected gaps and duplication in services and resources" (p. 48). Based on their study, DiMattia and Blumenstein identified four goals that information audits should help indentify:

1. Information needs to meet organizational targets,

2. Overall information resources,

3. The knowledge and expertise resources of the organization, and

4. Where information resources reside, who uses it, the barriers to its use, and the gaps that need to be filled (p. 48).

There are several other methods that are particularly good when addressing a small group environment such as found in the special library environment. Five such methods are: activities, data analysis, decision making, problem solving, and empirical analysis.

The *activities* approach uses an in-depth interview with an individual or group and its objective is to outline all of the activities of a typical day or project. The focus is on decisions made, actions taken, topics discussed, letters or memos written and received, and forms processed. The approach assumes that daily activities fall into a regular pattern, and once that pattern is clear, the librarian or information officer can translate these activities into information requirements. One problem with the method is that people often forget important but infrequently performed tasks. Another drawback is the tendency to overemphasize the most recent problems or activities.

Data analysis is a method in which the investigator examines information sources used and materials produced by the person or group. This approach circumvents the problems of forgetfulness and overemphasis on recent work. Reports, files, letters, and forms are the focal point of the study. The investigator examines the documents to determine what information was used in creating them. After finishing the examination, the researcher discusses each item in some depth with the person(s) concerned to determine which resources they consulted in preparing the documents. Through this process, it is possible to identify unnecessary information sources and to determine unmet needs.

The *decision-making* approach is similar to data analysis, but it focuses on the decision-making process. Again, the researcher is interested in the information used to formulate decisions and the origin of that information. The researcher also looks at the information received but not used. During the interview the researcher explores how the cost of not having the right information, or not having it as soon as required, affected the decision-making process. In the profit sector, either or both factors can have serious financial implications for the organization.

The *problem-solving* approach is similar to the decision-making approach, except the focus shifts to problem solving. Frequently, a problem-solving activity cuts across several departments or units and takes more time to complete than a decision-making process. The problem-solving approach provides a better organizational picture more quickly than the decision-making approach does.

All of the preceding approaches depend on the user providing accurate information about what she or he did or did not do. *Empirical studies*, in contrast, are based on observations of what is done (expressed needs), how users act, and information sources used. If a formal information center exists, it might conduct experiments, such as varying the location of information sources or removing them, to determine whether the users' perceptions of the value of an item translate into use.

Points to Keep in Mind

- You must understand the service community's interests in order to create a valued and sustainable collection.

- Collecting data about community interests is essential to developing the necessary understanding.

- Periodic large-scale studies are necessary; however, ongoing monitoring of the library's environment is the key to effective needs assessment.

- Data required to assist in collection management activities vary by type of library; several obvious categories are demographic, economic, and geographic.

- Methods of data collecting are also varied. Focus groups, field surveys, collection mapping, and information audits are among the most common approaches.

- Regardless of the data-collecting approach employed, the essential aspect of such projects is that if a sample rather than the entire service population represents the target study group, great care must be taken to ensure the sample will be statistically valid as a representation of the total.

Works Cited

Armstrong, Annie, Catherine Lord, and Judith Zelter. 2000. "Information Needs of Low-Income Residents in South King County." *Public Libraries* 39, 6: 330–335.

Bailey, Lea. 2009. "Does Your Library Reflect the Hispanic Culture? A Mapping Analysis." *Library Media Connection* 28, no. 3: 20–23.

Bradshaw, Jonathan E. 1972. "The Concept of Social Need." *New Society* 19, no. 496: 640–643.

Chadwell, Faye A. 2009. "What's Next for Collection Management and Managers? User-Centered Collection Management." *Collection Management* 34, no. 2: 69–78.

Crist, Margo, Peggy Daub, and Barbara MacAdam. 1994. "User Studies: Reality Check and Future Perfect." *Wilson Library Bulletin* 68, no. 6: 38–41.

DiMattia, Susan S., and Lynn Blumenstein. 2000. "In Search of the Information Audit: Essential Tool or Cumbersome Process?" *Library Journal* 125, no. 4: 48–50.

Everett, Jo Ann. 2003. "Curriculum Mapping and Collection Mapping: Otherwise Known as 'The Camel with Two Humps.'" In *Curriculum Connections Through the Library*, ed. Barbara Stripling and Sandra Hughes-Hassell, 119–137. Westport, CT: Libraries Unlimited.

Jones, Sherri, and Jessica Kayongo. 2008. "Identifying Student and Faculty Needs through LibQUAL+™: An Analysis of Qualitative Survey Comments." *College & Research Libraries* 69, no. 6: 493–509.

Jones, Wyman. 1978. *Response to the Report on Legality of Branch Library Funding Disparities*. Los Angeles: Los Angeles Public Library.

McDermott, John E. 1975. *Report on Legality of Branch Library Funding Disparities*. Los Angeles: Office of the City Attorney.

Mick, Colin, Georg, N. Lindsey, and Daniel Callahan. 1980. "Toward Usable User Studies." *Journal of the American Society for Information Science* 31, no. 5: 347–356.

Thorsen, Jeanne. 1998. "Community Studies: Raising the Roof and Other Recommendations." *Acquisitions Librarian* 10, no. 20: 5–13.

Todd, Julia. 2008. "GIS and Libraries: A Cross-Disciplinary Approach." *Online* 32, no. 5: 14–18.

Vlasis, Charlotte C. 2003. "Librarian Morphs into Curriculum Developer." In *Curriculum Connections Through the Library*, ed. Barbara Stripling and Sandra Hughes-Hassell, 105–119. Westport, CT: Libraries Unlimited.

Wortman, William A. 1989. *Collection Management*. Chicago: American Library Association.

Zweizig, Douglas. 1980. "Community Analysis." In *Local Public Library Administration*, 2nd ed., ed. E. Altman, 38–46. Chicago: American Library Association.

Selected Internet Resources

Boston College University Libraries—Community Analysis. http://libguides.bc.edu/communityanalysis.

Colorado Department of Education—Library Services to Diverse and Special Populations—Needs Analysis. http://www.cde.state.co.us/cdelib/diversity/Resources-Assess.htm.

Community Analysis for Libraries and Librarians. http://skyways.lib.ks.us/pathway/ca_homepage.html.

Idaho Commission for Libraries—Needs Assessment. http://libraries.idaho.gov/page/needs-assessment.

Libraryassessment.info. "A blog for and by librarians interested in library assessment, evaluation, and improvement supported by the Association of Research Libraries." http://libraryassessment.info.

Library Research Service—Public Library Resources for Community Analysis. http://www.lrs.org/public/community.php.

Nevada State Library And Archives—Community Analysis Resources on the WWW. http://*nsla.nevadaculture.org/dmdocuments/communityanalysis08.doc.*

New Pathways to Planning—Community Analysis Methods and Evaluation Options (CAMEO) Handbook. http://skyways.lib.ks.us/pathway/cameo/index.htm.

South Carolina State Library—Community Needs Assessment. http://www.statelibrary.sc.gov/community-needs-assessment.

Suggested Readings

Adkins, D., and D. Sturges. 2004. "Library Service Planning With GIS and Census Data." *Public Libraries* 43, no. 3: 165–170.

Charbonneau, Deborah H., and Vera P. Shiffman. 2007. "Demystifying Survey Research: Practical Suggestions for Effective Question Design." *Evidence Based Library and Information Practice* 2, no. 4: 46–56.

Doucett, Elisabeth. 2010. "10 Tips for Tracking Trends." *American Libraries* 41, nos. 6/7: 44–47.

Hertel, Karen, and Nancy Sprague. 2007. "GIS and Census Data: Tools for Library Planning." *Library Hi Tech* 25, no. 2: 246–259.

Ismail, Lizah. 2009. "What Are They Telling Us?: Library Use and Needs of Traditional and Non-traditional Students in a Graduate Social Work Program." *Journal of Academic Librarianship* 35, no. 6: 555–564.

Kim, Pan Jun, Jae Yun Lee, and Ji-Hong Park. 2009. "Developing a New Collection-Evaluation Method: Mapping and the User-Side h-index." *Journal of the American Society for Information Science and Technology* 60, no. 11: 2366–2377.

Lai, Katie, and Kylie Chan. 2010. "Do You Know Your Music Users' Needs? A Library User Survey that Helps Enhance a User-Centered Music Collection." *Journal of Academic Librarianship* 36, no. 1: 63–69.

Library Services to the Spanish-Speaking Committee, Reference Services Section of the Reference and User Services Association, American Library Association. 2007. "Guidelines for the Development and Promotion of Multilingual Collections and Services." *Reference and User Services Quarterly* 47, no. 2: 198–200.

Loertscher, David V., and Laura H. Wimberley. 2009. *Collection Development Using the Collection Mapping Technique: A Guide for Librarians*. San Jose, CA: Hi Willow Research.

Lynch, Mary Jo. 2002. "Economic Hard Times and Public Library Use Revisited." *American Libraries* 33, no. 7: 62.

Mehra, Bharat, and William C. Robinson. 2009. "The Community Engagement Model in Library and Information Science Education." *Journal of Education for Library and Information Science* 50, no. 1: 15–38.

Mentch, Fran, Barbara Strauss, and Carol Zsulya. 2008. "The Importance of 'Focusness': Focus Groups as a Means of Collection Management Assessment." *Collection Management* 33, nos. 1/2: 115–128.

Rajendiran, P., Arati U. Desphande, Indu Bhushan, and Y.S. Parihar. 2007. "Identification of Users' Information Needs: An Analysis of Inter-Library Loan Requests for Journal Selection." *DESIDOC Journal of Library & Information Technology* 28, no. 3: 56–59.

Raliphada, Lufuno, and Deonie Botha. 2006. "Testing the Viability of Henczel's Information Audit Methodology in Practice." *South African Journal of Library and Information Science* 72, no. 3: 242–250.

Spindler, Tim. 2009. "Statistical Analysis Models: Applications for Libraries." *Library Leadership and Management* 23, no. 1: 12–16.

Stoller, Michael. 2005. "Building Library Collections: It's Still About the User." *Collection Building* 24, no. 1: 4–8.

Worcester, Lea, and Lynn Westbrook. 2004. "Ways of Knowing: Community Information-Needs Analysis." *Texas Library Journal* 80, no. 3: 102–107.

4
Selecting Materials

Good book selection will help increase the use made of the
library. A library with 100 cheap but useful and used books is
much more valuable than one with an unlimited number of
costly but useless and neglected volumes.
—Lionel Roy McColvin, 1925

Besides familiarity with the community in its special characteristics and needs, there must be a broad general acquaintance
with the immediate problems of the day, general, national, and
local. . . . This aids especially in recognizing advancing currents
of popular interest and in anticipating requests by readers.
—Helen E. Haines, 1950

Selection is the heart of collection management. It is what keeps the CM
process alive. It is also one of the most enjoyable and challenging aspects
of being a librarian. As the opening quotations suggest, the issue of how to
select appropriate material for collections has been with us for some time.
Although both quotations only refer to books, the reality is that the underlying ideas remain valid in today's digital world.

One of the goals of selection is the creation of sustainable collections
that effectively meet the interests and needs of a library's service community. What constitutes a sustainable collection? William Walters (2008)
defined it as "one that can be maintained without significant degradation
over time" (p. 576). Although his focus was on the financial side of sustainability, the concept essentially applies to all aspects of collection management activities, not just acquisitions. And, the process begins with selection
activities.

In this chapter, our focus is on the content element in sustainability, not
on formats. Collection managers, at times, appear to forget that that content
is the "thing," and that various formats serve different purposes even when

conveying the same content. One such example is a Shakespearian play. It is one thing to read the play in a modern edition that also contains some commentary. It is a very different experience to read the same play as it appears in a first folio edition of Shakespeare's plays. An audio version allows the listener to concentrate on how one or more famous actors delivers the lines in the play without the distraction of seeing the actions. Various video recordings of the play as produced by different directors provide yet other perspectives. The variations in format all convey the same content. The cost to acquire the package/format will vary and ought to be assessed in terms of its purpose and potential usage. Ultimately it is content, purpose, and cost that matter in deciding what to add to the library's collection.

It is important to keep in mind that there is an interlinking of CM elements. Although textbooks, of necessity, must present the elements more or less independently, there is interplay between them in the real world of CM practice. Brian Quinn (2007) made that point when he wrote, "Decisions about whether to add new titles or to cancel existing ones are often complicated and stressful because they frequently involve the commitment or redistribution of limited funds" (p. 5). There are other examples one could use to illustrate the interlinking effect, such as having to decide between two useful titles and knowing that one of them might generate complaints regarding its content or the content relates to a topic of which you personally do not approve.

Quinn's focus in the article is not on the interlinking of CM activities, but on cognitive and affective decision making with an emphasis on collection management decisions. He makes the point that all writers on selection, including the current authors, only address the cognitive or "rational" aspects with no discussion of the affective (emotional) side of the process. We know, at least in the case of our text and probably in the cases of other writers he mentions, that he did not note that we had a final chapter that did touch on the emotional aspect of selection decisions. We must acknowledge that in the past, we did not emphasize the interconnection between the rational and emotional factors that are in fact part of many selection decisions.

The Quinn article motivated the authors and advisory board to think about what the "rational" factors are that can come into play in making selection decisions. The list ran to 37 factors, some were format specific but most were general in character. This chapter explores the general cognitive factors; later chapters address format-specific factors and Chapter 12 explores the emotional factors. However, before we explore the general selection factors, we must touch on the concept of CM policy.

Selection Starting Point: The Collection Management Policy and Its Value

An early task (within a day or two of assuming the post) for a person starting in a position with CM responsibilities is to read the library's collection policy document. This applies to both first-time selectors as well as those with years of experience. Labels for the concept vary: collection development policies, selection policies, acquisition policies, and collection management statements are a few examples. There is also a growing tendency to refer to the document as a "statement."

Not all libraries have such a document, but most do. The document has a good chance of being "dusty" when you read it, whether in paper or digital form. The digital copy's "dust" will be reflected in when it was last revised. Why would it be dusty if it is important to read and understand? A policy, as you may recall from your management 101 course, is a guide to thinking, it is not a set of rules or regulations (must dos). It gives the selector the broad framework of how the library approaches its collection building and maintenance activities. Thus, once you have assimilated the information in the document, you probably will rarely consult it again. One of the major functions of the document is to orient new selectors, in that library, to how CM is handled and the goals of the work at a given library.

Whatever label the library employs, the document has many uses, such as:

- Informing everyone about the nature and scope of the collection,

- Informing everyone of collecting priorities,

- Forcing thinking about organizational priorities for the collection,

- Generating some degree of commitment to meeting organizational goals,

- Setting standards for inclusion and exclusion,

- Reducing the influence of a single selector and personal biases,

- Providing a training and orientation tool for new staff,

- Helping ensure a degree of consistency over time and regardless of staff turnover,

- Guiding staff in handling complaints,

- Aiding in weeding and evaluating the collection,

- Aiding in rationalizing budget allocations,

- Providing a public relations document,

- Providing a means of assessing overall performance of the collection development program, and

- Providing outsiders with information about the purpose of collection development (an accountability tool).

Lois Cherepon and Andrew Sankowski (2003) noted:

> Collection development in the 21st century has become a balancing act for academic libraries. Deciding what to purchase in electronic format, what to continue to purchase in print, and what to purchase in both formats becomes increasingly difficult. . . . The answer involves compromise, keeping current with both technology and resources, and creating or re-creating a collection development policy. (p. 64)

Although their reference point was an academic library, the issues Cherepon and Sankowski raised are of concern to all types of libraries. We would also suggest that effective collection development always has been a balancing act of formats. What e-resources have done is add yet another layer of complexity to the process, albeit probably the most costly and complex layer. The complexity requires an up-to-date written policy statement for the reasons we outlined above.

Preparing, revising, and getting the document approved take time and effort. One of the largest time and effort components of the process is securing widespread input from the service community. You may go through several iterations of the document's content before there is a consensus. However, gaining that input and consensus helps ensure the document reflects both the service community and library needs. Having invested considerable staff time to preparing the document, it is important that the library's governing body (trustees or faculty library committees are examples of a governing body) approves that policy. With that body's approval, everyone has agreed on the ground rules for building and maintaining a collection that will serve the community.

Some people suggest that a collection development policy would be more practical if it consisted of minipolicies for subject areas or specialized service programs. Some libraries have developed a separate document for e-resources. One factor for the popularity of this concept is that preparing a single focus policy entails less time and effort than revising or creating a single comprehensive statement. We would suggest that taking the extra time, if the existing material has not been revised in the past five years, would help shake off the dust that may have accumulated over time.

What ought to be included in such a document? There is only limited consistency from library to library in what appears in a collection policy. However, some of the most common elements are statements:

- Linking CM to the library's and parent institution's mission and long-range plans,

- Providing an overview of the service population,

- Generating the goals for the collection management program,

- Detailing user types, subjects, and depth of coverage and formats collected,

- Identifying selectors and who has a voice in selection decision making,

- Spelling out any special requirements such as needing a positive published review before selecting,

- Outlining the relationship between a main or central library and any branches in terms of collection management,

- Detailing the role, if any, of gifts or donations in kind for collection building,

- Specifying the methods to employ to assess the collection and dispose of materials as appropriate,

- Stipulating the method(s) for handling complaints regarding collection items.

Linking the document to both the library's and parent institution's mission statement and long-term and strategic planning documents provides the context in which CM activities take place. The long-term and strategic plans are the most likely to assist in developing a policy statement that will be useful into the future. Such plans should reflect the current best thoughts about where the parent organization and the library hope to be some time in the future. (Most plans project five years into the future and many are "rolling plans"—that is they are revised every year based on accomplishments and changes in the operating environment.) Given that mission statements and strategic plans do evolve over time, it is wise to revisit the collection development policy whenever the parent organization issues a new plan or mission statement to be sure the policy continues to "map" to these documents.

Providing information about the service community (demographics, etc.) and any special groups of interest to CM activities, such as children, the home bound, and cultural/ethnic groups, is essential to help quickly orient new CM staff. Information about any reciprocal and collaborative programs related to CM work, subject areas (both breadth and depth) of primary interest to the service population, as well as formats collected gives newcomers a solid footing to start their CM work.

Generating a list of CM goals will take time and effort and almost always result in a long list before all interested parties are satisfied their hopes and concerns are properly reflected in the document. Every special interest party can, and probably will, submit a long list of needs for the CM staff to address. As a limited example, some years ago Evans (1993) developed some broad possible goals for creating collections for culturally diverse communities. A partial list includes collections that reflect:

- The root culture, to help maintain its heritage and social values.
- The experiences of the ethnic group in the United States.
- The survival skills and general information about life in the United States.
- The changing nature of society, with an emphasis on social changes in the root culture.
- The relations with other ethnic groups.
- The materials related to the current situation of the group in the United States.
- The future of the group in American society.
- The educational materials that will help adults and children in various formal and informal educational programs (pp. 26–27).

The process of reaching consensus takes time because having a 20-page list of goals is unrealistic as it will generate unrealistic expectations when funding realties impose severe limits on what can be acquired. Yes, it is possible to spread small amounts of money among all the goals; however, in most cases that amount will be so small as to be almost meaningless.

Who has responsibility for, and occasionally, who has the final authority to implement selection decisions must be very clear. Normally the two go together; however, there are situations in which a person or group may recommend items but someone else makes the final decision. When such a dual arrangement exists, it benefits everyone to define what the acceptable reasons are for rejecting a recommendation(s). The following are some of the possible selectors; many libraries use some combination of them:

- General librarians (today in a great many libraries CM work is just one element in a person's duties),
- Users (this is especially common in special libraries, but patron-driven selection is now being seen in public, school, and academic libraries as well),
- A committee of librarians (it is becoming more common for such committees to have user representatives as a part of the group),
- Library subject specialists (primarily in large research libraries where the individual has a graduate degree in the subject area and occasionally an MLS),
- Teaching faculty,
- Department/branch heads,
- Central library staff when there are branches.

When a library has some "must" and "must not" issues, such items should be spelled out so everyone knows what they are. Operating with an attitude that everyone "understands" or "knows" the rules usually causes problems from time to time. Often the problem arises when a person or persons in the service community questions a CM decision activity. Some of the more common dos and don'ts are:

- Select from standard or approved lists,
- Select items that have at least two positive reviews,
- Do not select items that have a negative review,
- Do not select textbooks, and
- Select only items of lasting literary merit or social value.

Branch library operations can complicate CM work unless the relationship to the main library is clearly spelled out. Are the branches fully dependent, partially dependent, or fully independent from the central facility in terms of collection management? The foregoing is essentially a continuum and most branches fall somewhere between the two extremes. We cover this in more detail later in the chapter.

Libraries receive gifts of books, journals/magazines, and media on a regular basis. Generally the bulk of such items are duplicates or out of the library's collecting scope. How to effectively handle gifts can be challenging at times, especially in the absence of a formal policy that addresses the issue. People hear the library is short of funds to buy material for the collection and think their gift of unwanted items is a valuable addition to the library's collection. Thus, how to dispose of the unneeded items may present a problem in terms of public relations. Having it clearly stated in the gift agreement (a form approved by the library's governing board) that the library has the sole right to dispose of unneeded items as it deems appropriate is a key policy issue. We explore gift implications in more depth in the next chapter.

From the Advisory Board

Carol Sinwell provided the following information about the Fairfax County (Virginia) Public Library's (FCPL) collection management policy:

The policy outlines 12 criteria to be followed in selecting material to be included in the library collection. The policy pertains to all of the collections, including any donated material. Amazon.com offers a way to make tax-deductible donations to the library (arranged by the Library Foundation) in which the donor chooses from a list of material which has been preselected by the library. As to monetary and other book donations, FCPL will accept money donations from patrons but does not accept "designated" donations that do not fit within the material collection guidelines and needs. Individuals often donate materials, especially books. If they pass muster, they may be added to the collection or included in a book sale.

Check This Out

Sample policies are available at AcqWeb's "Collection Development Policies" site at http://www.acqweb.org/cdv_policy.

Items in the collection can and do outlive their usefulness for the service community from time to time. A solid CM policy will cover both the methods of assessment to use when deciding if that time has come and how the library handles the disposition of such items. This can be a significant issue between an academic library and the teaching faculty who may have strong views about when, if ever, an item loses its usefulness. We look at the issue of collection assessment and withdrawal or storage of items in Chapter 6.

Every library will, at some time, have someone or a group of persons object to an item in the collection or available through an online database. Handling this situation in the absence of a policy will be much more stressful than it need be. The policy will not remove all the stress, but it will help. We cover ethical issues, complaints, and intellectual freedom in Chapter 12.

Engaging in Selection Activities

Earlier in this chapter we suggested that selection work can be one of the most enjoyable and rewarding library duties. While it is certainly enjoyable and rewarding, it can also be challenging and at times a little stressful. Over the next few pages we explore some of the things that lead to both the positive and negative sides of selection activities. We also indicated we had made a list of 37 "rational" factors involved in selection decision making. We cover 24 factors that apply to items regardless of format below; we review format-specific factors in Chapters 6 and 7. None of what follows is original; the factors discussed have been explored by many writers on collection building for many years (see Table 4.1).

Table 4.1.   Selection Process Theory Compared

McColvin	Drury	Haines	Ranganathan	Broadus	Curley & Broderick	Johnson
Theory of Book Selection (1925)	Book Selection (1930)	Living With Books (2nd ed., 1950)	Library Book Selection (1952; Rpt. 1990)	Selecting Materials For Libraries (2nd ed., 1981)	Building Library Collections (6th ed., 1985)	Fundamentals of Collection Development and Management (2nd ed., 2009)
1. Information should be as accurate as possible.	1. Establish suitable standards for judging all books.	1. Know the community's character and interests.	1. Books are for use.	1. Be aware of the impact of publicity that may stimulate demand.	1. Large public libraries with both a heterogeneous community to serve and a reasonable book budget can in theory apply most collection principles with little modification within the total library system.	1. Collection development activities may be broadly grouped into the categories of selecting, budgeting, planning and organizing, and communicating and reporting.
2. Items should be complete and balanced regarding subject and intended scope.	2. Apply criteria intelligently, evaluating the book's contents for inherent worth.	2. Be familiar with subjects of current interest.	2. Every reader his book.	2. Consider the duration as well as the intensity of the demand.		2. Formal planning for collections is the responsibility of the individual and the institution.
3. Authors should distinguish between fact and opinion.	3. Strive to get the best title on any subject, but add mediocre titles that will be read rather than superior titles that will be unread.	3. Represent subjects applicable to these conditions.	3. Every book its reader.	3. Weigh the amount of possible opposition to a title. Controversy stimulates demand.	2. Medium-sized libraries are similar, except that funding usually forces greater care in	3. Selection combines evaluation and
4. Information should be current. (Frequently *the determin-*	4. Information should be current.	4. Make the collection of local history materials useful and extensive.	4. Save the reader's time.	4. Include a reasonably high percentage of stan-		
			5. A library is a growing organism.			

(continued)

Table 4.1. (*Continued*)

McColvin	Drury	Haines	Ranganathan	Broadus	Curley & Broderick	Johnson
ing criteria for selection.)	4. Duplicate the best rather than acquire the many.	5. Provide materials for organized groups whose activities and interests can be related to books.		dards and classics in the collection.	selection. Mistakes are more costly.	assessment with personal knowledge, experience and intuition.
5. Writing style and treatment of the subject should be appropriate to the type of demand the book will answer.	5. Stock the classics and standards.	6. Provide materials for both actual and potential readers.		5. Consider past loans of specific titles and subjects. Past use is one of the most reliable predictors of future use.	3. Small public libraries are the most limited. Most can only hope to meet the most significant community demands, and they may lack both the professional staff and the money to do more.	4. Ongoing collection management involves deciding which materials to withdraw, store, preserve, digitize or cancel. It also involves protecting the collection from theft or damage.
6. The title should reflect the cultural values of its country of origin.	6. Select for positive use. 7. Develop the local history collection.	7. Avoid selecting books that are not in demand; withdraw books that are no longer useful.		6. Make some provision for serving the needs of potential users in the community. Having made such a provision, advertise it.	4. College libraries serve a more homogeneous population. In most cases, demand is the operative principle: college	5. Marketing, liaison and outreach activities are keys to obtaining information regarding user needs in order to develop
7. Consider physical characteristics when deciding between two books with similar content.	8. Be broad-minded and unprejudiced in selection. 9. Do select fiction. 10. Buy editions in bindings suitable for circulation and borrowing.	8. Select some books of permanent value regardless of their potential use.		7. Weigh the differences between true demand (which reflects		

(*continued*)

77

McColvin	Drury	Haines	Ranganathan	Broadus	Curley & Broderick	Johnson
	11. Know publishers, costs, and values. 12. Know authors and their works.	9. Practice impartiality in selection. Do not favor certain hobbies or opinions. In controversial or sectarian subjects, accept gifts if purchase is undesirable. 10. As much as possible, provide for the needs of specialists. 11. Strive not for a "complete" collection, but for the best: the best books on a subject, the best books by an author, the most useful		individual needs) and artificial demand (resulting from organized propaganda efforts).	libraries acquire materials needed to support the instructional program. No one questions the quality of the material if the request originated with a faculty member or department.	responsive collections. 6. Collection analysis is a means by which the utility or usefulness of a collection is measured. To be effective, such assessment activities should be ongoing. 7. Three components of cooperative collection development are physical access (resource sharing), intellectual (bibliographic) access, and coordinated collection development activities.

Table 4.1. (*Continued*)

(continued)

Table 4.1. (*Continued*)

McColvin	Drury	Haines	Ranganathan	Broadus	Curley & Broderick	Johnson
		volumes of a series.				8. The landscape of scholarly communication is undergoing rapid changes, most notably in the area of open access initiatives.
		12. Prefer an inferior book that will be read over a superior one that will not.				
		13. Keep abreast of current thought and opinion.				9. As scholarly communication continues to evolve, the need to support open access models, develop and manage institutional repositories, foster discovery and access, preserve digital content and provide outreach and liaison activities will continue to grow.
		14. Maintain promptness and regularity in supplying new books, especially for books that are both good and popular.				

What we have done is taken the factors that are scattered throughout the literature on CM and grouped them into 12 broad categories, some of which have subheadings, and have ordered them more or less in the sequence of the selection decision process.

1) Institutional setting

2) User interests/needs

3) Resources to consult to identify potential items

4) What exists in the collection

5) Known collection gaps (two subcategories)

6) Depth and breadth of subjects/topics based on library policy

7) Language of the material and local interest

8) Quality evaluation (10 subcategories)

9) Cost/usage assessment

10) Cost visa vie available funds

11) Availability of items elsewhere (locally)

12) Setting priorities for items to acquire

Institutional Setting and User Interests

It is the library's parent organization that creates its "type"—academic, public school, or special. The type immediately reduces the size of the information universe upon which a selector has to focus. The scope is further reduced by the characteristics of the service community that the selector is working with, such as having the assignment to work on the needs in the subject areas of anthropology and sociology, to build the children's collection, or provide curriculum support for grades K–4, and so forth. Only in the smallest libraries will the selector deal with a very broad range of topics and all classes of users.

Resources to Consult

With the above factors established, you can then look for resources that are likely to provide information about materials in your assigned area(s). In today's digital world, the range of possible useful resources is much greater than they were in the print-only environment.

One of the most obvious resources is bibliographies. They come in a variety of guises from the very general to the very narrow in scope. One of the most general "bibliographies" is the Online Computer Library Center's (OCLC) WorldCat™. In mid-2011, it contained 234 million records and over 1.7 billion bibliographic holdings, with more being added daily as libraries around the world add their new acquisitions to the database. Given the breadth and depth of the WorldCat™ database, it is not the best place to begin to look for new items that may be useful for your library. However, it is very useful when you need to verify some information about a known item such as which, if any, nearby libraries already hold the item. Such information may well impact your decision to add or not add the item to your collection. Another modestly useful feature is that each month, a list of the top 20 titles in terms of the number of views that title received is posted on the WorldCat™ blog (http://worldcat.org/blogs/)—a kind of library "top hits" list.

Its value is that the items on the list are very likely to be recent publications that libraries added to their collections.

On a slightly less grand scale are the online and printed catalogs of national libraries. Although not officially the U.S. national library, the Library of Congress (http://catalog.loc.gov/) performs many of the functions that other national libraries carry out. Some of the other national libraries that you might have occasion to use are:

British Library: http://www.bl.uk/

National Library of Australia: http://www.nla.gov.au/

Library and Archives Canada: http://www.collectionscanada.gc.ca/

Bibliothèque Nationale de *France:* http://www.bnf.fr/

Deutsche Nationalbibliothek: http://www.d-nb.de/eng/index.htm

Deutschen Zentralbibliothek für Wirtschaftswissenschaften (German National Library for Economics) http://www.zbw.eu/index-e.html

Biblioteca Nacional de México: http://bnm.unam.mx/

Access to these online catalogs, just as with WorldCat™, can be useful in verifying information about an item. The larger the library, the more likely you are to use these resources from time to time. However, any library with a large segment of its service population having a strong interest in reading material in languages other than English will find online catalogs useful for identifying new material to consider. (Almost all national libraries have the responsibility of acquiring and maintaining collections of material produced in their country. Some also have the even more ambitious goal of collecting everything in their language, regardless of where in the world it was published.)

For all their content, the large-scale databases and bibliographies do not provide availability information. A selector may not have the obligation to determining availability, leaving that task to the acquisitions unit. However, a selector can create goodwill with acquisitions staff when providing the availability information (that is, in print and possibly even vendor information).

Given print's long history, it is not surprising that the "bibliographic control" of that format is the strongest. Currently R.R. Bowker provides the broadest range of "availability tools." One such tool that you may know well is *Books in Print*® (*BIP*). A partner title, *Global Books in Print*®, includes Australian, Canadian, U.S., U.K., New Zealand, and South African publications and, like *BIP*, it covers books, audio books, and video titles. These products are available online as a subscription and are searchable by keyword, author, title, and ISBN/UPC (International Standard Book Number/Universal Product Code). We discuss such tools in more detail in the next chapter.

When a library has identified certain publishers as annually issuing a number of items that are of high interest, a selector will find going to those publishers' Websites a good method of identifying potentially useful items. Such sites almost always provide information about released titles as well as titles to be released in the near future ("Forthcoming Titles" is a common label for such pages). Almost every publisher of more than a dozen new titles per year and that has a backlist (items released in prior years but still in stock) will issue print catalogs and promotional flyers, although e-flyers and catalogs are becoming a more popular means of marketing. It is easy for a selector to get on the mailing list; it is often rather difficult to get off the list. You need to be cautious about any publishers' descriptions of their offerings. Needless to say, they are not likely to say anything bad about an item and rather often suggest the title is much better than it actually turns out to be. There are, from time to time, firms that libraries cannot trust—they simply put out totally misleading information. Another caution to keep in mind is that some announced forthcoming titles never do appear. Placing an order for such items may tie up much needed funds on something that never materializes in the acquisitions receiving unit. There are several common reasons for this to happen—the author fails to deliver the expected material or what is delivered in unacceptable. We explore such issues in more depth in Chapter 8.

There are thousands of subject bibliographies, best, recommended, "core," or "standard" lists in existence. Two such items are *Children's Core Collection* (H.W. Wilson, 20th edition, 2010) and *Nonbook Materials Core Collection* (online). Content of these identification tools varies from a single narrow topic to broad-based core lists that include fiction and nonfiction titles as well as a variety of formats. When using such tools you want to ascertain at least four key issues. First, what is the date when the tool first appeared; in a fast changing world what is "good" today may be useless in a year's time. Second, who produced the list, what were the person's or persons' qualifications for doing the work? Third, what criteria were employed in making the judgment to include an item? Fourth, and most important, just how relevant is the list to your library situation? Determining the answers for the first three questions is often more challenging than you might think. Patrick Jones (2003) had the following thoughts about core/best book lists produced by ALA, in this case his focus was on young adult collections: "While the various lists represent the best books published in one year for the young adult audience as chosen by a group of informed observers, they may or may not indicate which are the best books for the customers you serve, or want to serve" (p. 48).

What Is in the Collection, What Is Lacking

The collection policy will likely contain information about what your library does and does not collect and something about the level of interest or ability of the users. Such information supplies the broad context for your selection activities; what it does not do is tell you what already exists in the collection.

Although you can explore the library's holdings through the ILS, nothing matches spending time in the stacks looking at the items on the shelves in your area(s) of responsibility when it comes to knowing what you have. What titles are there in this or that narrow topic, what these titles contain, how old they are, and what usage patterns are discernable are some of the questions to keep in mind as you pull items off the shelf. Even the amount, or lack of, dust tells you something useful. This may seem like extra work, especially as you probably will have more job obligations than simply CM duties. However, doing this will save you more than the time you spend in the stacks as you engage in your ongoing selection work—you will have less and less need to check to see if you have or need this particular item.

Information about what is lacking or missing comes from several sources. Certainly some will come from your time in the stacks, especially if you know the subject area well. Any appropriate core/best/recommended list may provide other clues as to which voids to fill. However, one in-library source will provide significant input—public service departments. Interlibrary loan (ILL) requests can be very useful regarding current user interests that are unmet by the local resources. One caution, if you are in an academic library, is to make certain that a number of requests from one person reflects ongoing interest and not the needs of a onetime project.

Not long ago (late 1990s), academic libraries started using what is called a "books on demand" program, which uses ILL requests as the basis for acquiring items for the collection. Kristine Anderson and her colleagues (2002) reported on early results of one such program. They noted, "Five subject bibliographers analyzed 800 titles acquired through the program in their subject areas and compared them with titles acquired during the same time period through normal selection. The bibliographers concluded that the patron-driven *Books on Demand* program is a valuable complementary collection development tool" (pp. 1–2). In 2010, David Tyler and his associates wrote an article that looked at a similar program at another university. Their timeframe was five years' worth of acquisitions, and they noted in their conclusion that "The UNL [University of Nebraska, Lincoln] project confirmed findings in the literature indicating that purchase-on-demand programs at libraries of several types have been very successful at obtaining cost-effective materials that are not only suitable for their collections but also meet the needs of multiple patrons" (p. 174).

Circulation department records are another resource. One obvious category of information comes from the "lost and paid for" file. While it may or may not be the selector's responsibility to handle a replacement, in any event there may be a pattern of lost and paid for items that reflects a high interest level about a topic or particular work that needs some attention. Almost every circulation department has a "search file." That is, records of items users could not locate and have no record of being charged out to anyone. Circulation staff searches for the missing items, and they often find the item misshelved, lying on a table, or on a book truck waiting to be reshelved. However, some items do seem to disappear and eventually a decision about replacing the item must take place. As with lost and paid for items, CM staff may see a pattern in what is missing and need to answer the question, "What do we do about this?"

Earlier we mentioned that the CM policy provides, or may do so, information regarding subject breadth and depth. Although most libraries can and do benefit from such analysis, academic libraries often have the most complex tables of coverage and depth. Many academic libraries employ some variation of the *conspectus model* for addressing subject breadth and depth in their collections. The conspectus provides a coding system that all types of libraries can use. Small and medium-size libraries do not need as detailed an analysis as large libraries do. There are four possible subject levels in the conspectus model a library may select from (there is a Dewey conversion table available):

- 20 major Library of Congress divisions (the least detailed and most appropriate for small and medium-size nonspecialized libraries);

- 200 subject level (this is the level many colleges use);

- 500 field level (the most common level for medium-size academic and most large public libraries); and

- 5,000 topic level (this is the level one needs to employ with a research collection).

Setting the desired level is often a collaborative process between the CM personnel and other interested parties.

Generally, the library also indicates the desired level of collecting. One approach makes use of a five value system: 0—out of scope; 1—minimal; 2—basic information; 3—instructional level; and 4—research level. The *Pacific Northwest Collection Assessment Manual* (1992) offers a more detailed division of such coding: la, lb, 2a, 2b, 3a (basic), 3b (intermediate), and 3c (advanced). The process of assigning values is highly subjective and one of the reasons it is wise to have stakeholder involvement in making the decisions about levels. The *Pacific Northwest Manual* offers some quantitative guidelines to assist in assigning values. The following is a paraphrase of some of the suggested quantitative levels for making an assignment:

1. Monographs
   la = out of scope
   lb = fewer than 2,500 titles
   2a = 2,500–5,000 titles
   2b = 5,000–8,000 titles
   3a = 8,000–12,000 titles
   3b = over 12,000 titles

2. Percentage of holdings in major subject bibliographies
   lb = 5% or below
   2a = less than 10%
   2b = less than 15%
   3a = 15–20%
   3b = 30–40%
   3c = 50–70%
   4 = 75–80%

Elizabeth Futas (1993) wrote an interesting article about genre literature and public libraries in which she suggested employing collecting categories in the policy statement, such as recreational, informational, instructional, and reference, for genre materials:

> The level that makes the most sense for genre literature is the recreational level, which indicates the best current titles on the market. Some of the better known and still read genre authors might fall into one of two other levels available for public library selection, general information level, indicating a large number of current titles and a limited selection of retrospective titles, or instructional level, a good selection of current titles and a good selection of retrospective titles. (p. 42)

Language

For many selectors, the issue of adding items in languages other than English can cause some of the stress and emotion that Quinn wrote about. When funding is limited, do you select an item in a language you know has few readers in the service community when you know those few are active users and supporters of the library? What about selecting materials in a language you know has many potential, but very few active, users in the community, assuming the library can attract them? Some stress may surface as often the choice is between two or more equally good options.

There is the potential for some loud complaints from users who believe all users of U.S. libraries ought to be proficient in English, and libraries, especially public libraries, ought not offer anything but English language items. Not many years ago there was a pointed exchange of views in *American Libraries* (2007, vol. 38, no. 10) between Todd Quesada and Julia Stephens over the role, or lack thereof, Spanish language material and services have in public libraries. In 2010, concern about what rights non-English speakers or immigrants may or may not have became a powerful political issue. At the time we prepared this chapter, we had not read that libraries were being pulled into the debate. However, the exchange between Quesada and Stephens, as well as in later entries in the letters to editor section of *American Libraries*, suggests the issue is and has been a concern with the profession for some time.

Assessing Quality

This activity is the center of the selection process and perhaps the most complex. In this section we look at many of the elements that are part of estimating an item's quality for your collection. You rarely use all of the following quality factors for a single item, but you will need to use some of them. Different elements come into play as the character of the item changes (such as fiction or nonfiction, mass market or scholarly, adult or juvenile).

Reviews

One obvious and most frequently used starting point for quality assessment are published reviews, when they exist. Reviews are very helpful; however, there are limitations. Perhaps the most significant limitation is the percentage of new titles that actually receive a review. One large category of new items not reviewed is new or revised editions of a work. As most of the titles in this group are textbooks, the lack of reviews is less important as many libraries exclude textbooks from their collections.

Editors of review columns or journals receive hundreds to thousands of items from which they must select a few to review. The editors' primary limitation on the number of reviews is cost and the space they have for reviewing columns in journals and newspapers. Another limiting factor is having someone who is qualified and available to review an item within the timeframe the editor requires. (Good reviews require a person who knows the subject or genre very well, who has no personal interest regarding the author or creator of the item, and has adequate time for writing the review. Keeping such people available and being able to give people proper time for producing a sound review and usually for nothing more than "thanks, you can keep the review copy" is a challenge.) One trait of good selectors is they keep in mind the names of reviewers and how well their reviews matched up with the items after receipt in the library.

It is important to keep in mind the absence of a review does *not* mean an item lacks quality. Just how many items are or are not reviewed? Liz Johnson and Linda Brown (2008) provided some hard data to answer that question. Their sample was all of the books processed by the library vendor YBP for the OhioLINK consortium during the period of July 2004 through June 2005. (YBP was formerly the independent firm Yankee Book Peddler, and now is part of the Baker & Taylor firm under the title YBP. Its primary market is academic libraries.) Although the sample was heavily academic in character, it was not that far from the overall picture of reviewing, as we will illustrate below.

Johnson and Brown found that 89.9 percent of the titles in the sample received no review. They also grouped the titles by the size of the press that released them—small presses (1–18 titles), medium (19–69 titles), and large (more than 70 titles). Somewhat surprising was a higher percentage of the "small press" titles had a review (22 percent) than did the large presses (8.1 percent) (p. 99).

To gain some perspective on the above in terms of total U.S. production, we drew on data from Bowker's *Library and Book Trade Almanac* (*LBTA*, formerly *Bowker Annual*). Using 2009 preliminary data, one finds the reported U.S. production for the year was 175,443 titles (Bogart, 2010, p. 485) and 47,654 reviews (p. 525) published in the so-called gatekeeper review sources. Those figures suggest that 27.3 percent of the new titles received one review. The true number reviewed is far lower, as the assumption of one review per title is not valid; some titles get multiple reviews in sources such as *Publishers Weekly*, *Library Journal*, *Booklist*, and *Kirkus Reviews* as well as in newspapers such as the *New York Times* and *Chicago Tribune*. There are many reasons for a title being reviewed in several sources—it deals with a "hot topic," was written by a notable person, or it gets highly promoted for example. We did not attempt to determine just how many of the titles had more than one review. However, it is certain the actual number of titles that were reviewed in 2009 was less than 47,654 and the actual percentage of nonreviewed titles would be closer to the Johnson and Brown number than the implied 72.9 percent based on the Bowker reported reviews.

How many reviews does each of the gatekeeper review sources (those reported by Bowker) produce on average? The following are the top seven review sources listed in *LBTA* (Bogart, 2010, p. 525) in terms of number of reviews:

Booklist—8,279	*Library Journal*—5,741
Choice—6,632	*Publishers Weekly*—7,595
Horn Book Guide—4,373	*School Library Journal*—5,700
Kirkus Reviews—4,466	

The above discussion raises a question about library policies that require a selector to only consider items that have two or more reviews. Such a policy effectively eliminates more than 72 percent of U.S. annual production,

---

Check These Out

An excellent Website for identifying hundreds of sources for book reviews is http://www.complete-review.com/links/links.html. The site includes links to English and other foreign language review sites.

A good book that discusses U.S. book reviewing is Gail Pool's *In Faint Praise: The Plight of Book Reviewing in America* (Columbia: University of Missouri Press, 2007). Pool was a longtime book review editor for several journals and newspapers. Two very enlightening chapters are "Unnatural Selection" and "The Match." Unnatural selection deals with the issue of why the number of titles actually reviewed is so small, while the match chapter discusses the challenges in finding the right reviewer. The book is short, informative, and a "good read."

although (based on Bowker data about production and reviews) "juvenile" titles appear to have a significantly higher percentage (79 percent) receiving reviews (however, this percentage still does not take into consideration any duplication of reviews that may exist). A question to ponder is, "Is such a policy present to ensure collection quality or is it to protect the librarians from complaints about their decisions?"

Other Quality Factors

For many selectors, reviews help, but at the end of the day they must engage in a substantial amount of independent assessment. That activity draws on the same factors that good reviewers employ as well as additional factors of local concern. Some of those major factors are:

- Type of material (fiction or nonfiction for example),
- Subject matter,
- Content,
- Treatment (level and depth),
- Theme(s),
- Intended audience,
- Presentation style (writing quality),
- Accuracy,
- Utility (indexes, references, illustrations),
- Author's reputation,
- Publisher/producer's reputation,
- Point of view (evidence to support a view),
- Fiction (plot, characterizations, realistic/fantasy, etc.),
- Potential value for the service community,
- Final assessment.

The above are all useful when you have an item to examine, such as with an approval plan (we discuss such plans in the next chapter). The reality is that much of your assessment work will have to be done without having an opportunity to inspect or read the material.

You will have to make some judgment on the basis of a bibliographic citation or material supplied by the publisher or producer. Assessing the suitability of an item for your collection based on limited information is a challenge at first. Essentially, it takes time, experience, and making some poor calls before you get comfortable with this phase of collection management. It is also true that you will experience a similar learning curve when you change libraries. The following are a few tips that will help lessen the number of early poor calls.

Even with the most basic citation—author, title and subtitle, date of publication, publisher or producer, and price—you do have a number of clues as to the item's quality; this is especially true in today's online world. Start with the author or creator. Ask yourself, "Do I know the name from prior selection activities?" and "Are there other items in the collection by this person?" (The online public access catalog [OPAC] will quickly provide that answer.) If not, do some checking on the Web for information about the person and the individual's qualifications. Check WorldCat™ to see what other items the person is associated with and what libraries hold copies of prior titles as well as the current item under consideration. The more items the person has produced and that are widely held is a good clue to the general quality of the person's work. Another plus of such searches is you gain additional insight regarding the content from subject headings that have been assigned to the title and, on occasion, can even see the table of contents.

You can do the same type of checking regarding the publisher or producer, if you do not happen to know it. Some academic and large public libraries have developed "reputation data" for publishers they use with great frequency. There is the necessity to reassess the data on a regular basis as the pace of change in the publishing industry is no less than that in librarianship. In 1983, John Calhoun and James Bracken proposed an index of publisher quality. (See also a follow-up study by Goedeken (1993) and the definitions of *quality* and *relevance* offered by Metz and Stemmer in their 1996 study.) Although Calhoun and Bracken's article describes an index or model for an academic library, it is easy to apply to any type of library. Their concept was very straightforward:

1.   Determine the top 50 to 75 producers/publishers from which the library buys. Select a number of book awards, such as the Caldecott or a best-of-the-year award (e.g., *Choice*'s annual Outstanding Academic Books); or select a frequently updated list of recommended titles (e.g., Bill Katz's *Magazines for . . .*) that are appropriate for the library.

2.   Develop a table of award-winning titles by publisher based on the award lists. Total the number of award winners for each publisher over a period of time (e.g., two, three, or five years).

3.   Calculate a ratio based on each publisher's average output (during the time period covered by the award lists) and the number of award-winning titles published during that time (p. 257).

They also suggested that using this index could improve one's chances of selecting the best books without seeing reviews. For example, a person who blindly selected books from Academic Press stood a 1 in 46.67 chance of picking an award winner; the odds with Basic Books were 1 in 10.97 (p. 258). The effort to collect the data to create the index, though considerable, would familiarize selectors with the publishers from which the library frequently buys as well as with the publishers' track records in producing highly recommended titles.

Check This Out

An old but still very relevant article about using citation information in the selection process is Ross Atkinson's (1984) work "The Citation as Intertext: Toward a Theory of the Selection Process," in *Library Resources and Technical Services* 28, no. 2: 109–119. Atkinson was one of the best thinkers about collection management on both the theoretical and practical levels.

From the Authors' Experience

For most of his "selector career" Evans was responsible for materials in anthropology, archaeology, and often sociology. One such assignment was at Tozzer Library (Harvard University's anthropology library), which had at the time over 100 years of attempting to be one of the world's foremost anthropology libraries. Most of the selection work had to be done from citation information in bibliographies and out of print book dealer catalogs. Certainly teaching experience in both collection management and anthropology was a great help in making quality judgment calls. However, someone without such a background could also have done well using the ideas outlined above.

For example, reading a citation about conditions on the Lakota reservations in South Dakota, he had a different expectation regarding the content of the item with the place of publication as "Washington, D.C., 1986" or "Pine Ridge, S.D., 1977." The latter would have a much different perspective than would the former, and depending on the library's need for more information on the Lakota views, the latter would likely be the better choice. Another example of how a citation element could modify a judgment is a title implying comprehensive or comparative treatment of a broad or complex subject, with pagination indicating a much shorter book than would be reasonable for the topic.

When a citation string includes subject descriptors, profound modification in judgment can occur. An entry in a bibliography might seem appropriate for Tozzer Library until encountering the subject heading *juvenile*. Without the supplemental context, it is possible and even probable that the library would order some inappropriate items because of inadequate information—one of those poor calls that we all make.

Cost Issues

We ended our list of quality factors to consider with "your assessment." When that assessment is that the item "has potential for our collection," there are still a few more factors to think about before making the final decision to acquire the item—costs.

Although when you first start doing selection in a library the following will be difficult to do with any great confidence, you should make an estimate of the potential use of an item. Funds are limited and gaining maximum usage out of the items acquired shows good stewardship of the available funds. Essentially, you do a cost-benefit analysis for each item (will usage be proportional to cost), certainly not a formal analysis, but one in your mind based on your experience. (A hint to help with your assessment during the "early days" in a new library is to do a keyword search of the OPAC for items in the collection on that topic. What is their usage pattern?)

The second cost consideration is obvious, how much money is left to spend and how long must it last? (Most funding is for a fiscal year—FY.) The longer the timeframe before new funds are available, the more likely you will hold off on the "buy decision" as there is a chance even better items will appear later in the year. The question is—how long to wait? Near the end of a FY you often face the issue of not having enough money to acquire all the items you want or need. Which items can wait, which are "must acquire now," and how to make the call are questions that bedevil even the most experienced selectors.

With your assessment of potential value, cost to usage, and available funding, you have to prioritize the items—acquire now, can wait for a while, and those that may never be acquired. There is a continuum of importance from absolutely essential to the ultimate luxury, with almost all of the items falling somewhere in the midrange.

Another factor that may come into play in setting the priorities is the availability of the item locally and the existence of reciprocal borrowing or collection building agreements. There may be items that become essential due to more or less binding agreements, while items that would be nice to have in the collection are not purchased as they are available nearby. We explore collaborative CM in Chapter 7.

Variations in Selection by Library Type

For convenience of presentation, we employ the traditional categories of libraries: academic, public, school, and special. Certainly, there are great differences even within each category, and what follows provides only a broad overview of the thousands of variations that exist.

Academic Libraries—Community Colleges

In the United States there are two broad categories of postsecondary schools: vocational and academic. People usually think of publicly supported vocational programs in the United States as community colleges (CCs). However, the reality is that most CCs have both vocational and academic programs. The academic program is roughly equivalent to the first two years in a college or university and may lead to an associate of arts degree. Such programs also serve as a transfer program to a four-year college or university. If the transfer program is to succeed in providing the equivalent of the first two years of a four-year undergraduate degree, then the scope of the program must be just as comprehensive as that of the university program. That in turn has library collection implications.

Collection management personnel in a CC library have a challenging job. Not only must they focus on the academic programs, but they must also give equal attention to a wide range of vocational programs—and do so with a modest budget. Unfortunately, from a cost perspective, it is seldom possible to find materials that are useful in both programs. One factor is that the costs of materials to support some programs (such as health and medicine) tend to be higher than others (such as literature or history). Also, many vocational programs require more visual than print materials, which account in part for the fact that U.S. CC libraries tend to be leaders in the use of media materials. CC librarians normally have other duties assigned to them beyond their collection development responsibilities, such as reference and instruction. (However, this pattern is becoming more and more the norm for all types of libraries.)

Like other academic institutions, CCs also offer extensive adult continuing education programs. These programs often have little or no relationship to the degree programs. In most CCs the library, or learning resource center (LRC), must handle all programmatic information needs. Given the diversity of subjects and levels of user ability, the CC library more resembles the public library than it does its larger relation, the university library.

CC libraries serve a heterogeneous community, and their collections must reflect a diverse population with varying levels of language skills. Selection is usually item by item, with less use of blanket orders and approval plans than in other types of academic libraries. Collections generally contain at least a few items in all the standard educational formats. Selection personnel generally use a greater variety of selection aids than their colleagues in other types of libraries.

College Libraries

Although college libraries serving primarily bachelor's degree programs are diverse, each tends to serve a homogeneous user group. Only the small special library that caters to a company or research group is likely to have a more homogeneous service community. One characteristic of bachelor's degree programs is that, within a particular college, all the students who graduate, regardless of their major, complete some type of general education program. A program of core courses means that students select from a limited number of courses during their first two years. Less variety in course offerings makes library selection work less complex. Support of the curriculum is the primary objective of the college library collection. College libraries may offer some collection support for faculty research, but, unlike universities, colleges seldom emphasize research. With the curriculum as the focus for collection development activities, selectors have definite limits within which to work. Faculty members frequently play an active role in selection, more so than in the CC or university context.

Without question, the most widely used selection aid in U.S. college libraries is *Choice* (published by the ALA). ALA created *Choice* to meet the specific needs of college library collection development officers by reviewing publications aimed at the undergraduate market. Subject experts, including librarians, write the reviews with an emphasis on the subject content and the title's overall suitability for undergraduate, rather than research, use. With small staffs (typically 10 to 15 people), few college libraries have sufficient subject expertise to evaluate all the potentially useful titles published each year, even with help from the teaching faculty. Because *Choice* annually reviews more than 6,000 titles, primarily titles intended for the undergraduate student, and because of its widespread use as a selection aid, several librarians have studied *Choice* to determine how effective it is as a selection aid (see the Suggested Readings for a few such articles).

One study of the usage of *Choice*-reviewed titles in seven undergraduate liberal arts colleges by Margaret M. Jobe and Michael Levine-Clark (2008) concluded that:

> The undergraduate use rate of *Choice*-reviewed books is no different from that of the rest of the library collection. . . .
> Though these books may be used at the same rate as other books in the collection, a *Choice* review suggests a much higher possibility that the book will be used at least once. (p. 302)

University Libraries

University and research libraries' interests and needs dominate the professional literature, judging by the number of books and articles published about academic collection development. This domination arises from several types of numerical superiority. Although these libraries are not as numerous as libraries of other types, the size of their collections and the number of their staff, as well as monies expended per year on operations, far surpass the combined totals for all the other types of libraries. University and research libraries have collections ranging from a few hundred thousand to more than 10 million volumes. As an example, Tozzer Library (Harvard University) is a research library of about 320,000 items, a small library in the world of research libraries. However, it collects only in the fields of anthropology and archaeology. It is, as a result, one of the two largest anthropology libraries in the world. Like all research libraries, Tozzer spends a good deal of money on materials each year, does much work that is retrospective, and collects in most languages. Collection development and selection work require more time and attention in university research libraries than in other academic libraries. Typically, there are a few full-time CM staffers; although even in the largest research libraries there are fewer present today than in the past.

Looking at the history and development of U.S. academic libraries, one can see a changing pattern in regard to who does the book selection. In small libraries with limited funds, there is strong faculty involvement; sometimes the faculty has sole responsibility for building the collection. As the collection, institution, and budget grow, there is a shift to more and more librarian involvement and responsibility. At the university and research library levels, subject specialists come back into the selection picture, but they are members of the library staff rather than the teaching faculty.

A significant problem in large university and research library systems with departmental or subject libraries is coordinating CM activities. Budgets may be large, but there is always more material than money. Unintentional duplication is always a concern, but the biggest problem is determining whose responsibility it is to collect in a given subject. As the number of persons involved goes up and the scope of each person's responsibility diminishes, the danger of missing important items increases. Working together, sending one another announcements, and checking with colleagues about their decisions become major activities for university CM officers.

University libraries tend to depend heavily on standing and blanket orders, as well as approval plans, as means of reducing workloads while ensuring adequate collection building. Using such programs allows selectors more time for retrospective buying and for tracking down items from countries where the book trade is not well developed. Knowledge of one or more foreign languages is a must if one wishes to be a CM officer at the university level.

Public Libraries

Diversity is the primary characteristic of public libraries' selection practices (arising from the heterogeneous nature of the communities they serve). Communities of a few hundred people, with a small library open only a few hours per week with no professional or full-time staff, do not follow the same practices followed at large urban libraries. Collection sizes range from several hundred items (Mancos, Colorado) to large research collections of millions of volumes (New York City).

Despite this variety, some generalizations apply to most public libraries. The service community normally consists of unrelated constituencies: persons from various ethnic groups, of all ages, with various educational backgrounds and levels of skill and knowledge, and with a variety of information needs. "Wants" are the dominant factor in selection. Although librarians make the final selection decisions, they frequently employ a collection development committee that involves some users. Growth of the collection is modest because of limited stack space, and weeding activities focus on the removal of worn-out or outdated materials. Most selections are current imprints, with retrospective buying generally limited to replacement titles. Medium and large public libraries commonly collect audio and video recordings. Perhaps the main difference in collection development between public libraries and libraries of other types is the strong emphasis on recreational needs, in addition to educational and informational materials. Trade publishers count on a strong public library market for most of their new releases. Without the library market, book buyers would see even higher prices, because only a fraction of the new books published would become strong sellers, much less best sellers.

For larger libraries, there are two important issues in selection: speed and coordination. Most of the larger libraries are systems with a main library and several branches. The reading public likes to read new books while they are new, not six to nine months after interest wanes. Often interest is fleeting, especially in fiction. So, having the new books on the shelf and ready to circulate when the demand arises is important. With several service points, a system must control costs. One way to help control costs is to place one order for multiple copies of desired items rather than ordering one now, another later, and still more even later. Multiple copy orders tend to receive a higher discount for the library.

Anticipating public interest is a challenge for the public library, and it probably would be impossible without several aids. Unquestionably, the most important aid is the selector's inquiring, active mind and the commitment to read, read, read. In addition, one of the most useful aids is *Publishers Weekly*. Reading each issue cover to cover provides a wealth of information about what publishers plan to do to market new titles. Clues such as "30,000 first printing; major ad promo; author tour"; "BOMC, Cooking and Crafts Club alternative"; "major national advertising"; "soon to be a TV miniseries"; or "author to appear on the *Tonight Show*" can help the selector to identify potentially high-interest items before demand arises. Additionally, *Library Journal* and *Booklist* provide "Prepub alerts" and "upfront preview" listings. All three publications include such information in both their print and online publications. The McNaughton Plan (rental plan) is one way to meet high, short-term demand for multiple copies—we discuss this plan in more detail in the next chapter.

The need to coordinate order placement is one reason many public libraries use selection committees. Such committees, especially if they include a representative from each service location, reduce the problem of order coordination. In large systems with dozens of branches and mobile service points, such as the Los Angeles Public Library, total representation is impractical. In such cases, the selection committee develops a recommended buying list, and the service locations have a period of time to order from the list. Although it is not a perfect system, it does help achieve some degree of coordinated buying and cost control.

Small public libraries do not experience the above problems. Instead, their challenges involve finding the money and time to buy materials. Reviews play a vital role in helping selectors at the small library locate the best possible buys with limited funds. *Booklist* is the most important selection aid; although all the titles contained in *Booklist* are recommended, it also identifies highly recommended titles (called "the best buys"). *Booklist* also reviews a wide range of materials including reference titles. In the fall of 2010, *Booklist Online Video Newsletter* appeared as the newest of its online selection aid products.

Another distinctive feature of public library collection development is an emphasis on children's materials. In many public libraries, children's books get the highest use. Most libraries depend on positive reviews when making selection decisions about children's books. Often, the staff members examine the title when it arrives to make certain it fits collection guidelines, and some larger library systems receive review copies of just about all

---

Check This Out

The Cooperative Children's Book Center (CCBC, http://www.education.wisc.edu/ccbc/), a program of the School of Education at the University of Wisconsin–Madison, serves as a central source of review copies for librarians in Wisconsin. Although the titles do not circulate, the CCBC is used by school and public librarians to examine new books before purchasing them. The CCBC also provides a "Book of the Week" review of newly acquired titles (http://www.education.wisc.edu/ccbc/books/bowarchive.asp).

---

new titles from the major children's publishers. These copies can be made available for inspection by children's librarians before they make their purchases—although lately this practice has been curtailed in some places due to budgetary challenges.

One of the first specialist positions a growing public library tries to create is for children's materials and services. (Note: Traditionally, the overlap between children's materials in schools and those in public libraries has not been large. School libraries focus on curriculum support, while recreational materials have usually been the largest component of public library children's collections. This overlap may be growing, however, as homeschooling

---

From the Advisory Board

Virginia Walter provided the following observations regarding the challenges of going from the data side of learning about the service community to engaging in the world of selection. Like so many aspects of CM work, time and experience are keys to long-term success as well as getting out into the community and looking, talking, and thinking about what you see:

I have long noticed that my students often have difficulty making the leap from knowing the demographics to actually tailoring collections to those demographic considerations. And really, this involves knowing a wide variety of information and reading resources as well as the demographic data. I had no difficulty at the Malabar Branch figuring out how to meet the information needs of my elderly Jewish patron. He was very clear about his interest in reading the Yiddish newspaper. There was a greater learning curve involved in meeting the needs of the Latino community. I needed to learn more about them as individuals—not just as statistics. How many of them wanted to read Spanish language materials. What kind? Novelas? Spanish classics? Spanish comics? English classics translated into Spanish? (It turned out that car repair manuals in Spanish were particularly desirable.) What were the best sources for these materials? I found that taking my Spanish-speaking clerk with me to buy books, magazines, and records was the best way to be sure I was buying popular stuff. What kinds of ESL and citizenship materials were wanted? And that was just the adult material!

My students in children's library services are very good at identifying information needs or reading interests, but they need much more knowledge of the materials that are available to meet those needs and interests. To my mind, this is the essence of professional library work: knowing both the reader and information-seeker those materials that will potentially meet their need—and putting the two together.

becomes more popular and public libraries find themselves needing to meet both the research and recreational needs of younger clientele.) One review source that is frequently used is *School Library Journal* (http://www.school libraryjournal.com/). Another resource that can be helpful in the selection of these materials is the *Bulletin of the Center for Children's Books*, a publication from Johns Hopkins Press and the Graduate School of Library and Information Science at the University of Illinois at Urbana-Champaign (http://bccb.lis.illinois.edu/).

Two other special features of public library collection development are noteworthy. First, the public library, historically, has been a place to which citizens turn for self-education materials. Self-education needs range from basic language and survival skills and knowledge for the recent immigrant, to improving skills gained in schools, to maintaining current knowledge of a subject studied in college. In addition to the true educational function of the preceding, there is the self-help and education aspect exemplified by learning how to repair a car (as seen in the advisory board example above), how to fix a sticky door, how to prepare a special meal, or how to win friends and influence people. Selecting materials for the varied educational wants and desires of a diverse population can be a real challenge and a specialty in itself.

The last feature of note is the selection of genre fiction, a staple in most public library collections. Most people read only a few types of fiction regularly. Some readers will devour any western about range wars but will not touch a title about mountain men. Learning about the different categories and their authors is not only fun but also useful for anyone developing a public library collection.

Check These Out

A good resource that can be of help in learning about such fiction is the Genreflecting Advisory Series produced by Libraries Unlimited. The series currently contains over 30 titles covering genre types (Latino literature, historical fiction, horror, etc.) and some that focus on an age group. Another resource is the Readers Advisory Online blog, available at: http://www.readersadvisoronline.com/blog/.

School Library Media Centers

Curriculum support dominates school library media center collections. Some similarities exist among community college, college, and school media center selection and collection development. Each emphasizes providing materials directly tied to teaching requirements, and each uses instructor input in the selection process. An emphasis on current material, with limited retrospective buying, is also common. Community college and school media centers share the distinction of having the greatest number and variety of media materials in their collections. Both school and community college media centers must serve an immense range of student abilities.

Although similarities do exist, the differences between school media centers and other educational libraries far outweigh the similarities. Take curriculum support, for example. School media centers have very limited funding for collection building; in this area they resemble the small public library. With limited funds and limited staff (perhaps only a part-time professional with volunteers covering most of the work), most of the money goes to purchasing items that directly support specific instructional units.

From the Advisory Board

Sandra Hughes-Hassell recommends that school librarians check out *WOW Review: Reading Across Cultures* (http://wowlit.org/on-line-publications/review/), an electronic journal of critical reviews on children's and adolescent literature that highlights intercultural understanding and global perspectives, and the International Children's Digital Library (ICDL, http://en.childrenslibrary.org/) that as of mid-2011 contained more than 4,469 books in 55 languages.

Normally, teachers and media specialists serve on committees that review and select items for purchase. Some parent representation on the committee is desirable. Whatever the committee composition, the media specialist must take the responsibility for identifying potentially useful items, preparing a list of suggestions, and securing examination or preview copies for group consideration. Most importantly, the committee must have a clear sense of collection emphasis, of how the items under consideration support current curriculum, and of how the collection will grow as the curriculum evolves.

Published reviews play a significant role in media center selection. Often, school districts secure published reviews and also inspect items before making purchase decisions. The reasons for this are parental and school board interest in the collection's content and the need to spend limited funds on materials that will actually meet teachers' specific needs. The most widely used review sources are *Booklist*, *Horn Book*, *School Library Journal*, *Voice of Youth Advocates*, and H.W. Wilson's catalogs, such as the *Children's Core Collection*. As school populations have become increasingly diverse, consulting review sources, such as *MultiCultural Review*, a journal focused on race, ethnicity, and religious diversity that provides reviews of books and other media with multicultural themes and topics, and the Barahona Center for the Study of Books in Spanish for Children and Adolescents (http://www2.csusm.edu/csb/), a comprehensive, bilingual database for books published in Spanish-speaking countries or translated into Spanish from other languages, has become critical. Information about grade level and effectiveness in the classroom are two crucial concerns for the media specialist. Grade level information is generally available, but it is very difficult to locate data about classroom effectiveness. Usually, the time involved in gathering effectiveness data is too great to make it useful in media center collection development.

Special Libraries

Almost any general statement about special libraries and information centers is inaccurate for any individual special library because of the diversity of environmental settings. In a sense, this is a "catchall" category. As a result, this category is the largest and the least homogeneous. Dividing this category into three subclasses—scientific and technical, corporate and industrial, and subject and research—allows some useful generalizations. However, even these subclasses are not always mutually exclusive. A hospital library can have both a scientific and a corporate orientation if it has a responsibility to support both the medical and the administrative staff. In teaching hospitals, there is an educational aspect to collection building as well. There may even be a flavor of a public library, if the library offers a patient-service program. Some corporations establish two types of information centers, technical and management; others have a single facility to serve both activities. A geology library in a large research university may have more in common with an energy corporation library than it does with other libraries in its own institution. Large, independent, specialized research libraries, such as the Newberry, Linda Hall, or Folger libraries, fall into a class by themselves, yet they have many of the characteristics of the research university library.

Depending on which commercial mailing list one examines, the count of special libraries in the United States and Canada ranges from 12,000 to more than 19,000. Despite their substantial numbers, special libraries have not influenced professional practice as much as you might expect. This does not mean that special libraries have not made important contributions or developed innovative practices; it merely means that circumstances often make it difficult or impossible for special libraries to share information about their activities in the same manner as other libraries. Their diversity in character and operational environment is one reason for special libraries' modest influence. Another reason is that libraries and information centers in profit-oriented organizations frequently limit the reporting of activities and new systems for proprietary reasons; knowing what a competitor is working on may provide a company with an advantage. Such concerns often limit the amount of cooperative activities in which corporate libraries may engage. One way to learn about an organization's current interests is to study the materials in its library.

Most special libraries have very current collections and, in terms of collection policy, would be considered a level four (research), but without the retrospective element. Despite the heavy emphasis on current materials, the best-known selection aids provide little help to persons responsible for collection building in special libraries. Most of the material acquired for special libraries is very technical and of interest to only a few specialists; as a result, no meaningful market exists for review services. Recommendations of clients and knowledge of their information needs become the key elements in deciding what to buy.

Needs assessment activities are also a regular part of the special library program, to a greater degree than in other types of libraries. Selective dissemination of information (SDI) is a technique often used in special libraries. By developing and maintaining user interest profiles, the library can continually monitor the information needs and interests of its service population, allowing more effective collection building. The technique also serves as a public relations activity. Every SDI notification serves as a reminder of the library's existence and value. Usually, SDI services are ineffective for large service populations, because the services are too costly to operate; however, several commercial firms offer SDI-like services. The Institute for Scientific Information (ISI) is one commercial organization that has offered SDI-like services. ISI is now owned by Thompson Reuters and continues to publish several indexing and abstracting tools to which many special libraries subscribe (e.g., *Science Citation Index* on DVD or online).

Closing Thoughts on Selection—Quality or Demand

Librarians have been debating the question of what factor should be the primary driver of collection building—quality or demand—for more than 120 years. Some of our quotations in Chapter 2 reflect the very strong sentiment within the profession in the 19th century in favor of quality. Throughout the

20th century, the trend was more and more toward allowing demand to drive the selection decisions. Probably all librarians in the 20th century and perhaps even some in the 19th century would have agreed, it would be desirable to have both items of quality and material that reflected what people wanted to read, view, or listen to. The unfortunate reality is a library rarely has such luxurious funding for collections to be able to fully indulge both desires. For most, if not all, libraries, demand is the dominant factor.

This issue is still relevant to an extent when it comes to children's selection work. In most cases, this is more theoretical than actual. There are very few, if any, purely quality children's collections any longer. But many children's librarians still believe that it is their responsibility to lead children to books of some literary quality. They will use the more popular books as "bait" to get the kids into the library and then try to gently urge the award winners and other "good" books on the children. At the other end of the spectrum are librarians who say it is a triumph to get kids to read anything these days or that children have as much right to read trash as adults do.

Todd Kyle (2008) wrote about those issues, and although his reference point was children's collections in Canadian libraries, his views apply to the United States as well:

> The books that have immediate appeal in your collection are the ones that have the least apparent quality. . . . It is fair to say that the often-spirited debates over "junk" reading in our profession are largely finished, and most of us either accept pulp books as loss leaders, or even embrace them. . . . [W]hat to choose, quality or appeal? The answer is both—books that have one or the other, and especially books that combine the two. (pp. 257–258)

Points to Keep in Mind

- Selecting materials for a library collection is often one of the most enjoyable and satisfying activities a librarian performs, even if it is at times complex and difficult.

- Selection decisions are primarily based on rational information; however, there are times when emotional factors come into play (see Chapter 12).

- A useful starting point when taking on collections management responsibilities is to read the library's document/policy regarding the activities of CM staff in that library.

- Collection management policy documents are a valuable tool for orienting new CM staff as well as providing interested parties with information on how the library handles the work.

- Selection work involves a number of factors, some relatively simple and some rather complex.

- Selection decisions rest on a number of factors, some of which the policy will address, most of the rest will call for you to make a judgment.

- Factors up to the point of making the quality judgment are straightforward.

- Quality "calls" are the center of the selection decision-making process.

- Reviews are a help in making quality decisions, especially in smaller library settings.

- Always keep in mind only a very small percentage of the annual output of new materials ever gets a review.

- Assessing quality effectively takes time, but with practice it is possible to do so even from a basic citation string.

- Perhaps the most difficult call is the setting of priorities for acquiring an item—buy now, wait a while, put into the "someday file."

- Time, experience, and making some poor calls are what it takes to become an effective selector. The best of us had to learn from our mistakes. Enjoy the work.

Works Cited

Anderson, Kristine J., Robert S. Freeman, Jean-Pierre V. M. Hérubel, Lawrence J. Mykytiuk, Judith M. Nixon, and Suzanne M. Ward. 2002. "Buy, Don't Borrow: Bibliographers' Analysis of Academic Library Collection Development Through Interlibrary Loan Requests." *Collection Management* 27, nos. 3/4: 1–11.

Bogart, Dave, ed. 2010. *Library and Book Trade Almanac*, 55th ed. Medford, NJ: Information Today.

Broadus, Robert. 1981. *Selecting Materials for Libraries*, 2nd ed. New York: H. W. Wilson.

Calhoun, John, and James K. Bracken. 1983. "An Index of Publisher Quality for the Academic Library." *College & Research Libraries* 44, no. 3: 257–259.

Cherepon, Lois, and Andrew Sankowski. 2003. "Collection Development at SJU Libraries: Compromise, Missions, and Transitions." In *Collection Development Policies: New Directions for Changing Collections*, ed. Daniel C. Mack, 63–75. New York: Haworth.

Curley, Arthur, and Dorothy Broderick. 1983. *Building Library Collections*. 6th ed. Metuchen, NJ: Scarecrow Press.

Drury, Francis. 1930. *Book Selection*. Chicago: American Library Association.

Evans, G. Edward. 1993. "Needs Analysis and Collection Development Policies for Culturally Diverse Populations." *Collection Building* 11, no. 4: 16–27.

Futas, Elizabeth. 1993. "Collection Development of Genre Literature." *Collection Building* 12, nos. 3/4: 39–44.

Goedeken, Edward. 1993. "An Index to Publisher Quality Revisited." *Library Acquisitions: Practice and Theory* 17, no. 3: 263–268.

Haines, Helen E. 1950. *Living with Books: The Art of Book Selection*, 2nd ed. New York: Columbia University Press.

Jobe, Margaret M., and Michael Levine-Clark. 2008. "Use and Non-Use of *Choice*-Reviewed Titles in Undergraduate Libraries." *Journal of Academic Librarianship* 34, no. 4: 295–304.

Johnson, Liz, and Linda A. Brown. 2008. "Book Reviews by the Numbers." *Collection Management* 33, nos. 1/2: 83–113.

Johnson, Peggy. 2009. *Fundamentals of Collection Development and Management.* 2nd ed. Chicago: American Library Association.

Jones, Patrick. 2003. "To the Teen Core: A Librarian Advocates Building Collections that Serve YA readers." *School Library Journal* 49, no. 3: 48–49.

Kyle, Todd. 2008. "Children's Collection Development: Good Books, or Books Kids Like?" *Feliciter* 54, no. 6: 257–258.

McColvin, Lionel Roy. 1925. *The Theory of Book Selection for Public Libraries.* London: Grafton.

Metz, Paul, and John Stemmer. 1996. "A Reputational Study of Academic Publishers." *College & Research Libraries* 57, no. 3: 234–247.

Pacific Northwest Collection Assessment Manual. 1992. 4th ed. Lacey, WA: Western Library Network.

Quesada, Todd Douglas. 2007. "Spanish Spoken Here." *American Libraries* 38, no. 10: 40, 42, 44.

Quinn, Brian. 2007. "Cognitive and Affective Process in Collection Development." *Library Resources and Technical Services* 51, no. 1: 5–15.

Ranganathan, S. R. 1952. *Library Book Selection.* New Delhi: India Library Association.

Stephens, Julia. 2007. "English Spoken Here." *American Libraries* 38, no. 10: 41, 43–44.

Tyler, David C., Yang Xu, Joyce C. Melvin, Marylou Epp, and Anita M. Kreps. 2010. "Just How Right Are the Customers? An Analysis of the Relative Performance of Patron-Initiated Interlibrary Loan Monograph Purchases." *Collection Management* 35, no. 3: 162–179.

Walters, William H. 2008. "Journal Prices, Book Acquisitions, and Sustainable College Library Collections." *College & Research Libraries* 69, no. 6: 576–586.

Suggested Readings

Alabaster, Carol. 2010. *Developing an Outstanding Core Collection: A Guide for Libraries.* Chicago: ALA Editions.

Anjejo, Rose. 2006. "Collection Development Policies for Small Libraries." *PNLA Quarterly* 70, no. 2: 12–16.

Calvani, Mayra, and Anne K. Edwards. 2008. *The Slippery Art of Book Reviewing.* Kingsport, TN: Twilight Times Books.

Campbell, Sharon A. 2006. "To Buy or to Borrow, That Is the Question." *Journal of Interlibrary Loan, Document Delivery and Electronic Reserve* 16, no. 3: 35–39.

Chen, Kristine. 2010. "Give Them What They Want." *School Library Journal* 56, no. 10: 29–32.

Comer, Alberta, and Elizabeth Lorenzen. 2006. "Is Purchase on Demand a Worthy Model? Do Patrons Really Know What They Want?" In *Charleston Conference Proceedings 2006*, ed. Beth R. Bernhardt, Tim Daniels, and Kim Steinle, 171–179. Charleston, SC: Libraries Unlimited.

Corrigan, Andy. 2005. "The Collection Policy Reborn: A Practical Application of Web-Based Documentation." *Collection Building* 24, no. 2: 65–69.

Davidson, Glenn, and Dan Dorner. 2009. "Selection Criteria for Mobile Library Collections." *Collection Building* 28, no. 2: 51–58.

Douglas, C. Steven. 2011. "Revising a Collection Development Policy in a Rapidly Changing Environment." *Journal of Electronic Resources in Medical Libraries* 8, no. 1: 15–21.

Foss, Michelle. 2007. "Books-on-Demand Pilot Program: An Innovative 'Patroncentric' Approach to Enhance the Library Collection." *Journal of Access Services* 5, no. 1: 306–315.

Franklin, Pat, and Claire Gatrell Stephens. 2009. "Use Standards to Draw Curriculum Maps." *School Library Media Activities Monthly* 25, no. 9: 44–45.

Hoffmann, Frank W., and Richard John Wood. 2007. *Library Collection Development Policies: School Libraries and Learning Resource Centers*. Lanham, MD: Scarecrow Press.

Jud, Edie. 2007. "Whoever Would Have Thought Book Shopping Might Raise Eyebrows?" *Knowledge Quest* 36, no. 2: 30–32.

Knievel, Jennifer E., Heather Wicht, and Lynn Silipigni Connaway. 2006. "Use of Circulation Statistics and Interlibrary Loan Data in Collection Management." *College & Research Libraries* 67, no. 1: 35–49.

Levine-Clark, Michael. 2010. "Developing a Multiformat Demand-Driven Acquisition Model." *Collection Management* 35, nos. 3/4: 201–207.

Levine-Clark, Michael, and Margaret M. Jobe. 2007. "Do Reviews Matter? An Analysis of Usage and Holdings of *Choice*-Reviewed Titles Within a Consortium." *Journal of Academic Librarianship* 33, no. 6: 639–646.

Peck, Dale. 2004. *Hatchet Jobs: Writings on Contemporary Fiction*. New York: New Press.

Pickett, Carmelita, Jane Stephens, Rusty Kimball, Diana Ramirez, Joel Thornton, and Nancy Burford. 2011. "Revisiting an Abandoned Practice: The Death and Resurrection of Collection Development Policies." *Collection Management* 36, no. 3: 165–181.

Schmitt, John P., and Stewart Saunders. 1983. "An Assessment of *Choice* as a Tool for Selection." *College & Research Libraries* 44, no. 5: 375–380.

Smith, Karen M. 2006. "The Power of Information: Creating a YA Nonfiction Collection." *Young Adult Library Services* 5, no. 1: 28–30.

Williams, Karen Carter, and Rickey Best. 2006. "E-book Usage and the *Choice* Outstanding Academic Book List: Is There a Correlation?" *Journal of Academic Librarianship* 32, no. 5: 474–478.

Zhu, Qin, and Sophia Guevara. 2009. "A Practical Guide for Building a User-Focused Digital Library Collection." *Computers in Libraries* 29, no. 4: 6–10.

5
Acquiring Materials

The definition of "acquire" has evolved far beyond purchasing, subscribing, and licensing. Acquisitions activities now include—and in the future will increasingly include—issues of rights management.

> —Vera Fessler, 2007

During the course of my regular work day, I spend a lot of time contacting vendors to resolve problems, claim missing serial issues, order replacements, set up new standing orders and subscriptions, obtain price quotes, sort out billing questions, and track down problems with online access. No two vendor customer service operations are alike and many of them are slowly driving me up a wall.

> —Anne Myers, 2009

It is impossible for many libraries to fulfill all their patrons' needs and wants. So they'll have to be prudent, keep watch on local priorities, and remind funders of the library's value as they navigate a challenging future.

> —Norman Oder, 2010

If selection work is the heart of collection management, acquisitions is the blood that keeps CM a functioning and growing process. Acquisitions work translates selection decisions into materials available on the library's shelves or accessible on its network.

There are three broad categories of acquisition work—making decisions regarding how to acquire an item, working with vendors and suppliers to secure the desired materials, and maintaining the appropriate financial and other records related to each acquisition transaction. Although not as enjoyable as seeking out new items for the collection, acquisitions work can be satisfying and occasionally challenging.

Some years ago, S. R. Ranganathan (1988) formulated several "laws" of librarianship. His fifth law was "a library is a growing organism" (p. 326). Acquisitions activities are one of the driving forces in a library's growth. A growing organism is almost always also a changing one. For acquisitions, the basic functions remain unchanged today despite changes in technology, the economy, and the ever-changing information environment. This is not to imply that things are not changing within acquisitions, they are. Although the basic issues may be unchanged, the ways of addressing those issues have and are changing. The skills, abilities, and background required to be effective in acquisitions work are very different today from what they were not all that many years ago.

As you might guess, it is the electronic resources—more specifically the networked or Web materials—that are creating the most changes for acquisitions units. E-resources call for a different acquisitions approach, such as having trial periods and leasing rather than owning materials. While you might think of a trial period as somewhat like an approval plan for books or previewing other media—in other words looking before buying—it is very different, especially when you consider the complexity of the process that involves a number of libraries and even more people. We explore these issues more fully in Chapter 7.

In the past, an acquisitions librarian needed basic skills such as rapid decision making and fiscal management. Today, in addition to these skills, a person must be technologically savvy, be able to deal with the "legalese" found in licensing and leasing agreements, and be more and more a diplomat when dealing with consortia members.

To be fully effective, collection management and acquisitions personnel must have a very cooperative working relationship. Poor coordination will result in wasted effort, slow response time, and high unit costs. Achieving coordination requires that all parties understand the work processes, problems, and value of the others' work.

Acquisitions departments have several broad goals. Four common goals are:

1. To acquire material as quickly as possible.

2. To maintain a high level of accuracy in all work procedures.

3. To keep work processes simple, in order to achieve the lowest possible unit cost.

4. To develop close, friendly working relationships with other library units and with vendors.

Speed is a significant factor in meeting user demands as well as improving user satisfaction. An acquisitions system that requires three or four months to secure items available locally in bookstores will create a serious public relations problem. A system that is very fast but has a high error rate will increase operating costs and will waste time and energy for both departmental staff and suppliers. Studies have shown that, in many medium-size and large libraries, the costs of acquiring and processing an item are equal to or greater than the price of the item. By keeping procedures simple, and by periodically reviewing workflow processes, the department can help the library provide better service. Speed, accuracy, and thrift should be the watchwords of acquisitions departments. Certainly, online ordering, electronic invoicing, and credit card payments greatly enhance the speed with which the department can handle much of the traditional paperwork.

The underlying key to successful acquisitions programs is developing and maintaining good relationships both within and outside the library. Good internal working relationships with the entire library staff are of course important; however, there are three areas where these relationships are of special importance—with the selectors, the catalog department, and with senior administrators.

Needless to say, the selectors are the most important group for the department as it is their input that generates the department's primary work activities. Librarian selectors and teaching faculty are generally good at accurately supplying 80 to 90 percent of the information necessary to order an item. Tensions can develop if that percentage drops by very much and the department staff has to spend more time tracking down required information. When users submit requests, the amount of time establishing what is really wanted and the library's need for the item goes up dramatically. The flow of material into and out of the department can become an issue in technical services, especially the cataloging department. Both departments seek to have a reasonably smooth flow throughout the year— with few peaks and valleys. However, the incoming requests are the driving force behind that flow, and keeping that flow constant is often a challenge, especially near the end of the FY.

Another tension point that is becoming more and more common is the use of outsourcing for a substantial amount of technical service processes. That is, ordering items to arrive shelf ready and with the cataloging record already loaded or ready to be loaded into the library's OPAC. The tension arises over whose responsibility it is to check on the quality of the incoming material. Catalogers generally do not have the background to deal with the financial aspect of the "preprocessed" material, while acquisition personnel rarely have the background to verify the cataloging data. Working out a reasonable solution may take time and cause tensions in previously good relationships.

Senior administration is another group with a vested interest in the department's operation, especially its fiscal management. The most senior administrator (director) is responsible for everything that takes place in the library. For almost all libraries, the two top components in the operating expense (OE) budget are salaries and the funds for collection development. The two categories often represent 80 percent or more of the OE. Needless to say, senior administrators must closely monitor those expenditures. In some larger libraries, the administrative office has taken on handling the acquisition unit's financial record keeping in order to have a better day-to-day picture of the total budget situation.

Beyond the senior administration there are outside groups that have an interest in the department's fiscal activities. Certainly the most prominent of those is the business office of the library's parent institution. Its interest is in ensuring that the acquisitions department's financial record keeping is in compliance with its regulations as well as using proper accounting practices. It does not have an interest in what materials are acquired for the collection as long as the purchases fall within the permitted categories— books, journals, and so forth. Normally there is at least monthly interaction between the units as the parent business office sends out a monthly report on what it has on record as the expended and unexpended library funds.

Other business offices that the department interacts with fairly frequently are the vendors and acquisition departments in libraries in a consortium that acquires material for the group. Perhaps the more challenging of the two are the other libraries where the sharing of the payment to the vendor of the product has to be coordinated. It is likely that a consortium with more than a dozen members will have libraries operating on different FY calendars. Making a payment for a shared purchase may be a challenge for a member or two near the end of their FY. We explore consortial activities in more detail in Chapter 7.

Acquiring Collection Materials

There are five steps in the overall acquisitions process:

- Request processing
- Verification
- Ordering
- Reporting (fiscal management)
- Receiving orders

The first four phases of the process are described in this chapter. The process of receiving orders is described in more detail in Evans and his colleagues' *Introduction to Technical Services* (2011).

At the start of the acquisitions process (request processing), before the departmental staff can decide on what method to employ to acquire an item, they must engage in some preliminary sorting and checking activities. Staff members must review incoming requests, be they paper or virtual in format, to establish both the need for the item and that all of the required ordering information is there. (This is not to suggest the department should override selectors' decisions when we say "the need for the item.")

Requests for the library to acquire this or that item for the collection arrive in various forms, even though the library may have a standard format available in both paper and electronic versions. A few examples of the way items are requested include via a conversation or telephone call with a selector or faculty member, on a slip of paper, on a napkin, or on the back of an envelope. A staff member converts such requests to the department's standard format and the verification work begins. Verification is perhaps the most interesting and challenging duty in this department. The attempt to establish an item's existence when there is very little information is similar to detective work.

When the requests are from CM personnel, there is only a modest need for verification work. There may be some missing ordering information such as the ISBN (a unique number for each title) or its format (paperback or hard cover) because the source the selector used did not contain the information. Also the department must check to determine if the item is already on order. Many, if not most, nonfiction works cover more than one topic. For example, for a book with the title *History of the Political Impact of the Women's Movement in the United States*, three or more selectors might have seen information about this title at nearly the same time and each submitted a request. Even when the integrated library system (ILS) allows selectors to see the status of an on-order title, it is possible that an earlier request for the item has not been entered, so no record exists and the selector submits a duplicate request. In addition, there are times when announcement of a new release does not mention it is part of a series to which the library has a standing order. Thus, the department checks all requests to determine the need for the item, not to second guess selectors, but to avoid unwanted duplication and waste limited funds.

When the request is from users, however, the department must not only check to see if the item is in the queue to be ordered, on order, or received and being processed, but also if it is already in the collection. Users often think of editors as the author of such items as conference proceedings or symposia when library cataloging rules call for a corporate entry. Such confusion is much less common today as OPACs allow keyword searching.

User requests are also very likely to lack all of the necessary ordering information as well as sometimes having inaccurate information about the item. Thus, establishing the existence of the requested item becomes essential. Online services such as *Books in Print.Com*™ or YBP Library Services' GOBI® (Global Online Bibliographic Information) system speed up the necessary preorder checking. WorldCat™ is also a great source for establishing the existence of the requested item.

Acquisition Methods

Before placing an order, the staff must make three important decisions:

- Which acquisition method to use.
- What vendor to use.
- What funding source to use.

Essentially there are eight standard methods of acquisition—firm order, standing order, approval plans, blanket order, subscriptions (for serials departments), leases, gifts, and exchange. A *firm order* (orders in which desired items are individually named) is the usual method for titles that the library *knows* it wants. An order is a legal contract, something that many don't realize, between the library and the vendor. This means a vendor could force payment even if the library experiences a financial setback. The all too common setback is for the parent institution to take back some of the funds allocated to the library. The parent body does not usually specify where the library finds the required amount, merely that it deliver the called for funds. In most cases, the only uncommitted funds in the amount required are those for collection building. Most library vendors are well aware of this type of event and almost never press their legal right to payment for items that were on order when the financial "claw back" occurred. Firm orders are also the best method to use for the first volume in a series, even if the selectors believe they are likely to order the entire series.

Standing orders (an open order for all titles fitting a particular category) are best for items that are serial in character and the library is confident it wants all the publications as they appear. Some examples are a numbered or unnumbered series from a publisher that deal with a single subject area. Often publishers issue annual volumes (for example, *Oceanography and Marine Biology: An Annual Review* [Boca Raton, FL: CRC Press, 2009]) that the library knows it will want on an ongoing basis. Other broad categories are the irregular publications of a professional society, memoirs or special commemorative volumes, for example. The library places the order for the series or items rather like it places a journal subscription. The supplier (vendor or producer) automatically sends the items as they appear along with an invoice. There is a distinction between "thinking about" and "planning on" when considering series items. When the selector knows that the reputation of the publisher or editor of the series is sound, it is probably best to place a standing order. (A standing order will save staff time and effort due to the automatic shipments.) However, especially in academic libraries, standing orders are often the result of a faculty member's request, and if the library does not periodically review its standing orders, it may find that the requester left the institution years before or there is no longer an interest in the series' subject. The result is money being spent on less useful items.

The greatest drawback to standing orders is their unpredictable nature in terms of both numbers and cost. Certainly there are fewer problems about numbers for the regular series, but their cost per item may vary. When it comes to publishers' series or irregular series, a library may go years without receiving a title, then receive several in one year. Looking at past experience and using an average amount is a safe approach; however, the library is seldom able to set aside exactly the right amount. Committing (encumbering) too much money for too long may result in lost opportunities to acquire other useful items. Committing too little can result in having invoices arrive and not having the funds available to pay them. Standing orders are a valuable acquisition method, but one that requires careful monitoring throughout the year.

Approval plans are, in a sense, a variation of the standing order concept. They involve automatic shipment of items to the library from a vendor along with automatic invoicing, after the library accepts the item. The differences are that the approval plan normally covers a number of subject areas, and the library has the right to return titles it does not want within a contractually specified timeframe (unless the approval plan items arrive preprocessed or shelf ready, in which case returns are normally not permitted). The underlying assumption is that collection management staff can make better decisions about an item's appropriateness by looking at the item before committing to its purchase.

After that time has elapsed, unreturned items must be paid for. Although approval plans can save staff time and effort when properly implemented, they can also be costly when not thoughtfully established and carefully monitored. Robert Alan and colleagues (2010) spelled out the broad advantages of such plans: "Approval plans have been considered an efficient and cost-effective way for libraries to acquire books in large quantities across many disciplines. Through approval plans, vendors supply current imprints as well as notification slips or forms to libraries on the basis of selected publisher output, subject profiles, and nonsubject categories such as readership level, country of origin, and format" (p. 64). However, there is research evidence that indicates the approval plan can result in a substantially higher number of very low or no-use items being added to the collection (Evans, 1970, 1974).

The key element in making the approval plan a cost-effective acquisition method is creating a sound "profile" with the plan vendor. The profile can be created by the subject selector alone or can also be created in conjunction with the acquisition librarian. It is also important to consult with those parties interested in CM, such as teaching faculty or selectors from related fields or subjects. A profile outlines the parameters of the plan and covers issues such as subjects desired, levels of treatment (undergraduate, graduate, etc.), languages or countries coverage, no reprints, no collections of reprinted articles, and so forth. The more time devoted to profile definition, as well as monitoring the actual operation of the plan and making adjustments, the greater the value of an approval plan to the library and the acquisitions department.

A *blanket order* is a combination of a firm order and an approval plan. It is a commitment on the library's part to purchase all of something, usually the output of a publisher, or a limited subject area, or from a country. In the case of a subject area or country, there is a profile developed between the library and the blanket order vendor. The materials arrive automatically along with the invoice, thus saving staff time. Another advantage, for country blanket order plans, is that they ensure the library acquires a copy of limited print runs. (It is not uncommon to have very limited print runs of scholarly items in many countries. Waiting for an announcement or a listing in a national bibliography may mean that there are no copies left to purchase.) Like the standing order, the major drawback of blanket order plans is predicting how much money the library will need to reserve to cover the invoices. There is even less predictability with blanket order plans because there are more variables.

Subscriptions, for journals, newspapers, and many other serials, are a combination of standing and blanket orders. A library may enter a subscription for a given timeframe just as an individual does for personal magazines. However, rather than going through an annual renewal process, many libraries enter into an agreement with a serials vendor to automatically renew subscriptions until the library requests a cancellation (until forbidden orders). This saves both the library and vendor staff time and paperwork. This is a cost-effective system for those titles the library is *certain* are of long-term interest to end users.

Leases are now commonplace for handling e-resources, especially those that are Web based. The decision to lease is almost always in the hands of the supplier rather than the library, although sometimes a library can "buy" the product, usually at a substantially higher price. The difference between buying and leasing has significant implications for the library and its users. Essentially the library pays for *access* to the information for as long as it pays the annual fee. At the end of a lease, the library generally loses all access to the material it was paying for, although some suppliers will provide long-term access to the material that was available during the lease period. Chapters 7 and 9 provide more information about this and other issues related to electronic resources.

Frequently, the acquisitions department is the library's designated recipient of unsolicited *gifts* of books, serials, and other materials (sometimes accompanied by a variety of molds and insects) that well-meaning people give to the library. Both solicited and unsolicited gifts can be a source of important out-of-print materials for replacement, extra copies, and the filling of gaps in the collection. The collection development policy statement on gifts will help acquisitions personnel process the material quickly.

Reviewing gifts is important, as a library cannot afford to discard valuable or needed items that arrive as gifts. Selectors normally make the call to keep or dispose of such items. Selectors ought to keep in mind that they should not add an item just because it is "free." Processing and storage costs are the same for a gift as for a purchased item. Older books require careful checking, as variations in printings and editions may determine whether an item is valuable or worthless. (Usually, a second or third printing is less valuable than the first printing of a work.)

Steven Carrico (1999) provides an excellent summary of the advantages and disadvantages of gift programs:

Positive Points of Gifts

1. Gifts can replace worn and missing items in a library.

2. Out-of-print desiderata often surface from gift donations.

3. Gifts can foster communication and goodwill in a library community.

4. Gifts may become heavily used or important research additions to a collection.

5. Some titles that are not available by purchase are available as gifts.

6. Worthwhile gift material not selected for a library collection can be put in a book sale, sold to dealers, or given away to underfunded libraries and institutions.

Negative Points of Gifts

1. Gifts require staff time and are costly to process.

2. Dealing with even well-meaning gift donors is frequently an aggravation to staff.

3. Gifts take up precious space in a library.

4. Many collection managers give gifts low priority, so they may sit on review shelves for a long time.

5. A large percentage of most gifts are not added to a collection, which creates disposal problems.

6. Overall, since most gift books added to a collection are older editions, they will be less frequently used by library patrons (p. 210).

There are some legal aspects about gifts that staff must understand. One Internal Revenue Service (IRS) regulation relevant to libraries has to do with gifts and donations to a library or not-for-profit information center. Any library, or its parent institution, that receives a gift in-kind (books, journals, manuscripts, and so forth) with an appraised value of $5,000 or more must report the gift to the IRS. A second regulation forbids the receiving party (in this case the library) from providing an estimated value for the gift in-kind. A disinterested third party or organization must make the valuation. Normally, an appraiser charges a fee for valuing gifts, and the donor is supposed to pay the fee. Most often, the appraisers are antiquarian dealers who charge a flat fee for the service unless the collection is large or complex. If the appraisal is complex, the appraiser either charges a percentage of the appraised value or an hourly fee. Typically, with gifts thought to be worth

---

Check This Out

Janet Bishop, Patricia A. Smith, and Chris Sugnet discussed how the Colorado State University Libraries decided to eliminate its general gift program and restrict future gifts to materials supporting its archives and special collections in their 2010 article "Refocusing a Gift Program in an Academic Library," in *Library Collections, Acquisitions, and Technical Services* (34, no. 4: 115–122).

From the Advisory Board

Carol Sinwell reminds us of the true impact Friends' groups can have on libraries:

Fairfax (Virginia) County Public Library has an enormously successful (non-profit) Friends Group. Each library has the option for their own group, but the George Mason Regional Library is a particularly well-organized group meeting daily at the library to process gifts (http://www.georgemasonfriends.blogspot .com/). The group has made major donations to the library system for over 25 years, earning service awards from Fairfax County and the Virginia Library Association.

   This Friends group has developed an excellent relationship with the county government, whereby the county provides storage space for processed and boxed gifts and the sheriff's office's community service workers provide the labor when the Friends need help setting up for their three-day book sales—held four times a year. For many years this one group provided the funds for the library system's Children's Summer Reading Game—plus having additional funds to support a circulating art collection, renovations, special collections, etc.

---

less than $4,999, the library may write a letter of acknowledgment indicating the number and type of items received. For gifts of less than $250, the IRS does not require a letter.

   Donations and gifts also present an acquisitions option that can be appropriate at times. Sometimes a library user or board member donates certain materials on a regular basis, making it unnecessary to order the item if there is no immediate demand for the material. Occasionally, an appropriate series or set costs so much a library cannot buy it with regular funding sources. Seeking a donor to assist with funding or to pay for the purchase is not unheard of, but again, there may be substantial delays in acquiring the item. Most often this takes place with rare books and special collections items. An active (and well-to-do) Friends of the Library group may be the answer to a special purchase situation. Friends groups, used judiciously, can significantly expand the collection and stretch funds. Deciding to use the gift method of acquisition will almost always result in a long delay in receiving the desired item.

   The final acquisition category is the *exchange* method. There are two basic types of exchange activity: the exchange of unwanted duplicate or gift materials and the exchange of new materials between libraries. Usually, only research libraries at institutions with publication programs engage in exchange of new materials. Occasionally, libraries use this system to acquire materials from countries in which there are commercial trade restrictions. Where government trade restrictions make buying and selling of publications from certain countries difficult or impossible, the cooperating libraries acquire (buy) their local publications for exchange. Exchanges of this type are complex and difficult to manage, and this is an acquisition method of last resort.

   James Marcum (2008) wrote about a variation on the exchange method—barter. Essentially, for years libraries have, from time to time, offered exchange lists whereby a library offers to another library anything on the list for the cost of shipping. Handling unneeded material this way is labor intensive—creating the list, distributing and posting the list, monitoring the requests, shipping the material, and finally collecting the shipping cost. Marcum suggests a more formal approach whereby several libraries

---

From the Authors' Experience

Since retiring from full-time work, Evans has been in charge of a small research library at the Museum of Northern Arizona. The museum has a publication program that includes both popular and research report publications. Currently the library has 63 exchange partners in the United States and Europe. Given the very tight economic conditions, which is reflected in an almost nonexistent acquisitions budget, if it were not for the exchange program, the library would have been able to add very few newly published items to the collection.

---

work together to essentially trade lots or collections of low-use materials. Marcum states: "To treat those little-used volumes as having no value will be the administrative method more often than we would like to think. A lot of marginal material was added in the years when volume count equaled library 'goodness.' . . . But chances are somebody else needs the collection to provide background for its current collection emphasis. It would have real value for them, if we could just make the right connection" (p. 50).

Selecting the Vendor

The following material focuses on vendors who support the library's acquisition functions. There are six broad factors that come into play in making a selection: what is commonly carried (normal stock), the firm's technological capability, how quickly the firm is likely to deliver material(s) (order fulfillment), the firm's financial condition and discounts offered, the range of services available, and customer service. It is essential to remember that in most instances there will be a contract prepared, with all the legalities that such documents entail, once a choice is made. The contract will specify all the terms and conditions, many of which could have serious financial consequences for the library should the library wish to cancel or otherwise modify the agreement.

What the Firm Stocks

When looking for a source for collection items a key concern is what the company usually carries in stock. You will often see statements on vendors' Websites that read "Over xxx million items in our warehouse" or something very similar. That is not useful information; it could mean there are many copies of a few thousand titles. What is useful is having a list of all the producers and publishers the firm regularly carries in its warehouse(s), as well as what series/producers/publishers they do *not* carry—such a listing may be surprisingly long and have unexpected names. What are its specialties, if any? For example, Baker & Taylor specializes in public and school library markets while YBP Library Services (a Baker & Taylor subsidiary) and Midwest Library Service focus on academic libraries. Sales representatives often say the firm can supply *any* title from *any* publisher, with only minor exceptions. Although it may be possible for a general (primarily mass market titles) book supplier to secure STM (scientific, technical, medical) titles, the delays in delivery may be excessive. Knowing which publishers the vendor does not handle helps maintain good working relations in the long run, although securing that information may prove to be challenging.

Vendor Technological Capabilities

In this category, probably the key question is, does the firm's system have an interface that will work effectively with the library's ILS? If the answer is yes, could the library have a free test period to determine those capabilities prior to signing a contract? Other technology concerns are, does the firm offer free online preorder checking, electronic ordering, invoicing, payments, claiming, technology support or troubleshooting and what are the hours of availability, and so forth? Today, the technological issues are almost as important as the firm's stock.

Speed of Delivery

We have mentioned several times that speed of fulfillment is one measure by which the user community judges the quality of the library's service. Thus, it is not surprising that vendor fulfillment speed is a factor in making a final decision on which vendor to employ. Information about the average delivery time from the vendor ought to be cross-checked with some of the vendor's current customers. There should be no hesitation on the vendor's part in supplying a list of current customers. It also often pays to contact customers not on the list as a further cross-check.

Many vendors promise 24-hour shipment of items in stock. Do they make good on such claims? Generally, yes; however, the key phrase is *in stock*. Frequently, there can be delays of three to four months in receiving a complete order because one or more titles are not in stock.

Financial Considerations

There is more to consider in this category than what the discount rate for purchases may be, if any. Certainly the discount rate is important; what is equally important is to what percentage of the items that discount rate applies. A related issue is, are there classes of material that carry service charges rather than a discount? There is also the possibility the rate will be dependent on the contracted dollar amount spent with the firm within a specified period (the greater the amount spent, the higher the discount).

Discounting is a twisting and turning maze in the book trade. The discount the library receives is dependent on the discount the vendor receives from the producers or publishers. Because vendors buy in volume, they receive a substantial discount from producers. When they sell a copy of the highly discounted title to the library, the library receives a discount off the producer's list price. However, that is substantially lower than the vendor received. Clearly there must be a profit margin for the firm to stay in business. For example, if the vendor received a 40 percent discount from the producer, the discount given the library is likely to be 15 to 20 percent. If the library ordered the title directly from the producer, there is a slight chance the discount may be about the same level (10 to 15 percent). The advantage for the library of going with a vendor rather than ordering directly comes about from staff savings. That is, being able to send the vendor one order for titles from dozens of producers rather than creating dozens of orders going to each producer.

Every publisher's discount schedule is slightly different, if not unique. Some items are *net* (no discount); usually these are textbooks, STM titles, or items of limited sales appeal. *Short discounts* are normally 20 percent or less; these are items the producers expect will have limited appeal but have more potential than the net titles. *Trade discounts* range from 30 to 60 percent or more; items in this category are high-demand items or high-risk popular fiction such as first-time authors. Publishers believe that by giving a high discount for fiction, bookstores will stock more copies and thus help promote the title. Vendors normally receive 40 to 50 percent discounts, primarily because of their high-volume orders (hundreds of copies per title rather than the tens that most libraries and independent bookstore owners order).

Another financial concern is with the firm's financial stability. Like everyone else, vendors have encountered financial problems during the current recession. Some publishers are requiring prepayment or have placed vendors on a *pro forma* status. Pro forma status requires prepayment, and suppliers extend credit on the basis of the current performance in payment of bills. Much of the credit and order fulfillment extended by publishers depends on an almost personal relationship with the buyer. That in turn impacts the vendor's ability to fulfill orders as quickly as it did in the past. Thus libraries must select a vendor with care. It is not inappropriate to check a prospective vendor's financial status (through a rating service, such as Dun and Bradstreet).

Additional Vendor Services

Many of today's major vendors offer a variety of services that go beyond supplying items for the collection. They offer almost one-stop technical services, from preorder checking to cataloging to shelf-ready (processed) material. Some of the larger U.S. library book vendors are Baker & Taylor, Brodart, Follett, and Midwest Library Service. EBSCO is probably the largest U.S. serials vendor; although another firm that is especially good for non-U.S. titles is Blackwells (UK). In addition, there are smaller firms that provide good-quality service; however, their numbers are decreasing in tight economic times.

Baker & Taylor, Brodart, and Follett focus on public and school library needs. YPB Library Services (via Baker & Taylor) and Midwest Library Service handle primarily the academic library market. Almost all vendors offer some combination, if not all, of the following in addition to the basic order fulfillment service:

- Preorder searching and verification—many allow a search and direct downloading into an order form.

- Selection assistance such as access to reviews of items from major review journals.

- More than one type of format (printed books, e-books, audio/video recordings, for example).

- Electronic table of contents (TOC) and/or book jacket art for ordered titles. Academic libraries like the TOC service as it becomes searchable in the OPAC and is a valued service by researchers. For a public or school library, the cover art, attached to the OPAC record, helps attract a reader to the item, rather like bookstores displaying many titles with the jacket facing out rather than having the spine showing.

- Cataloging and "shelf-ready" processing—cataloging can take the form of downloading a Library of Congress MARC (machine readable cataloging) record into the library's ILS for catalogers to modify as necessary or having the vendor actually do the cataloging and forwarding the final record. Shelf ready means the items arrive with labels and any necessary book pockets, property stamps, date due slips, and so forth in place and ready to go into the collection.

- Customized management data (see below).

In addition to materials, Brodart is a major resource for library furniture and equipment (book trucks, step stools, shelving units, etc.) as well as supplies (bar codes, date due slips, for example).

Brodart also offers a rental service, the McNaughton Plan, which is designed to help solve the problem of providing an adequate number of high-demand titles for both books and audio recordings. Most public libraries face the challenge of having a high demand for popular titles; however, that high demand only lasts a short time. The challenge is how to meet the demand and yet not spend too much money on short-term interest items. One solution libraries employ is to buy two or three copies and set up a reservation/request queue for those wishing to read/listen to the item. The public understands the challenge, but they still express frustration with the reservation system. McNaughton offers another alternative: rent multiple copies for the duration of the title's popularity and return the unneeded copies. Brodart describes the plan as a *leasing* program. The plan offers high-demand items that Brodart's staff selects. A library cannot order just any book; it must be on Brodart's list of high-demand titles. Some financial savings occur as there are no processing costs because the books come shelf ready and the leasing fee is substantially lower than the item's purchase price. Further, users are happy because of shorter wait times for the latest bestseller. All in all, anyone involved in meeting recreational reading needs will find the program worth investigating.

Customer Service Considerations

As our second quotation for this chapter suggests, customer service is no small issue for libraries. The list of activities Myers (2009) identifies as being customer service related is long but not comprehensive in terms of all the challenges that arise and require staff interaction between the library and vendor. Long-term relationships are the result of respectful dealings by both parties as well as taking some time to learn about the other party's challenges and needs. It is also based on having realistic expectations of one another.

Acquisition departments have a right to expect that a vendor will provide:

- A large inventory of titles in appropriate formats,
- Prompt and accurate order fulfillment,
- Prompt and accurate reporting on items not in stock,
- Personal service at a reasonable price,
- Prompt technical support for problems with shared technology, and
- Timely correction of faulty services such as incorrect cataloging or incorrectly processed shelf-ready items.

Most vendors are reasonably good at meeting those expectations once they become aware of the library's specific issues. Getting to "once they become aware" is sometimes a challenge. Telephone trees are a bane for almost all customers, not just library staff. E-mail and "contact us" boxes often seem to lead to black holes rather than service. In defense of the vendors, the current economic conditions are sometimes to blame as many libraries deal with staffing issues. Layoffs, furloughs, and frozen vacant positions force organizations to employ technology to help address some of the personnel shortfalls. Patience is key to maintaining civil working relationships.

Vendors also have a right to expect the following:

- A reasonable time to gain an understanding of the library's needs,
- Cooperation in placing orders using the firm's system rather than "we did it this way with our former vendor,"
- Paperwork being kept to a minimum and an attempt to streamline operations,
- Prompt payment for services, and
- Not requiring too many exceptions to the firm's normal processes.

Libraries sometimes employ practices that are somewhat outmoded and reflect an attitude of "we always do it this way" and expect the vendor to change its practices to conform to the library's approach. Unless there is a parent institutional requirement involved, the library should be open to at least consider modifying its practices. Being open from the start about the average invoice payment cycle, having the ability to authorize partial payments, and similar matters will also create a more positive relationship.

Vendor Evaluation

Acquisitions departments should engage in ongoing monitoring of vendor performance. In the past, monitoring vendors was time consuming and difficult, and it still is if a library is working with a manual acquisitions system. However, today's automated acquisitions systems can produce a variety of useful management and vendor reports very quickly and in various formats. Knowing what to do with the quantity of data the systems can produce is another matter.

There are two types of evaluation acquisitions staff undertake. One is more of a monitoring of vendor performance with an eye to identifying small concerns that, if left unnoticed, could become a major issue. The other is a formal assessment of the vendor with an eye toward changing vendors or renewing a contract.

One obvious issue that arises in the evaluation process is which vendor performs best on a given type of order (examples are conference proceedings, music scores, or video recordings). The first step is to decide what *best* means. Does it mean highest discount? Fastest delivery? Most accurate reports? Highest percentage of the order filled with the first shipment? All of the above? The answer varies from library to library depending on local needs and conditions. Once the library defines *best*, it knows what data to get from the system. Other evaluation issues are:

- Who handles rush orders most efficiently?
- Who handles international orders most effectively—a dealer in the country of origin or a general international dealer?

- Are specialty dealers more effective in handling their specialties than are general dealers?

- Who handles claims the quickest?

We have mentioned speed of acquisitions is one measure users take into consideration when judging library quality. Typically a 30-day window for delivery is standard for vendors, after which the library may reasonably start a claiming process. Paul Orkiszewski (2005) did a comparative study of Amazon.com and a library vendor and found that Amazon's average delivery time was two weeks, while the major vendor's average was four weeks. However, Amazon's cancellation rate was more than twice that of the vendor; further, of the 5,134 titles in the study sample, 327 were not available for ordering through Amazon (p. 205).

Libraries expect vendors to report the status of titles not delivered upon receipt of a claim. Most ILS acquisitions modules have the ability to generate claim forms based on the order and expected delivery date the department establishes. Vendors should respond with a meaningful report within a reasonable period. Most vendors are quick to report because they understand most libraries cannot authorize any payment until the full order is in the library. In addition, the sooner the selector learns that a requested title is not available the better, as this allows the selector to decide whether or not he or she wishes to find an alternative title or pursues other means of acquiring it (such as through the out-of-print market, discussed later).

One of the less-than-helpful status reports that vendors occasionally use is temporarily out of stock (TOS). How long is "temporarily"? What has the vendor done to secure the item? Poor or inaccurate reporting costs the library money, as Audrey Eaglen (1984) pointed out in her article "Trouble in Kiddyland: The Hidden Costs of O.P. and O.S." In periods of rapid inflation, each day the funds remain committed but unexpended erodes buying power because producers and suppliers raise prices without notice. Recommended vendor reports should indicate that an item is "not yet received from publisher" (NYR); "out-of-stock, ordering" (OS, ordering); "claiming"; "canceled"; "not yet published" (NYP); "out-of-stock, publisher" (OS, publisher); "out-of-print" (OP); "publication canceled"; "out-of-stock indefinitely" (treat this one as a cancellation); "not our publication" (NOP); "wrong title supplied"; "defective copy"; and "wrong quantity supplied." After staff members learn how long, on average, a vendor takes to supply titles reported in one of the recommended categories, it is possible to make informed decisions regarding when to cancel and when to wait for delivery.

Check This Out

In her 2008 article "Advanced Collection Development Project in Partnership with a Vendor" (*Collection Building* 27, no 2: 56–62), Suzanne Gyeszly described an engineering collection building effort in which a vendor (YBP) assisted in what was called the "Advanced Collection Development" project. Its purpose was to quickly build an engineering collection at a new campus of Texas A&M University in Qatar. In this effort, YBP provided access to a special database from which to select material and shipped shelf-ready volumes to the new library. Although the project was not unique, the article provides a good overview of what excellent working relationships with a vendor can accomplish.

When dealing with U.S. publishers, allowing for the normal "snail mail" time, it is reasonable to send a second claim in 60 days after the first claim, if there has been no status report. Many order forms carry a statement reading "cancel after *x* days." Although such statements are legally binding, most libraries send a separate cancellation notice.

A common occurrence is unexpected budget cuts; unfortunately, in the past and certainly recently such cuts have occurred with some frequency. Most vendors have been cooperative about making the adjustments. By establishing a regular cancellation date, libraries that must expend funds within their FY can avoid or reduce the last-minute scramble of canceling outstanding orders and ordering materials that the vendor can deliver in time to expend the funds.

Retail Outlets

Retail outlets are a source of material to a limited extent for libraries, however, they are generally less able to accommodate the special fiscal requirements that most libraries must follow. Libraries in large metropolitan areas generally have a good bookstore nearby. Although most libraries will spend only a small portion of the materials budget in such stores, the possibility is worth exploring. The large U.S. national chains, such as Books-A-Million and Barnes & Noble, operate very different from local stores and are not likely to be able to accommodate library needs beyond occasionally allowing a "corporate" or "educational" discount on some of the titles they carry.

Amazon.com is a resource for some libraries that need a quick turnaround time when it comes to popular titles. One challenge for libraries is developing a workable means of payment. The online shopping sites are based on credit card payments. Libraries and their parent organizations operate on a purchase order or invoice system. Although the situation is changing, many libraries cannot get a credit card in the departmental name due to regulations or reluctance on the part of the library's parent organization. Some departments will use a personal card and go through a reimbursement process; however, this is not a long-term or high-volume solution. Evans did work at one academic library where, after a significant passage of time and effort, it was able to secure a corporate account with Amazon. Overall, the effort was of only marginal value to the acquisitions department.

From the Advisory Board

Sandra Hughes-Hassell provides her insight as to how independent bookstores can be partners in the collection process:

In my experience both as a school librarian and as the manager of a children's bookstore, independent bookstores are happy to work with libraries to provide quick access to titles, especially to eclectic titles that the larger chain bookstores might not carry. When I managed a children's bookstore in Chapel Hill in the early 1990s, for example, school librarians in the area used us for the "need it now" purchases—the titles that teachers or students requested on the spur of the moment—or the "hard to find" titles. We not only provided these titles overnight, but we also offered a 20 percent discount (unless the title was short discounted, of course).

As mentioned previously, Orkiszewski (2005) conducted a comparative study of Amazon and a traditional library book and media vendor. In addition to raising the issues mentioned earlier relating to order fulfillment, he found that on average the Amazon discount was lower (8.75 percent) compared to the traditional vendors (15.24 percent). One of his conclusions was, "Libraries interested in using Amazon should find it useful for trade and popular press books, DVDs, and book and media items that need to be acquired quickly" (p. 208). Although e-stores are not *the* answer to the challenges facing busy acquisition departments, they can be of assistance and should not be totally dismissed.

Out-of-Print and Antiquarian Dealers

Retrospective collection building is one of the most interesting and challenging areas of CM work. Libraries buy retrospectively for two reasons: to fill in gaps in the collection and to replace worn out or lost copies of titles. There has been a steady decline in retrospective buying on the part of libraries over the past 20 years due to limited budgets, as well as the need to increase purchases of nonprint and electronic resources. Another factor in the decline has been the proliferation of bibliographic databases such as OCLC, which make locating a copy of an out-of-print title to borrow through ILL much easier. As a result, acquisitions staff and selectors have decreasing experience to draw upon when they need to work in this field. Dealers in this field are a "special breed," unlike other vendors with which the library has more experience.

One outcome of the decline is that the field, which has always been very dependent on collectors, is even more driven today by collector interests than by library needs. Allowing for overlap, there are two broad categories of OP dealers. (It should be noted that most of these individuals dislike the label "secondhand dealer.") One category focuses primarily on general OP books, that is, on buying and selling relatively recent OP books. Often these books sell at prices that are the same as, or only slightly higher than, their publication price. The other category of dealer focuses on rare, antiquarian, and special (for example, fore-edged painted, miniature, or private press) books. Prices for this type of book can range from around $10 (U.S.) to thousands of dollars.

Many acquisitions librarians and book dealers classify OP book distribution services into three general types: (1) a complete book service, (2) a complete sales service, and (3) a complete bookstore. The first two may operate in a manner that does not allow, or at least require, customers to come to the seller's location. All contact is by E-mail, telephone, and occasionally by regular mail. The owner may maintain only a small stock of choice items in a garage or basement. In a *complete book service*, a dealer actively searches for items for a customer even if the items are not in stock. In the past this was the standard approach for serious retrospective collection development. Today, with several OP Web search sites, such as Bookfinder (http://www .bookfinder.com), many libraries handle all the work themselves.

A *sales service* is just what the name implies: A dealer reads the "wanted" sections of book trade Websites and publications and sends off quotes on items in his or her stock. Such services seldom place ads or conduct searches for a customer. The *complete bookstore* is a store operation that depends on in-person trade. Stores of this type often engage in book service and sales service activities as well.

Since the late 1990s, the OP trade has become very dependent on the Web. Today there are thousands of OP dealers with a Web presence. To some degree the Web has kept prices down, or slowed their increase. Checking prices through a site such as AbeBooks.Com® (http://www.abebooks.com) is very easy.

An example of the power of Web searching for OP titles is one done in November 2010 for Charles Dickens titles. A general search turned up 106,000-plus copies ranging in price from $1.50 (U.S.) to tens of thousands of dollars. Narrowing the search to first editions brought the results to 1,959 titles. The lowest price was $3.97; however, item number 1,959 on the list was a presentation copy of *Nicholas Nickleby* inscribed by Dickens to a close personal friend. Its asking price was $185,000 (U.S.). Sellers with first editions were from many countries (a total of 21—for example, Australia, Canada, Denmark, India, Norway, Scotland, and the United Kingdom) and in cities across the United States; the inscribed copy was from a dealer in New Hampshire.

An example of a title that might reflect the interest of a science library that was searched was Henry Fairfield Osborn's two-volume set *Proboscidea: A Monograph of the Discovery, Evolution, Migration and Extinction of the Mastodons and Elephants of the World* (American Museum of Natural History, vol. 1, 1936 and vol. 2, 1942). Only one set turned up in a search of AbeBooks and Bookfinder. The set was available from a dealer in Edinburgh, Scotland, with an asking price of $3,614 (U.S.). Before OP online searching was possible, such a search could have progressed for years before there was success. Now in a matter of minutes you can have rather definitive results. If you don't get a hit, in most cases dozens of hits, you can be reasonably sure the item is not available or you are lacking some critical data about the title. One reason for suspecting the item is not available is that sites such as AbeBooks and Bookfinder have tens of thousands of dealer members worldwide, and the Web has become their major source of business. One online OP dealer with pages and services focusing on library needs is Alibris™ (http://library.alibris.com/about-library?cm_sp=lhs-_-info-_-aboutlib). This site makes the point "we accept library purchase orders" as well as offering a "want list" matching service.

As is true of OP dealer's print catalog descriptions, one must be careful to read the description provided online with a critical mind, at least for the rare book purchases. Despite the need for caution, the Web has indeed changed the nature of retrospective collection development. Dealer descriptions and condition statements can be very idiosyncratic, and one must read them with a degree of caution. There are no official standards for such information. Some years ago *AB Bookman's Weekly* put forward some suggested terms and their definitions. What follows can only be thought of as broad meanings to help assess what a dealer may be describing.

Two of the top-level condition terms you may see are *as new* and *fine*. Presumably an "as new" implies a flawless item—the identical condition as when published—including a perfect dust jacket, if that was part of the original. Sometimes a dealer will use *mint* for this state. "Fine" is a slightly less perfect state, perhaps there is a little evidence of shelf wear and use but of a very minor nature. *Very good* and *good* are conditions that most libraries find acceptable for general collection replacement copies—there is evidence of wear. *Fair* and *poor* condition states probably are not suitable for libraries except when nothing else is available and the need is very strong as they imply some defects in the item. *Ex-library*, as the term indicates, means the copy has the usual stamping, perforations, spindling, and other mutilations that libraries use to property mark an item.

A library may assume that most OP dealers sell their stock as described or "as is." If there is no statement about the item's condition, it should be in good or better condition. A common statement in catalogs is "terms—all books in original binding and in good or better condition unless otherwise stated." The OP dealer's reputation for honesty, service, and fair prices is important. To gain such a reputation requires a considerable period of time in this field. In today's Web-based environment, this issue is a challenge for libraries. If one is only purchasing a $20 or $30 (U.S.) replacement copy, the risks of dealing with an unknown dealer are not all that high. For higher priced materials, there are real risks. The risks were there in the preelectronic environment as well, but ease of posting an item for sale on the Web has magnified the opportunities for less-than-honest sellers to make a sale. One clue of a good reputation is membership in organizations such as Antiquarian Booksellers Association of America (http://www.abaa.org) or the International League of Antiquarian Booksellers (http://www.ilab.org); members usually state that information on their Websites.

One element in the OP trade is very mysterious to the outsider and even to librarians who have had years of experience with dealers: How do dealers determine the asking price? (The rule of thumb of paying one-third or less of the expected sales income is probably ignored more than it is practiced. The "or less" is the key.) Sol Malkin (1974) summed up the outsider's feeling about pricing in the OP trade: "Many new-book dealers think of the antiquarian bookseller as a secondhand junkman or as a weird character who obtains books by sorcery, prices them by cannibalistic necromancy, and sells them by black magic" (p. 208).

As amusing as Malkin's theory may be, prices are actually based on a number of interrelated factors:

1. How much it costs to acquire the item.

2. The amount of current interest in collecting a particular subject or author.

3. The number of copies printed and the number of copies still in existence.

4. The physical condition of the copy.

5. Any special features of the particular copy (autographed by the author or signed or owned by a famous person, for example).

6. What other dealers are asking for copies of the same edition in the same condition.

In the past, it might have appeared that magic was the essential ingredient in successful OP operations—getting the price right. To a large degree, dealers set prices after they know the answers to the questions of supply and demand. Without question, the current asking price is the major determining factor—given equal conditions in the other five areas. In today's online environment, determining how many copies are available and what their asking price is has simplified pricing for both the dealer and the buyer.

Fiscal Management

The next phase of acquisitions work relates to what amounts to very careful record keeping activities, most of which are financial in character. There are records of orders placed, items received, and amounts paid. There is also an accountability aspect (audits) that draw on the records. Two other monetary related activities involve projecting/estimating price increases for materials and allocating the available funds for acquiring materials.

Tight economic times translate into tight acquisition funding for libraries. Norman Oder's article (2010), quoted at the opening of the chapter, reported on *Library Journal*'s annual survey of public library budgets. Results of the survey, not surprisingly, showed a downward trend—with a 2.6 percent reduction in the overall average budget, a 3.5 percent reduction in the materials budget, and, for the first time in several years, a 1.6 percent decline in the per capita expenditure (p. 44). The percentage drops on overall and collections funding, while not dramatic, have been on a downward slope for some time now. The cumulative impact of year after year reductions is beginning to show in ways that service communities are noticing.

One of the survey questions reported in Oder's article asked about what coping strategies the libraries had implemented for addressing the shortfalls. The top six responses were:

Cutting travel and training funds—51 percent

Freezing salaries—41 percent

Seeking more "outside" funding (grants, donations)—36 percent

Cutting/reducing programming activities—28 percent

Reduced service hours—26 percent

Increased use of volunteers—26 percent (p. 46).

When asked about which cuts or reductions users would probably miss the most, the vast majority of libraries expected service hour changes to be the most common concern (74 percent), followed by fewer new titles added (14 percent), and then reductions in services (12 percent) (Oder, 2010, p. 44). "Making do" with less has become a fact of life for most U.S. libraries, and it seems likely to continue for some time. Thus, understanding the issues of financial control and making the most effective use of the available funds are critical. With collection funds usually being the second-largest component in a library's budget, acquisitions staff must commit themselves to handling the funds properly and thoughtfully.

Estimating Costs

Given the significance of the acquisitions budget in terms of the overall institutional budget, projections about what funds it will take to at least maintain the current level of purchasing in the next budget cycle become important to senior administrators as they formulate the overall budget request. Thus it is incumbent on the department to provide the most accurate estimates as possible. Libraries often have difficulty establishing credibility with funding authorities regarding the different nature of the materials purchased with collection funds. Some funding officials have difficulty accepting the fact that the Consumer Price Index (CPI) numbers do not apply to library materials. The notion that each item is one of a kind— almost monopolistic in nature—seems hard to get across. In reality, library collection items do not fit the classic economic pricing model where there is competition between similar products. As a result, the producers of the materials can and do set their prices with only modest thought about competitive prices. For many years there was a double-digit percentage price increase for library material when the CPI was a modest single digit. Today the increases are not double digit, but still well above the CPI rate.

Starting in the 1970s, U.S. librarians made an all-out effort to create useful library price indexes that measure rates of change. A subcommittee of the American National Standards Institute, the Z39 Committee (1974), was able to develop guidelines for price indexes. By the early 1980s, it was necessary to revise the guidelines, which were later published as Z39.20 (National Information Standards Organization, 1999). Another group effort was that of the Library Materials Price Index Committee (Association for Library Collections and Technical Services of ALA). The committee has produced a price index for U.S. materials and some international publications (http://www.ala.org/ala/mgrps/divs/alcts/resources/collect/serials/spi.cfm). These efforts provide consistent data on price changes over a long period, which, when averaged, are as close as anyone can come to predicting future price changes.

The most recent U.S. price data are in journals; historical data appear in *Library and Book Trade Almanac*. Using this source is adequate for some purposes, but one needs to be aware that the information that appears in the "current" volume is almost two years old. Preliminary data for books published during a calendar year appear in *Publishers Weekly* (often in late February or early March). Final data appear some months later (September or October). The major problem with the published indexes is that when preparing a budget request, up-to-date information may not be readily available.

Just as libraries prepare budget requests at different times of the year, pricing data appear at various times during the year in a variety of sources. The challenge is to find the most current data, which may determine the library's success in securing the requested funding.

Libraries that purchase a significant number of foreign publications also need to estimate the impact of exchange rates. Volatile exchange rates affect buying power almost as much as inflation. For example, in January 1985, the exchange rate for the pound sterling was $1.2963 (U.S.); in January 1988 it was up to $1.7813 (U.S.); in 1992 it was $1.7653 (U.S.); by January 1994 it was down to $1.4872 (U.S.), in March 1999 it had moved up to $1.6064 (U.S.), and it was at $1.60554 (U.S.) by July 2011. Although it is impossible to accurately forecast the direction and amount of fluctuation in the exchange rates 12 months into the future, some effort should go into studying the previous 12-month rates and attempting to predict future trends. (One source for historic data on exchange rates is the Federal Reserve Board: http://www.federalreserve.gov/releases/g5a/.) It is important to have good data about the amounts spent in various countries during the previous year. The country of publication is less important than the vendor's country. For example, if the library uses the vendor Harrassowitz, prices will be in euros, regardless of the country of origin of the items purchased. After collecting the data, the library can use them as factors in

---

Check This Out

Sheila Smyth examined the utility of creating systematic programs to be more responsive to shifts in currency trends in her 2010 article "Currency Trends and Collection Building: Implications for Acquisitions" (*College & Research Libraries News* 71, no. 10: 547–549, 566).

estimating the cost of continuing the current acquisition levels from the countries from which the library normally buys.

Allocating Funds

You would be correct to think that dividing up the materials budget is a rather complicated process. Today, there are usually three broad slices to the materials budget "pie": books, serials, and e-resources. Mark Estes (2009) noted that he "used the pie in describing my library budget to an information vendor. My library book and computer research budget is a pie—for me to give you some more of my pie I must make another information vendor's piece smaller" (p. 1). And, just as in Estes's vendor scenario, when one slice of the allocation increases, more often than not all of the other slices get smaller.

If there were only three slices of the budget pie to consider, the process would not be all that complicated; although the individuals in charge of the three areas might well disagree about the size of their respective slices. In most libraries, there are many more slices to consider. While there may always be some disagreement about who gets how much money for materials, today's stable or shrinking materials budget makes for interesting, even heated, debates regarding who should or must get what.

Ordinarily, the method of allocation reflects, at least to some degree, the library's collection development policy statement priorities. If the library employs a collecting intensity ranking system in the collection development policy, it is reasonable to expect to find those levels reflected in the amount of money allocated to the subject or format. Almost all allocation methods are complex, and matching the needs and monies available requires that the library consider several factors.

From the funding authority's point of view, it has no interest in how the library decides to allocate the funds provided they purchase material for the collection. However, except in the smallest library, there are usually several staff members who would like to have a voice in the allocation discussion or debate. Each person will come to the table with her or his case for why "this year" his or her area must receive a bigger slice of the pie. Just as the library's budget request to the funding authorities is a political process, so too is the internal materials budget an allocation process.

Each library will have its own categories for allocation. However, some of the more common categories are:

- Adult monographs (fiction/nonfiction)
- Adult serials
- Adult media
- Children's books
- Children's magazines
- Children's media
- Young adult (YA) books
- YA magazines
- YA media
- Reference department
- Replacement items
- Rental/lease titles
- E-resources

This list reflects the public library environment. When it comes to academic and school libraries, the list of categories becomes even more complex. Educational libraries not only have to address the three broad categories (print, media, and electronic) as well as some of the above listed items such as reference and replacements, but they also may have teaching departments or faculty members lobbying for a slice of an ever-smaller pie. (There may even be cases where more than one department wants their own copy of a particular title—which can complicate how many copies to order and to which fund code to charge the title.)

Among the issues that factor into the allocation process are past practices, differential publication rates, unit cost and inflation rates, level of demand, and actual usage of the material. Implementing a formal allocation system takes time and effort. Some professionals question whether it is worthwhile allocating the monies. Opponents to allocation claim it is difficult to develop a fair allocation model, and it is time consuming to calculate the amounts needed. Certainly allocations add to the workload in the acquisitions department as they have to track more expenditure categories. Those opposed to the process also claim that, because the models are difficult to develop, libraries tend to leave the allocation percentages or ratios in place too long and simply add in the next year's percentage increase rather than recalculating the figures annually. They suggest that selectors may not spend accounts effectively because there is too much or too little money available. Finally, they argue that it is difficult to effect transfers from one account to another during the year. Proponents of allocation claim that it provides better control of collection development, and it is a more effective way to monitor expenditures.

A good allocation process provides at least four outcomes. First and foremost, it matches, or should, available funds with actual funding needs. Second, it provides selectors with guidelines for how they should allocate their time. That is, if someone is responsible for three selection areas with funding allocations of $15,000, $5,000, and $500, it is clear which area requires the most attention. (In many cases, it is more difficult to spend the smaller amount, because one must be careful to spend it wisely.) Third, the allocation process provides a means of assessing the selector's work at the end of the fiscal year. Finally, it provides the service community with a sense of collecting priorities, assuming the allocation information is made available to them. The library can communicate the information in terms of percentages rather than specific monetary amounts if there is a concern about divulging budgetary data.

Alternatives to traditional allocation models have been examined, and in some cases implemented. Dinkins (2011) notes that "with the explosion of online resources since the late 1990s, academic libraries are struggling to make a traditional allocation formula, based on academic disciplines and purchase of tangible materials, also work for the purchase or lease of online resources supporting multidisciplinary research needs" (p. 121). Dinkins's article describes how Stetson University chose to base its collections allocation decisions on the results of examining historical data and usage statistics, as it was discovered this method was as effective as using a more complex formula.

Check This Out

Virginia Williams and June Schmidt's (2008) article "Determining the Average Cost of a Book for Allocation Formulas" (*Library Resources and Technical Services* 52, no. 1: 60–70) provides a good review of the various allocation formulas libraries, especially academic and school, employ as well as the pros and cons of each.

Check These Out

Two good resources for gaining an understanding of library accounting and budgetary practices are:

G. Stevenson Smith, *Managerial Accounting for Libraries and Other Not-for-Profit Organizations*. 2nd ed. Chicago: American Library Association, 2002.

Anne M. Turner, *Managing Money: A Guide for Librarians*. Jefferson, NC: McFarland, 2007.

Financial Records

We noted earlier that much of the acquisition department's work involves financial record keeping. One of the key people in the department is the bookkeeper who may or may not have a background in library work. Regardless of his or her background, the bookkeeper will quickly pick up the requisite knowledge, as most of the bookkeeping follows standard accounting practices. There is one library-related process that is unlike most business bookkeeping practice—encumbering.

Encumbering

Encumbering is a process that allows the library to set aside monies to pay for ordered items. When the library waits 60, 90, or 120 days or more for orders, there is some chance that the monies available will be over- or underspent if there is no system that allows for setting aside funds.

The following chart shows how the process works. Day 1 (the first day of the FY) shows the library with an annual allocation of $1,000 for a particular subject area. On day 2, the library orders an item with a list price of $24.95. Although there may be shipping and handling charges, there probably will be a discount. Because none of the costs and credits are known at the time, the list price is the amount a staff member records as encumbered. (Some departments add a fixed percentage of the list price in order to more closely match what will be the invoice price.) The unexpended column reflects the $24.95 deduction, with zero showing in the expended category. Sixty-two days later, the item and invoice arrive; the invoice reflects a 15 percent discount ($3.74) and no shipping or handling charges. The bookkeeper records the actual cost ($21.21) underexpended and adds the $3.74 to the unexpended amount. The amount encumbered now is zero.

	Unexpended	Encumbered	Expended
Day 1	$1000.00	0	0
Day 2	$975.05	$24.95	0
Day 62	$978.79	0	$21.21

This system is much more complex than the example suggests, because libraries place and receive multiple orders every day. With each transaction the amounts in each column change. *Neither the acquisitions department nor the selectors know the precise unexpended balance, except on the first and last day of the fiscal year.* If the funding body takes back all unexpended funds at the end of the FY (a *cash accounting* system), the acquisitions department staff must know the fund(s) balances as they enter the final quarter of the year.

Several factors make it difficult to learn the exact status of the funds, even when encumbering funds. One factor is delivery of orders. Vendors may assure customers they will deliver before the end of the FY but fail to do so. Such a failure can result in the encumbered money being lost. With a cash system, the acquisitions department staff must make some choices at the end of the FY if there are funds in the encumbered category. The main issue is determining if the items still on order are important enough to leave on order. An affirmative answer has substantial implications for collection development.

Using the foregoing example and assuming that day 62 comes after the start of a new FY and the new allocation is $1,000, on day 1 of the new FY, the amount unexpended would be $975.05 ($1,000 minus $24.95), encumbered $24.95, and expended zero. In essence, there is a reduction in the amount available for new orders and the library lost $24.95 from the prior year's allocation. (One of the authors once took over as head of a library on June 25, and the system's financial officer reported the entire acquisitions allocation was encumbered for the coming fiscal year, starting July 1. To have some funds for collection development over the next 12 months, it was necessary to cancel 347 orders.) With an *accrual system*, the unexpended funds carry forward into the next FY. Under such a system, using the previous example, the day 1 figures would be unexpended $1,000, encumbered $24.95, and expended zero.

There is a problem in leaving funds encumbered for long periods under either system, especially when there is rapid inflation or exchange rates are unfavorable. The latter are two reasons why a firm but reasonable date for automatic cancellation of unfilled orders is important.

The point of all this work is to allow the library to expend all the materials funds available in a timely manner without overordering. Remember that an order is a legal contract between the library and the supplier. Certainly most suppliers who have a long-standing relationship with libraries will understand an occasional overcommitment of funds, but they have a legal right to full, prompt payment for all orders placed. One way they allow libraries to address the problem is to ship the order on time but hold the invoice until the start of the next FY.

A major problem confronting an acquisitions bookkeeper is the number of allocation accounts. In some libraries, the number may run over 200. Restricted funds are especially problematic because the library may charge only certain types of materials to such accounts. Although the bookkeeper's job may be to assign charges to the various accounts, that person also must know approximately how much money remains as free balance, as encumbered, and as expended. As the number of accounts goes up, so does the bookkeeper's workload.

Stewardship

Many libraries have "special" funds available for collection building. The two most common are grant monies and endowment funds. Grants almost always have clearly specified reporting requirements regarding how the library used the money. Endowment or gift funds may or may not have such requirements.

With grants, you may be expected to provide detailed information on items acquired (list price, discount, tax if any, etc.). The reason is some categories of cost may not be allowed under the terms of the grant. In other cases, all you need to report is the number of items acquired. We would recommend generating a detailed accounting, even if not required, as there is always a chance the grant usage may be audited.

Endowments and special gifts, such as for memorial purposes, are another matter when it comes to reporting. They may or may not call for informing the donor what was acquired. However, it is a best practice to send such a report regardless of the necessity.

Special gifts may be annual or onetime in character. Memorial gift funds usually call for placing a book plate in the item indicating the name of the person being memorialized. The same is often the case with endowed funds. Many academic libraries have numerous endowed book accounts, most of which specify a subject area where you may have used the monies. In the case of narrowly defined topics, you may not identify an appropriate item for a year or more.

Telling donors, whether required or not, not only what was acquired but where to find it in the collection—call number—offers the donors a chance to look at the items and judge your stewardship of their monies. That "extra" step can result in additional gifts for collection building. It does mean that acquisitions and cataloging departments must keep good records of what was selected and processed for several, if not dozens, of separate accounts.

Audits

Are audits really necessary in libraries? Must we remember how, where, when, and on what we spent every cent? (An enjoyable short poem by Robert Frost titled the "Hardship of Accounting" addresses the issue of accounting and audits: http://varietyreading.carlsguides.com/forwards/hardship .php.) Unfortunately, the answer is *yes* when it comes to library funds. Some years ago, Herbert Snyder and Julia Hersberger (1997) published an article outlining embezzlement in public libraries. The article makes it clear why regular financial audits are necessary.

There are three basic audit types. *Operational audits* examine an organization's procedures and practices, usually with the goal of making improvements. *Compliance audits* examine how well an organization is following procedures established by some higher level body. An example might be to determine if the acquisitions department has followed the procedures for funds received through a federal government LSCA (Library Services and Construction Act) or LSTA (Library Services and Technology Act) grants. The *financial audit* is what comes to people's minds when they hear "audit." It is often a yearly event for the acquisitions department, wherein its records are examined by nonlibrary personnel to assure the funding authority, as well as other parties, that the monies were in fact expended in the expected way and that the records of those transactions comply with standard accounting practices and guidelines. One aspect of having the power to manage and expend substantial amounts of money is fiscal accountability. The amount of money does not need to be "substantial" if it involves public or private funds. For acquisitions departments, the auditor's visit is probably second only to the annual performance appraisal process in terms of worry and stress for the staff. The worry is not that they have done something wrong, but rather their not being able to find some type of documentation that an auditor wishes to check.

A legalistic definition of an *audit* is the process of accumulation and evaluation of evidence about quantifiable information of an economic entity to determine and report on the degree of correspondence between the information and established criteria. More simply put, it is the process of ensuring that the financial records are accurate and that the information is presented correctly using accepted accounting practices and of making recommendations for improvements in how the process is carried out. The basic questions and required records relate to whether a purchase was made with proper authorization, was received, and was paid for in an appropriate manner, and whether the item is still available. (If the item is no longer available, there should be appropriate records regarding its disposal.) With automated acquisitions systems, undergoing an audit is less time consuming than in the past, where the paper trail was in fact a number of different paper records that had to be gathered and compared. At least now, an ILS can pull up the necessary information fairly quickly.

Points to Keep in Mind

- Acquisition departments secure the items that selectors identify as important to add to the collection.
- Acquisition activities are almost always related in some manner to financial matters.
- Three key areas of acquisitions work are determining how to acquire an item, acquiring the items, and creating and maintaining the financial records associated with the acquisition activities.
- There are eight broad methods for acquiring collection materials: firm order, standing order, blanket order, approval plan, subscriptions, leases, gifts, and exchanges.
- Developing and maintaining a good working relationship with vendors is key to having a successful acquisitions program.
- Encumbering is a method that assists the library in not over- or underexpending the funds available for collection development.
- Audits and accountability go hand in hand; the audits demonstrate to funding authorities and other stakeholders that the library expended the funds entrusted to it in an appropriate manner.

Works Cited

Alan, Robert, Tina E. Chrzastowski, Lisa German, and Jynn Wiley. 2010. "Approval Plan Profile Assessment in Two Large ARL Libraries: University of Illinois at Urbana-Champaign and Pennsylvania State University." *Library Resources and Technical Services* 54, no. 2: 64–76.

Carrico, Steven. 1999. "Gifts and Exchanges." In *Understanding the Business of Acquisitions,* 2nd ed., ed. Karen A. Schmidt, 205–223. Chicago: American Library Association.

Dinkins, Debbi. 2011. "Allocating Academic Library Budgets: Adapting Historical Data Models at One University Library." *Collection Management* 36, no. 2: 119–130.

Eaglen, Audrey B. 1984. "Trouble in Kiddyland: The Hidden Costs of O.P. and O.S." *Collection Building* 6, no. 2: 26–28.

Estes, Mark E. 2009. "Slicing Your Pieces of the Pie." *AALL Spectrum* 13, no. 4: 1.

Evans, G. Edward. 1970. "Book Selection and Book Collection Usage in Academic Libraries." *Library Quarterly* 40, no. 3: 297–308.

Evans, G. Edward. 1974. "Approval Plans and Collection Development in Academic Libraries." *Library Resources and Technical Services* 18, no. 1: 35–50.

Evans, G. Edward, Sheila S. Inter, and Jan Weihs. 2011. *Introduction to Technical Services*, 8th ed. Santa Barbara, CA: Libraries Unlimited.

Fessler, Vera. 2007. "The Future of Technical Services." *Library Administration and Management* 21, no. 3: 139–144.

Malkin, Sol. 1974. "Rare and Out-of-Print Books." In *A Manual on Bookselling.* New York: American Booksellers Association.

Marcum, James W. 2008. "Collection Building Barter: A Proposal." *Bottom Line: Managing Library Finances* 21, no. 2: 49–51.

Myers, Anne. 2009. "Lament for Lost Customer Service." *AALL Spectrum* 13, no. 7: CRIV Sheet 3–4.

Oder, Norman. 2010. "Permanent Shift?" *Library Journal* 135, no. 1: 44, 46.

Orkiszewski, Paul. 2005. "A Comparative Study of Amazon.com as a Library Book and Media Vendor." *Library Resources & Technical Services* 49, no. 3: 204–209.

Ranganathan, S. R. 1988. *The Five Laws of Library Science*. Bangalore, India: Sarada Ranganathan Endowment for Library Science.

Snyder, Herbert, and Julia Hersberger. 1997. "Public Libraries and Embezzlement: An Examination of Internal Control and Financial Misconduct." *Library Quarterly* 67, no. 1: 1–23.

Selected Websites of Note

AcqLink: http://bubl.ac.uk/link/linkbrowse.cfm?menuid=1026

AcqWeb: http://www.acqweb.org/

Association for Library Collections and Technical Services (ALCTS), Guidelines and Standards for Technical Services, http://www.ala.org/ala/mgrps/divs/alcts/resources/guides/index.cfm

H. W. Smith Bookstore: http://www.bookshop.co.uk/

Suggested Readings

Allen, Sydney K. 2000. "Libraries on the Book Buying Merry-Go-Round: Internet Book Seller vs. Library Book Vendor." *Against the Grain* 12, no. 2: 1, 16–22.

Allen, Sydney K., and Heather S. Miller. 2003. "The Merry-Go-Round Revisited: Libraries Buying Books Online." *Against the Grain* 15, no. 4: 58, 60, 62, 64.

Anderson, Colleen D. 2008. "Accounting and Auditing Resources." *College & Research Libraries News* 69, no. 2: 96–100.

Appavoo, Clare. 2007. "Size Doesn't Matter: Book Approval Plans Can Be Catered to Tight Budgets." *Feliciter* 53, no. 5: 238–240.

Barnes, Matt, Jon Clayborne, and Suzy Szazz Palmer. 2005. "Book Pricing: Publisher, Vendor, and Library Perspectives." *Collection Building* 24, no. 3: 87–91.

Branche-Brown, Lynne C. 1995. "Vendor Evaluation." *Collection Management* 19, nos. 3/4: 47–56.

Brantley, John S. 2010. "Approval Plans, Discipline Change, and the Importance of Human Mediated Book Selection." *Library Collections, Acquisitions, and Technical Services* 34, no. 1: 11–24.

Copper, Tom. 2010. "Getting the Most from Donations." *Public Libraries* 49, no. 2: 31–36.

Furr, Patricia. 2006. "Electronic Acquisitions: How E-Commerce May Change the Way that Your Library Buys Books." *Mississippi Libraries* 70, no. 2: 26–27.

Gray, David, and Malcolm H. Brantz. 2003. "Out of the Box and Into the Bookstore: Nontraditional Use of the Bookstore." *Against the Grain* 15, no. 3: 36, 38, 40, 42.

Hirko, Buff. 2004. "Get Vendor Savvy." *Library Journal Net Connect* 124, Spring: 12–13.

Hoffert, Barbara. 2007. "Who's Selecting Now? *Library Journal* 132, no. 14: 40–43.

Holden, Jesse. 2010. *Acquisitions in the New Information Universe: Core Competencies and Ethical Practices*. New York: Neal-Schuman.

Howard, Jennifer. 2010. "Reader Choice, Not Vendor Influence, Reshapes Library Collections." *Chronicle of Higher Education* 57, no. 12: A11–A12.

Linn, Mott. 2007. "Budget Systems Used in Allocating Resources to Libraries." *Bottom Line* 20, no. 1: 20–29.

Massey, Tinker. 2005. "Management of Gift Materials in an Academic Library." *Collection Building* 24, no. 3: 80–82.

Newcomer, Nara L. 2009. "Back to Basics: International Collection Development on a Shoestring." *Collection Building* 28, no. 4: 164–169.

Pomerantz, Sarah, and Andrew White. 2009. "Re-modeling ILS Acquisitions Data to Financially Transition From Print to Digital Formats." *Library Collections, Acquisitions, and Technical Services* 33, no. 1: 42–49.

Riley, John. 2009. "Are Any Books Still Out-of-Print?"*Against the Grain* 21, no. 5: 1–14.

Smith, A. Arro, and Stephanie Langenkamp. 2007. "Indexed Collection Budget Allocations: A Tool for Quantitative Collection Development Based on Circulation." *Public Libraries* 46, no. 5: 50–54.

Somsel, Larisa. 2004. "Buying Books Online Is No Mystery." *Collection Management* 29, nos. 3/4: 41–52.

Stamison, Christine, Bob Persing, Chris Beckett, and Chris Brady. 2009. "What They Never Told You About Vendors in Library School." *Serials Librarian* 56, no. 1: 139–145.

Steele, Kirstin. 2008. "Are Budget Limitations Real? Perspective, Perceptions, and a Plan." *Bottom Line* 21, no. 3: 85–87.

Ward, Judit H. 2009. "Acquisitions Globalized: The Foreign Language Acquisitions Experience in a Research Library." *Library Resources and Technical Services* 53, no. 2: 86–93.

6
Assessing Collections and the Library

Many years ago libraries were simply judged by the number of volumes on the shelves, no matter what the condition or usefulness of the item.
> —Marvene Dearman and Elizabeth Dumas, 2008

One way to determine the value of anything is to determine its usefulness. Nowhere is this truer than in libraries and, in turn, their collections. More and more, libraries are encompassing large percentages of their collections as electronic, and this begs the question about its value.
> —Douglas King, 2009

Collection assessment, at its best, is an art not a science, and the numbers that it generates are a means not an end.
> —Jennifer Z. McClure, 2009

Collections are a major factor in a library's service program. As such, they also play a significant role in any assessment or evaluation of the quality of the library. Collection evaluation is not new; it has been something librarians and others have done for the better part of 100 years. One example of how long libraries have been evaluating their collections comes from Robert Downs (1941) when he wrote about his "years of experience" examining library collections:

> From the internal point of view, the survey, if properly done, gives one an opportunity to stand off and get an objective look at the library, to see its strengths, its weaknesses, the directions in

133

which it has been developing, how it compares with other similar
libraries, how well the collection is adapted to its clientele, and
provides a basis for future planning. (p. 113)

Downs believed that, in addition to their internal value, surveys are an
essential step in preparing for library cooperative acquisitions projects and
resource sharing.

Providing the highest quality service is a key component in demonstrating value for money spent and for gaining user support. Some years ago,
Brian Quinn (1997) wrote:

> The concept of service quality is somewhat elusive and resists
> easy definition, but essentially it emphasizes gap reduction—
> reducing any gap that may exist between a customer's expecta-
> tions and the customer's perception of the quality of service
> provided. More traditional measures of academic library quality
> such as collection size are considered to be of secondary impor-
> tance. (p. 359)

In the recent past, the term *assessment* has become almost a buzzword
in both the professional and popular press. People apply it to almost every
type of organization and activity. People also tend to use assessment and
accountability interchangeably. Although the two terms are related, they
are not identical, except in the very broadest meaning.

One way to think about the differences is that *assessment* is a process
that an organization undertakes to look at its own activities, services, or
operations. *Accountability*, on the other hand, is when an outside agency
or group looks at an organization's activities, services, or operations. For
libraries, there is almost always a parent body to which it is accountable.
The parent body can and occasionally does look at some or all of the library's
activities. The most common occurrence is the one we discussed in the previous chapter—fiscal management and conducting audits of the library's
financial transactions. For educational libraries, there is another outside
group that engages in examining a library's activities—accreditation groups.
Accrediting agencies represent one of the largest stakeholder groups with
an interest in library service and quality—the general public.

In 2005, John B. Harer and Bryan R. Cole published an article on the
importance of stakeholders' interest in measuring performance and service. They engaged in a Delphi study "to determine the importance of a
list of critical processes and performance measures relevant to measuring quality in academic libraries" (p. 149). Their results suggested that, in
an academic context, students, faculty, and the general public, at least in
terms of publicly financed institution's interests, were significant factors
in assessing quality (p. 160). Other types of libraries have equally diverse
stakeholders.

There are a variety of reasons for a library to undertake collection
assessment projects. Some are internal and others are external in character.
At other times, both become factors. The following are some of the factors
that come into play from time to time:

Collection Development Needs

- Determining the true scope of the collections (that is, what is the
  subject coverage).

- Determining the depth of the collections (that is, what amount and type of material comprise the collection).

- Determining how the service community uses the collection (that is, what is the circulation and use within the library).

- Determining the collection's monetary value (which must be known for insurance and capital assessment reasons).

- Determining the strong areas of the collection (in quantitative and qualitative terms).

- Determining the weak areas of the collection (in quantitative and qualitative terms).

- Identifying problems that exist in the collection policy and program.

- Determining changes that should be made in the existing program.

- Determining how well the collection development officers are carrying out their duties.

- Provide data for possible cooperative collection development programs.

- Provide data for deselection (weeding) projects.

- Provide data to determine the need for a full inventory.

Budgetary Needs

- Assist in determining allocations needed to strengthen weak areas.

- Assist in determining allocations needed to maintain areas of strength.

- Assist in determining allocations needed for retrospective collection development.

- Assist in determining overall allocations.

Local Institutional Needs

- Determine if the library's performance is marginal, adequate, or above average.

- Determine if the budget request for materials is reasonable.

- Determine if the budget provides the appropriate level of support.

- Determine if the library is comparable to others serving similar communities.

- Determine if there are alternatives to space expansion (for example, weeding).

- Determine if the collection is outdated.

- Determine if there is sufficient coordination in the collection program (that is, does the library really need all those separate collections).

- Determine if the level of duplication is appropriate.

- Determine if the cost/benefit ratio is reasonable.

Extraorganizational Needs

- Provide data for accreditation groups.

- Provide data for funding agencies.

- Provide data for various networks, consortia, and other cooperative programs.

- Provide data to donors.

More often than not, collection assessment projects address several of the above factors, if for no other reason than doing a project takes time and effort, so meeting more than one objective makes good sense. There are times when projects provide unexpected dividends by providing information about a factor that was not part of the original project goals.

Successful assessment projects are those with clearly defined goals and with researchers who are alert for the serendipitous findings. When the project is undertaken for accreditation purposes, the initial work is straightforward as there are clear goals—address the areas of interest to the accrediting body. A challenge in this area is when the visiting team is "on site" and requests information now—often in a timeframe of less than 24 hours. (Visiting teams are rarely on site for more than five days, and a rough average is closer to three days.) To address such requests, those who conduct the collection assessments for the library must understand the pros and cons of the various methods available for conducting such work.

No one suggests that it is possible to determine the adequacy of a library's collection solely in quantitative terms. However, in the absence of quantitative guidelines, budgeting officers, who cannot avoid the use of quantitative data—such as volumes added—for decision making, adopt measures that seem to have the virtue of simplicity but are essentially

---

From the Authors' Experience

Chapter 1 included a description of one of Evans' consulting projects undertaken at a private university regarding student complaints about the campus library. Although the objections raised by on-campus students covered a wide range of issues concerning the quality of library service, the collection was the topic most often mentioned in some manner.

The students complained about lack of material without being more specific. Thus, the initial focus was collection depth, breadth, and usage patterns and a request for a random sample of collection base for analysis. The request for the sample was intended to look at holdings by subject areas and the institutions' degree programs and determine some ratios of holdings to usage on the chance that it was just a few areas that were causing the complaints. As we noted in Chapter 1, the surprise finding was the fact that there was a 13-year "hole" in the collection in which no (or very few at best) new monographs had been added to the collection. Students tend to want the newest information for their course assignments. What the analysis showed was the holdings prior to 1984 were balanced across the degree program areas, but were totally skewed toward later material.

Perhaps the outcome of an increase in the budget for on-campus library resources would have been the same; however, the dramatic nature of the totally unexpected data very likely made the increases larger and quicker than might have happened otherwise. Unexpected findings are not all that rare.

irrelevant to the library's function. Therefore, it is necessary to develop quantitative approaches for evaluating collections that are useful in official decision making and that retain the virtue of simplicity while being relevant to the library's programs and services.

Collection Assessment Methodologies

Some years ago, the ALA issued the *Guide to the Evaluation of Library Collections* (1989). Although this title has not been updated, it continues to provide a useful framework for collection assessment by dividing evaluation methods into two broad categories: collection-centered measures and use-centered measures. Each category consists of several evaluative methods. The methods focus on print resources, but there are some that can be employed with e-resources as well. The categories, along with their associated methodologies, are:

Collection-Centered Methods

- List checking, bibliographies, and catalogs,
- Expert opinion,
- Comparative use statistics,
- Collection standards.

Use-Centered Methods

- Circulation studies,
- User opinion/studies,
- Analysis of ILL statistics,
- Citation studies,
- In-house use studies,
- Shelf availability,
- Simulated use studies,
- Document delivery tests.

Each method has its advantages and disadvantages. A good approach to an assessment project is to employ several methods that will counterbalance one another's weaknesses. (We cover e-resource assessment in Chapter 9.)

Collection-Centered Methods

List Checking

List checking is an old standby for collection evaluators; it may well be the first method that libraries employed after realizing there was a need to assess their collections. It can serve a variety of purposes. Used alone or in combination with other techniques—usually with the goal of coming up with some numerically based statement, such as "We (or they) have X percentage of the books on this list"—one of its advantages is that it provides objective data. Consultants frequently check holdings against standard bibliographies (or suggest that the library do it), which allows a person to make some comparisons that provide some insight about the overall collection.

Self-surveys frequently make use of checklist methods. M. Llewellyn Raney (1933) conducted the first checklist self-survey, at least the first reported in the literature, in a book published by the University of Chicago libraries. This survey used 300 bibliographies to check the entire collection for the purpose of determining future needs. It was carried out from 1929 to 1933, which provides some insight into how labor intensive such projects were and continue to be. There is little question that this pioneering effort demonstrated the value of using checklists to thoroughly examine the total collection—it lead to seven years of increased acquisition funding for the library.

Regardless of collection size, it is worthwhile to take time to review some of the best-of-the-year lists published by various associations and journals. Such reviews will help selectors spot titles missed during the year and serve as a check against personal biases playing too great a role in the selection process.

Checklisting rests on several assumptions; one is that the selected list reflects the goals and purposes of the checking institution. A second assumption is that the sample size, assuming that the entire list is not checked, is such that it is both valid and reliable. That is, the data are only as good as the sampling method employed. Another assumption is there is some correlation between the percentage of listed books held by a library and the percentage of quality books in the library's collection. This assumption may or may not be warranted. An equally questionable assumption is that listed books not held necessarily constitute desiderata, and that the proportion of items held to items needed (as represented on the list) constitutes an effective measure of a library's adequacy.

Certainly there are shortcomings of the checklist method. Eight criticisms that appear repeatedly in the literature are:

- Checklists are developed for a broad range of libraries and never are a complete match for any particular library.

- Almost all lists are selective and omit many worthwhile titles.

- Many titles have little relevance for a specific library's community.

- Lists may be out of date.

- A library may own many titles that are not on the checklist but that are as good as the titles on the checklist.

- Document delivery services carry no weight in the evaluation.

- Checklists approve titles; there is no penalty for having poor titles.

- Checklists fail to take into account special materials that may be important to a particular library.

Obviously, the time involved in effectively checking lists is a concern. Spotty or limited checking does little good, but most libraries are unable or unwilling to check an entire list. Checklist results show the percentage of books from the list that is in the collection. This may sound fine, but there is no standard proportion of a list a library should have. How would you interpret the fact that the library holds 53 percent of some list? Is it reasonable or necessary to have every item? Comparisons of one library's holdings with another's on the basis of percentage of titles listed are of little value, unless the two libraries have almost identical service populations.

This lengthy discussion of the shortcomings of the checklist method should serve more as a warning than a prohibition. There *are* benefits from using this method in evaluation. Many librarians believe that checking lists help reveal gaps and weaknesses in a collection and that the lists provide handy selection guides if the library wishes to use them for this purpose. They think that the revelation of gaps and weaknesses may lead to reconsideration of selection methods and policies. Often administrators outside the library respond more quickly and favorably to information about gaps in a collection when the evaluators identify the gaps by using standard lists than when they use other means of identifying the weaknesses.

Expert Opinion (Impressionistic Assessment)

Today, experts primarily play a role in collection assessment by helping CM staff formulate a sound assessment project using a variety of techniques. In the past, people such as Robert Downs, who we cited earlier, came in and conducted the assessment for the library. Such "experts" did employ best or recommended lists as part of their assessment, but also drew on their experience and opinions about strengths and weaknesses. There are still occasions when the outside expert is needed, most often when the library believes that such a person will have more credibility with funding authorities or other outside bodies. There are also rare occasions when the outside group hires an expert to do the assessment if the group thinks an unbiased judgment is necessary.

Today it is rare for this to be the sole technique used for assessment. The most common time this occurs is during accreditation visits, when a visiting team member walks into the stacks, looks around, and comes out with a sense of the value of the collection. No consultant who regularly uses this technique limits it to shelf reading. Rather, consultants prefer to collect impressions from the service community as well as from CM staff. Although each person's view is valid only for his or her own areas of interest, in combination, individuals' views should provide an overall sense of the service community's views. (This approach falls into the category of user satisfaction.) Users make judgments about the collection every time they look for something. They will have an opinion even after one brief visit. Thus, the approach is important, if for no other reason than providing the evaluator with a sense of what the users think about the collection.

The obvious weakness of the impressionistic technique is that it is overwhelmingly subjective. Certainly the opinions of those who use the collection regularly as well as the views of subject specialists are important. However, impressions are most useful as one element in a multifaceted evaluation project.

Comparative Use Statistics

Comparisons across a number of institutions can offer useful, if limited, data for assessing a collection. The limitations arise from institutional variations in objectives, programs, and service populations. For instance, a community college with a strong emphasis on transfer programs will have a library collection that reflects that emphasis, whereas a community college that focuses on vocational programs requires a rather different collection. Comparing the two would be like comparing apples to oranges.

From the Authors' Experience

Evans worked at a library that used an early version of the service now owned by OCLC (it used the AMIGOS version and the data were delivered on a set of CD-ROMs that the library could use in various ways). At that time, a library could create a peer group of up to 40 libraries, which was the number the library selected for comparison. The library used the resulting data to guide campus departments how to strengthen their holdings in their subject area, as input for new program proposals, as well as for accreditation reports. A small sample of the type of data generated follows.

Subcollection Proportions
Peer Group: PEER GROUP 1 (40)
LC Division: B-BJ Philosophy/Psychology

NATC	Titles Evaluator	Avg Mbr	Comparative Size	Peer Group	% of Subcollection Evaluator
B1-B68	80	54	148.15	2.23	2.09
B69-B789	386	241	160.17	9.96	10.08
B790-B5739	937	606	154.62	25.00	24.47
BC1-BC9999	60	49	122.45	2.01	1.57
BD1-BD9999	336	196	171.43	8.08	8.78
BF1-BF1000	1,500	939	159.74	38.71	39.17
BF1001-BF1400	48	37	129.73	1.54	1.25
BF1401-BF1999	38	37	102.70	1.51	0.99
BH1-BH9999	68	44	154.55	1.81	1.78
BJ1-BJ1800	372	217	171.43	8.95	9.72
BJ1801-BJ2195	4	5	80.00	0.19	0.10
Totals	3,829	2,425	157.88	100.00	100.00

The term *peer* in the table refers to the group used for comparison; the term *evaluator* refers to the assessing library. The Subcollection Counts notes that in the areas denoted B1-BJ2195 (LC classification) the peer group held 2,425 titles while the evaluating library held 3,829. That result suggests that, at least in terms of titles held, the evaluating library had great strength in the subject area.

Some useful comparative evaluation tools have been developed as a result of technology and growth of bibliographic utilities. A widely used product or service is OCLC's WorldCat Collection Analysis™ (http://www.oclc.org/us/en/collectionanalysis/default.htm). As the name implies, the service draws on the WorldCat™ database. With it, a library can select a peer group—up to 10 peers—for comparison purposes. It is possible to compare your collection with the group as a whole or library by library. You can identify your unique holdings and strengths and weaknesses based on volume counts in a class number in your collection. Only OCLC members can use the service since it draws on OCLC's cataloging database. The data produced from doing such analysis are very useful, if somewhat expensive.

Jennifer McClure (2009), cited in one of this chapter's opening quotations, published an interesting article about doing essentially the same type of analysis just using WorldCat™. If her methodology remains workable was unknown at the time of this printing. She cites two studies, Knievel, Wicht, and Connaway (2006) and White (2008), who also developed a methodology to engage in assessment using WorldCat™ alone. In both cases, the methods these individuals employed are no longer possible. OCLC made changes to the WorldCat™ displays so that White's method can no longer be replicated. The approach taken by Knievel, Wicht, and Connaway required technical assistance from the OCLC's Office of Research, not something that would be widely available to most libraries. McClure does provide detailed instructions about her technique—which still worked in mid-2011.

Another relatively new assessment tool that public and some academic libraries are using is the Bowker Book Analysis System™ (BBAS). The service combines material from *Choice* and the *H.W. Wilson Standard Catalogs* to form the assessment database. The system assists in identifying gaps and duplication in the collection. Bowker's Webpage describing the service states:

> Spend more time focusing on selection decisions and create a custom core collection with confidence. Maintain your collection on an ongoing basis so you can provide the most current and appropriate titles to your library patrons.
>
> Using four matching methods (ISBN, LCCN & Title & Author, Title & Author, or LCCN & Title), the comparison between your collection and the core list you choose allows you to instantly recognize by subject area where the strengths and weaknesses lie in your collection. Depending on the core list selected, reports are grouped either Dewey Decimal classification, LC classification or RCL taxonomy. (http://www.bbanalysis.com/bbas/)

An academic colleague provided the following comments about using BBAS:

> One thing I did was review the overall percentages for titles held. Our percentage of Core titles held is about 14.5 percent. It provides a break down by call number range 000s–900s and I can see if everything is around 14.5 percent or if there are stronger and weaker areas. We are strong in Philosophy and Religion (19–20 percent). We are weak in Technology and Arts and Recreation (6.7 and 9.5 percent). Not surprising results for what started as a Catholic liberal arts college, I think. So I have a sense that the collection, while small, has been consistently built up.
>
> Aside from the overview, I am using it to provide lists of current materials (post-2000) that we don't have to faculty. My plan is that it will generate a response on what they believe we need to add to the collection to support the curriculum. The faculty have consistently responded to library surveys that the collection is weak and has gaps. In terms of support the numbers have actually gone down since I got here even though we are buying more books. (I think that might be influenced by a large number of new faculty as we try to grow and who are used to larger research libraries from their Ph.D. programs.) Generally, it will be a point of departure for conversations between the library and faculty on what needs to be added. More specifically, as the university is trying to grow from 2,500 FTE [full-time

equivalents] to 4–6,000 FTE, we are adding new programs, both undergraduate and graduate. We have used this tool to identify appropriate materials for new programs, again focusing on the most recent, often the new programs in areas where we have not have traditionally collected. (John Stemmer, personal communication, 2009)

Using Collection Standards as an Assessment Method

As mentioned in Chapter 2, there are published standards for almost every type of library. The standards cover all aspects of library operations and services, including collections. Some standards have a section about print collections and sections dealing with other formats. The standards vary over time, and they sometimes shift from a quantitative to a qualitative approach and back again. These shifts make long-term comparisons problematic. Quantitative standards have proven useful, in some instances, especially for libraries that do not achieve the standard.

The *Standards for Libraries in Higher Education* (Association of College and University Libraries, 2004) is a document that suggests using ratios, such as "ratio of volumes to combined student (undergraduate and graduate, if applicable) and faculty" as one means of assessing adequacy. The standards, at the time this was written, also list questions regarding outcomes of the type accrediting agencies often ask. One such question is, "Does the library have a continuing and effective program to evaluate its collections, resources and online databases, both quantitatively and qualitatively?" The point of the questions is to emphasize why assessment is a vital part of a sound CM program. Patricia Iannuzzi and Jeanne M. Brown (2010) reported on the results of a 2010 survey of academic directors regarding what they thought should be revised in the 2004 document. Their article concluded with them noting, "our colleagues have clearly indicated a need to align library standards with regional accreditation standards" (p. 487).

School library standards appear in state documents, as ALA and its American Association of School Libraries do not issue standards or guidelines. A school media center standard related to collections is *School Library Programs: Standards and Guidelines for Texas* (Texas State Library and Archives, 2005). As indicated in the document, "The library media program provides a balanced, carefully selected, and systematically organized collection of print and electronic library resources that are sufficient to meet students' needs in all subject areas and that are continuously monitored for currency and relevancy" (p. 16). The standards also provide guidance on determining how that statement translates into realty by outlining four levels: exemplary, recognized, acceptable, and below standard. The levels identify quantitative and qualitative issues such as collection size and formats, age of materials, and evaluative tools.

Similarly, public library standards also appear in state documents, as the ALA and its Public Library Association do not issue standards or guidelines. In the case of Wisconsin, for example, it is the Wisconsin Department

---

Check This Out

The following site provides links to many of the state standards for school libraries: http://www.sldirectory.com/libsf/resf/evaluate.html.

of Public Instruction that produces public library standards. Section 5 of the standards (5th edition, 2010) covers collections and resources. There are levels for conducting a review of how well a library meets the standards. The basic level is to answer a series of questions; more advanced evaluations call for in-depth study and data collecting. Two of the basic questions regarding collections are:

Yes___ No___   20. The library establishes and meets a service target for total collection size per capita (including print volumes and audio and video materials) not lower than the Basic Level for its population group.

Yes___ No___   22. Every item in the library's collection is evaluated for retention, replacement, or withdrawal at least every five years to determine its usefulness and accuracy according to the library's collection development policy. Outdated, unnecessary, or damaged materials are removed from the collection. The library establishes and attains a measurable annual weeding plan based on local conditions and the library mission. (p. 27)

Use-Centered Methods

Circulation Studies

Studying collection use patterns is a very common method for evaluating collections. Two basic assumptions underlie usage studies: (1) the adequacy of the print collection is directly related to its use, and (2) circulation records provide a reasonably representative picture of collection use. Use data, normally viewed in terms of circulation figures, are objective, and the differences in the objectives of the institution that the library serves do not affect the data. They also serve as a useful check on one or more of the other evaluation methods. Usage data are essential in deselection projects (we cover deselection later in this chapter). Today's ILS can easily and quickly generate reams of data regarding item usage. Although the system can output the data quickly, the staff time that goes into assessing the data and deciding what to do about the results is substantial.

Check This Out

In the early 1980s, Paul Metz (Virginia Tech Libraries) conducted what was then considered the first full-scale study analyzing circulation data in order to determine library collection use. Metz recently repeated the study and reported the results in his 2011 article "Revisiting the Landscape of Literatures: Replication and Change in the Use of Subject Collections" (*College & Research Libraries* 72, no. 4: 344–359). Metz found the results of the current examination strongly correlated with those of the original study and noted: "Even the fairly significant shifts in the overall use of subject literatures appear to result, as was argued in *Landscape*, not from micro-level changes in library use within the disciplines, but rather from demographic changes in the population of active users" (p. 359). The original study was published as *The Landscape of Literatures: Use of Subject Collections in a University Library* (Chicago: American Library Association, 1983) and is also worth reviewing.

What to do with all the data generated by an ILS can be a challenge, so thinking about what the purpose of the project is—withdrawal or storage—can help keep the data to a manageable size. There are problems in interpreting circulation data in terms of the value of a collection. Circulation data cannot reflect use generated within the library, such as reference collections and noncirculating journals. Even for circulating items, there is no way of knowing how the material was used; perhaps the book was used to prop open a window or press flowers. Nor can you determine the value derived by the person from a circulated item.

In the public library setting, circulation and in-house use data can be useful in determining the need for multiple copies as well as subject areas of high use in which the library has limited holdings. School libraries have very limited collection space, and having "deadwood" (unused items) occupying valuable shelf or floor space is rarely acceptable.

Customer Perceptions

Users' opinions about collection adequacy, in terms of quantity, quality, or both, are significant factors in their overall view about library quality. On the positive side, users know, or think they know, if the material in the collection has met their needs; on the negative side, past experiences will affect users' assessments for good or bad. A person who has used material from only one collection may be more positive about the collection than it warrants because of lack of experience with any other collection. Likewise, a person who has experience with a large research collection may be overly critical of anything less. Knowing something about the individuals' past library experiences can help evaluators assess the responses more accurately. One must also be careful in interpreting self-selected samples; those volunteering information are often part of a small but vocal segment of the user population and may unduly influence the evaluation.

There are at least two commercial products for helping libraries gauge users' attitudes regarding service quality, including collections. One product is LibQUAL+®, which is a set of tools for soliciting, tracking, understanding, and acting "upon users opinions of service quality" (http://www.libqual.org) of libraries. Although some people (e.g., Edgar, 2006) have raised questions about the adequacy of LibQUAL+® as the sole assessment method, it is a useful tool. Conducting such a study can provide data that are both local and comparative with other libraries. It is, in essence, a gap measurement process of the type Quinn (1997) mentioned. Individuals filling out a survey form are asked to indicate, using a nine-point scale, three responses to each question: the person's minimal expectation for a service, the person's desired expectation, and the perceived level of service. A "gap" is present when there are differences between expectations and perceptions.

Some libraries are now using the product Counting Opinions. The organization's statement of purpose or service is to provide "comprehensive, cost-effective, real-time solutions designed for libraries, in support of customer insight, operational improvements and advocacy efforts" (http://www.countingopinions.com). Their list of customers includes both academic and public libraries. Two of the company's products are LibSat™ ("the means to measure customer satisfaction") and LibPAS™ (library performance assessment).

Focus groups are another commonly employed method for gathering user views on collections and other services. Mentch, Strauss, and Zsulya (2008) reported on a project that combined LibQUAL+® with the results of

---

Check This Out
An excellent resource for learning about using focus groups, which is a more complex process than just talking to people, is the six-volume *Focus Group Kit* by David Morgan and Richard Krueger (Thousand Oaks, CA: Sage, 1998).

---

focus group input. As they noted, "surveys are good at gathering breadth of data; focus groups are good at gathering depth of data" (p. 118). In their conclusion, they observed that, "Pursuing an area of concern in LibQUAL+® surveys by conducting focus group sessions on the library's collections, access to it and its use was an appropriate and informative research activity, which yielded usable results" (p. 127).

One point to keep in mind is that normally focus groups pull from an active, interested population. If only actual users are sampled, the institution may leave out a large number of people in the service population and fail to discover the answer to two basic questions: Why are nonusers nonusers? Is it because of collection inadequacies?

Use of ILL Statistics

One factor that people occasionally overlook in the assessment process is the frequency of use of ILL or document delivery services. Heavy use of such services may or may not signal a collection issue for the users. There are at least three aspects to use of "other library resources": physical access to other facilities, traditional ILL, and document delivery services. People often use several libraries to meet their various information requirements: educational libraries for academic needs, special libraries for work-related information, and public libraries for recreational materials. They may also use such libraries for a single purpose, because no one type to which they have access can or does supply all the desired data. It is this latter group that has implications for collection development officers. Just knowing that some segment of the service population is using two or more libraries is not enough. The issue is why they are doing so. Again, the reasons may be something other than collection adequacy—closer proximity to where they live or work, different or more convenient service hours, more or better parking, and so forth. However, it is also possible that the problem *is* the collection, and learning from the users their reasons for securing information from other libraries will be of assistance in thinking about possible adjustments in collecting activities.

CM staff should periodically review ILL data for journal articles, if for no other reason than copyright compliance. There should be a careful consideration of whether it is better to add a print or electronic subscription or depend on a commercial service that pays a royalty fee for each item delivered. An overall review of ILL data may reveal areas of the collection that are too weak to meet all the demands or that may need greater depth of coverage.

Likewise, document delivery data may also provide useful clues for collection development officers, assuming one employs a broad definition that includes full-text materials in online databases. The library needs to review or assess the use of the databases. Who is using what and for what purpose? The key issue is long-term versus short-term needs and how the archiving of the electronic information is or is not handled by the vendor(s).

Check These Out

There are a number of articles describing "on demand" purchasing as a result of ILL use. Three recent articles worth reviewing are:

Judith M. Nixon and E. Stewart Saunders's 2010 article "A Study of Circulation Statistics of Books on Demand: A Decade of Patron-Driven Collection Development, Part 3" (*Collection Management* 35, nos. 3/4: 151–161), which describes the results of the 10-year review of the purchase-on-demand program in place at the Purdue University Libraries.

David C. Tyler, Yang Xu, Joyce C. Melvin, Marylou Epp, and Anita M. Kreps's (2010) piece "Just How Right Are the Customers? An Analysis of the Relative Performance of Patron-Initiated Interlibrary Loan Monograph Purchases" (*Collection Management* 35, nos. 3/4: 162–179), which describes the review of on-demand activities at the University of Nebraska–Lincoln Libraries.

Gerrit van Dyk's (2011) article "Interlibrary Loan Purchase-on-Demand: A Misleading Literature" (*Library Collections, Acquisitions, and Technical Services* 35, nos. 2/3: 83–89), which discusses the overhead costs of accessioning materials in a "Purchase on Demand" environment, including acquisitions, cataloging, and maintenance costs.

Bibliometric Studies

Bibliometric methods are particularly valuable for assessing serial collections. Two of the most common techniques are citation and content analysis. Of those two, citation analysis is what most CM personnel employ when working with their serial collections. Ben Wagner (2009) noted, "Librarians have long consulted journal impact factors (JIFs) in making journal acquisition and cancellation decisions. Given the misuse of these impact factors by many tenure/promotion committees and national governments as a surrogate evaluation of the quality of an individual's publications, it is also one of the few bibliometric tools well known to many within the scholarly community." The misuse Wagner mentions arises from the not uncommon use in tenure and promotion process for academics as well as to assess the "value" or importance of the research activities of a department or even an entire institution.

A JIF is a number derived by calculating the number of citations to articles in a journal over a two-year timeframe and dividing by the number of articles the journal publishes in one year. The underlying assumption of JIFs is the more influential or important an article is to a field, the more often it will be cited by others, and, by extension, the more important articles a journal publishes, the more important the journal is. CM personnel use the impact factor when looking at what journals they ought to have in their collection; however, the most common time to use it is during the very painful and, in academic libraries, politically sensitive time when journal subscriptions must be reduced. As Wagner suggested, academic administrators and faculty are reasonably aware of the impact factor, thus, its use as a major consideration in the "keep or drop" decisions is generally accepted.

Knowledge of the concept does not ensure there will be no complaints about decisions made employing JIFs from faculty or departments impacted

---

Something to Watch

J. Richard Gott III proposed an alternative to the standard citation ranking system, named the E-Index (*Physics Today*, November 2010, vol. 63, no. 11, p. 12). This system factors in the efforts of all contributors, something that is lacking in the current system of ranking. It will be interesting to see as time passes whether or not the E-Index becomes as popular as earlier citation ranking methods.

---

by the decisions. There are many complaints about the nature and use of JIFs. Two of the common complaints about the impact factor that do have some validity are citation usages do vary from discipline to discipline and journals may and do make editorial decisions, unrelated to research quality, in order to enhance their impact number.

So, where do those JIFs come from? Although there are a few sources (such as Science Gateway http://www.sciencegateway.org/rank/index.html, and Journal-Ranking.Com www.journal-ranking.com), the primary resource is Thomson Reuters's *Journal Citation Reports*® (http://thomsonreuters.com/products_services/science/science_products/a-z/journal_citation_reports/). The *Reports*, as of mid-2011, covers over 9,000 journals—including over 6,500 science titles and 1,900 social science serials. The service provides a variety of options to consider when making selection or cancellation decisions in addition to the impact number. There are subject groups, which help address the issue of differentials in citation patterns between disciplines. There is also a feature titled the "cited half-life," which provides some insight in how long the citation impact lasts. When used with careful thought regarding limitations, JIFs can be another useful tool for assessing a collection.

From the Authors' Experience

When the authors have engaged in a collection assessment project of their own collections or when serving as consultants, we employ the following steps after determining the library's goals and objectives:

1. Develop an individual set of criteria for quality and value.

2. Draw a random sample from the collection and examine the use of the items (database sample).

3. Collect data about titles wanted but not available (document delivery requests).

4. Check records of in-library use if available and compare with circulated use to determine if there is a variation by subject.

5. Find out how much obsolete material is in the collection (for example, science works more than 15 years old and not considered classics).

6. Use the database sample to determine the average age of items in a given subject area.

7. If checklists have some relevance to the library, check them, but also do some research concerning the usefulness of these checklists.

Citation analysis can also be employed when working on projects related to starting a new program that will require collection support. Compiling a sample of appropriate reports or studies recently completed elsewhere and then checking the cited references against holdings records to determine which items already exist in the collection provides useful information. If the collection lacks a substantial percentage of the sample citations, the collection will not adequately support the new program without additional funding for acquisitions in the area of interest.

Deselection—Weeding

Deselection work is important, if often the last of many tasks, in a sound CM program. "Selection in reverse" is one way to think about the process. The older term for the process, and one still often used, is weeding. Without an ongoing deselection program in place, a collection can quickly age and become less and less attractive and more difficult to use. Different library types have different goals for the process. For example, public, school, and special libraries carry out the process primarily for replacement or withdrawal purposes. Academic libraries, on the other hand, engage in the process to perhaps withdraw some items, but most often to identify items that could be stored in less costly space.

All libraries ultimately face collection storage space problems. The need for collection space is almost as old as libraries themselves. One of the earliest references to the problem in the United States is in a letter from Thomas Hollis (Harvard's president at the time) to Harvard College's Board of Governors in 1725. He wrote, "If you want more room for modern books, it is easy to remove the less useful into a more remote place, but do not sell them as they are devoted" (Carpenter, 1986, p. 122). More than 100 years passed before Harvard followed Hollis's advice; today, like most major research libraries, remote storage is part of everyday collection development activities at Harvard.

Selection and deselection are similar activities: first, they are both necessary parts of an effective collection development program; and second, both require the same type of decision making. The same factors that lead to the decision to add an item could lead to a later decision to remove the item. As suggested in Chapter 4, the book selection policy in place should also govern deselection projects.

Some time ago, in *Current Contents*, Eugene Garfield (1975) noted that weeding a library is like examining an investment portfolio. Investment advisers know that people don't like to liquidate bad investments. Just like frustrated tycoons, many librarians can't face the fact that some of their guesses have gone wrong. They continue to throw good money after bad, hoping, like so many optimistic stockbrokers, that their bad decisions will somehow be undone. After paying for a journal for 10 years, they rationalize that maybe someone will finally use it in the 11th or 12th year. We explore some of the psychological issues related to deselection or weeding later in this chapter.

Before implementing a deselection program, the CM staff should decide on the goals of the project. This process should include an analysis of the present staffing situation (as such projects are time consuming), as well as user interest, concerns, and cooperation. Time should also be spent developing a clear picture of project costs and what to do with the materials identified as less useful for the active collection.

Frequently the withdrawal of less useful items becomes a matter of public concern. Withdrawal can take the form of placing the items in a gifts and exchange program or through a book sale. Although putting the items in the dumpster can raise questions about the library's stewardship, in actuality, many school districts have deselection policies that prohibit selling items that have been weeded. In these cases, the only way to dispose of these materials is through recycling or by placing them in the dumpster. Occasionally, the material goes into a recycling program after it has gone through numerous sales or exchange efforts.

Storing, in contrast, retains the item at a second level of access. Second-level access normally is not open to users and is frequently some distance from the library. Most second-level access storage systems house the materials as compactly as possible to maximize storage capacity. Compact shelving for low-use material is coming into widespread use as libraries attempt to gain maximum storage from existing square footage. Generally, a staff member retrieves the desired item from the storage facility for the user. Depending on the storage unit's location and the library's policy, the time lapse between request and receipt ranges from a few minutes to 48 hours. Nevertheless, this arrangement is normally faster than ILL.

Below is a more detailed discussion of how deselection or weeding varies by library type. We look at academic libraries last because of their focus on storage rather than withdrawal.

Deselection Variations

Public Libraries

Public libraries have an overarching goal of supplying materials that meet the current needs and interests of the service community. In the public library, user demand is an important factor influencing selection and deselection. Therefore, materials no longer of interest or use to the public are candidates for withdrawal. A public library rule of thumb is that collections should completely turn over once every 10 years.

Certainly there are differences due to size. Small and branch public libraries generally focus on high-demand materials, with little or no expectation that they will have preservation responsibilities. (An exception would be in the area of local history, where the library may be the only place one might expect to find such material.) Large public libraries have different responsibilities that often include housing and maintaining research collections. Thus they have to consider a wider range of issues, more like those confronting academic libraries, when undertaking a deselection program. Chris Jones (2007) made the point that public libraries must consider every factor in its deselection activities. He noted that, "Yes, size does matter—but freshness cannot be ignored. Weeding is as important to a library collection as it is to a healthy and attractive garden" (p. 172).

Sometimes a deselection project can have unexpected results; an example was the Free Library of Philadelphia. In Chapter 5, we noted that auditors expect to find items purchased still available or a solid paper trail explaining their absence. When the Philadelphia City Controller's office conducted its review of the library, it concluded that the library was in violation of the city charter by "destroying hundreds of thousands of books." Although the report acknowledged that weeding was a generally accepted practice in libraries, it also stated that "this practice had gone awry" (St. Lifer and DiMattia, 1979, p. 12). At issue was the library's failure to try to find takers

---

From the Advisory Board

Virginia Walter provides this perspective on the deselection process in public libraries:

Publication date is definitely a factor in much of the nonfiction where librarians must be sure that they no longer stock books identifying Pluto as a planet or Brontosaurus as a dinosaur. Good children's librarians will remove these as soon as the errors of fact are noted, rather than waiting for a burst of deselection activity.

Public librarians who still engage in hands-on collection development (rather than having it done centrally) tend to rely on their own knowledge of their customers and the books to assess the usefulness of their collections. They have their own set of questions they might use to assess the collection when they are assigned to a new branch:

- Do I have enough California mission books to satisfy the perennial fourth-grade homework assignment need?

- How many copies of *Diary of a Wimpy Kid* are available?

- Do we have copies of the books that I use over and over again for family story time and class visits?

- Does the number of books in other languages seem likely to meet the needs of this community?

Experienced children's librarians can also tell a lot by a quick perusal of the sorting shelves to see what has been checked out or cleared from the tables. For most, it really is more of an art than a science.

---

for the worn books it had withdrawn (admittedly the numbers involved were substantial—360,000 volumes).

Three resources are especially useful in planning public library weeding projects: Stanley J. Slote's (2000) *Weeding Library Collections*, which is a good starting point for planning and implementing a deselection project in any type of library. Joseph P. Segal's (1980) *Weeding Collections in Small and Medium-Sized Libraries: The CREW Method* provides a foundation for the use of the CREW method (which stands for Continuous Review Evaluation and Weeding). The CREW concept was revisited by Jeanette Larson (2008) for the Texas State Library and Archives Commission in *CREW: A Weeding Manual for Modern Libraries*.

Both Slote and Segal emphasize the use of circulation data, with Slote's system relying on circulation data (shelf life) to identify candidates for weeding. Segal's system uses age of the publication, circulation data, and several subjective elements he labels MUSTY (M = misleading, U = ugly [worn out], S = superseded, T = trivial, and Y = your collection no longer needs the item). Larson's title updates the MUSTY criteria to MUSTIE (M = misleading, U = ugly, S = superseded, T = trivial, I = Irrelevant [to the clientele of the library], and E = May be obtained Elsewhere).

The ideas and methods described in these resources are useful in all types of small libraries, especially school media centers.

School Library Media Centers

School library media centers employ highly structured collection development practices. In most schools and school districts, the media center expends its funds with the advice of a committee consisting of teachers, administrators, librarians, and, occasionally, parents. The need to coordinate collection development processes with curriculum needs is imperative. Typically, media centers lack substantial floor space for collections. Thus, when there is a major shift in the curriculum (new areas added and old ones dropped), the library must remove most of the old material. To some degree, the media center's deselection problems are fewer because there usually are other community libraries or a school district central media center that serve as backup resources.

In addition to the Slote, Segal, and Larson titles previously mentioned, there are two older articles that provide sound advice about weeding school media collections. Anita Gordon's (1983) "Weeding: Keeping Up with the Information Explosion," and the Calgary Board of Education, Educational Media Team's (1984) "Weeding the School Library Media Collection." Gordon's article, though short, provides a good illustration of how one may use some standard bibliographies in a deselection program. The Calgary article provides a detailed, step-by-step method for weeding the school collection. Newer resources available on the topic include Donna Baumbach and Linda L. Miller's (2006) *Less Is More: A Practical Guide to Weeding School Library Collections*.

Special Libraries

As stated earlier, the category "special libraries" is so heterogeneous that meaningful general statements are almost impossible to make. Special libraries have to exercise the most stringent deselection programs because of strict limits on collection size, usually the result of fixed amounts of storage space. It is not surprising, given that the cost of corporate office space is so high that libraries must make efficient use of each square foot they have allocated to their operations. Thus, the special library must operate with the businessperson's eye toward economy and efficiency. Also, the collections of such libraries usually consist of technical material, much of it serial in character and often with a rapid and regular rate of obsolescence, at least for the local users.

A major concern of special libraries is meeting the current needs of its clients. In such a situation, deselection is easier because of comparatively straightforward and predictable use patterns, the small size and homogeneous nature of the clientele, and the relatively narrow service goals for the library. Deselection takes place with little hesitation because costs and space are prime considerations. The bibliometric measures we covered earlier in the chapter are valuable in establishing deselection programs in special libraries.

Academic Libraries

Traditionally, the purposes of the academic research library have been to select, acquire, organize, preserve (this has had special emphasis), and make available the full record of human knowledge. CM officers in such institutions seldom view current demand as a valid measure of an item's worth. Potential or long-term research value takes highest priority. That said, why are deselection programs part of research library collections or other academic libraries activities?

The role of the college and university library is evolving. Whenever librarians discuss the changing role, they cite the information explosion as one cause along with the ever-increasing availability of e-resources. Most CM officers understand that it is futile to expect any one institution to locate and acquire all of the relevant material that comes into existence. Nor can they organize it, house it, or make it readily accessible to their users.

One challenge is the inevitable lack of collection space for academic libraries while needing to both retain existing items as well as add new material. Certainly the increasing availability of new e-resources (born digital) as well as ongoing digitization efforts ease the space challenges. However, most academic libraries have substantial "legacy" collections of print material, and printed scholarly titles are continuing to appear and be acquired. Slowly but surely the collection space shrinks and eventually disappears. CM or access services/circulation personnel can make fairly accurate estimates of when the shelving space will be gone. More often than not, expansion of on-campus collection space before the existing space is gone is not too likely, especially under tight economic conditions. Thus, it is imperative to plan on how to handle the situation before it actually happens. The usual plan is through a deselection project.

Barriers to Deselection

One piece of library folklore helps slow or stop many deselection programs. That is, no matter how strange an item may seem, at least one person in the world will find it valuable—and that person will request the item 10 minutes after the library discards it. We have never met anyone who has had it happen, but people insist that it does. There is the proverb: one person's trash is someone else's treasure, and CM staff faces this issue when undertaking a deselection project. It is almost guaranteed that someone, given the chance, will object to the withdrawal or storage of any item in the collection.

Deselection, especially for withdrawal purposes, is not something librarians enjoy. There is the issue of a bad investment or judgment call, as Garfield wrote about. When it is about withdrawing worn-out items or material you know will become out of date at some point and need to be replaced, the process is easy; however, when an item had not been used or not used in many years, it is much more time consuming and difficult to do.

Most of us were taught by parents and teachers to treat books and magazines with respect. In fact, we learned to have great respect for anything printed. The idea of tearing pages or otherwise damaging a book or magazine goes against all we learned. The problem is that we are confusing the information contained in a package with the packaging. Some material becomes dated and must go, or people will act on incorrect information (prime examples are a loose-leaf service with superseding pages or dated medical or legal information). Travel directories and telephone books are other examples of materials that should go. Long-term value of other materials is less clear, and it is easy to find reasons to save them. In essence, our childhood training adds to the difficulties in removing items from a collection. If the library's goal is to purge rather than store the item, the problem is even bigger. Some of the more common reasons for not thinning a collection are:

- Lack of time,

- Procrastination,

- Fear of making a mistake,

- Concern of being called a "book burner,"

- Concern about dealing with opposition to such a project, especially common in academic library settings.

These reasons are, to a greater or lesser extent, psychological.

The issue of time to conduct such work is very real and significant. Today all library staff members are asked to do more and more tasks, especially when economic conditions force hiring freezes or loss of a full-time equivalent when a person resigns. There is no question that properly done deselection projects take a substantial amount of time. Where to find that time is difficult. However, as Brice Austin (2002) noted, "While selecting materials for storage is never easy, our experience confirms what Lee Ash (1963) suggested long ago: that the longer the process goes on, the more difficult it becomes" (p. 58). We would add to that thought, the longer you delay in starting such a project, the more difficult it will be and the more time it will require.

Sometimes librarians never suggest deselection because they assume there will be opposition from faculty, staff, general users, board members, or others. Naturally, there will be opposition. However, if no one raises the issue,

---

From the Authors' Experience

The last library where Evans worked full time faced a serious collection space challenge. Although the university was committed to building a new library, everyone knew that five or more years of fund raising would be required before there would be any hope of starting construction. The library knew that at current annual rates of acquisitions, the collection storage space would be exhausted in less than two years. A further complicating issue was that 240,000 books that were in a cooperative storage facility would be returned to the library in less than 12 months due to the cooperative's regulations. The 240,000 books had been selected for storage over a four-year period in which librarians and faculty made book-by-book decisions. The university had decided to use a document storage firm (Iron Mountain) to store low-use items until such time as there was a new library.

The problem: How to select 600,000 volumes to store in less than 18 months.

The solution: Store the existing 240,000 remotely stored items and store all bound journals.

The solution was far from easy, nor would it be quickly accomplished. Librarians heatedly debated the pros and cons but finally decided to recommend the bound journal move to the faculty library committee. Two factors helped make the final choice. First, the library had electronic versions of almost all the print titles and students much prefer using those resources to having to find the bound volume and make photocopies. Second, and probably most important, the librarians realized there was not enough time for an item-by-item selection process of monographs while still carrying out their other duties. The faculty library committee and faculty senate debated the matter for some time and eventually signed off on the project.

This is a small example of the challenges and time commitment required for a "simple" storage project.

there is no chance of gaining user support. The possibility also exists that the assumed opposition will never materialize, and that users from whom one least expects help turn out to be strong supporters. Putting off deselection to avoid a conflict just increases the problem as well as the likelihood that when deselection does occur, the process will generate opposition. Fear of possible political consequences has kept libraries from proposing a deselection program. However, it is likely that a deselection process, done in a routine manner, will not be noticed or opposed by users. As Ginny Collier (2010) noted, "There will always be books that people ask for that your library won't have. You need to be strong, and do what's best for your collection. Books that languish, unused, on the shelf are of no use to anyone" (p. 51).

Occasionally, libraries encounter legal barriers. Although not common, they can arise and they are time consuming. The problem arises in publicly supported libraries where regulations may govern the disposal of any material purchased with public funds. In some cases, the library must sell the material, even if only to a pulp dealer. Any disposal that gives even a hint of government book burning will cause public relations problems; this stems from general attitudes toward printed materials. The library should do all it legally can to avoid any such appearance.

Deselection Criteria

Deselection is not an overnight process, and it is not a function that one performs in isolation from other collection development activities. Those involved in deselection must consider all library purposes and activities. Some of the most important issues are library goals, the availability of acquisition funds for new titles, the relationship of a particular book to others on that subject, the degree to which the library functions as an archive, and the potential future usefulness of an item. Only when one considers all the factors can one develop a successful deselection program. After the staff recognizes the need for a deselection project, several lists of criteria can help in the deselection process. The following is a fairly comprehensive list:

- Duplicates,
- Unsolicited and unwanted gifts,
- Obsolete books, especially in the areas of science, medicine, and law,
- Superseded editions,
- Books that are infested, dirty, shabby, worn out, juvenile (which wear out quickly), and so forth,
- Books with small print, brittle paper, and missing pages,
- Unused, unneeded volumes of sets,
- Periodicals with no indexes,
- Low/nonused items.

The mere fact that a book is a duplicate or worn out does not necessarily mean that one should discard it. Past use of the item should be the deciding factor. Also, consider whether it will be possible to find a replacement copy.

Three broad categories of deselection criteria exist, at least in the literature: physical condition, qualitative worth, and quantitative worth. Physical condition, for most researchers, is not an effective criterion. In most cases,

---

From the Advisory Board

Carol Sinwell notes one process she has used to successfully address "reluctant deselectors":

One of the challenges all libraries face is staff reluctance to "weed" items that have been part of the historical core collections. One approach I used was to move the "items" from the main floor to a temporary holding location in the back room. That way, if the librarian was right and the item was indeed needed it was easily available; but, if the item was not asked for in a while (and out of sight of the librarian) for a time—it was easier to migrate to the "weeded" pile.

---

poor physical condition results from overuse rather than nonuse. Thus, one replaces or repairs books in poor physical condition. (There is little indication in the literature on deselection that poor condition includes material with brittle paper. As discussed in Chapter 10, brittle paper is a major problem.) Consequently, if the library employs physical condition as a criterion, it will identify only a few items, unless brittle paper is part of the assessment process.

Qualitative worth as a criterion for deselection is highly subjective. Because of variations in individual value judgments, researchers do not believe that this is an effective deselection method. Getting people to take the time to review the material is difficult. Any group assessment will be slow. Researchers have shown that a library can achieve almost the same outcome it would from specialists' reviewing the material as by using an objective measure, such as past circulation or other usage data, if one wishes to predict future use. Also, the deselection process is faster and cheaper when past-use data are available.

The problems that arise in monograph weeding also apply to serials. A major difference, however, is that journals are not homogeneous in content. Another difference is that the amount of space required to house serial publications is greater than that required to house monographs. Thus, cost is often the determining factor in weeding (that is, although there may be some requests for a particular serial, the amount of space that a publication occupies may not be economical or may not warrant retaining the full set in the collection).

Of course, one should not forget users. Considering the benefits and drawbacks, in terms of customer service, that result from an active deselection program is a step in the process. Based on personal research projects, the percentage of librarians who think that a user should be able to decide which materials to use out of all possible materials available (that is, no deselection) is much smaller than the percentage of librarians who strongly believe that a no-weeding policy is detrimental to the patron. Even academic faculty members lack complete familiarity with all the materials in their own subject fields; faced with a million volumes or more in a collection, how can we expect a student to choose the materials most helpful to his or her research without some assistance?

Storage

Large libraries, particularly research libraries, generally deselect for storage rather than withdrawal. These are two different processes. Often criteria useful in making discard decisions do not apply to storage decisions.

It is important to recognize that the primary objective of these two different forms of treatment is not necessarily to reduce the total amount of money spent for library purposes. Instead, the primary objective is to maximize, by employing economical storage facilities, the amount of research material available to the patron. The two main considerations for a storage program are: (1) What selection criteria are most cost-effective? and (2) How will the library store the items?

In *Patterns in the Use of Books in Large Research Libraries*, Fussler and Simon (1969) reported some interesting ideas and statistical findings concerning the use factor in selective weeding of books for storage. Although they recognized that frequency of circulation or use of books is not always an accurate measure of the importance of books in large research libraries, Fussler and Simon hoped to determine whether some statistical method could identify low-use books in research library collections. One of their goals was to sort the collection into high- and low-use materials. High-use items would remain in the local collection, and low-use items would go to a remote storage facility (p. 3). They found that use and circulation data were effective for the first cut, that is, to identify potential materials. The final judgment of what to send to storage or discard remained with the collection development staff and other interested persons. Blindly following use data can create more problems than it solves. The authors concluded that past use of an item was the best predictor of future use (p. 143). Given the nature of a large research library, they thought a 15- to 20-year study period provided the best results, but a 5-year period provided adequate data.

Fussler and Simon's findings indicate that their methods would produce similar percentages of use in libraries, regardless of type, clientele, and collection size. They concluded that scholars at various institutions have similar reading interests. Finally, they identified three practical alternatives for selecting books for storage:

1. Judgment of one or a few expert selectors in a field.

2. An examination of past use of a book and/or its objective characteristics.

3. A combination of these two approaches (p. 145).

Of these alternatives, they concluded that an objective system (that is, a statistical measure) ranks books more accurately in terms of probable value than does the subjective judgment of a single scholar in the field. They did recommend, however, that subject specialists and faculty review the candidate books identified using objective means before moving the books to remote storage.

Richard Trueswell (1965) quantitatively measured the relationship between the last circulation date of a book and user circulation requirements and their effect on weeding. He hoped to determine a quantitative method of maintaining a library's holdings at a reasonable level while providing satisfactory service to the user. (One can also use his method to determine the need for multiple copies, thus increasing the probability a user finds the needed books.)

Trueswell's basic assumption was that the last circulation date of a book is an indication of the book's value. He determined the cumulative distribution of the previous circulation data, which he assumed represented the typical circulation of a given library. Next, he determined the 99th percentile, which he used as the cutoff point for stack thinning. By multiplying the previous monthly circulation figures and the distribution for each month after establishing the 99th percentile, he was able to calculate the expected size of the main collection (p. 22).

In applying this method to a sample from the Deering Library at Northwestern University, Trueswell predicted that a library could satisfy 99 percent of its circulation requirements with just 40 percent of its present holdings (p. 24). That is, the library could move 60 percent of its collections to storage without significantly affecting the majority of users. Trueswell did admit that many of his basic assumptions were questionable and that future research would yield more reliable data. Additional research, including that by Trueswell, supported his initial results.

Many other deselection studies exist, and they all generally agree that deselection based on past-use data provide the most cost-effective results. Although most of the studies were from academic libraries, Stanley Slote (2000) found that the method also worked in public libraries.

Although circulation data are as sound a predictor of future use as you can find, they rest on several assumptions that staff must understand and accept. One assumption is that circulated use is proportional to in-house use. What that proportion is depends on local circumstances. A second assumption is that current use patterns are similar to past and future patterns. (Trueswell revisited the same library over a period of 10 years and found the same results each time. Of course, that does not mean that the patterns would be the same 50 or 100 years from now.) A third assumption is that statistically random samples provide an adequate base for determining use patterns. A known limitation of circulation data is that a few customers can have a major impact on circulation (otherwise known as the 80/20 rule). Failure to take in-house use into account in a deselection program dependent on use data as the main selection criterion will have skewed results.

One factor to keep in mind is that the automated circulation systems now in use in many libraries will make it possible to collect valuable data for a project. With many systems, it is possible to collect data about in-house use by using a handheld reader and then downloading the data to the system. In the past, in-house use data was particularly time consuming to collect. The fourth edition of Slote's (2000) book has an excellent chapter on using computer data in a deselection project.

Points to Keep in Mind

- Assessment is a process that a library employs to look at its collections, services, and other activities to make judgments about quality and effectiveness.

- Accountability is when an outside body looks at library operations to make judgments regarding the library, such as its quality and compliance with regulations, to determine its effectiveness and overall value.

- Ongoing collection assessment is an indication of a healthy CM program.

- Assessment methods may be divided into two broad categories: collection-centered and use-centered.

- Each assessment method has its pros and cons; employing a number of methodologies that will balance out the cons is a sound assessment practice.

- Deselection is a necessary component of any sound CM program.

- There are two broad outcomes of a deselection project—withdrawal from the collection or storage in a low-cost facility, off site in most instances.

- Past usage (circulated and in-house) data are the best predictors of future use.

Works Cited

Ash, Lee. 1963. *Yale's Selective Book Retirement Program*. Hamden, CT: Archon Books.

Association of College and University Libraries. 2004. *Standards for Libraries in Higher Education*. Chicago: American Library Association.

Austin, Brice. 2002. "Establishing Materials Selection Goals for Remote Storage: A Methodology." *Collection Management* 27, nos. 3/4: 57–68.

Baumbach, Donna, and Linda L. Miller. 2006. *Less Is More: A Practical Guide to Weeding School Library Collections*. Chicago: American Library Association.

Calgary Board of Education, Educational Media Team. 1984. "Weeding the School Library Media Collection." *School Library Media Quarterly* 12, no. 5: 419–424.

Carpenter, Kenneth E. 1986. *The First 350 Years of the Harvard University Library*. Cambridge, MA: Harvard University Library.

Collier, Ginny. 2010. "The Reluctant Weeder." *Children and Libraries: The Journal of the Association for Library Service to Children* 8, no. 2: 51–53.

Dearman, Marvene, and Elizabeth Dumas. 2008. "Weeding and Collection Development Go Hand-in-Hand." *Louisiana Libraries* 71, no. 2: 11–14.

Downs, Robert. 1941. "Technique of the Library Resources Survey." *Special Libraries* 32, April: 113–115.

Edgar, William B. 2006. "Questioning LibQUAL+: Expanding Its Assessment of Academic Library Effectiveness." *Portal: Libraries and the Academy* 6, no. 4: 445–465.

Fussler, Herman H., and Julian L. Simon. 1969. *Patterns in the Use of Books in Large Research Libraries*, rev. ed. Chicago: University of Chicago Press.

Garfield, Eugene. 1975. "Weeding." *Current Contents* 15 (June 30): 26.

Gordon, Anita. 1983. "Weeding: Keeping Up with the Information Explosion." *School Library Journal* 30, no. 1: 45–46.

Harer, John B., and Bryan R. Cole. 2005. "The Importance of the Stakeholder in Performance Measurement: Critical Processes and Performance Measures for Assessing and Improving Academic Library Services and Programs." *College & Research Libraries* 66, no. 2: 149–170.

Iannuzzi, Patricia, and Jeanne M. Brown. 2010. "ACRL's Standards for Libraries in Higher Education: Academic Library Directors Weigh In." *College & Research Libraries News* 71, no. 9: 486–487.

Jones, Chris. 2007. "Maintaining a Healthy Library Collection." *APLIS: Australasian Public Libraries and Information Services* 20, no. 4: 170–172.

King, Douglas. 2009. "How Can Libraries Determine the Value in Collecting, Managing, Preserving, and/or Cataloging E-Resources?" *Journal of Electronic Resources Librarianship* 21, no. 2: 131–140.

Knievel, Jennifer E., Heather Wicht, and Lynn Silipigni Connaway. 2006. "Use of Circulation Statistics and Interlibrary Loan Data in Collection Management." *College & Research Libraries* 67, no. 1: 35–49.

Larson, Jeanette. 2008. *CREW: A Weeding Manual for Modern Libraries*. Austin: Texas State Library and Archives Commission. http://www.tsl.state.tx.us/ld/pubs/crew.

McClure, Jennifer Z. 2009. "Collection Assessment Through WorldCat." *Collection Management* 34, no. 2: 79–93.

Mentch, Fran, Barbara Strauss, and Carol Zsulya. 2008. "The Importance of 'Focusness': Focus Groups as a Means of Collection Management Assessment." *Collection Management* 33, nos. 1/2: 115–128.

Public Library Development Team, Wisconsin Department of Public Instruction. 2010. *Wisconsin Public Library Standards*. 5th edition. Madison: Wisconsin Department of Public Instruction. http://www.dpi.state.wi.us/pld/standard. html.

Quinn, Brian. 1997. "Adapting Service Quality Concepts to Academic Libraries." *Journal of Academic Librarianship* 23, no. 5: 359–369.

Raney, M. Llewellyn. 1933. *The University Libraries*. Chicago: University of Chicago Press.

Segal, Joseph P. 1980. *Evaluating and Weeding Collections in Small and Medium-Sized Public Libraries: The CREW Method*. Chicago: American Library Association.

Slote, Stanley J. 2000. *Weeding Library Collections*, 4th ed. Englewood, CO: Libraries Unlimited.

St. Lifer, Evan, and Susan DiMattia. 1979. "City Rebukes Philadelphia Library on Weeding Practices." *Library Journal* 121, no. 9: 12.

Texas State Library and Archives. 2005. *School Library Programs: Standards and Guidelines for Texas*. Texas Administrative Code, Title 13. Cultural Resources, Part I. Texas State Library and Archives Commission, Chapter 4. School Library Programs, Subchapter A. Standards and Guidelines, Section 4.1. http://www.tsl.state.tx.us/ld/schoollibs/slsAdopted2005.pdf.

Trueswell, Richard. 1965. "Quantitative Measure of User Circulation Requirements and Its Effects on Possible Stack Thinning and Multiple Copy Determination." *American Documentation* 16, no. 1: 20–25.

Wagner, A. Ben. 2009. "Percentile-Based Journal Impact Factors: A Neglected Collection Metric." *Issues in Science and Technology Librarianship* 57, Spring. http://www.istl.org/09-spring/refereed1.html.

White, Howard D. 2008. "Better than Brief Tests: Coverage Power Tests of Collection Strength." *College & Research Libraries* 69, no. 2: 155–174.

Suggested Readings

Agee, Jim. 2005. "Collection Evaluation: A Foundation for Collection Development." *Collection Building* 24, no. 3: 92–95.

Allen, Melissa. 2010. "Weed 'Em and Reap: The Art of Weeding to Avoid Criticism." *Library Media Connection* 28, no. 6: 32–33.

Banks, Julie. 2002. "Weeding Book Collections in the Age of the Internet." *Collection Building* 21, no. 3: 113–119.

Baumbach, Donna J., and Linda L. Miller. 2006. *Less Is More: A Practical Guide to Weeding School Library Collections.* Chicago: American Library Association.

Bhatt, Jay, and Dana Dwenick. 2009. "JISC's Academic Database Assessment Tool as a Collection Development and Management Tool for Bibliographic Databases." *Collection Management* 34, no. 3: 234–241.

Bishop, Kay. 2007. *The Collection Program in Schools. Concepts, Practices, and Information Sources,* 4th ed. Westport, CT: Libraries Unlimited.

Blake, Julie C., and Susan P. Schleper. 2004. "From Data to Decisions: Using Surveys and Statistics to Make Collection Management Decisions." *Library Collections, Acquisitions, and Technical Services* 28, no. 4: 460–464.

Crosetto, Alice, Laura Kinner, and Lucy Duhon. 2008. "Assessment in a Tight Time Frame: Using Readily Available Data to Evaluate Your Collection." *Collection Management* 33, nos. 1/2: 29–50.

Dubicki, Eleonora. 2008. "Weeding: Facing the Fears." *Collection Building* 27, no. 4: 132–135.

Greiner, Tony. 2010. "Performing Collection Use Studies with Microsoft Excel 2007." *Collection Management* 35, no. 1: 38–48. [Note: This is an update of the 2007 Greiner and Cooper text listed below, focusing on performing a collection assessment using Excel 2007.]

Greiner, Tony, and Bob Cooper. 2007. *Analyzing Library Collection Use with Excel.* Chicago: American Library Association.

Hibner, Holly, and Mary Kelly. 2010. *Making a Collection Count: A Holistic Approach to Library Collection Management.* Oxford: Chandos Publishing.

Howard, Jennifer. 2010. "Reader Choice, Not Vendor Influence, Reshapes Library Collections." *Chronicle of Higher Education* 57, no. 12: A11–A12.

Japzon, Andrea C., and Hongmian Gong. 2005. "A Neighborhood Analysis of Public Library Use in New York City." *Library Quarterly* 75, no. 4: 446–463.

Lugg, Rick, and Ruth Fischer. 2008. "Future Tense—The Disapproval Plan: Rules-Based Weeding and Storage Decisions." *Against the Grain* 20, no. 6: 74–76.

Martin, Heath, Kimberley Robles-Smith, Julie Garrison, and Doug Way. 2009. "Methods and Strategies for Creating a Culture of Collections Assessment at Comprehensive Universities." *Journal of Electronic Resources Librarianship* 21, nos. 3/4: 213–236.

Mix, Vickie. 2010. "Documents Journey Through Time: Weeding a History." *Collection Building* 29, no. 4: 131–136.

Wiersma, Gabrielle. 2010. "Collection Assessment in Response to Changing Curricula: An Analysis of the Biotechnology Resources at the University of Colorado at Boulder." *Issues in Science and Technology Librarianship* 61. http://www.istl.org/10-spring/refereed1.html.

7

Cooperation, Collaboration, and Consortia Issues

Of all the buzz words used in the school library media profession, "collaboration" evokes the strongest feelings—and not all of those feelings are positive.

—Carl A. Harvey II, 2008

Collaboration, as someone once said, is an unnatural act. It is natural for institutions to be concerned with protecting their own interests but unnatural for them to voluntarily compromise their interests. Even if consortia representatives agree to work together, because of differing needs and capabilities, getting them to all arrive at the same decision is difficult, thus making the purchase of a database very time consuming.

—Gayle Chan and Anthony W. Ferguson, 2002

As collection development decisions become more of a group phenomenon, understanding the group and its dynamics becomes more important.

—Brian Quinn, 2008

Cooperation, collaboration, and consortia share an underlying base—two or more people or organizations working together to achieve common goals or purposes. There are, however, some important differences. Cooperation involves the exchange of something (work, money, etc.) between the partners with each gaining something from the cooperative effort, but not necessarily equal benefits. Collaboration calls for combining resources with others in order to produce a "new value" that equally benefits all the partners. Consortia are formal structures that pool the resources of members to achieve benefits that are, or may be, too costly or at a lower cost than any one member

161

could realize independently. All three have and do play a role in collection management activities.

One of the factors that separates cooperation from the other two concepts in the process is usually informality—no bylaws or other formal structures. The activities undertaken are usually very low risk and ceasing to be a partner is easy and carries no penalties or obligations. Cooperative projects tend to be narrow in focus and involve low resource costs (staff, time, and funding). One such low cost cooperative activity is agreeing to let other library users have access to your collection in return for your users having borrowing rights in their libraries (reciprocal borrowing agreements). Two examples are reciprocal agreements at Northern Virginia Community College and George Mason University, and borrowing privileges for graduate students at Chesapeake Information and Research Library Alliance member institutions (http://www.cirla.org/). Benefits are likely to vary between partners (library A may gain more than libraries B, G, and F); however, the low resource costs make the varying benefits less important to the lower benefit libraries as they see obvious benefits from working together. Successful cooperative efforts can lead to collaboration and even the creation of a consortium.

From the Authors' Experience

Evans was heavily involved in a group that evolved from being a collaborative effort of a few private academic libraries into a statewide consortium. Based on conversations with founding members, the original group met the definition of a cooperative during its first few years of existence. From the earliest days, the purpose was to help libraries get better prices for their acquisition of online databases. Initially, a large research library carried the leadership responsibilities with the other libraries playing little or no role in the operations.

When Evans' library joined the group (Southern California Electronic Libraries), there were eight members. By then there were some problems when it came to handling the funds to pay for purchases—some business offices raised questions about sending funds to another institution for the acquisition of something for their campus. As a result, the group became more formal, creating a set of bylaws, formally sharing the workload (group chairperson, secretary, and treasurer) and establishing a business checking account to handle payments to vendors. It also added the word Consortia to its name.

The new structure worked well for some years until the membership grew and the dollar amounts for purchases reached six and, occasionally, seven figures. Given the success of what was first a local (Los Angeles) and then expanding to a fully regional (southern California) collaborative group, private academic libraries across the state started requesting membership. The group realized it was becoming ever more risky to operate as a voluntary group, and the library directors were in effect committing their home institutions to being totally responsible for the full cost of any contract the group signed with a vendor.

Members recognized the need to incorporate in order to limit individual member financial liabilities. It was equally clear the workload was getting too great to be handled by library directors voluntarily committing hours of time to the group's activities (now called the Statewide California Electronic Libraries Consortium—SCELC; http://scelc.org). A membership dues structure was created to provide funding for hiring staff of a SCELC office. Today, SCELC has 109 members, including a few institutions outside of California, and includes special libraries in addition to its original academic library base.

Collaborative projects are more formal. They usually have bylaws, officers, assigned roles or obligations, and other organizational elements. Group projects are focused on one or two goals, and there is the expectation of equal or very close to equal benefits for all members. An older example of a major collection building project that "added value" for scholars, researchers, and research libraries was the Farmington Plan—we will touch on that program later in this chapter. Most collaborative efforts carry higher risks and greater costs than do most cooperative ventures. Leadership is much more shared than in cooperative programs where there is usually one dominant library leading the way. Collaborative programs almost always require the active participation of senior managers on an ongoing basis.

Consortia are highly structured, often being legally incorporated entities, with elected officers and boards of directors. Most have mission and goal statements that do not fully match any one of the member libraries' statements. There is very often an annual cost for being a member that helps pay the group's operating costs. Partners expect to realize substantial benefits from their membership. Resource requirements are high, especially for those groups that negotiate prices for databases, and there are substantial risks for all partners when one or more members fail to contribute their share of the funding.

Background

Libraries have been engaging in joint ventures for a long time—well over 100 years in the United States. Many of the joint venture projects, successful and not so successful, relate in some manner to library collections. Thus, you would expect libraries would have mastered the process. Overall, they do know what is necessary for achieving a successful joint venture. They have also learned that each new effort will bring with it some new challenges, and that the truly successful programs must change with the changing times. Robert Kieft and Bernard Reilly (2009) provided a good summary of CM joint ventures when they wrote:

> The arduous, variegated, and occasionally distinguished history of collections cooperation on scales large and small is as old as Melvil Dewey, with interest in the last ten years moving from the periphery of specialized materials to the heartland of electronic journals and reference works. This interest now seems poised to move from that heartland to the back yard of librarians' everyday work on the development of circulating collections. (p. 106)

The efforts that the authors referred to range from something as simple as ILL activities to projects to preserve the ever-growing mountain of digital materials. Outside factors generally play a key role in motivating the start of joint venture activities as well as impact the way in which those activities change over time.

Most of the early efforts focused on internal library operations; certainly they led to service improvements, reduced library costs, and improved collection depth and breadth, but they were not very visible to the majority of users. Many of today's projects are often something users see and appreciate. Shirley Kennedy (2008) reflected the visibility aspect when she wrote:

> Up until a couple of months ago I had not set foot in a public library in more than five years. . . . But one day, a colleague passed along some information about the county public library cooperative upgrading its online system, and I had to take a look. It's awesome. . . . What is cool is that we have the Pinellas Automated Library System, which lets you browse or search through the collections of all 15 member libraries, select or reserve materials, and have them sent to a library convenient to you. (pp. 18, 19)

Sharing Collection Items

One of the oldest resource sharing activities was the loaning of books between libraries. Loans to libraries may have occurred in ancient Egypt and Greece, but the evidence is sketchy. There was a famous "loan" of the Athenian state copies of the works of Aeschylus, Sophocles, and Euripides to the library of the Egyptian Pharaoh Ptolemaios III Euergetes (ruled 247–222 BCE). However, Ptolemaios kept the valuable originals and returned only copies to Athens. Cooperative loaning of materials from library to library in Western Europe goes back at least as far as early medieval times, if not the so-called Dark Ages (Jackson, 1974). Monasteries often loaned out books for copying to the scriptoria of other monasteries, sometimes hundreds of miles distant. These libraries sometimes never recovered the loaned materials, due to the exigencies of medieval travel, warfare, fire, barbarian raids, and the occasional thief.

U.S. libraries started an informal ILL program in the early 1900s, and the operating rules were codified in 1917. Borrowing activity remained low until the 1950s when a standardized request form was adopted by the ALA. The development of union catalogs and serials lists in the 1960s containing the holdings of multiple libraries greatly aided the ability to locate wanted materials, and the introduction of the OCLC ILL subsystem in the 1970s allowed the electronic transmission of requests. ILL continues to evolve today through the medium of the Internet, resulting in speedier fulfillment of requests, more user control over the process, as well as greater satisfaction. Without much doubt, ILL is a prime example of cooperation—no bylaws, no officers, no membership fees, just a sharing of collections between libraries

---

Something to Watch

As we have seen in this chapter, collaborative efforts can take many forms. One group that has emerged is the Rethinking Resource Sharing Initiative (RRSI), formed to "advocate for a revolution in the way libraries conduct resource sharing" (http://rethinkingresourcesharing.org/index.html). Such efforts are likely to become more in demand, for as noted by Beth Posner (2007) in her article titled "Library Resource Sharing in the Early Age of Google" (*Library Philosophy and Practice* 9, no. 3: 1–10: http://www.webpages.uidaho.edu/~mbolin/posner.htm), "Because of an increased awareness of online information, people may request more obscure items from more ILL departments, which will encourage more libraries to get involved in resource sharing" (p. 6).

Another collaborative effort to watch is the Rethinking Resource Sharing Policies Committee, a part of the Reference and User Services Association in ALA (http://www.ala.org/ala/mgrps/divs/rusa/sections/stars/section/rrscomm/rrscomm.cfm), whose work is closely aligned to the RRSI.

on a voluntary basis. ILL document delivery activities are beyond the scope of this book; however, there is an obvious link between CM and those activities. And, there is a link between those services and CM resource sharing.

Although ILL remains an important component of library service and a form of resource sharing, a new type of service probably generates the highest volume of items being shared between libraries. ILS products have allowed for the creation of a fast, effective, and easy to use means for libraries to share items in their collections without significantly increasing staffing costs. Local and regional consortia have expanded the use of other libraries' collections by local users through several approaches.

Some consortia are single library types. Perhaps the most widely known is OhioLINK (http://www.ohiolink.edu/), which is comprised of 88 academic libraries and the State Library in Ohio. Three examples of multitype consortia are LINK+ (California), TexShare (Texas), and the Northern Lights Library Network (Minnesota). LINK+ (http://csul.iii.com/screens/linkplusinfo.html) is a group of academic (both public and private) and public libraries with a union catalog database of the members' holdings. The system allows local users to conduct a search of both the local OPAC and the union catalog. If the local library does not hold the item sought, a user who is in good standing may request the item from a member library that does have the item. Delivery time to the local library is, on average, less than three days.

TexShare is "a consortium of Texas libraries joining together to share print and electronic materials, purchase online resources, and combine staff expertise. TexShare services are available to patrons of participating member libraries across Texas, regardless of institution type, size, or location" (http://www.texshare.edu/generalinfo/about). One feature of the program is a TexShare library card that allows a patron to borrow from any member library.

Membership in the Northern Lights Library Network "includes more than 300 libraries: academic libraries (private and public), school libraries, public libraries in 4 regional public library systems and a variety of special libraries" (http://www.nlln.org). It employs a courier service similar to the LINK+ program for getting items to its users. Two special features of Northern Lights is its 24/7 reference service and the Research Project Calculator, a

> project funded jointly by MINITEX and MnLINK to develop Cool Tools for Minnesota secondary school students and their teachers. It is based on the original Assignment Calculator from the University of Minnesota Libraries. It includes a cool calculator for research projects, as well as supplementary resources for teachers. Always available. Always free! (http://www.nlln.org/libtools.html)

There are hundreds of such consortia, far too many for us to cover in all their various forms and services. Consortia have become a mainstay in collection sharing activities. Users especially like the speedy delivery of documents that often took weeks or months to secure through a standard ILL service. We should note that not all such consortia succeed in difficult economic times. One example is Nylink (New York, http://nylink.org), which told its 300-plus members in mid-2010 that it was closing its operations due to financial shortfalls. It ceased operations in May 2011. Such announcements serve to remind people that while everyone loves resource sharing and the other benefits of collaborative consortia programs, there is *no* "free lunch." It takes people, time, effort, and a good amount of money to make these projects work.

Shared Collection Building

An early example of a major national collection building/resource sharing project was the Farmington Plan. A very large percentage of today's research library collections are a direct result of that plan and other post–World War II cooperative acquisition programs. The Farmington Plan and several other joint ventures had grand hopes and scale. Essentially the hope was for U.S. research libraries to never again face the lack of information about other parts of the world that became painfully clear at the onset of World War II.

How did the Farmington Plan address the ambitious goal of having at least one copy of research or intelligence interest material in a U.S. research library? The basic structure used the model that the Library of Congress (LC) and research libraries created to distribute the books gathered from postwar Germany. If there was only one copy available, LC retained it; additional copies were allocated on the basis of having a wide regional distribution and existing collection strengths. Essentially, the plan concept was to distribute collection and subject responsibility among libraries based on their institutional research interests and existing collection strength. The plan operated until 1972, when it became too complex, costly, and operationally difficult for libraries to manage. The Farmington Plan was a collaborative venture with officers, assigned roles, bylaws, and other organizational structures.

Today, we have nothing as grand in scope or hope as the Farmington Plan. That does not, however, mean there are no joint efforts in shared collection building under way. Some that actually preceded Farmington are very much alive and doing rather well. One such effort is the Triangle Research Libraries Network (TRLN; http://www.trln.org/), based in North Carolina. TRLN began in the 1930s when Duke and North Carolina universities decided to combine some of their collection funding to expand collection depth for both institutions. TRLN's purpose "is to marshal the financial, human, and information resources of their research libraries through cooperative efforts in order to create a rich and unparalleled knowledge environment that furthers the universities' teaching, research, and service missions" (http://www.trln.org/about/trlnfact.pdf). The economic times of today are not quite as tough as they were during the Great Depression, but they are tough enough to warrant continued efforts to share building activities.

TRLN provides a solid example of the benefits of collaborative collection building. In 2006, the group undertook an overlap study—such studies indicate the percentages of titles held by multiple libraries. In TRLN's case, there are currently four member libraries. The study indicated that 71 percent of the titles in the database were held by just one library; the number of records in the database was 5,158,309. Only 2 percent were held by all four members (http://www.trln.org/TaskGroups/CollectionAnalysis/TRLN_CollAnalysis_June2Report.pdf). Similar studies in consortia such as OhioLINK and LINK+ have produced similar results. The notion that each

---

Check This Out

For readers interested in gaining a better understanding of the true legacy of the Farmington Plan and later cooperative efforts, see Ralph D. Wagner's detailed monograph *A History of the Farmington Plan* (Lanham, MD: Scarecrow Press, 2002).

library, large and small, has something unique to bring to the table for users when it comes to resource sharing is accurate.

On a smaller scale, there are cases where libraries in consortia with an online union catalog and courier services are entering into very informal cooperative collection building arrangements. Most simply agree to check the union catalog prior to ordering an item. If the item is not in the database, the library moves ahead with the acquisition process. Should it already be in the system, the selector makes a judgment regarding the need for additional copies. Such arrangements do cut down on the number of lower-use items in the system, stretching limited funds for the collection building.

One area where the issue of duplication is a challenge is with e-resources. Many of these items are acquired through consortial purchases. The result is a growing homogeneity in e-resources, which may not be sustainable in

---

From the Authors' Experience

One of the newest collaborative efforts to develop is the HathiTrust (http://www.hathitrust.org), which the University of Maryland (UMD) Libraries joined in the fall of 2010. HathiTrust was originally formed in 2008 by the 13 universities of the Committee on Institutional Cooperation, as well as the University of California system and the Library of Virginia primarily as a repository for digital collections. Since that time, membership in HathiTrust has grown to over 50 individual institutions (universities and public libraries), including the Biblioteca de la Universidad Complutense de Madrid.

HathiTrust provides preservation and access capabilities for both public domain and in-copyright works provided by member institutions as well as from Google, the Internet Archive, and Microsoft. Member institutions can take part in HathiTrust either by depositing their own digital content or by "participating in the long-term curation and management of the depository in return for enhanced services for accessing and using materials in the digital library" (http://www.hathitrust.org/partnership). The size of HathiTrust allows it to forge partnerships that one institution alone would be unable to do.

Patricia Steele, dean of the UMD Libraries, sees HathiTrust as "a model for the future in collections, both physical and digital," and as a "mechanism that allows libraries to take responsibility for preservation in a digital world" (personal interview, January 2011). At the time this volume was being prepared, UMD efforts were concentrated on establishing authentication mechanisms to allow for "discovery" of HathiTrust materials in the catalog (http://catalog.umd.edu), as well as via WorldCatUM (http://umaryland.worldcat.org/) and ResearchPort (http://researchport.umd.edu). Future involvement in HathiTrust will continue to be explored by the UMD Libraries, as HathiTrust continues to grow and evolve. As noted by Dean Steele, membership in HathiTrust "allows us [the libraries] to think differently about what we do and our collections" (personal interview, January 2011).

A number of presentations and articles on the background and activities of HathiTrust may be found on their Website (http://www.hathitrust.org/news_publications). One publication that provides an overview of the development of HathiTrust as well as its operations is Jeremy York's 2010 IFLA conference presentation "Building a Future by Preserving Our Past: The Preservation Infrastructure of HathiTrust Digital Library" (http://www.hathitrust.org/documents/hathitrust-ifla-201008.pdf). Another article that reviews the history and future goals of HathiTrust is Heather Christenson's (2011) "HathiTrust: A Research Library at Web Scale," in *Library Resources and Technical Services* (55, no. 2: 93–102).

the current economic climate. Some state libraries, such as Arizona (http://www.lib.az.us/azlibrary/res.aspx), Minnesota (http://www.elm4you.org/), and Louisiana (http://lalibcon.state.lib.la.us/), have purchased access to selected journal databases that are made freely accessible to state residents, thus reducing the need for numerous libraries to pay for access. Others, such as North Carolina (NCLive, http://www.nclive.org/about), have gone beyond purchasing access to journal databases to include other materials such as e-books, primary source materials, and reference tools. We will explore the issues related to cost, access, and duplication of e-resources in Chapter 9.

Sharing Collection Storage

A long-standing collaborative program that addresses storage of low-use materials and collaborative collection building is the Center for Research Libraries (CRL; http://www.crl.edu). CRL started out as the Midwestern Inter-Library Center (MILC), founded in 1949 as a regional cooperative remote storage facility. (Research libraries have been remotely storing collections for many years and had discussed the concept for even longer.) From the outset, MILC/CRL acquired some low-use materials on behalf of its membership (for example, college catalogs and state government publications). Rather quickly, CRL became a national library asset that continues to acquire and lends a variety of low-use materials. It often picked up Farmington Plan subject responsibilities when a library wished to drop the subject from its collection. Today, membership is open to any library willing to pay the annual membership fee.

Some individual campuses have created large storage facilities for their own collections; Harvard is a prime example. The University of California library system created two such facilities—the Northern and Southern Regional Library Facilities. The Southern facility was established in 1987 and

> provides space for University of California library materials, archives and manuscript collections. Utilizing high-density shelving, the collections are stored in a climate-controlled environment that is designed to preserve the collections. (http://www.srlf.ucla.edu/default.aspx)

To gain an understanding of the scale of such units, according to SRLF's 2009–2010 annual report, it held 6,739,892 items from just the five southern California campuses (http://www.srlf.ucla.edu/AnnualRpt/SRLFannualRpt20092010.pdf).

Where does one place one of the world's largest library cooperative projects—OCLC? Certainly it began as a library cooperative. During the 1960s, U.S. librarians engaged in a variety of efforts to create cooperative or centralized technical service centers (acquiring, cataloging, and process collections items). Some projects focused on a type of library, such as academic or public. Later efforts focused on multitype regional or statewide programs. Today we see the results of those efforts in OCLC as well as state and regional "networks" that go well beyond offering technical service activities.

Today, OCLC does business globally and at times refers to its activities as "enterprise based." However, today it remains a library membership body. There is an elected Board of Trustees representing the 27,000-plus member libraries. OCLC's activities go well beyond the type of services we discussed in the preceding sections, such as engaging in research projects. There is an international body, the International Coalition of Library Consortia

---

Something to Watch

The following thoughts come from Virginia Walter:

When I was in Charlotte, North Carolina, a couple of weeks ago, I heard a lot about their relatively new policy of floating collections. I had heard the term before but didn't really know how it works except in limited situations, such as foreign language collections that were rotated to various branch libraries. At the Charlotte Mecklenberg Library, when a book is returned to any of their agencies, it stays there regardless of where it was checked out from. Their collection manager hails this as a mechanism that has enabled them to survive the latest round of draconian budget cuts. (Not sure why—saving on delivery costs perhaps?) The librarians at the brilliant ImaginOn facility, an innovative destination library in the downtown area for families from the greater Charlotte area, see it differently. Families come to ImaginOn, check out books and return them to their local library. The librarians at ImaginOn thus never know what books are actually in *their* collection at any given time. Books go out, but they don't come back in. Every now and then branches send surplus "duplicate" copies to ImaginOn; these are not necessarily the most popular or useful titles.

(ICOLC), which OCLC does not belong to according to the ICOLC Website membership list, although OCLC Canada and the OCLC Western Service Center are both listed (http://www.library.yale.edu/consortia/icolcmembers .html). In many ways, OCLC today is more like other traditional library vendors than what most people would think of as a library consortia.

Reasons for Engaging in Joint Ventures

You can identify several benefits that can arise from any library joint venture. One such benefit is the potential for improving both user and staff access to information as well as to the materials themselves. Earlier we noted that lack of information about holdings was a problem in the past for ILL "resource sharing." Some networks that include a variety of library types, for example, Northern Lights and LINK+ in California, share their collections through maintaining an online union catalog and using a courier service.

A second benefit of collection sharing is that it vastly increases the breadth and depth of material available to users of member libraries. For example, when Loyola Marymount University (LMU) library joined LINK+, the result was the campus library users went from having access to a collection of just over 500,000 volumes to having online access to a collection of more than 4 million titles and 6 million copies. Although the LMU collection was the smallest added to the database up to the time it joined, more than 37 percent of the LMU items were unique to the system. As we noted earlier, almost every new member to such consortia, regardless of size, will add some unique titles to the database.

An obvious third benefit is that a joint project may assist in stretching limited financial resources. Too often, people view cooperative collection building ventures as a money-saving device. In truth, they do not save money for a library; rather they help broaden the range of materials available.

There are times when collaborative projects can lead to a benefit in terms of greater staff specialization. In such cases, a person can concentrate on one or two activities rather than on five or six. The resulting specialization should produce better overall performance. Naturally, better performance should lead to better service and thus greater user satisfaction.

By actively promoting the existence of collaborative efforts and services, a joint project can enhance the visibility of the library in a positive manner. It may also be useful in demonstrating the library's stewardship of the funding it was given for collection building purposes as well as value for monies spent (more items, and better, faster service, for example).

A final benefit, although one not frequently discussed, is the improvement in the working relationships among cooperating libraries. This is particularly true in a multitype system. People can gain a better perspective about other libraries' problems as a result of working together on mutual problems or goals. Also, learning about the special problems that another type of library encounters helps a person to know what its staff can or cannot do. Some systems have found this to be so valuable a benefit that they have set up exchange internships for staff members, both professional and nonprofessional. Mark and Allan Scheffer and Nancy Braun (2009), in writing about people working in groups and the challenges in doing so effectively, suggested, "The real issue, it seems, lies far more in the attitudes people bring to the process of working together toward a commonly-held goal. The major sticking point, in other words, is not so much what people do in groups, but who they are in groups" (p. 3). The more people get to know and trust one another, the more effective they become at working together.

Murray Shepard (2004) outlined four advantages that three Canadian academic libraries (one large, one medium, and one small sized) identified as arising from their collaboration:

- Remote storage of little used materials,
- Development of web-based, unified and integrated online "catalogue,"
- Joint purchases of online resources, and
- Rationalization of information resources. (p. 1)

His essay provides good information on what it takes to have a successful joint venture.

Collaboration on the Personal Level

Collection management staff always has a need to work closely with users in order to create practical collections. Finding ways to get busy people to take time to work with you on such matters takes some ingenuity.

Eleanor Howe (2008) wrote about a collaborative effort she participated in with a high school English teacher. The teacher was interested in expanding the library collection for doing research papers in the honors English classes he taught. Howe and this teacher developed an exercise for the students in which they were given broad latitude in selecting a research topic. Once the students selected their topics, they were to prepare a written recommendation for the purchase of one item for that library that would be useful in writing a paper on their selected topic. Although the budget would not allow for the purchase of all the recommended items, it did average about 10 such purchases a year. At the time Howe submitted the article, the effort was successful enough that another teacher asked to have her students involved. Howe reported on the outcome of the effort: "The students, of course, were the ones who gained the most: they improved their search, resource evaluation, and writing skills; they developed ownership and pride in their library by contributing to its collection; and they created a more relevant collection available for all students" (p. 9).

Anthony Fonseca and Van Viator (2009), in writing about academic librarians and faculty collaboration as a means of enhancing librarians and the library's visibility, concluded, "These collaborative efforts lead to better recognition of librarians on the academic campus, especially in the realms of information literacy and collection development" (p. 87). While it is theoretically possible to build appropriate academic collections without the active input from faculty, the process is much more effective when there is a collaborative effort. Fonseca and Viator's article provides some sound ideas for how to go about gaining such relationships. Melissa Campbell (2010) expanded on the subject of librarian-teacher collaboration by suggesting the following roles in the process: "Within the framework of faculty-librarian collaboration . . . faculty [are] responsible for providing the source material as well as the internal framework for interpretation. Librarians serve as the 'hyperlink,' i.e., the 'click through' in that they understand what the ideas are connected to as well as how they are connected" (p. 33).

Making Collaborative Projects Work

Several times in this chapter we have stated that successful collaborative-consortia activities require time, effort, and money from each participant. There is no doubt that these are three of the keys to success, but they are not the only ones.

In 1994, Rosabeth Kanter identified eight "I's" as the elements necessary for partnerships to succeed:

- Individual Excellence
- Importance
- Interdependence
- Investment
- Information
- Integration
- Institutionalization
- Integrity (p. 100)

"Individual excellence" means each partner or member has something of value to contribute to the joint effort. This does not mean that all contributions must be equal, just that each does have something to add to the mix. We already noted that for consortia that maintain online catalogs, even the smallest collection added to the database contributes at least a few unique items. Kanter also made the point that the motivation for the effort must be positive rather than negative, thus the "values" of the input must be for that positive purpose.

"Importance" relates to the positive motivation for the partnership. It also implies that the purpose(s) of the program matches some or all of the participants' long-term goals and their organizational missions. When that is the case, you have in place something that will drive the group forward to achieve the program's goals. This is not as easy as it appears; it is especially challenging when it comes to multitype library consortia. For example, all the participants may agree that acquiring online databases at a reasonable cost is a goal, but which products the effort(s) should focus on first can be contentious.

"Interdependence" is almost self-explanatory; there needs to be a reorganization so that all the participants will gain something they would not if they "went it alone." What that something is will likely vary somewhat from library to library and consortia to consortia (lower costs, deeper collections, faster document delivery, etc.).

"Investment" is something we have mentioned several times in this chapter—in terms of time, effort, and money. As Kanter (1994) noted, such investments become tangible evidence of the participants' long-term commitment to the venture (p. 100). Without such a commitment, the probability of the effort failing is very high.

"Information" is, as is true for any work situation, essential for success. The exchange of accurate, timely information and communications is essential for consortial activities. The reason is libraries do not have much latitude when it comes to shifting resources during a fiscal year and consortia have even less flexibility. Often those individuals who most actively look after consortial operations are part-time workers, or, if full time, they are few in number. Keeping members informed about the bad and good news in terms of a library's contribution(s) as soon as possible helps the group make adjustments more effectively.

"Integration" is vitally important to a consortia's long-term success as well as a major factor in its demise (lack of integration). Collection sharing requires some adjustments in local practices, regardless of what form that "sharing" takes. The greater the changes required, the greater the challenges for achieving integration. Many consortia have started with small steps and have waited until all the members have integrated those steps before moving on to larger-scale projects. For example, just instituting a courier service calls for local shifts in who does what when or even who takes on new duties. Change, especially in the workplace, is not something some people accept willingly. Just one member having problems getting the service up and running can cause others to question the value of that member, the service, or both. Such doubts can erode the trust necessary for successful consortial operations.

"Institutionalization" refers to a point we made early in this chapter, the fact that collaboration and consortia ventures call for a formalization of roles. One factor that you see in long-lasting efforts is that assigning of roles is done in a manner that reduces the risk that the departure of one person (not that person's home institution) from the group will cause the group to have serious operational problems. This can be a challenge to accomplish as individuals with strong leadership skills are naturally going to come to the forefront. If the group recognizes the need to truly share leadership, they have a good chance of staying successful in the long term.

"Integrity" and trust are the foundations upon which strong collaborative and consortia ventures are built. Building trust takes time, and often such ventures at least start with senior managers leading the effort. This also generally means there are some strong personalities involved and individuals who may not be used to having to be too accommodating at their home institutions. During the early days, there may be a fair amount of "I'm (my library) is the big fish in this pond" with an implied threat of "I will take my marbles and go home if I don't get my way." It takes more than a meeting or two to work through such issues, time together is the best way to reduce such problems. To have a successful partnership there must be trust and compromises as well as true teamwork (Evans, 2002a, 2002b; German, 2008). Generally the members of the controlling board are the library directors. There is a practical reason for this; there must be the authority to commit a library to new or modifications to a program element. However, there must be thoughtful, meaningful, and ongoing consultation with all the partners in order to have success in any cooperative effort.

Group Decision Making

Collection management personnel have to think about several categories of decision making—their own, colleagues they work with on an individual basis, internal library groups (committees and teams), and external groups (collaborations, consortia, professional associations, etc.). If anything, group decision making is even more complex than decisions made by an individual.

As we noted in Chapter 4, effective decision making is about making a choice from a number of possible options when several good possibilities exist. As the number of options increases, it often appears as if the choice is harder to make. That is somewhat true; however, the more options you consider, the more likely the final selection will be the best, or one of the best. When you are part of a group the process is more complex, and such group decisions are becoming increasingly more common in the workplace. As Alexander Chizhik, Robert Shelly, and Lisa Troyer (2009) wrote, "In the modern world, even endeavors that were considered individualistic a decade ago, like computer programming, are now collaborations among large and small groups" (p. 251).

In the past, making selection decisions was probably 75 to 80 percent an individual's choice to make. Yes, public and school librarians did and do employ selection committees where group decisions are the norm. However, more often than not they are composed of internal staff with, occasionally, user representation. Such groups are something of a "middle ground" between total individual decision making and total outside group decision making. They share many of the external group aspects; however, the composition of the internal selection committee normally comprises people with whom you have worked and interacted with over some time. That characteristic means that trust and shared cooperative efforts are much easier to achieve. The balance of this chapter focuses on the external group decision-making issues.

You should not think of decision making as an "event," for either individual or group decisions. The vast majority of decisions develop over time. Yes, there is the moment of choice, but generally there is an elapse of time between knowing a decision is necessary and the decision point. Even quick "gut" decisions usually draw on some prior knowledge related to the circumstances calling for a decision. Research suggests that people who view decision making as a process rather than an event are more effective (Garvin and Roberto, 2001).

What the group views as the goal for the decision is important—a search for the best outcome or as making a case for a position. In the case of collaborative/consortia ventures, many times there is a need for doing both, which adds another layer of complexity to the process. Although this may exist for an individual's decision, it becomes critical in the group setting. When a group views its goal as advocacy or making the case, there is often a sense of competition to see if one's personal view can prevail. When it comes to multitype consortia, there are several "constituencies" to factor in to the process as well. That type of atmosphere does not lend itself to optimal decisions or at least not ones that are made rapidly. Strong personal views, values, biases, and hidden agendas get in the way of meaningful and open exchanges. These also have a tendency to limit the number of alternatives developed and evaluated.

Another issue is advocacy or vigorous debate about positions or alternatives that can generate some degree of conflict. Eden King, Michelle Hebl, and Daniel Beal (2009) noted, "The characteristics of interactions within teams, including the amount of conflict and cooperation that exists, are of utmost importance in determining team effectiveness, and thus are the focus of a great deal of scholarly research" (p. 265). Conflict is where the concepts of fight, flight, and flow often come into play. Some people will fight very hard for their position(s) on matters, while others, in the face conflict, simply give up (flight) and refuse to discuss the issue further. Neither situation is likely to result in good decision making. What is needed are those who are willing to keep things moving (flow) and actively seek the middle ground. In a group setting, it is likely there will be two, if not all three, of these three behaviors present, and this will impact the group process and the quality of the decision reached.

Conflict, in and of itself, is not a problem. It can be beneficial when it is cognitive rather than emotional in character. The challenge is to achieve the highest possible cognitive and the lowest level of emotional conflict. One way to help achieve this is to carefully frame the decision goals for the group. Another technique is to monitor the group, and when emotions are running high, essentially call a "timeout" for the group.

Groups can easily fall into the trap of "groupthink." Two factors frequently play a role in groupthink. Perhaps the most common is the desire to get or keep things moving along. This often results in too quick of a decision, without much effort to develop much less assess multiple options. The second common factor is the desire to be a "team player"; this too can reduce options and very likely limit thoughtful critical assessment or idea generation.

Generally in consortia, and like groups, decisions become a situation where concessions and consensus are the keys to a resolution. Another "C" for such decision making is consideration—you should not always get what you would like if the group is to succeed. A final "C," often the most significant, is the presence or absence of coalitions. In many ways, the existence of coalitions assists in moving matters forward as they normally reduce the number of variables in play with a large group.

Check This Out

A good article that provides guidance on group or team decision making is H. Frank Cervone's 2005 article "Managing Digital Libraries: The View From 30,000 Feet. Making Decisions, Methods for Digital Library Project Teams," in *OCLC Systems and Services* (21, no. 1: 30–35).

Check This Out

An outstanding article, if complex for those uncomfortable with quantitative methods, is Robert M. Hayes's 2003 piece titled "Cooperative Game: Theoretic Models for Decision-Making in the Context of Library Cooperation," found in *Library Trends* (51, no. 3 [Winter]: 441–461).

A major challenge for such groups, as the authors can attest to from personal experience, is determining what is "best." The number of bests is substantially greater in a consortial environment than for a single library. There are the bests for each institution, the bests for coalitions, and, of course, the bests for the group as a whole.

Building trust is always a factor in group decision making, but it becomes more of a challenge for consortial members as they have less time together. Time is a key factor in creating trust, and it is in limited supply in such situations. A related factor is that, more often than not, institutional representatives at such meetings are senior, if not, the senior manager. Generally such people are not used to having their ideas or views as openly challenged as may take place in such a consortial setting. Time together, trust, concessions, and consensus are the key elements for successful consortial decision making.

Points to Keep in Mind

- Cooperation involves the exchange of something (work, money, etc.) between the partners with each gaining something from the cooperative effort but not necessarily equal benefits.

- Collaboration calls for combining resources with others in order to produce a "new value" that equally benefits all the partners.

- A consortia is a formal structure that pools the resources of members to achieve benefits that are, or may be, too costly than any one member could realize independently.

- All of the above can provide benefits for users and libraries; however, to be effective, they require committed people, lots of time and effort, as well as significant financial resources.

- Joint ventures do not save money, they stretch existing resources. There is no "free lunch" for libraries.

- The benefits of joint ventures vary from library to library as well as by the nature of the project. Most librarians agree that the benefits gained far outweigh the resources required to make the venture a success.

- The elements that help ensure success are individual excellence, importance, interdependence, investment, information, integration, institutionalization, and integrity.

- Group decisions must be based on concessions, consideration, consensus, and trust.

Works Cited

Campbell, Melissa. 2010. "Collaborations Between Librarians and Faculty in a Digital Age." *Education Digest* 75, no. 6: 30–33.

Chan, Gayle, and Anthony Ferguson. 2002. "Digital Library Consortia in the 21st Century: The Hong Kong JULAC Case." *Collection Management* 27, nos. 3/4: 13–27.

Chizhik, Alexander W., Robert K. Shelly, and Lisa Troyer. 2009. "Intragroup Conflict and Cooperation: An Introduction." *Journal of Social Issues* 65, no. 2: 251–259.

Evans, G. Edward. 2002a. "Management Issues of Co-operative Ventures and Consortia in the USA. Part One." *Library Management* 23, nos. 4/5: 213–226.

Evans, G. Edward. 2002b. "Management Issues of Consortia. Part Two." *Library Management* 23, nos. 6/7: 275–286.

Fonseca, Anthony J., and Van P. Viator. 2009. "Escaping the Island of Lost Faculty: Collaboration as a Means of Visibility." *Collaborative Librarianship* 1, no. 3: 81–90.

Garvin, David A., and Michael A. Roberto. 2001. "What You Don't Know About Making Decisions." *Harvard Business Review* 79, no. 8: 108–116.

German, Lisa. 2008. "It's All About Teamwork: Working in a Consortial Environment." *Technicalities* 28, no. 3: 1, 12–15.

Harvey II, Carl A. 2008. "Collaboration Connections." *School Library Media Activities Monthly* 24, no. 9: 20–22.

Howe, Eleanor B. 2008. "Collaborating With Teachers to Empower Students @ Your Library®: Building a Relevant Collection With Student Recommendations." *Learning and Media* 36, no. 3: 8–9.

Jackson, Sidney L. 1974. *Libraries and Librarianship in the West: A Brief History*. New York: McGraw-Hill.

Kanter, Rosabeth Moss. 1994. "Collaborative Advantage: Successful Partnerships Manage the Relationship Not Just the Deal." *Harvard Business Review* 72, no. 4: 96–108.

Kennedy, Shirley Duglin. 2008. "True Confessions." *Information Today* 25, no. 9: 17–19.

Kieft, Robert H., and Bernard F. Reilly. 2009. "Regional and National Cooperation on Legacy Print Collections." *Collaborative Librarianship* 1, no. 3: 106–108.

King, Eden B., Michelle R. Hebl, and Daniel J. Beal. 2009. "Conflict and Cooperation in Diverse Workgroups." *Journal of Social Issues* 65, no. 2: 261–285.

Quinn, Brian. 2008. "The Psychology of Group Decision Making in Collection Development." *Library Collections, Acquisitions, and Technical Services* 32, no. 1: 10–18.

Scheffer, Mark, Allan Scheffer, and Nancy Braun. 2009. "Collaborative Consultation: A Principled Foundation for Collective Excellence." *Supervision* 70, no. 9: 3–5.

Shepard, Murray. 2004. "Library Collaboration: What Makes It Work?" *IATUL Annual Conference Proceedings* 14: 1–11. http://www.iatul.org/doclibrary/public/Conf_Proceedings/2004/Murray20Sheperd.pdf.

Suggested Readings

Borek, Dian, Brian Bell, Gail Richardson, and Walter Lewis. 2006. "Perspectives on Building Consortia Between Libraries and Other Agencies." *Library Trends* 54, no. 3: 448–462.

Buchanan, Leigh, and Andrew O'Connell. 2006. "A Brief History of Decision Making." *Harvard Business Review* 84, no. 1: 32–41.

Buckland, Michael K. 1975. *Book Availability and the Library User*. New York: Pergamon.

Bullington, Jeff. 2009. "About ICOLC and the ICOLC Statement on the Global Economic Crisis and Its Impact on Consortial Licenses." *Collaborative Librarianship* 1, no. 4: 156–161.

Chadwell, Faye A. 2009. "What's Next for Collection Management and Managers? Successful Collaboration." *Collection Management* 34, no. 3: 151–156.

Connell, Ruth R. 2008. "Eight May Be Too Many: Getting a Toe-Hold on Cooperative Collection Building." *Collection Management* 33, nos. 1/2: 17–28.

Conner, Tiffani, Ken Middleton, Andy Carter, and Melanie Feltner-Reichert. 2009. "Volunteer Voices: Tennessee's Collaborative Digitization Program." *Collaborative Librarianship* 1, no. 4: 122–132.

Dovidio, John F., Tamar Saguy, and Nurit Shnabel. 2009. "Cooperation and Conflict Within Groups: Bridging Intragroup and Intergroup Processes." *Journal of Social Issues* 65, no. 2: 429–449.

Edwards, Phillip M. 2004. "Collection Development and Maintenance Across Libraries, Archives, and Museums: A Novel Collaborative Approach." *Library Resources and Technical Services* 48, no. 1: 26–33.

Fisher, Steve P. 2009. "Research Library Collaboration in Colorado—The Birth and Early Evolution of CARL, the Colorado Alliance of Research Libraries." *Collaborative Librarianship* 1, no. 3: 91–98.

Hart, Richard L. 2007. "Collaboration and Article Quality in the Literature of Academic Librarianship." *Journal of Academic Librarianship* 33, no. 2: 190–195.

Lammers, Glenda. 2007. "Cooperative Collection Development: Can It Really Be that Easy?" *IFLA Conference Proceedings* 1–14.

Pan, Denise, and Fong Yem. 2010. "Return on Investment for Collaborative Collection Development: A Cost-Benefit Evaluation of Consortia Purchasing." *Collaborative Librarianship* 2, no. 4: 183–192.

Paul, Souren, Carol Stoak Saunders, and William David Haseman. 2005. "A Question of Timing: The Impact of Information Acquisition on Group Decision Making." *Information Resources Management Journal* 18, no. 4 (October–December): 81–100.

Prottsman, Mary Fran. 2011. "Communication and Collaboration: Collection Development in Challenging Economic Times." *Journal of Electronic Resources in Medical Libraries* 8, no. 2: 107–116.

Rogers, Paul, and Marcia Blenko. 2006. "Who Has the D?" *Harvard Business Review* 84, no.1: 52–61.

Sanville, Tom. 2008. "Do Economic Factors Really Matter in the Assessment and Retention of Electronic Resources Licensed at the Library Consortium Level?" *Collection Management* 33, nos. 1/2: 1–16.

Tong, Min, and Cynthia Kisby. 2009. "A Partnership Approach to Multi-Campus Library Services." *Collaborative Librarianship* 1, no. 4: 133–144.

8
Print, Media, and Related Issues

Print on Demand, Publish on Demand, or POD services, are terms which refer to the printing technologies and associated business model under which smaller numbers of books, as few as a single copy, are printed only after an order has been received. More conventional printing methods such as letterpress and offset, do not provide an economical way to produce small runs of a title.
—William C. Dougherty, 2009

From an author's perspective as well as that of a reader, one could say: Whoever decides to present a body of complex knowledge, regardless on what subject, be it fiction or non-fiction, text or other, will consider a book as the best vehicle. And whoever, as a reader, needs a body of complex knowledge, regardless on what subject, be it fiction or non-fiction, text or other, will be most likely to turn to a book.
—Ruediger Wischenbart, 2008

Magazines for kids pose one of the great conundrums in juvenile collection development in public libraries. Of all the material we provide, magazines are probably the most ephemeral, expensive, flimsy, difficult to shelve, attractive to steal, and inviting to mark up. We could just ignore these magazines, but with an estimated readership of sixty million, we do so at our peril.
—Susan Patron, 2006

Why are board games suddenly hot? For starters, new board games involve a sophisticated thought process that challenges kids to think critically.
—Christopher Harris, 2009

> For more than 150 years, the United States Government Printing Office (GPO), along with its Federal Depository Library Program (FDLP), has supported an informed citizenry and democracy by ensuring access and preservation to a broad swath of federal government information.
> —John A. Shuler, Paul T. Jaeger, and John Carlo Bertot, 2010

Much is made in the popular press, as well as in the professional press (if less strident and certain), about what the future holds for nondigital formats. As we will discuss in the next chapter, the digital age is changing and will continue to change both the composition of library collections as well as how libraries go about their business. In Chapter 1, we included an extended discussion about libraries, reading, and their futures. It is our belief that libraries, with materials in both print and electronic formats, and reading do in fact have long-term futures. Finally, we believe that the so-called legacy or traditional formats will remain a vital part of library collections for a long time.

Books, serials, and nonprint formats have been the major components of library collections for some time. Each of those broad format types encompasses a wide range of materials. Books range from the most popular to the most scholarly titles and appear in hardback, paperback, large print, and today, electronic format. Each subtype has slightly different factors to consider when deciding whether to add it to the collection.

For example, in a public library setting, you might get some debate about adding traditional comic books (serials) to the collection, but few would argue against having some Manga titles (a subset of graphic novels) for young adults. However, even what may seem like a fairly straightforward selection (due to the item's popularity) may still have complicating factors surrounding it. Challenges to the material are one factor to recognize. As reported by Stacy Creel (2008), "Graphic novels are some of the most frequently circulated materials in teen collections, and they are also often most challenged" (p. 197). The impact of adding such materials, in terms of demand for them, is another factor. Mary Simmons and Beth O'Briant (2009) experienced such an unexpected increase in demand and noted, "You begin to feel claustrophobic as the hoards of high school students encircle

---

Check These Out

An age rating system similar to the one used by the motion picture industry was developed by Michele Gorman, the "Getting Graphic" columnist for *Library Media Connection*, and implemented in 2007 by TOKYOPOP—a Manga publisher. The rating system was based on five levels: E for everyone, Y for young adult—over 10 years old, T for teen—13 years old and up, OT for older teen—over 16 years old, and M for mature—over 18. TOKYOPOP announced in early 2011 that it was closing down its U.S. offices. As such, the future of the rating system was uncertain at the time we prepared this edition.

A detailed list of resources on graphic novels, including Manga, compiled by Michele Gorman is available at http://comixlibrarian.com/resources/links/. Also worth visiting is the "Graphic Novels" page (http://www.education.wisc.edu/ccbc/books/graphicnovels.asp) maintained by the Cooperative Children's Book Center (CCBC) at the University of Wisconsin–Madison, which includes review sources, awards, and recommended lists of readings on the genre.

you like buzzards on a road kill. Could this scenario be real—and happen in your media center? It happened to us, and it can happen in your media center, if you begin to add graphic novels and manga" (p. 16). This is just one example of issues surrounding the selection of print materials. Nonprint materials are equally varied in content and issues, as we will discuss later in the chapter.

Producers of Library Collection Resources

Organizations that produce information or recreational materials that libraries collect also face challenges in today's digital world. These organizations, for-profit and not-for-profit, must generate at least enough income to continue to operate. Just as libraries struggle with technology's rapidly changing character, so too do the producers. Which development will last? How soon should a "hot new" development be adopted? Adopting too soon may result in financial losses; while waiting until it is too late may result in the market being saturated by the early adopters. Even with ideal timing, determining the best pricing model is difficult. We explore digital issues in some detail in Chapter 9.

When it comes to products to offer, everyone (producers, librarians, and users) would like to have top-quality, low-cost items, covering almost all subjects and user interests. However, cost and income are the driving forces in what producers decide to issue. Perhaps the concept of publish on demand (POD, discussed later in this chapter) will be able to help control such costs while maintaining the income stream by reducing inventory, storage, and distribution costs. Barbara Fister (2009), in an article that compared the views of a publisher's editor and a librarian about the publishing industry, wrote the following about book quality from the editor's perspective:

> I don't want to publish schlock. I'd much rather publish quality books, and I fight really hard to get attention for my authors, but we have to publish what people want. The fact is, seven out of ten books don't recoup their costs. It's the best sellers and the steady sellers on the backlist that pay the bills. (p. 24)

Even the not-for-profit producers, such as university presses, have to attempt to break even each year. Such presses know that very few of the new titles they produce will sell well enough to recover production costs. Thus, a few titles must do well enough to generate the income that allows for a break-even year. In good economic times, the university may be willing to cover any losses in a year as part of its obligation to scholarship; however, in difficult times it may not be able to underwrite a series of losing years. For-profit presses have even less leeway, their shareholders and owners expect positive annual returns.

Librarians sometimes complain that the producers do not release enough titles on this or that topic. Again the issue goes back to the need to at least break even to stay in business. Again, this is where POD could increase the availability of modest- and low-demand titles.

It would be difficult for most producers to stay operational if all they could depend on were sales to libraries. This is not to say library purchasing is insignificant, it is—amounting to over $2 billion in 2003 (St. Lifer, 2004, p. 11). Even ALA's publication program is not solely dependent on library sales—there is an expectation that there will be at least some sales to individuals and perhaps even some sales as textbooks. Commercial publishers that have "lines" that focus on librarianship spread their focus between several markets, especially on textbooks. Editors must make their decisions, at least in part, on what the sales potential may be for a title, not just the content—so schlock may sell well.

What is a "typical" return for a 250-page trade book selling for $25 (U.S.)? The following are the costs for a hypothetical first press run:

Suggested Retail Price	$25.00
Printing/binding	−2.00
	23.00
Warehouse/distribution	−2.00
	21.00
Discount to retailer	−12.50
	8.50
Overhead (including editorial)	−2.00
	6.50
Marketing	−1.50
	5.00
Author royalty (10–15%)	−1.25*
Profit	3.75

*Most royalties are based on the net sales income, not the list price. Also, neither publishers nor authors receive any income from resales.

Types of Producers

The publication *Book Industry Trends* (Book Industry Study Group) employs a 10-category system for grouping the book publishing industry in the United States:

Trade	Mass market
Book clubs	Mail order (including E-mail)
Religious	Professional/specialty presses
University presses	El-Hi (elementary and high school textbooks)
College textbook	Publisher/distributor

Four of the above are firms that CM personnel interact with, to some degree, on a regular basis—trade, mass market, university presses, and professional. We include the religious category in the professional/specialty category. School media centers may have occasional dealings with an El-Hi press; however, since the main focus of these publishers is on textbook series, it is more likely that the school district will deal with such firms. We will also touch on several other types of presses such as vanity, serial, and government.

Keep in mind that most of today's "publishers" issue more than books. Most of the "majors" have a number of lines—trade, textbook, paperback (mass market), for example. Some publishers, such as Academic Press and

Sage, have rather extensive lists of serial titles. Presses with a trade line often have an audio book division to capitalize on new book titles. A few may issue books and DVDs; certainly national government presses issue information materials in almost all formats.

Trade publishers produce a wide range of titles, both fiction and nonfiction, that have wide sales potential. HarperCollins; Alfred A. Knopf; Doubleday; Macmillan; Little, Brown; Thames & Hudson; and Random House are typical trade publishers. Many trade publishers have divisions that produce specialty titles, such as children's, college textbooks, paperback, and reference titles. Trade publishers have three markets: bookstores, libraries, and wholesalers.

Professional/specialty publishers restrict output to a few areas or subjects. Facts on File is an example of a specialty publisher in the field of reference titles. These publishers' audiences are relatively small and more critical of the material than are trade publishers' audiences. Some of the specialties include reference, paperback, children's, religious, music, cartographic, and subject areas such as librarianship. Some examples are art (e.g., Harry N. Abrams), music (e.g., Schirmer), science (e.g., Academic Press), technical (e.g., American Technical Publishers), law (e.g., West Publishing), and medical (e.g., W.B. Saunders). Many professional/specialty books require expensive graphic preparation or presswork. Such presswork increases production costs, which is one of the reasons art, music, and science, medical, and technology titles are so costly. Discounts tend to be low for titles in this category.

Mass market/paperback publishers produce two types of work: quality trade paperbacks and mass-market paperbacks. A trade publisher may have a quality paperback division or may issue the paperbound version of a book through the same division that issued the hardcover edition. The publisher may also publish original paperbacks, that is, a first edition in paperback.

The majority of mass-market paperbacks are reprints of titles that first appeared in hardcover. Some of the genre fiction series are original in paper such as Harlequin titles and are low cost because of their mass-market appeal. Their distribution differs from that of other books. Their low price is based, in part, on the concept of mass sales. Therefore, they sell anywhere the publisher can get someone to handle them. The paperback books on sale in train and bus stations, airline terminals, corner stores, and kiosks are mass-market paperbacks. These books have a short shelf life compared to hardcovers.

El-Hi publishers occupy one of the highest risk areas of publishing. Most publishers in this area develop a line of textbooks for several grades, for example, a social studies series. Preparation of such texts requires large amounts of expertise, time, energy, and money. Printing costs are high because most school texts feature expensive color plates and other specialized presswork. Such projects require large, up-front investments that must be recouped before realizing a profit. If enough school districts adopt a text, profits can be substantial, but failure to secure adoption can mean tremendous loss.

University/scholarly presses, because they are part of a not-for-profit organization, receive subsidies that help underwrite their costs. Most are part of an academic institution such as the University of California Press, a museum such as the Museum of Northern Arizona, a research institution such as the Battelle Memorial Institute, or a learned society like the American Philosophical Society. The subsidies come through two main sources—institutional and authors.

The role of the scholarly press in the economical and open dissemination of knowledge is critical. Without scholarly presses, important works with limited appeal do not get published. Certainly there are times when a commercial house is willing to publish a book that will not show a profit because the publisher thinks the book is so important, but relying on that type of willingness will, in the long run, mean that too many important works would never appear.

Institutional subsidies take a variety of forms such as free space or utilities for the press's operation, underwriting some or all of the cost of salaries and benefits, and covering marketing expenses. Today there is a growing use of "page charges" as a means of underwriting publication costs. This is very common in the field of scientific and technical journal publishing. The author must pay a set fee for each published page. In some cases, the author built that cost into a research project; in other cases the author's home institution pays the fee. Unlike "vanity publishing," the reason for the charges is to help recoup what can be very costly presswork such as complex charts and graphs or color requirements. Discounts for scholarly press titles are normally modest at best.

Although they are not listed by the Book Industry Study Group, *small presses* are important for academic, public, and school libraries. Small presses are often thought of as literary presses by some people, including librarians. Anyone reading the annual "Small Press Round-Up" in *Library Journal* could reasonably reach the same conclusion. The reality is that small presses are as diverse as the international publishing conglomerates. Size is the only real difference. Many address regional interests and topics that are not of interest to their bigger brothers.

A good guide to the output of small presses is *Small Press Record of Books in Print (SPRBIP)*, published by Dustbooks. The *SPRBIP* is the definitive record of books in print by the small press industry, listing more than 40,000 titles from more than 4,600 small, independent, educational, and self-publishers worldwide and is available on CD-ROM or online (http://www.dustbooks.com/sr.htm). Many of these presses are one-person operations, a sideline from the individual's home. Such presses seldom publish more than 10 titles per year. The listings in *SPRBIP* show the broad range of subject interests of small presses and that there are both book and periodical presses that fall in this category. Some people assume that the content of small press publications is poor. This is an incorrect assumption, for small presses do not produce, proportionally, any more poor quality titles than do the large publishers. Often it is only through the small press that one can find information on less popular topics.

Government presses are the world's largest publishers. The combined annual output of government publications—international (UNESCO); national (U.S. Government Printing Office); and state, provincial, regional, and local jurisdictions—dwarfs commercial output. In the past, many people

---

From the Advisory Board

Sandra Hughes-Hassell notes that small presses are also critical in developing collections for school and public libraries that have large minority populations. One resource she recommends is the listing of small presses that publish books by and about "people of color" (http://www.education.wisc.edu/ccbc/books/pclist.asp), produced by the Cooperative Children's Book Center (CCBC) at University of Wisconsin–Madison.

thought of government publications as being characterized by poor physical quality or as uninteresting items that governments gave away. Today, some government publications rival the best offerings of commercial publishers and cost much less. (The government price does not fully recover production costs, so the price can be lower.) Most government publishing activity goes well beyond the printing of legislative hearings or actions and occasional executive materials.

Before we move on from producers of books, we should identify two other types of presses—vanity and private—and further discuss the "on demand" concept. *Vanity presses* (self-publishing firms) differ from other publishing houses in that they receive almost all of their income from the authors whose works they publish; an example of such a press is Exposition Press. Another example is CreateSpace™ (https://www.createspace.com/), an Amazon.com company that facilitates book, CD, and DVD production. Vanity presses always show a profit and never lack material to produce. They offer editing assistance for a fee, and they arrange to print as many copies as the author can afford. Distribution is the author's chore, although some firms, for a fee, will handle this work as well. Many authors who use vanity presses donate copies of their books to local libraries, but such items frequently arrive with no indication that they are gifts. (Note: Although vanity publishers do not vet the titles they print in the same manner as the above publishers do, not all vanity titles are lacking in merit. Thus, when unsolicited titles do arrive at the library, a selector is well advised to examine the item.)

There is an exponential rise in self-publishing due to POD, e-books, and the ease of self-distribution through the Internet. Keep in mind that when selecting self-published books there is rarely any third-party assessment of the content's quality. Thus, there is reason to be cautious when thinking about self-published nonfiction titles. We suggest checking the "publisher" information in WorldCat™ to see if other libraries have the title in question or if there are other items produced by the publisher. If not, the best approach is to ask for an approval copy and do some fact checking of the content.

Self-publishing is still a major no-no in the education field, especially in higher education. Just as on the Web, anyone can claim anything in a self-published title.

As for *on-demand* initiatives, such activities can conceivably allow publishers to produce single copies of a wider variety of titles at an affordable cost. William Dougherty noted, "although 'self publishing' has been around since publishing began, and 'vanity presses' are nearly as old, the advent of digital printing both simplifies and complicates the situation for everyone" (p. 184). These advances in digital publishing certainly make it much easier, faster, and more economical for titles to be printed in smaller batches—or even one title at a time, as seen with the advent of the Espresso Book Machine® (EBM) from On Demand Books (http://www.ondemandbooks .com/). Some of the features of the EBM include its ability to "print, bind, and trim on demand at point of sale perfect-bound library-quality paperback books with full-color covers . . . in minutes for a production cost of a penny a page" (http://www.ondemandbooks.com/images/EBM_Brochure.pdf, p. 1). Institutions that cannot afford the high purchase price may look at leasing options available from On Demand.

For these advantages, Dougherty does caution that because the technology is still relatively new, items produced in such a manner may not be the same quality as those generated by a "traditional" publisher, and "equally unclear is how much marketing or promoting of titles may be available" (p. 184), particularly for first-time authors (a problem seen with traditional

---

Check These Out

For more information on the University of Michigan's EBM experience, see Terri Geitgey's 2011 article "The University of Michigan Library Espresso Book Machine Experience" (*Library Hi Tech* 29, no. 1: 51–61). In addition, Rick Anderson related the story of the University of Utah's experience with their EBM in his 2010 article "The Espresso Book Machine: The Marriott Library Experience" (*Serials* 23, no. 1: 39–42).

---

vanity presses). In addition, Arlitsch (2011) notes that once produced, EBM titles still require some technical processing on the part of libraries. However, in terms of quickly meeting the needs of a patron, he notes that "the immediate requirement is simply to attach a temporary bar code and scan it into the circulation system, thereby keeping the user service as expedient as the EBM makes possible" (p. 65).

Although the original offerings from On Demand were modest, in 2009, the company announced a partnership with Google Books (*Advanced Technology Libraries*, 2009, p. 1) that effectively expanded its catalog by over 2 million public domain titles, thereby making the service more intriguing. At the time we were preparing this text, the EBM had limited installations in library settings, most notably the University of Michigan (http://www.lib.umich.edu/espresso-book-machine), the University of Utah (http://www.lib.utah.edu/services/espresso-book-machine.php), and Riverside (California) Public Libraries. As on-demand services become more popular, they are likely to make a very real impact on the way CM is approached, and this certainly bears watching.

Private presses are not business operations in the sense that the owners do not always expect to make money. Most private presses are an avocation rather than a vocation for the owners. Examples are Henry Morris, Bird, and Poull Press. In many instances, the owners do not sell their products but give them away. Most private presses are owned by individuals who enjoy fine printing and experimenting with type fonts and design. When an owner gives away the end product (often produced on a hand press), only a few copies are printed. In the past, many developments in type and book design originated with private presses. Some of the most beautiful examples of typographic and book design originated at private presses. Large research libraries often attempt to secure copies of items produced by private presses.

Check This Out

For an in-depth look at the challenges facing publishers, visit ReadWriteWeb.com and review its four-part series "Bits of Destruction Hit the Book Publishing Business" (http://www.readwriteweb.com/fastsearch?search=bits+of+destruction&x=18&y=16).

Serial Producers

Serial publishers are different in that they often have staff writers to produce their material. Many serial producers also count on advertising for a portion of their operating income. Certainly more and more are expecting to realize much of their revenue from the digital versions of their print publications. For many types of serial producers, the institutional market is their financial foundation. Library users' interest in serials is an important element in the serial producers' long-term success.

For some library users, serials are the most frequently consulted library resource. In the not-too-distant past, it was print-based serials, and today it is a combination of print and digital that many people expect and want. People still subscribe to some paper-based newspapers and magazines, but turn to libraries for many titles they had subscribed to in the past. Professional associations still issue information in paper, but they also release it in an e-format. How long this dual process will last is an open question. However, it seems likely it will exist to some extent for the lifetime of this edition.

Currency is very important for those who use serials on a regular basis. Serial update intervals can be very short, daily in the case of many newspapers. Articles in a serial are short (compared to book-length treatments of the same topic) and focus on a fairly narrow subject. Readers with very specific information needs frequently find that serials provide the desired data more quickly than books. Finally, serials are often the first printed source of information about a new subject or development. People use serials as a source for learning about new things. Also, the sheer volume of new information appearing in serials far exceeds that of books.

What Is a Serial?

Users and librarians employ words such as *journal*, *magazine*, and *periodical* interchangeably. Such usage masks some significant differences in the category of serial and fails to denote the many variations that exist. Thomas Nisonger (1998), in his book on serials management, devoted more than six pages to how different groups have attempted to define serials. The electronic world is changing the nature of serials and the way libraries process them. The Internet has even changed what a library should consider a serial. T. Scott Plutchak (2007) suggested that "The serial as defined by librarians is an anachronism in the digital age, and will not survive for long. . . . This matter of definitions bedevils us all, and I'm sure you've had the same kinds of discussions in your institutions that we've had in mine as we try to figure out how to shoehorn these new information resources that we're dealing with into the same old categories" (p. 81). For our purposes, the following definition will suffice: a serial is a publication issued as one of a consecutively numbered and indefinitely continued series.

Plutchak's point is well taken, that is, the library focus has been, and still is to a large extent, on the physical format rather than content. However, at present the old definitions still exist and are widely used in libraries. We draw upon the early work of Fritz Machlup, Kenneth Leeson, and their associates (1978) for our discussion of serial types. They developed an 18-part classification system for serials. Their system covered all types of serials, including serials "not elsewhere classified." We have yet to encounter a serial that does not fit into one of these categories.

The first category is *institutional reports*, which are annual, semiannual, quarterly, or occasional publications of corporations, financial institutions, and organizations serving business and finance as well as most organizations. Academic and public libraries serving business programs and interests frequently need to acquire this type of serial. Corporate libraries actively collect this category. Most of the reports available to libraries and information centers are free for the asking. Collecting in this area is labor intensive, because it requires maintaining address and correspondence files, especially if a library collects much beyond the large national corporations.

Thanks to online resources, such as EDGAR Online (from the Securities and Exchange Commission, http://www.sec.gov/edgar.shtml), filings are now available from a number of sources.

Yearbooks and proceedings are annuals, biennials, and occasional publications, bound or stapled, including yearbooks, almanacs, proceedings, transactions, memoirs, directories, and reports of societies and associations. Many libraries collect these serials, especially academic, special, and large public libraries. The more libraries that collect a particular society's or association's publications, the more likely it is that a commercial vendor will handle a standing order for the material. Unfortunately, a significant number must be obtained directly from the society or association. Again, this category normally requires setting up and maintaining address and correspondence files, which is only slightly less labor intensive than doing the same for annual reports of organizations.

Superseding serials fall into one of two categories, both of which are labor intensive in their paper-based format. One group consists of the superseding serial services (each new issue superseding previous ones). These include publications such as telephone directories and product catalogs. The second group consists of the nonsuperseding serial services, many of which were print-based looseleaf publications that provided information such as changes in accounting rules or government regulations. In the past, both groups often required careful filing of new material and the removal of other (older or superseded) material. Most of the services are now available online, reducing most of the staffing and training issues. Most of these publications are only available from the publisher. Examples of such services are the *Labor Relations Reporter* from the Bureau of National Affairs and the *Standard Federal Tax Reporter* from the Commerce Clearing House.

Nonsuperseding serials are less of a problem and some are available from serial jobbers. However, the materials in this class tend to be expensive, and many must be ordered directly from the publisher. Indexing and abstracting services fall into one of these two classes. All types of libraries need a few of these reference serials. As the serial collection grows, there is an increasing demand from users for more indexing and abstracting services. Certainly online journal databases have reduced the need for such services.

Newspapers are one of the obvious serials that libraries acquire in both print and electronic formats. Serial jobbers handle subscriptions to major domestic and international newspapers for libraries. Selectors must decide how soon users want or need access to nonlocal newspapers. The greater the need for speedy access, the greater the cost for the library. For example, the *London Times* is available at several different speeds, each with a different cost: daily airmail edition by air freight, daily airmail edition by airmail (the most expensive option), daily regular edition by air freight, daily regular edition in weekly packets (the least expensive option), or microfilm edition. The *New York Times* offers an even wider variety of editions: city edition, late city edition, national edition, New York edition, large-type weekly, same day, next day, two day, weekly packets, microfilm, and others.

Almost all major newspapers are somewhat available online; we say somewhat because at the time this was written, newspapers were struggling with the issue of staying in business. They are trying to develop a workable model for generating income to replace revenue lost due to rapidly declining paper subscriptions and advertising. As a result they often allow free access to a limited version of a story and provide access to the full story when a reader pays a fee—per-story fee, monthly fee, and annual fee are some of the models in use in 2011. Libraries can also provide online access to newspapers through several database vendors such as NewsBank (http://www.newsbank.com/) or ProQuest (http://www.proquest.com); some of the serials databases include some newspaper coverage as well, for example EBSCO*host*® (http://www.ebscohost.com/).

Newsletters, leaflets, news releases, and similar materials are a form of serial that some libraries actively acquire. Corporate libraries are the most active in gathering material in this category, especially those supporting marketing, lobbying, and public relations activities. Many of the items in this class are free; all a library needs to do is ask to be placed on the distribution list. Other items, especially newsletters containing economic or trade data, can be exceedingly expensive. A number of U.S. services cost in excess of $20,000 for quarterly newsletters of only a few pages. It is at that point that one can begin to fully appreciate the difference between the cost of the information and the cost of the package in which it comes.

Magazines are the most common serials and the category that most often comes to mind when thinking about serials. Magazines are mass-market or popular serials; Machlup and his colleagues divided them into five subgroups. These are the titles that almost any serial jobber will handle for a library. Following are the five subgroups:

- Mass-market serials and weekly or monthly news magazines (such as *Newsweek* and *The Economist*)

- Popular magazines dealing with fiction, pictures, sports, travel, fashion, sex, humor, and comics (such as *Sports Illustrated* and *Harpers Bazaar*)

- Magazines that popularize science and social, political, and cultural affairs (*Smithsonian* and *National Geographic*)

- Magazines focusing on opinion and criticism—social, political, literary, artistic, aesthetic, or religious (examples are *Foreign Affairs* and *New Yorker*)

- Other magazines not elsewhere classified. An example of such a title is an organization publication (governmental or private) that is really a public relations vehicle, sometimes called a "house organ." These publications often contain general-interest material, but there is usually some clearly stated or implied relationship between the subject covered and the issuing organization (e.g., *Plain Truth*). Another type of publication in the "other" category is the magazine found in the pocket of airline seats.

Libraries may receive a substantial number of house organs because their publishers give them away. Vendors seldom handle this type of magazine.

Journals are titles that are of interest to a narrower segment of the population, sometimes referred to as "informed laypeople," researchers, and scholars. This category has four subcategories:

- Nonspecialized journals for the intelligentsia who are well informed on literature, art, social affairs, politics, and so on (*Science* and *American Indian Art Magazine* are examples)

- Learned journals for specialists—primary research journals and secondary research journals (*American Indian Culture and Research Journal* and *Applied Physics Research*, for example)

- Practical professional journals in applied fields, including technology, medicine, law, agriculture, management, library and information science, business, and trades (*RQ* or *School Library Journal*, for example)

- Parochial journals of any type but addressed chiefly to a parochial audience—local or regional (*Kiva* or *Arizona Highways*).

Most titles in these categories are available from library vendors, although the library must place direct orders for some of the more specialized learned journals. Most parochial journals must be purchased directly from the publisher; local history and regional archaeological publications are examples of this class of serial. Sometimes a library must join an association to obtain its publications.

The final serial category consists of government publications, reports, bulletins, statistical series, releases, etc. by public agencies, executive, legislative and judiciary, local, state, national, foreign and international. With these variations in serials in mind, it is clear why there is confusion about terms and why there are challenges in collecting and preserving them. Each type fills a niche in the information dissemination system. Although they do create special handling procedures and problems, they are a necessary part of any library's collection. Patrick Carr (2009) opened his article with the following:

> The literature of serials librarianship published in 2006 and 2007 reveals a field in rapid transition. The changes occurring range from the shifting nature of serial collections to evolving models, initiatives, and management strategies used to acquire and administer access to these collections. (p. 3)

Serials Selection Issues and Models

One can make a few broad generalizations about serials selection. The fields of science, technology, and medicine (commonly abbreviated as STM in the literature) are very dependent on serial publications. They are on average the most costly and have a habit of splitting into ever narrower topics. (The notion of scholars adding new knowledge results in what some skeptics say is fewer and fewer people knowing more and more about less and less. The end result is generally more and more titles about ever narrower subjects.) At the opposite end of the spectrum are the humanities, which depend more on books than on serials. Between these two are the social sciences, some of which are more similar to the science disciplines (e.g., psychology, linguistics, physical anthropology), and others of which are more similar to the humanities (e.g., political science, education, and social anthropology).

Serials change over time as new editors, governing boards, or owners make major and minor shifts in the content and orientation. From a selector's point of view, a change in a print title is a signal to rethink the title's appropriateness for the collection. For some journals, there is a long history of title changes, which can be confusing for end users who may not know of the changes over time and may think the library has fewer holdings than it actually does. Steve Black (2009) succinctly summed up the library view regarding the changing character and titles of serials by noting, "Since changes in title create work for librarians and confusion for patrons, librarians want title changes to occur only for compelling reasons" (p. 200).

Although his comment focused on titles, other changes also create the issues he mentioned—such as frequency of publication, scope of coverage, and, in the case of scholarly journals, even splitting into two titles with slightly different coverage.

A decision to subscribe to a serial is a much bigger decision than monographic purchase decisions. Several factors account for the difference. Because serials are ongoing, they can become a standing commitment for the library and thus become a more-or-less fixed element in the materials budget. Because serials arrive in parts or issues, there must be an ongoing process for receiving the material and maintaining records about what did or did not arrive. Unfortunately, few serials arrive in a form that allows for easy long-term storage or heavy use; therefore, libraries must develop a means to preserve them such as binding—an additional cost factor—or securing an additional copy in a microformat. In addition, print serials occupy large amounts of storage space, which over time becomes scarce.

Gaining access to the contents of print serials usually requires subscribing to one or more indexing and abstracting services, which are in themselves serials. A serials collection that does not provide for quick, easy, and inexpensive scanning or photocopy services will quickly become a collection of covers and advertisements as the articles disappear. When adding a title that has been published for some time, one must also consider the question of back files—prior volumes.

There are five serial selection models: cost, citation analysis, worth or use, polling, and core lists. There are many variations, but the five listed form the basis for models for selecting serials. Much of the work done in this area is relatively recent and more the result of having to cancel rather than to start subscriptions.

Cost models of selection are the oldest and have the greatest number of variations. One of the most complex models deals with the real annual cost of a serial. The annual cost consists of six elements: acquisition cost, processing cost, maintenance cost, storage cost, utility or use cost, and subscription price. *Acquisition costs* include such things as selection, order placement, and time spent in working with the subscription agent or publisher. *Processing costs* cover check-in, claiming, routing, cataloging or other labeling, adding security strips, and shelving in public service for the first time. *Maintenance costs* involve binding, microfilming or acquiring microform, selecting for remote storage, and possibly discarding. *Storage costs* entail calculating the linear feet of storage space (either or both shelf and cabinet space) used by the title and the cost of the space. *Utility* or *use costs* are the most complex to calculate. They incorporate costs of time for such things as retrieval from a storage location (library staff only), pick-up and reshelving, answering questions about the title ("Do you have . . . ?", "I can't find . . .", and "What is the latest issue you have?"), and all other required assistance (assistance with microform readers, for example). The last, and often the lowest, cost is the *subscription price*. The sum of these costs represents the real annual cost of the title for the library. Looking over the list of costs makes it clear that it will take some time to calculate the individual cost centers. However, once one determines the unit costs (for example, the average time to shelve an issue), it is fairly easy to calculate the cost for a given number of issues of a title. With an annual cost for each title, selectors can determine which titles to continue or discontinue.

Like cost models, citation analysis paradigms take several forms. The main objective, from a selection point of view, is to identify frequently cited titles. Citation analysis can help identify a core collection for a field and

---

Check This Out

To learn more about Bradford's Law of Scattering and its applications, see Jeppe Nicolaisen and Birger Hjørland's 2007 article "Practical Potentials of Bradford's Law: A Critical Examination of the Received View" in *Journal of Documentation* (63, no. 3: 359–377).

---

provide a listing of titles ranked by the frequency with which they are cited. Another collection development use of citation analysis is in evaluating a collection. (Could a set of papers or reports have been done using this collection?) Citation analysis information is most useful in large or specialized research collections, although core collection information is valuable to smaller and nonspecialized collections as well. (See Chapter 6 for a fuller discussion of citation analysis.)

Using the Bradford Distribution, one can rank titles to develop information for collection policy use as well to make decisions regarding current subscriptions. The goal of this ranking is to identify all journals containing articles relevant to a given subject and to rank them in order based on the number of relevant articles they publish in a year. The pattern, according to Bradford's Law of Scattering, will show that a few journals publish the majority of articles and a large number of journals publish only one or two cited articles. If one equates a basic collection with holding journals that contain 20 percent of the relevant material, one might subscribe to only three or four titles. For libraries with a comprehensive collecting goal, the subscription list may contain several hundred titles. For example, Tozzer Library (Harvard) has a current subscription list of more than 1,200 titles just for coverage of anthropology and archaeology.

Journal-worth models usually involve some information about title usage along with other data. The model involves cost, use, impact factor, and information about the nature of the publication (core subject, for example) to calculate a cost-benefit ratio.

As one might assume, most of the models require a substantial amount of data collection. If their only utility lay in making selection decisions, few libraries would use them. Their major value comes into play when the library must cut subscriptions. Having collected data that are similar for all the titles makes the unpleasant task a little easier. What librarians hoped would be a rare occurrence has, for some libraries, become an almost annual task. Each time the task becomes more difficult, and the models demonstrate their value.

Polling experts and using lists of recommended journals are other methods for identifying what to buy or keep. Both suffer from being less directly linked to the local situation, unless the experts are local users. One can find lists of journals in relatively narrow subjects, often listed with recommendations, or at least comments, in journals like *Serials Librarian* (Routledge) and *Serials Review* (Elsevier).

Identifying Serials

Serials employ a different bibliographic network than that used for monographs. Few of the selection aids for books cover serials, and reviews of serials are few and far between. However, there are several general and specialized guides to serial publications. In the past, when publishers would supply several free sample copies of a title for the library to examine, the lack of reviews was not a problem. Today, many publishers charge for sample issues, and though it depletes the funds for subscribing to serials and adds to the time it takes to acquire them, it is useful to get sample issues before committing the library to a new serial. Three useful general guides are *ULRICHSWeb™ Global Serials Directory* (https://ulrichsweb.serialsso lutions.com/), *Serials Directory™* (EBSCO, http://www.ebscohost.com/public/ the-serials-directory), and *Standard Periodical Directory* (Oxbridge Communications, http://www.oxbridge.com/SPDCluster/theSPD.asp).

Newspapers, newsletters, and serials published at least five times a year are identifiable in guides like *Gale Directory of Publications and Broadcast Media* (Gale Research, http://www.gale.cengage.com/pdf/facts/ GDofPub&Broad.pdf). For literary publications, one should use *International Directory of Little Magazines and Small Presses* (Dustbooks, http:// www.dustbooks.com/d.htm) and *MLA International Bibliography* (Modern Language Association, http://www.mla.org/bibliography).

Serials Review (http://www.elsevier.com/wps/find/journaldescription.cws_ home/620213/description#description) publishes some reviews prepared by serials librarians and, occasionally, subject experts. The journal started as both a reviewing journal and a professional journal for serials librarians. Today it is primarily a professional journal, with only a few pages of serials reviews in each volume. Occasionally, *Serials Review* reviews an established serial. Such reviews help librarians monitor changes in the editorial policy of titles to which the library subscribes.

You can also use "core" or recommended lists for a variety of subject fields such as Julie Bartel's (ALA, 2004) *From A to Zine: Building a Winning Zine Collection in Your Library*. Some caution is in order when using core lists; one must understand the methodology employed to generate the list and know that it fits the needs of your library.

Media Formats

Much like the debate over quality versus demand as the driving force of CM, so too has the profession had differences of opinion regarding the role, if any, of media in a library's collection. Some librarians held the belief that media formats distracted libraries from their primary mission—the promotion of lifelong reading—especially the reading of quality literary titles. Further, they believed such collections drain essential resources from print material. Essentially, such people viewed libraries as being in the "book" rather than the "information" business. Will Manley (1991) went so far as to suggest that "Videos are the 'Twinkies' of library collections" (p. 89).

Others, such as Sally Mason (1994), for example, held the view that media formats are as central to collections as print materials. She noted that "Clearly, the visual media will only become more important to library service in the future. . . . It is not enough for librarians to 'capitulate' on the issue of visual media. We must become leaders and advocates . . . helping the public to learn what is available, to sort through multiple possibilities, and offering guidance in the use of media to obtain needed information" (p. 12). Likewise, Myra Brown (2006) suggested, "It is counterproductive to stigmatize one format while deifying print. We dilute our energy by imposing such artificial distinctions" (p. 84).

Regardless of differences in philosophy, various nonprint formats have been present in libraries for the better part of 100 years. (Music recordings were one of the first nonprint items added to library collections.) Media resources have been an interesting, varied, and challenging component of collections. In today's digital environment, they remain interesting and challenging, if perhaps not as varied as in the past.

There is a general recognition that other media play an important role in having an informed society. Anyone reading *Publishers Weekly* (*PW*) or shopping on Amazon.com knows that publishers and booksellers no longer limit themselves to just books and magazines. They see themselves as being in the information business. Regular columns in *PW* on audio and video releases indicate that producers and vendors view this field as an important market. The use of computerized typesetting and scanning equipment opened the way for products such as Kindle and Nook e-readers.

It appears that we are entering into what some call the "postliterate age." Jones-Kavalier and Flannigan (2008) noted, "Prior to the 21st century, *literate* defined a person's ability to read and write, separating the educated from the uneducated. With the advent of the new millennium and the rapidity with which technology has changed society, the concept of literacy has assumed new meanings" (p. 13). Doug Johnson (2009) went on to suggest that a postliterate society is one in which a person can read and write but who also chooses to gather information and learn through additional mechanisms, including "audio, video, graphics, and gaming" (p. 20).

Media Issues

Media formats present several challenges for the library and its acquisitions budget. Unlike print materials, in most cases media formats require some type of equipment in order to access their content. Thus, there is the cost of both buying the equipment and maintaining it on an ongoing basis. Failure to maintain the equipment will damage the medium used with it, which is much more fragile than paper-based content. There is also, at times, an issue of equipment compatibility when ordering new titles (such as DVD or Blu-ray).

Because media items are generally used with equipment, they wear out or are damaged more quickly than print materials, especially when the public may check them out for home use. For example, libraries circulating video formats expect to get fewer than 25 circulations before the title is too worn to remain in circulation. Also, unlike print, some media, such as video, often have restrictions on how they may be used. A concept called "performance rights" affects library usage. Performance rights are addressed later in this chapter and in Chapter 11.

One ongoing media issue for libraries is the speed of technological change. Those working with end users have to keep pondering the question, "How many times must we purchase a copy of Beethoven's Fifth Symphony or the movie *Gone With the Wind*?" Since the 1960s, the music recording collections have moved from vinyl disks (in several different sizes and speeds) to cassettes (in several variations) to CDs, and now to downloadable files. A similar series of changes took place in terms of motion pictures—from film (16 mm and 8 mm) to cassette (VHS and Beta) to DVD and now Blu-ray. Changes in technology leave libraries with legacy collections of items many users view as dinosaurs. Moving too quickly into a format (for example Beta) that does not last is a waste of funds, yet waiting too long can also be costly, if for no other reason than losing users' goodwill and support.

Long-term preservation of media can become an issue for some libraries—the material wears out quickly and the equipment changes very fast as well—but there are also short-term issues related to wear, damage, and security to consider as well.

Given media's changing formats, your work life in this area will be interesting, to say the least. As Alan Kaye (2005) wrote, "Now picture and sound seem to having their way with computers and the Internet. Multimedia information has become almost native to computers, collapsing the market for analog formats and creating a digital world" (p. 62). He went on to discuss how libraries like his have already eliminated or are in the process of eliminating filmstrips, slide sets, 16 mm and 8 mm films, Super 8 mm films, and all phonograph records and music audiocassettes. Not all libraries have gone that far, and many still have some legacy collections. If you are interested in more information about such formats, consult the previous edition of this book.

Video Formats

As noted above, most libraries have been or are weeding their film collections in terms of 16 mm and 8 mm formats. About the only environment in which such films are found are special collections and archives. Like many of the other formats, film content has migrated to a digital form (DVDs and increasingly to streaming video). Videocassettes (VHS) are still in collections and are available for purchase, primarily because much of the content is not yet available in a digital form.

Format battles in the video field have been ongoing for some years now. As mentioned previously, one well-known battle was between Beta and VHS, with VHS being declared the winner. A more recent struggle was between DVD, Blu-ray, HD-DVD, and now 3D formatting. By 2008, the HD-DVD format had fallen out of the contest, leaving DVD and Blu-ray to continue the competition. Today, libraries are once again caught in the middle of a commercial battle where they must bet on a winning side or spend limited funds duplicating the same content in competing formats. One issue is that a DVD player cannot play a Blu-ray disk; however, most Blu-ray players can play the older DVD format. Although prices for Blu-ray players have fallen, less than 10 percent of U.S. households had a Blu-ray player by late 2009 (Dick, 2009, p. 33), so at the present time, there is still a limited user base for this format. This is expected to change in the future, however.

Notwithstanding the Blu-ray issue, most libraries still have substantial collections of VHS material and DVDs. According to Norman Oder (2005, p. 38), until fairly recently, many libraries were still purchasing VHS cassettes in large numbers. By 2007, DVD purchases had overtaken the VHS format, at least for feature film titles. As Netherby (2007) noted, "Part of the growth in the DVD era comes down to simple economics. [Libraries] can buy more movies with their budgets than they could in the VHS era" (p. 5). Most of the video circulation comes from movies in the public library setting, while curriculum-related videos dominate educational library usage.

Given the quick release of DVDs after a film is in theaters, DVD collections generate some of the same issues as best-seller books. Everyone wants it now, not next month after all the talk has faded. In terms of circulation, feature-film videos beat nonfiction videos hands down; theatrical films represent roughly 68 percent of the collections, 72 percent of the expenditures, and 80 percent of the circulations (Oder, 2005, p. 40). Brodart offers the DVD equivalent of the McNaughton book-rental plan where a library may lease multiple copies of a popular DVD title for a short time and return all or some of the copies after the demand has died down (http://www.books.brodart.com/Content3.aspx?P=95).

Another option to meet patron demand for video materials that may be on the horizon is downloadable video. Downloadable e-video was being tested by some larger public libraries as of 2006 and had proved rather successful by 2011. Libraries providing this service do so via contracts with vendors such as OverDrive, which provides a wide range of resources including audio books, movies, and concert videos (http://www.overdrive.com/Resources/MediaFormats/). The Denver Public Library once reported that they had more than 1,200 downloads of their "e-Flicks," although they had only 82 titles available at that time (Kim, 2006, p. 62). Content available for downloading was limited in 2011, but will probably increase rapidly as the demand grows. One appealing aspect of the service is that people can download the movies from their homes.

Cost containment is an issue for most of the libraries offering this type of service. Vendors charge the library a fee based on the community's population. Another concern may be monitoring who is doing the downloading; to address this, some libraries have restricted e-movie files to residents of the service area only. Finally, there are often fees to collect from users of the service—in late 2007 they ranged from $2.99 to $49.99 for libraries that do charge a fee (Spielvogel, 2007, p. 12).

One of the educational usage issues with video is that an instructor often only wants to use a segment from several videos in a class session. Although it is possible to have several video players available, having all the equipment present and having all the videos properly queued is a nuisance and a distraction. With streaming video, it is possible to select the desired segments and put them together in the desired sequence. An example might be demonstrating how different actors or directors interpret a scene for a Shakespeare play. With video streaming it is possible to

- select segments for an entire class or an individual student,
- select segments for student or teacher presentations,
- bookmark segments for future use,
- control the video the same as on a player (play, pause, rewind, and fast-forward), and
- use selected elements in student assignments (Redden, 2005, p. 14).

Video streaming is reaching all levels of education from kindergarten to Harvard's Business School. School media centers and academic libraries can use programs such as Windows Media Player, RealTime, or Quicktime to deliver the material to the classroom. The difference between streaming and downloading is that with streaming, one has the ability to immediately view images as they arrive rather than waiting for an entire download to be completed before viewing anything. (Maximizing teaching time is a factor for instructors.) Some educational video content providers offer video-streaming services and occasionally material from other producers who are not yet offering such services. Generally, the charge for the streaming service is an annual fee based on school enrollment.

One concern, especially for public libraries, is the potential for complaints about its video collection. Public libraries usually address movie and other ratings (such as graphic/Manga novels and video games) in their collection development policy. School library media centers have somewhat less exposure to challenges because of the instructional nature of the collections; however, even in these libraries it is possible to have a parent complain

---

Check These Out

For more information on the issue of performance rights, see Judy Salpeter's article in *TechLearning*, "The New Rules of Copyright" (October 15, 2008; http://teachnology.pbworks.com/f/The_New_Rules_of_Copyright.pdf), and "How Do I Find Out If a Movie Has Public Performance Rights" from the Enoch Pratt Free Library (http://www.prattlibrary.org/locations/sightsandsounds/index.aspx?id=11096).

---

about a video, such as one dealing with evolution. Very often the complaint will raise the question about the suitability of certain titles for young viewers and the need for "protecting the children." This was the major factor in the creation of the movie rating system.

The Motion Picture Association of America (MPAA) has a rating system for its releases—the familiar G, PG, PG-13, R, and NC-17 one sees in the movie section of the newspaper. The Classification and Rating Administration (CARA) within MPAA establishes each film's rating. Although these ratings have no legal force and, in fact, are based on the somewhat subjective opinion of the CARA rating board, the general public accepts them as appropriate. The key is the content of each film in terms of its suitability for children.

The unfortunate fact is that even a collection of G- and PG-rated titles does not ensure that there will be no complaints. One possible way to handle the situation, although it is not always easy to accomplish, is to create two sections for video, one in the children's/young adult area and another in the adult area. This will not forestall all complaints, but it could help. In addition, some public libraries have restricted minors from checking out R-rated materials—but they still have to deal with the issue of adults watching these materials on public machines, so such issues need to be considered and if possible addressed in the collection development policy. You might want to check the video polices of some other libraries such as those for the Weyauwega Public Library (http://www.wegalibrary.org/VideoPolicy.asp) or the Oscoda County Library (http://www.oscoda.lib.mi.us/video.html) for examples of how these libraries addressed the issue.

Videos are an important source of programming for public libraries, although such programming can be somewhat of a problem because of performance rights, which are a component of the copyright law. For libraries in educational settings, performance rights can be an even greater issue. We cover the legal aspects related to collection usage in Chapter 11.

Other Image Formats

As mentioned earlier, many libraries, because of space, maintenance, and low-user interest, are disposing of their collections of reel film, filmstrips, slides, and flat pictures. (We hope they do so with care and don't discard items of long-term societal value solely because of storage space concerns.) Most filmstrips were designed as instructional material and required special projectors, but many of the items are now digitized and available online. The same is true of many of the slide sets. Flat pictures have always presented challenges in organization and access. Scanning images is an approach to keeping pictorial materials in order and increasing access, especially if available via the library Web site, assuming there are no outstanding copyright issues.

Maps

Maps are a form of pictorial material, and most libraries have traditionally held at least a small collection, in addition to atlases in the reference collection. Internet map sites, such as MapQuest, Google Maps, or Multimap, have significantly reduced the demand for road maps in libraries. Information found on such sites provides what most people were seeking when they came to the library "looking for a map"—street and highway information.

Maps actually come in a variety of forms and content. Large public libraries, academic libraries, and many business and industrial libraries have extensive collections. Maps take the form of graphic representations of such things as geological structures, physical features, economic data, and population distributions. They may be in a variety of forms—folded, sheets, raised relief, globes, and even aerial or satellite images—although print maps are currently seeing a decline in popularity as users are showing a preference for computerized maps. Selectors must have clear guidance as to a map collection's scope and purpose. Although a collection might incorporate aerial photographs, including satellite photographs, should it also house remote sensing data from satellites? Are raised relief maps worth including, or are they a commercial product of no real informational value? Clearly the users' requirements will determine the answers to these and many other questions about the collection.

Audio Recordings

Returning to a widely held format, audio recordings, again there is great diversity and incompatibility concerns, at least in terms of the legacy collections. In public libraries, the music recordings are usually part of the circulating collection. For educational libraries the purpose is usually instructional, with limited, if any, use outside the library. This is the media category that most clearly reflects the long-term influence of a changing technology on library collections: vinyl records—various speeds, tapes—various speeds, cassettes—various tracks, CDs, and downloading.

The widespread use of Internet audio streaming, iPods, and other electronic gear has made music recordings a low-use item in most libraries. Many libraries retain their older recordings because often the performance has not yet migrated to a digital form. A few libraries are purchasing relatively low-cost equipment and software that allows earlier recording formats to be converted to an MP3 format; however, the library must be careful to do this in compliance with copyright laws.

For public libraries, audio books have become almost as important as the video collection. Automobile players, portable handheld CD and MP3 players, and other portable digital media players (like iPods) have created a significant market for audio books. Even reading a small paperback on a crowded subway or bus can be difficult. Listening to a pocket-sized player with a headset allows the listener to close out the noise, to some degree, and enjoy a favorite piece of music or listen to a best seller. The same is true for those commuting in their cars or just out for a power walk. Audio books are popular with individuals learning English as a second language and are frequently purchased by community colleges and public libraries for these purposes. Another value of audio books is providing those with vision impairments additional opportunities to enjoy print material that goes beyond those available through the National Library Service for the Blind and Physically Handicapped.

Books-on-tape cassettes and CDs as well as digital audio books (DABs) are very popular. The cassette still has a small niche in the audio collection for commuters whose vehicle CD player does not provide dependable playback (road bumps can translate into sound bumps, perhaps skipping the key information in a whodunit). Tape decks do not suffer from this problem, but fewer and fewer vehicles have them as a standard feature.

Many libraries are forming collaborative DAB services. Some examples of existing programs in 2011 include Illinois Kids Zone (http://www .ilkidszone.info), ListenOhio (http://www.listenohio.org), and the Midwest Collaborative for Library Services (http://www.mlcnet.org/cms/sitem.cfm/ databases_econtent/digital_books/). Unlike the digital music field, DAB is much more stable and does not, at least in 2011, face the same copyright issues as music. In 2011, four major vendors offered DAB products: Audible (http://www.audible.com), OverDrive (http://www.overdrive.com), EBSCO*host*®, formerly netlibrary/Recorded Books *(http://support.ebsco host.com/ebooks/audiobook_faqs.php),* and TumbleBookLibrary (http:// www.tumblebooks.com). Tom Peters and his colleagues (2005) provided an overview of the differences between the services. There are other smaller services that offer very few titles, but as they grow they may well become significant market players.

There are major advantages to having DABs as part of a library's audio service program. Most notably, DABs

- Are available 24/7,

- Are never lost or damaged (at least for the library),

- Require no processing,

- Require no shelf space,

- Never require overdue notices or fines (files automatically delete at the end of the loan period),

- Provide the visually impaired with another means of access to popular titles,

- Allow for simple weeding,

- Allow for easy collaboration, and

- Offer easily obtainable usage data from the vendors.

Games

Should libraries acquire games? Are they an example of Will Manley's "Twinkies"? Our opening quotation from Christopher Harris suggests that even board games have a place in some collections. The reality is that public and school libraries have ever-growing collections of games—both educational and recreational in character. As noted by Farmer (2010), "Video games are now a part of the culture and the fabric of our society. We would not think of denying our customers the latest fiction, but regularly deny them storylines that are just as relevant to the daily conversations and lives of library users" (p. 33). Even academic libraries, including at least one large research library, are beginning to collect games (Laskowski and

Ward, 2009). Further evidence of the growing importance of games in library collections was that 2011 saw the seventh academic Games, Learning, and Society (GLS) conference, while the second American Library Association–sponsored Gaming, Learning, and Libraries symposium was held in 2008. "Twinkies" or not, games are a growing segment of library collections.

Nonboard games are among the most complex items to select, acquire, and support of all the media formats in a collection. Two of the major reasons for the complexity are the fact that there are multiple platforms (each widely owned by users) for playing games and there are often multiple releases for a title. Certainly both issues exist, to some extent, for video titles. However, as of 2011 there are at least 10 platforms for electronic games. Although the platforms compete for market share, the competition has not focused on whose standards or technology will win; rather, it is whose games attract and hold players' attention longest and money spent on products for a given platform. Following are the game platforms available on retail store shelves in 2011:

- Nintendo DS™
- Nintendo GameCube™
- Playstation 2™
- Playstation 3™
- Game Boy Advance®
- PC/MAC based games
- Xbox®
- Xbox 360®
- PSP® (PlayStation portable)
- Wii™

When such a variety of platforms is combined with cross-platform releases of a title, you can see where there would be serious collection budget concerns for selectors. Few traditional library vendors handle games, and at the time of this writing there was no source for placing a standing order.

Like motion pictures, games have a rating system. Most video games released in North America carry a rating from the Entertainment Software Rating Board (ESRB), a nonprofit, self-regulatory, third-party entity formed in 1994 by what is now the Entertainment Software Association. ESRB ratings consist of two parts: a rating symbol on the front of the box addressing age appropriateness, and one of more than 30 different content descriptors (e.g., alcohol reference, blood and gore, etc.) on the back of the box elaborating on elements that may be of interest or concern to users and their guardians. The seven ratings on the box front are EC, early childhood; E, everyone six and up; E10, everyone 10 and up; T, teen 13 and up; M, mature 17 and up; AO, adults only 18 and up; and RP, rating pending. The rating system complexity and the need to provide information about system requirements exemplify the types of challenges that face libraries that are collecting games. Games also raise some serious policy issues, in particular how to monitor who uses what rating.

Check This Out

A good discussion of the whys of having a nonbook collections is Meghan Harper's 2009 article "H. W. Wilson *Nonbook Materials Core Collection*," in *School Library Monthly* (26, no. 2: 35–37).

Government Documents Information

In the not too distant past, government documents were a common element in many library collections. There are still legacy copies of such items in collections; however, all levels of government have shifted their efforts to disseminate information from print to digital formats. (Note: government information did and still does exist in a variety of formats—print, videos, graphic, and microforms as well as digital.) Not only are their communication efforts more and more based on the Internet and Web, but so are their services. One result is that libraries acquire fewer and fewer hard copies of government information while playing a greater role in providing access to such information and services. Donna Blankinship (2010) reported on a study, funded by the Bill and Melinda Gates Foundation, of computer use and libraries. She noted that the study "confirms what public librarians have been saying as they compete for public dollars to expand their services and high speed Internet access: library computer use by the general public is widespread and not just among poor people" (p. A23). The usage is certainly wide ranging, and some of the usage is for gaining access to government information.

When it was just a print world, Federal Depository Library Program (FDLP) libraries were the primary source for government information (many of which were and are academic libraries), and a person had to visit the library to gain access. Today, Web searches provide government information alongside other sources of information. What has changed is that public libraries are now the most active in providing people with access to government information and services. This is largely due to the limits academic libraries must place on outside users when it comes to computer access. Almost by default, public libraries, because of the open access to their facilities and services, have become a major interface between citizens and government information.

Government information has been, and to a large extent still is, a mysterious and frequently misunderstood part of the information world. Because government publications arise out of government action or a perceived need to inform citizens about some matter, and appear in either print or digital form, these materials can confuse library staff and user alike. As mentioned previously, most current government information is accessible through the Web. Online searches, regardless of the search engine used, produce thousands of hits for most queries. Where government information will appear in the search results is a matter of the search engine's relevance algorithm and the search terms used. Regardless of perceived limitations in locating the materials, government information constitutes an important, current, and vital part of having an informed citizenry.

Because government information is a product of many branches and governmental agencies, they have no special subject focus and usually reflect the concerns of the agency that produced them. Predictably, a document produced by the U.S. Department of Agriculture (USDA) probably deals with a subject related to agriculture, such as livestock statistics, horticulture, or irrigation. However, the relationship may be less direct, because the USDA also publishes information about nutrition, forestry, and home economics. As remote as the connection may seem, most government information has some connection to the issuing agencies' purpose.

E-government refers to how all levels of government are attempting to more actively engage their citizens in the governance process through the use of the Web and technology. Government agencies use the Web to disseminate information and provide services. Rose and Grant (2010) noted, "As the scope of E-Government capabilities has grown and the concept has evolved, the definition of E-Government has evolved with it. E-Government is no longer viewed as a simple provision of information and services via the Internet, but as a way of transforming how citizens interact with government" (p. 26).

Currently, what is perhaps the most user-friendly site for accessing U.S. Federal government information is the portal USA.gov, which is called the "U.S. Government's Official Web Portal" (http://www.usa.gov). In addition to the expected search box at the top of the page, the home page offers a tab labeled "Explore Topics" listing a set of broad topical selections (such as "Consumer Guides" and "Health and Nutrition") that provide links to government information on the topic from any agency. There is also a "Find Government Agencies" tab that provides links to the three main branches of government and their agencies, as well as online sites for the states and U.S. territories, local jurisdictions, and tribal governments. The state, local, and tribal pages also offer more search options.

Access to, and identification of, state and local government information was difficult in the past, but sites such as GovEngine.com (http://www.govengine.com) provides links to such information, which has greatly enhanced access. The Library of Congress (http://www.loc.gov/rr/news/stategov/stategov.html) also provides a detailed list of links to state government Websites and some local government sites. Yet another service is the State and Local Government on the Net Website (http://www.statelocalgov.net/).

Since 9/11, the U.S. federal government has rethought what and how much government information ought to be available to the general public. Paper documents may not have the most current information, but the reader knows that the document has not been modified by some unknown, perhaps third nongovernment party. Also, a paper document is not likely to vanish in the blink of an eye. Neither is true of the digital format. Kathy Dempsey's (2004) editorial titled "The Info Was There, Then—Poof" sums up the issue of the permanence of digital information. Her editorial prefaced a themed journal issue dealing with government information, in which she highlighted a key concern: "Where do you draw the line between which data should be public and which should be kept private?" (p. 4). We might add who should make that critical call? In her piece, Dempsey related how one of the articles intended for that issue went "poof" when the White House requested a final review process. (The authors of the article in question worked in a federal information center and their piece was to describe the factors that determine what information is deemed classified.) Klein and Schwal (2005) also discussed the delicate balance society must achieve between maintaining free access to information and security, if its citizens are to effectively participate in a meaningful democracy.

Klein and Schwal (who themselves are federal government employees) in their concluding section made the following points: "Newly generated government information will be evaluated against established criteria for review for public release, the same as always. This is a decentralized process. There is no core group making these decisions, although there may be a tendency on the part of those responsible to err on the side of caution" (p. 23).

Something that is frequently overlooked in the debate about security and access is the fact that depository libraries (the largest holders of print government publications) do not *own* the material. Although they invest significant sums of money in the long-term storage of the material and in staff effort to service the collections, they do not have ownership. The government can and has at various times withdrawn material from depository collections—that process is not just a post-9/11 phenomenon. Further, the federal government can do so without consultation, and libraries have no recourse.

Acquiring Government Information

Many documents are available free from issuing agencies and congressional representatives. They are also available as gifts or exchanges from libraries that have held them for the statutory period and wish to dispose of them or from other libraries with extra nondepository copies. Another common method of acquisition is to purchase needed items through the agency's official sales program. The agency may or may not offer a standing order program. Some commercial jobbers and bookstores deal in government documents, and some booksellers, especially used or rare booksellers, may stock some government documents. To locate Government Printing Office (GPO) federal material, the source to consult is the Catalog of U.S. Government Publications (http://catalog.gpo.gov) the successor to the *Monthly Catalog*. Another resource is the GPO's Online Paper Store (http://www.gpo.gov/cus tomers/store.htm).

One large commercial vendor of government documents is Bernan Associates of Maryland. As noted on its Website:

> Bernan is a leading distributor of essential publications from the United States government and intergovernmental organizations, and a respected publisher of critically acclaimed reference works based on government data. The two businesses are intertwined; for ease of description, we will describe them as distinct activities.
>
> Bernan offers easy, one-stop access to a world of government and international agency books, journals, and CD-ROMs for academic and public libraries in the U.S., as well as law and corporate libraries. (http://www.bernan.com/General/About_ Bernan.aspx)

Bernan Associates handles federal documents and offers several standing-order programs.

Through the United Nations (UN) Publications Website (https://unp .un.org/), a library may acquire items issued by such entities as UNESCO, as well as other UN and international organization publications. Although it does not offer a depository plan, it does have a deposit account service:

> Any customer, non-account or account holder, wishing to estab-lish a deposit account should submit their request in writing. A minimum initial deposit of US$500.00 should be maintained. Upon receipt of your deposit, an account number will be assigned. . . .
>
> All prices are quoted in US dollars, prices are subject to change without notice. [A] shipping and handling fee will be added to each order. Special shipping instructions can usually be accommodated and these will be charged on an individual basis. Discounts are offered to wholesalers, retailers and agents. (https://unp.un.org/Librarians.aspx)

Standing order and subscription services are also available. In addition, some titles are available online. A full listing of agencies that release their publications through this program is available online (https://unp.un.org/Agency.aspx).

Federal Depository Library Program

The concept of a national system of libraries holding national government documents has a long history—Congress passed the first legislation for what is now the FDLP in 1813. Certainly, the program succeeded in getting government information into libraries across the nation where the public has access to the material, even if the indexing of the material left much to be desired. There are two types of depository libraries, full and selective. A full depository agrees to accept all items available to FDLP participants (essentially those materials handled by the GPO; selective institutions take only a portion of the material). The selective libraries are encouraged to take at least 15 percent of the items available—the depository program does *not* include all publications issued by federal agencies and organizations. A list of member libraries is available from the GPO Website (http://catalog.gpo .gov/fdlpdir/FDLPdir.jsp).

At one time, there were 1,365 depository libraries in the United States, but as of 2011 the number had dropped to about 1,250. The number has been declining over the past 15 years because many libraries that were selective members dropped out of the program as collection space and staffing problems grew and electronic access increased.

The composition of the FDLP is heavily weighted toward academic libraries (50 percent), with public libraries a distant second (20 percent). The balance consists of academic law libraries (11 percent), community college libraries (5 percent), state and special libraries (5 percent), federal and state court libraries (5 percent), and federal agency libraries (4 percent).

As the federal government moves toward increasing dependence on electronic dissemination of information, the following types of questions are being raised with regard to the FDLP:

- Is the FDLP still necessary?

- Is the FDLP a remnant of the 19th century?

- Is the FDLP the best way to get information to people in the 21st century?

- Is there a way to change the system to make it more cost-effective?

Peter Hernon and Laura Saunders (2009), in writing about the future of the FDLP, concluded by noting, "Finally, by 2023, there might be a new future that involves a decentralized network of libraries" (p. 366).

At the same time the Hernon and Saunders article appeared, the Depository Library Council (2009) released a draft strategic plan covering 2009–2014. That document made the point that, "At the same time, any strategic vision needs to embrace new ways of collaboration and partnership among depositories and with GPO. This cooperation may include ways of building and sustaining future digital collections of published Federal information sources, but it also must include the deliberative preservation of significant paper and print collections of Federal information" (p. 3). One of the concluding points of the strategic plan was that, "The successful model will be a careful blend of the program's traditional accessibility and technological innovation" (p. 9). An announcement was made by the GPO in June 2011 that they had requested buyouts/early retirement packages for over 2,000 of the agency's employees (http://www.fdlp.gov/component/content/article/19-general/960-gpo-buyout-earlyouts). The ultimate result of this request and how it will impact the FDLP, and CM activities related to government information, remains to be seen.

Depository practices and requirements differ from state to state. The statutes of any particular state will provide the frequency and the statutory framework of the depository program. The state library can provide more detailed information about its state depository program, including a list of depositories, sales and acquisition information, and information about which materials are available from a central source and which are available only from individual agencies.

Points to Keep in Mind

- "Traditional" formats are likely to be produced and acquired by libraries through the lifetime of this book.

- Print books will continue to be published for the foreseeable future.

- Serials are a high demand component of any library collection. A major factor in that demand is the currency of information contained in serials.

- Serials require a significant amount of staff time to select, process, manage, and preserve.

- Media formats have been and will be an important element in a library collection; especially as we go deeper into what some label the "postliterate age."

- Media selection must not only consider content and potential usage, but also technology issues, which are in a state of rapid change, as well as the selection constant of cost considerations.

- Government information is an important element in any library's collection or service program.

- All types of libraries can acquire useful information from government agencies at a reasonable cost.

- By providing users with Web access to government information, libraries will increase the use of the valuable information and data that exist from such sources.

Works Cited

Arlitsch, Kenning. 2011. "The Espresso Book Machine: A Change Agent for Libraries." *Library Hi Tech* 29, no. 1: 62–72.

Black, Steve. 2009. "Editors' Perspectives on Current Topics in Serials." *Serials Librarian* 57, no. 3: 199–222.

Blankinship, Donna. 2010. "Library-Computer Use Common." *Arizona Republic* March 28: A23.

Brown, Myra Michele. 2005. "Video Libraries: More Than a Lure." *American Libraries* 36, no. 11: 41.

Carr, Patrick L. 2009. "From Innovation to Transformation: A Review of the 2006-7 Serials Literature." *Library Resources and Technical Services* 53, no. 1: 3–14.

Creel, Stacy L. 2008. "Graphic Novels and Manga and Manhwa . . . Oh, My!" *VOYA* 31, no. 3: 197.

Dempsey, Kathy. 2004. "The Info Was There, Then—Poof." *Computers in Libraries* 24, no. 4: 4.

Depository Library Council. 2009. Federal Depository Library Program Strategic Plan, 2009–2014. Washington, DC: Library Services and Content Management, Superintendent of Documents, U.S. Government Printing Office. http://www.fdlp.gov/component/docman/doc_download/37-fdlp-stratigic-plan-2009-2014-draft-3?ItemId=45.

Dick, Jeff T. 2009. "Bracing for Blu-ray." *Library Journal* 134, no. 19: 33–35.

Dougherty, William C. 2009. "Print On Demand: What Librarians Should Know." *Journal of Academic Librarianship* 35, no. 2: 184–186.

Farmer, Sandy. 2010. "Gaming 2.0." *American Libraries* 41, nos. 11/12: 32–34.

Fister, Barbara. 2009. "Publishers and Librarians: Two Cultures, One Goal." *Library Journal* 134, no. 8: 22–25.

"Google Signs Agreement With On Demand Books." 2009. *Advanced Technology Libraries* 38, no. 10: 1, 9.

Harris, Christopher. 2009. "Meet the New School Board: Board Games Are Back—And They're Exactly What Your Curriculum Needs." *School Library Journal* 55, no. 5: 24–26.

Hernon, Peter, and Laura Saunders. 2009. "The Federal Depository Library Program in 2023: One Perspective on the Transition to the Future." *College & Research Libraries* 70, no. 4: 351–370.

Johnson, Doug. 2009. "Libraries for a Postliterate Society." *Multimedia and Internet @ Schools* 16, no. 4: 20–22.

Jones-Kavalier, Barbara R., and Suzanne I. Flannigan. 2008. "Connecting the Digital Dots: Literacy of the 21st Century." *Teacher Librarian* 35, no. 3: 13–16.

Kaye, Alan. 2005. "Digital Dawn." *Library Journal* 130, no. 9: 62–65.

Kim, Ann. 2006. "The Future Is Now." *Library Journal* 131, no. 9: 660–663.

Klein, Bonnie, and Sandy Schwal. 2005. "A Delicate Balance: National Security vs. Public Access." *Computers in Libraries* 25, no. 3: 16–23.

Laskowski, Mary, and David Ward. 2009. "Building Next Generation Video Game Collections in Academic Libraries." *Journal of Academic Librarianship* 35, no. 3: 267–273.

Machlup, Fritz, Kenneth Leeson, and Associates. 1978. *Information Through the Printed Word*. New York: Praeger.

Manley, Will. 1991. "Facing the Public." *Wilson Library Bulletin* 65, no. 6: 89.

Mason, Sally. 1994. "Libraries, Literacy and the Visual Media." In *Video Collection Development in Multitype Libraries,* ed. G.P. Handman, 9–13. Westport, CT: Greenwood.

Netherby, Jennifer. 2007. "Slow to Become a Shelf Staple, DVD Is Still Growing." *Library Journal* 132: 5–6.

Nisonger, Thomas. 1998. *Management of Serials in Libraries*. Englewood, CO: Libraries Unlimited.

Oder, Norman. 2005. "The DVD Predicament." *Library Journal* 130, no. 19: 35–40.

Patron, Susan. 2006. "Children's Magazines and Collection Development." *Children and Libraries* 4, no. 3: 39, 44.

Peters, Tom, Lori Bell, Diana Brawley Sussman, and Sharon Ruda. 2005. "An Overview of Digital Audio Books for Libraries." *Computers in Libraries* 25, no. 7: 7–8, 61–64.

Plutchak, T. Scott. 2007. "What's a Serial When You're Running in Internet Time?" *Serials Librarian* 52, nos. 1/2: 79–90.

Redden, Linda. 2005. "Videostreaming I-in K–12 Classrooms." *Media and Methods* 42, no. 1: 14–15.

Rose, Wade R., and Gerald G. Grant. 2010. "Critical Issues Pertaining to the Planning and Implementation of E-Government Initiatives." *Government Information Quarterly* 27, no. 1: 26–33.

St. Lifer, Evan. 2004. "Your Impact on Book Buying." *School Library Journal* 50, no. 9: 11.

Shuler, John A., Paul T. Jaeger, and John Carlo Bertot. 2010. "Implications of Harmonizing the Future of the Federal Depository Library Program Within E-Government Principles and Policies." *Government Information Quarterly* 27, no. 1: 9–16.

Simmons Mary, and Beth O'Briant. 2009. "Journey into the World of Manga and Graphic Novels." *Library Media Connection* 27, no. 4: 16–17.

Spielvogel, Cindy. 2007. "Libraries Lead the Way to Movie Downloads." *Library Journal* 132, no. 10, Hi-Def supplement: 11–12.

Wischenbart, Ruediger. 2008. "Ripping Off the Cover: Has Digitization Changed What's Really in the Book?" *Logos* 19, no. 4: 196–202.

Suggested Readings

Allgood, Julian Everett. 2007. "Serials and Multiple Versions, or the Inexorable Trend Toward Work-Level Displays." *Library Resources and Technical Services* 51, no. 3: 160–178.

Bergman, Barb, Victoria Peters, and Jessica Schomberg. 2007. "Video Collecting for the Sometimes Media Librarian: Tips and Tricks for Selecting, Purchasing, and Cataloging Videos for an Academic Library." *College & Undergraduate Libraries* 14, no. 1: 57–77.

Canepi, Kitti, Andrea Imre, Harold Way, and Christina Torbert. 2007. "Open Access and Conscious Selection." *Serials Librarian* 52, nos. 3/4: 331–334.

Chapman, Bert, and John A. Shuler. 2009. "Letters to the Editor." *College & Research Libraries* 70, no. 5: 419–420. (Comments regarding the Hernon and Saunders survey as referred to in the chapter.)

Cheney, Debora. 2010. "Dinosaurs in a Jetson World: A Dozen Ways to Revitalize Your Microforms Collection." *Library Collections, Acquisitions, and Technical Services* 34, nos. 2/3: 66–73.

Cole, Louise. 2009. "The E-Deal: Keeping Up to Date and Allowing Access to the End User." *Serials Librarian* 57, no. 4: 399–409.

Davis, Roger. 2009. "A Web-Based Usage Counter for Serials Collections." *Serials Librarian* 57, nos.1/2: 137–148.

Derry, Sebastian. 2009. "Biz of Acq—Shooting the Rapids—Navigating Changing Video Formats." *Against the Grain* 21, no. 1: 63–64.

Englert, Tracy. 2009. "Biz of Acq—'Free' Access to Subscription Databases Through the FDLP: Government Documents and Acquisitions." *Against the Grain* 21, no. 5: 66, 68.

Faran, Ellen W. 2011. "Sustaining Scholarly Publishing: University Presses and Emerging Business Models." *C&RL News* 72, no. 5: 284–287.

Frey, Nancy, and Douglas Fisher, eds. 2008. *Teaching Visual Literacy: Using Comic Books, Graphic Novels, Anime, Cartoons and More to Develop Comprehension and Thinking Skills.* Thousand Oaks, CA: Corwin.

Garvin, Peggy. 2006. "The Government Domain: FirstGov Becomes First in Government Search." *Law and Technology Resources for Legal Professionals.* http://www.llrx.com/columns/govdomain13.htm.

Handman, Gary. 2010. "License to Look: Evolving Models for Library Video Acquisition and Access." *Library Trends* 58, no. 3: 324–334.

Haynes, Elizabeth. 2009. "Getting Started With Graphic Novels in School Libraries." *Library Media Connection* 27, no. 4: 10–12.

Helgren, Jamie E. 2011. "Booking to the Future." *American Libraries* 42, nos. 1/2: 40–43.

Hoy, Susan. 2009. "What Talking Books Have To Say: Issues and Options For Public Libraries." *APLIS* 22, no. 4: 164–180.

King, David Lee. 2009. "Video on the Web: The Basics." *Multimedia and Internet @ Schools* 16, no. 1: 14–16.

Lee, Scott, and Carolyn Burrell. 2004. "Introduction to Streaming Video for Novices." *Library Hi Tech News* 21, no. 2: 20–24.

Lin, Chi-Shiou, and Kristin R. Eschenfelder. 2008. "Selection Practices for Web-based Government Publications in State Depository Library Programs: Comparing Active and Passive Approaches." *Government Information Quarterly* 25, no. 1: 5–24.

McElfresh, Laura Kane. 2007. "When a Journal Isn't a Journal." *Technicalities* 27, no. 1: 1, 11–13.

Mitchell, Nicole, and Elizabeth R. Lorbeer. 2009. "Building Relevant and Sustainable Collections." *Serials Librarian* 57, no. 4: 327–333.

Morrison, Andrea M., ed. 2008. *Managing Electronic Government Information in Libraries: Issues and Practices.* Chicago: American Library Association.

Priebe, Ted, Amy Welch, and Marian MacGilvray. 2008. "The U.S. Government Printing Office's Initiatives for the Federal Depository Library Program to Set the Stage for the 21st Century." *Government Information Quarterly* 25, no. 1: 48–56.

Schroeder, Rebecca, and Julie Williamsen. 2011. "Streaming Video: The Collaborative Convergence of Technical Services, Collection Development, and Information Technology in the Academic Library." *Collection Management* 36, no. 2: 89–106.

Smith, Debbi A. 2009. "Format Overlap of the 'New York Times': A Collection Management Case Study." *Collection Management* 34, no. 2: 94–111.

Stamison, Christine, Bob Persing, and Chris Beckett. 2009. "What They Never Told You About Vendors in Library School." *Serials Librarian* 56, nos. 1/4: 139–145.

Widzinski, Lori. 2010. "'Step Away from the Machine': A Look at Our Collective Past." *Library Trends* 58, no. 3: 358–377.

Wilson-Higgins, Suzanne. 2011. "Could Print On-Demand Actually Be the 'New Interlibrary Loan'?" *Interlending and Document Supply* 39, no. 1: 5–8.

Withey, Lynne, Steve Cohn, Ellen Faran, Michael Jensen, Garrett Kiely, Will Underwood, and Kathleen Keane, et al. 2011. "Sustaining Scholarly Publishing: New Business Models for University Presses." *Journal of Scholarly Publishing* 42, no. 4: 397–441.

9
E-Resources and Technology Issues

E-books have been quietly taking their place beside more traditional materials, and many academic libraries now count hundreds of thousands of electronic books as part of their collections.
—William Miller, 2008

Reading on screens, especially on small dedicated ereading
devices such as Kindle and Sony Reader, is causing ripples of
interest and unrest in the reading population, not to mention
among authors, publishers and librarians. The effects and
efficacy of ereading is hotly discussed.
—Tom Peters, 2010

Historically, libraries have acquired material through purchase
or gifts. Once the material is acquired, it becomes the property of
the library. . . . Today, the licensing of electronic resources is
replacing the traditional acquisition of printed material. The
nonownership licensing of digital material and electronic resources from publishers and service providers is the current
state of affairs, without any warranties of long-term access.
—Shona Koehn and Suliman Hawamdeh, 2010

Library technology issues are far broader than collection management.
Libraries' employment of technology has done much to blur their traditional administrative and operational structures. A great many staff members wear several hats that do not fit nicely into the concepts of public or
technical services. Also, there is no question that electronic resources have

contributed their share to the blurring process. E-resource management calls not only for a sound subject/content background, but some understanding of several legal issues and more than a little technological knowledge. We explore some of the impact e-resources have on libraries and their staff in this and later chapters.

One reflection of technology's impact on the field is in ALA's "Core Competencies of Librarianship" adopted in 2009. The statement outlines eight core areas, one of which focuses on technology. Section 4 ("Technological Knowledge and Skills") consists of four subtopics that relate in one way or another to collections. For example, competency 4A relates to "Information, communication, assistive, and related technologies as they affect the resources, service delivery, and uses of libraries and other information agencies" (http://www.ala.org/ala/educationcareers/careers/corecomp/corecompetences/finalcorecompstat09.pdf). The concept of electronic resource management will be explored later in this chapter.

Sarah Pritchard (2008) made the point that "In the digital environment, we still have resources, staff, and facilities that combine in various ways to acquire and provide information. These recombinations challenge traditional definitions of library organization. . . . All parts of a library are involved, not just some pieces that we can conveniently segregate as a special type of content or a special service" (pp. 219–220). In her article, she explored, in some detail, what these recombinations are and how they will possibly change in the near future.

Certainly Lizabeth Wilson (2008) was correct in stating, "Collaboration and collective action will be the defining characteristics of the twenty-first century library. We can no longer feel complacent about artificial boundaries among our libraries. The most urgent issues—scholarly communication, digital libraries, and information literacy—require the contributions of many" (p. 130). Although her focus was on the research library environment, her point regarding collaboration and collective action applies to any type of library in the 21st century. Further, the point also applies to library operations as the digital world cuts across traditional department boundaries and requires a higher level of cooperation than in the past, if end users are to be served effectively. As Jesse Holden (2010) wrote, "Navigating the information universe is complex in that it requires maximizing resources in a way that simultaneously *expands* and *narrows* the available content that is required by an end user by distilling the most useful content from the broadest number of sources" (p. 11). Accomplishing such tasks calls for many skills and, more often than not, several people.

What do we mean by e-resources? We believe materials either converted to or "born" digital fall under the e-resources umbrella. In today's digital world, almost all new materials might well be thought of as born digital as few people are using typewriters to prepare reports, articles, or book manuscripts, at least in developed countries. Current usage of born digital relates to material first appearing in a digital form. Some such items may later be issued in a paper format, but the initial release was electronic. We address the following in this chapter:

- Books
- Digital video
- Web links

- Serials
- Digital music
- Institutional repositories

Differences Between Traditional and E-Resources

There are at least seven major differences between print and digital collection management. Perhaps the most important difference is that a library rarely owns the electronic materials. With e-resources, what a library pays for is access, not a physical product over which it has full control. As long as the library pays the appropriate fees and its usage complies with the legal agreement (license or contract), the access remains in place. However, should there be a failure on the library's part, the vendor can, and occasionally does, "pull the plug" on availability for the library's users. Even in the days when libraries did receive a physical product (CD-ROMs, for example) containing digital content such as an indexing service, the library agreed to either return or destroy the CD-ROM upon receipt of an updated version. Today's e-environment makes it much easier for the vendor to control library compliance by simply cutting the connection to the database.

A second difference is the existence of licenses or contracts that govern what the terms of access are. (We examine licenses and contracts in some detail in Chapter 11.) Many of these legal agreements contain clauses outlining to whom and how to provide access to the e-material. Often these limitations—a third difference—go against the library's philosophy of service such as open to all or sharing resources. What the limitations are varies from vendor to vendor. Some of the more common are restrictions that limit or forbid the use of the content for interlibrary lending, limits on the number of individuals who may access the material at the same time (simultaneous users), restrictions on the use of the material by nonlibrary cardholders (any user group not identified in the license), remote access availability (proxy server issues and in-library usage), and even restrictions that make the library liable for how an individual uses the information gathered after leaving the building.

Another difference is the final decision to purchase access to most e-resources comes after a trial period. That is, the vendor allows access to the product for a period of time. How long that period is varies, but almost always it is 30 days or more. There are several reasons for wanting or even demanding a trial:

- The relatively high cost of e-products (except for e-books, which can be substantially less expensive than print),

- The variety of search platforms available from vendor to vendor,

- The actual content of the database or product,

- The ease of use in terms of staff and users,

- The technical requirements that need to be met to make the product available given a library's infrastructure.

To be effective, from a decision-making perspective, the trial ought to allow full end-user access. Few vendors have trouble allowing such access as they expect or hope that the end users will add pressure to the library to provide ongoing availability to the product.

A complicating factor in making a final acquisition decision is that many such e-products are acquired through a consortial arrangement (a fifth difference). As mentioned in earlier chapters, such purchases are based on group decision making that tends to be complex (many voices, many opinions) and drawn out. More often than not, the library's costs to take part in

---

Something to Watch

In spring 2011, HarperCollins announced a plan to place a "cap" on the number of views possible for e-books purchased from them. In this plan, "new titles licensed from library ebook vendors will be able to circulate only 26 times before the license expires" (http://www.libraryjournal.com/lj/home/889452-264/harpercollins_caps_loans_on_ebook.html.csp). Brian Kenney noted the decision "generated one of the biggest storms in our profession in years—complete with calls to boycott the publisher" ("The Harper-Collins Kerfuffle," 2011. *School Library Journal* 56, no. 4: 9). Initially, some consortia did react by voting to suspend purchases from HarperCollins (http://www.libraryjournal.com/lj/home/889582-264/library_consortia_begin_to_vote.html.csp). How this scenario is ultimately resolved remains to be seen, but it is definitely an issue to watch.

HarperCollins is not alone. As noted in *ShelfLife* ("Will Harper Collins Policy Change Libraries?" 2011. *ShelfLife* 6, no. 1: 1–3), "Others of the Big Six, Macmillan and Simon & Schuster, for example, currently do not offer their electronic titles for sale to libraries" (p. 2).

"the deal" are unknown until almost the last minute—needless to say, cost is a critical decision factor. The final cost is generally governed by the number of libraries taking part and a last minute drop out or joiner can impact the price, which in turn may influence a library's decision to participate.

When it comes time to assess an e-service, the library may find that it is highly dependent on data supplied by the vendor—a sixth difference. Such data may not really address the evaluation issues that are important to the library. Assessment of e-services was addressed in Chapter 6.

The final difference is permanence. There are three aspects to this in terms of e-resources. First, and foremost, as we noted above, the library does not own the product or service. When it becomes necessary to cancel a service, it may be possible to retain access to the material that was available during the time the library paid for access. That, however, is something the library must address at the time of purchase. A second issue is that what is there today may not be there tomorrow, even though the library is fully paid up. Vendors can and do pull material from their product without notifying the library. Naturally, there is the issue of long-term preservation of electronic resources in general—they are actually less permanent than traditional formats. We will cover all these issues in more detail in Chapter 10.

Selection Issues

Almost all of the factors that you consider for traditional formats apply, to some degree, to e-resources. However, e-selection decisions are a little different. Broadly speaking there are seven categories of e-selection—content, limitations, costs, people factors, technical, cancellations/archival issues, and assessment.

One major difference that needs to be considered is whether the e-product would or could replace something that already exists in the collection. The most common place for this issue to arise is with e-serial packages. In the early days of such packages, libraries thought about and sometimes did cancel their print subscriptions for titles in the package with the idea the monies freed up by the cancellation would help pay for the package. This rarely worked as intended as often the e-version was not identical to the paper version. Another factor that arose was that some publishers place an "embargo" on the e-version—not allowing it to appear for some time period after the paper copy appeared. Essentially the notion of saving money by canceling a paper subscription to help cover the cost of an e-package has not worked as hoped. When you have paper-based copies of a high percentage of the package titles, a reasonable question is, will the electronic versions provide a true enhancement of service?

Content

Depending on what the e-product is—book, serials, music, video—one of the first questions to ask is does this product fill a real need or gap in collection or is it just a means of showing others that the library is moving into the digital world? The latter reason is not good stewardship of limited funding. You should be able to identify some e-products that you actually need, thus demonstrating forward-looking collection building and good stewardship. An obvious related question is what is the quality of the content and reputation of those who put the package together? When it comes to packages, there are two aspects of content quality to think about. First is the traditional quality of each title in the package, followed by the package's total quality.

Yet another question that is rather important is, what does a vendor or producer mean by the phrase "full text"? Does it mean everything that appears in the print version(s) of the titles, including advertisements? Often, all that is meant is the text of the article in the case of serials. Some vendors do not include article graphics in their context but rather create separate files of figures, photographs, and charts making it highly inconvenient for readers. What about color graphics? If the product does not handle color, images using color may be very difficult to interpret in various shades of gray.

A second quality issue is illustrated in Table 9.1. There is a significant amount of duplication between aggregator packages. The data in the table was collected from an academic library that has made a major commitment to providing e-resources. The first three titles in the table are in all of the major aggregator packages. As Table 9.1 illustrates, not only is there duplication of titles, but there are also differences in time periods covered by the packages.

Although not all that common, a few publishers have chosen to only allow one aggregator to include a title in its package, *Harvard Business Review* (*HBR*), for example. That means if you need access to an electronic version of *HBR* you must subscribe to one of a select number of EBSCO databases (such as *Business Source Complete*) and all the other titles in that package. An individual can subscribe to the journal at three different levels, paper only, online only, or a combination of both methods ($129 a year as of mid-2011). *HBR*'s individual subscription options are not intended for corporate or library settings.

All of the above makes for complex decision making; it is especially hard when the package under consideration is through a consortia arrangement. There are time pressures as well as information questions to handle, and this is just the start of the selection process.

Limitations

Limitations related to e-resources fall into two broad categories: access and rights. Access issues can be numerous in some contracts. Some of the most common are who can have access to the material—some examples are "authorized" (only registered borrowers), "walk-in" users, in library access

Table 9.1.   Title Overlap and Coverage Time Frames

Library Journal
from 05/01/1976 to present in Academic Search Complete
from 05/01/1976 to present in Business Source Complete
from 05/01/1976 to present in Health Source: Nursing/Academic Edition
from 05/01/1976 to present in MasterFILE Premier
from 01/01/1996 to present in ABI/INFORM
from 01/01/1996 to present in ProQuest Research Library
from 01/01/1998 to present in Education Full Text
from 01/01/1998 to present in Wilson OmniFile Full Text Mega Edition
Journal of Academic Librarianship
from 03/01/1975 to 05/31/2004 in Academic Search Complete
from 03/01/1975 to 05/31/2004 in Business Source Complete
from 01/01/1984 to 05/31/2004 in MasterFILE Premier
from 1993 to 1994 in ScienceDirect
from 01/01/1995 to present in ScienceDirect
from 01/01/1996 to present in Education Full Text
from 01/01/1996 to present in Wilson OmniFile Full Text Mega Edition
Teacher Librarian (Vancouver)
from 11/01/1996 to present in ProQuest Research Library
from 09/01/1998 to present in Academic Search Complete
from 09/01/1998 to present in Education Full Text
from 09/01/1998 to present in MasterFILE Premier
from 09/01/1998 to present in Wilson OmniFile Full Text Mega Edition
from 10/01/1998 to present in LexisNexis Academic
The Economist (London)
from 1843 to 2006 in The Economist Historical Archive
from 07/07/1990 to present in Academic Search Complete
from 07/07/1990 to present in Business Source Complete
from 07/07/1990 to present in MasterFILE Premier
from 08/04/2001 to present in ABI/INFORM
from 08/04/2001 to present in ProQuest Research Library
Harvard Business Review
from 10/01/1922 to present in Business Source Complete
People (New York, N.Y.: 2002)
from 01/10/1994 to present in Academic Search Complete
from 2002 to present in MasterFILE Premier
from 02/15/2010 to present in ProQuest Research Library

only, and passworded or authenticated access for remote users. Sometimes there are restrictions on the number of simultaneous users. Almost always there is a sliding scale of fees for increasing the base number of users beyond the number in the standard agreement. The good news about this fee is that you can always start with the base number and increase it if usage indicates there is a need. Almost all the access limitations may be dealt with by paying more for the service. However, there are almost always issues beyond the cost that complicate the decision process—the library having to address its technological infrastructure, for example.

Which rights or obligations are tied to the package or service varies, but they are often more difficult to resolve than those of access. Limiting or forbidding the use of the material for resource-sharing activities such as ILL are fairly common and hard to nearly impossible to modify. One limit to which a library should not agree to is one that holds the library liable for the usage a person makes of the material accessed after leaving the library. Even the copyright laws do not try to impose such an obligation on libraries.

Cost

In many ways, purchasing a new automobile is the closest activity that we all do that mirrors the process of a library acquiring an e-service. There is a starting price and after going through a series of possible additions or subtractions, a final price. Getting to final cost always seems to take longer than expected. Cost considerations are significant, and often cost is the determining factor in the decision to acquire an e-product or service. However, you often have to wait until after all the issues are known before the cost is finalized. That final figure may turn an otherwise positive decision process into a negative one.

What are some of the cost factors you must resolve before getting to the final cost figure? One of them is the discount that may be available. Like a new automobile, there is a suggested retail price; however, everyone knows that price is rarely the final cost. If the vendor is a firm with which the library has done substantial business over a number of years, there is likely to be some discount for the library "going it alone." When the library is part of a consortia, the final price is often not settled until well after the trial period ends as the number of participants is finally settled.

Also, like a new car, products may offer optional extras or upgrades; this is especially true of journal full-text databases. Usually the base product offers access to articles from the current issue to some point back in time. For example, base coverage may be for the previous 10 years; however, the journals in the database probably have a history much longer than that. The vendor usually offers back-issue coverage at an additional cost. Some vendors break down back files into increments of 10 to 15 years, each at an added charge. It might seem obvious that a library with an interest in certain titles might well have the back issues in paper form and there would be no need to purchase access to a digital format as well. That is often the case; however, more and more users are becoming accustomed to having 24/7 remote access to journals, and they pressure the library to have key titles available in digital format as far back as possible.

People Issues

With traditional print materials, you do not have many "people issues" to think about. Perhaps the only real concern might be whether a title selected will cause complaints about its inclusion in the collection. Such is not the case with e-resources. There are both end-user and staff factors to take into account.

Ease of use is a major consideration regarding almost all e-resources. Questions to consider include will the product require staff training? How easy will it be for the public to use, or will users require staff assistance? Each e-vendor will try to differentiate its product(s) from other vendors by employing a proprietary search engine and features. Each new vendor, for the library, is likely to have something different regarding access methods for their material. How easy or complex that process is should be put into the selection thought process. Clearly, more intuitive search processes are better for both the user and staff.

Products or services that involve downloading, such as e-books, music, or videos, often call for staff involvement. First-time users of the product or service are likely to require some assistance even when the person has experience with downloading materials, as the vendor is likely to have some special requirements. There are some services that require creation of a user account or individualized password by the library staff. In addition, there may be fees associated with the service that the library is responsible for collecting. All of these activities add to the staff workload, which seems to grow exponentially with little prospect of adding new staff. Thus, what may seem like a very small increase for one or more staff members from the addition of one new e-service can grow into a sizable workload issue. Another related matter is, given extended library service hours and the fact that most users assume anyone working in a library is a "librarian," more public service staff will need detailed training for the new product. It is no longer just the reference librarians who must know more than a little about each e-product or service. As we noted in this chapter's opening paragraph, work roles are blending more and more in most libraries.

Technical Issues

In some ways, technical issues along with fiscal concerns are the driving forces in the final selection decision for e-resources. One technical issue is where the content will reside. Factors to consider include whether or not the e-resource will exist on the library's server, the vendor's server, or if it otherwise Web-based. Servers have maximum limits on simultaneous access, after which point response time begins to decline, and in extreme cases, shuts down. Thus, having a sense of how great the load would be, if the product is housed on the library's server, may be critical to reaching a decision regarding whether or not to acquire a product. If the load is too great, the library may be able to have the database hosted elsewhere, for an extra fee. Another technical consideration is the robustness of the library's information communication technology infrastructure. Certainly the library could upgrade both the server and infrastructure, but this will increase overall costs.

Another question to answer is how much technology support is needed or available from library staff. For most libraries today, staffing can be a challenge, and committing any significant amount of time to maintaining or sustaining a new product, beyond user support, is problematic. Knowing what is required beforehand is essential for making an informed purchase decision.

Similarly, clarifying what, if any, special equipment or software will be needed is an important issue. In addition, the question of accessing the content must be fully understood. Access options range from password access to Internet protocol–secured access, barcode access (such as the code on a person's borrower card), or proxy-server access, all of which may require ongoing staff attention. Another concern is whether or not the resource allows for remote access or is only accessible within the library. Either option has staffing implications.

Assessment Options

Although circulation and processing statistics have long been kept for print library materials, e-materials can present special challenges when it comes to quantifying their use. Such challenges were succinctly described by Martha Whittaker (2008) who observed:

> On the face of it, keeping track of usage in the digital environment should be much easier than in the print environment. . . . Computers are good at counting things. It is not easy, however, because there are so many variables in the way people access and use digital materials. We cannot just look at circulation statistics or scan the unshelved books and journals on tables at the end of the day for accurate usage information. (p. 443)

Assessment challenges or not, given that more and more libraries commit 50 percent or more of their materials budget to electronic resources, means serious assessments must occur as these expenditures are usually long-term commitments. Bertot, McClure, and Ryan (2001) noted: "Without the development, collection, analysis, and reporting of electronic resource and service measures . . . libraries are misrepresenting their overall service usage and potentially damaging their ability to compete for scarce funding resources in their communities" (pp. 1–2). Although almost every vendor *claims* to provide usage data, few provide what a library actually needs in order to determine the actual value to end users. Thus, libraries have been taking on the job. One big question is what constitutes "usage"—is any search, including mistakes in spelling, considered a search? Do gross numbers really provide much useful information?

Several assessment initiatives have been undertaken in response to the need for gathering solid informative usage data for e-resources. Two such efforts are Project COUNTER (Counting Online Usage of NeTworked Electronic Resources, http://www.projectcounter.org/) and the International Coalition of Library Consortia's (ICOLC) "Revised Guidelines for Statistical Measures of Usage of Web-Based Information Resources" (2006, http://www.library.yale.edu/consortia/webstats06.htm). Project COUNTER was launched in 2002 as a means of setting standards for "recording and reporting of online usage statistics in a consistent, credible and compatible way" (http://www.projectcounter.org/about.html), and it operates through the publication of a series of Codes of Practice, which are guidelines for the production of vendor reports. ICOLC's Guidelines, on the other hand, establish consistent "boundaries" for what should be included in vendor statistical reports, without compromising user privacy or confidentiality.

COUNTER and ICOLC address usage data from the vendor side of the equation. Additionally, the implementation of a local electronic resource management system (ERMS) allows individual libraries to track acquisitions, usage data, and licensing efforts. ERMSs are largely credited to the work of Tim Jewell (2001; Jewell et al., 2004) at the University of Washington and the Digital Library Federation. Vendors currently offering such systems include Innovative Interfaces (ERMS) and Ex Libris (Verde). Unfortunately, such systems can be cost-prohibitive for some libraries. However, low-cost

---

Check This Out

Rachel A. Fleming-May and Jill E. Grogg discuss the concepts surrounding use and usage studies for e-resources in their 2010 article "Chapter 1: Assessing Use and Usage" (*Library Technology Reports* 46, no. 6: 5–10).

Check These Out

Two fairly comprehensive books on e-resource assessment are Richard Bleiler and Jill Livingston's *Evaluating E-Resources* (Washington, DC: Association of Research Libraries, 2010), and Andrew C. White's *E-Metrics for Library and Information Professionals: How to Use Data for Managing and Evaluating Electronic Resource Collections* (New York: Neal-Schuman, 2006).

---

alternatives are available, ranging from open-source products (Doering and Chilton, 2009), to Web 2.0 applications (Murray, 2008) or the use of simple spreadsheet software.

John Bertot and his colleagues (2001) provided the most comprehensive approach for evaluating e-resources. They suggest a matrix approach that incorporates many of the elements one uses in the electronic selection process: technical infrastructure, information content, support issues, and management issues. To that, they add the importance of assessing those elements in terms of their extensiveness, efficiency, effectiveness, service quality, impact, usefulness, and adoption (pp. 62–73). (One should read their publication, as we only very briefly outline their major ideas.) *Efficiency* and *effectiveness* elements encompass what they sound like. *Extensiveness* is how much of the electronic service users access; this can be a major factor with aggregator packages. *Service quality* is how well the activity is accomplished; one suggested measure would be the percentage of users who find what they need. *Impact* is a measure of what, if any, difference the service makes to other activities. *Usefulness* is a measure of how appropriate the service is for a class of users or an individual. *Adoption* is a measure of how much, if at all, users incorporate the service into individual or organizational activities.

Many electronic products provide, as part of the package or as an optional addition, report software that allows one to easily monitor who is using what when. You can and should load management report software onto the servers that provide access to electronic resources. Management reports will provide some of the data needed to evaluate electronic resources and the "value" of different products and services to local as well as remote users.

Cancellation or Loss of Service

With the purchase of e-resources comes some special considerations regarding product cancellation or loss of service. Some issues to consider include what happens if a library must drop an e-product or service? What happens if the e-vendor goes out of business? What happens if the e-vendor merges with another firm? The first "what if" unfortunately is just as common an occurrence today as it was when there were no e-products or services. The latter two, while not that common, do take place from time to time. In the past, when the library possessed and owned a book, journal, recording, and so forth, it retained something for the monies spent when one of the above scenarios occurred. With e-products, unless you are careful during the selection process, the likely outcome of any of the above situations is "poof," you have nothing. The money is gone, and with it, so is the information.

Robert Wolf (2009) summed up the budgetary situation and e-journals as follows: "We have spent the last decade building our electronic journal subscriptions without seriously considering the real obstacles to perpetual access. We know publishers offer perpetual access [at least some do], and that is good, however, we have not taken steps necessary to ensure that it is in a format we can actually use" (p. 34). There are three broad aspects to the above "what ifs" situation—legal, technical, and long-term preservation. In this chapter we look at technical issues, in Chapter 10 we cover long-term preservation, while Chapter 11 addresses the legal side of the picture.

The "what ifs" apply to almost all e-products and services; however, e-serials, given their popularity with users, are the format most often addressed in the literature. The technical issues are the same for e-books, music, serials, and video. Libraries have three common methods for gaining access to e-materials—through aggregator packages such as EBSCO's *Kids Search* (http://www.ebscohost.com/schools/kids-search) and Gale's *Biography In Context* (http://www.gale.cengage.com/InContext/bio.htm); via publishers' packages, for example Sage's *Sage Reference Online* (http://www.sage-ereference.com/) and offerings from Alexander Street Press, including *Ethnographic Video Online* and *Music Online* (http://alexanderstreet.com/products/anth.htm and http://alexanderstreet.com/products/muso.htm); and title by title from publishers.

Early in the new e-product and service consideration process, it is wise to request a copy of the vendor's standard contract or license. As noted in the Wolf quotation above, not all e-vendors include perpetual access in their service agreements. Some who do will offer it as an added cost feature. Those that do not have such a clause may be willing to add it. Such access rights may be included in agreements in rather ambiguous terms. Jim Stemper and Susan Barribeau (2006) quoted one such vague statement: "Licensor and Licensee shall discuss a mechanism satisfactory to the Licensor and Licensee to enable the Licensee to have access . . . and the terms of such access" (p. 102). Their article reports on an analysis they conducted of 50 e-agreements for journals from both aggregators and publishers. Knowing the content of an agreement, and not just in reference to long-term access, is very useful during your deliberations regarding an e-acquisition.

So what if you and the vendor do reach a satisfactory agreement regarding perpetual access? What is it that the library will have should it become necessary to cancel a subscription or service? Actually, the library will be better off in the case of a vendor or publisher having problems than when the library has budget problems. At best, the library will receive one or more DVD-ROMs, or the material in some other format—PDFs, HTML, or XML text files, for example. However, what should be remembered is that you will end up with lots of data but not the search interface. The only access to the data will be when a person knows the full citation for the desired item. Essentially, the library will have to pay someone to create some type of search capability—not something many libraries could afford. There would also be some potential copyright issues as there are only a finite number of ways to search databases.

Although they may be seen as an alternative in such a situation, archival services such as LOCKSS (Lots Of Copies Keep Stuff Safe, based at Stanford University Libraries) and Portico (a digital preservation service) are of limited value in the above circumstances. In the case of LOCKSS, the library must have an active subscription for the title or service. That does not help in cancellation times, which are likely to continue well into the future. Portico services are also not useful for cancellation access. We will discuss these services as well as others in more detail in Chapters 10 and 11.

At the time this volume was being prepared, few good options existed to protect the library's investment in e-resources when the library falls on hard economic times and must start canceling titles and services. There are better protections, if far from ideal, available to cover circumstances that are vendor or publisher related. Giving serious thought to the "what if the library has to cancel" question during the selection phase is rather important.

E-Formats

Electronic collections go beyond those purchased from vendors and publishers. Diane Kovacs (2007) noted that "Some digital collections are preservation projects designed to ensure that fragile historical materials are available for future generations. Libraries participate in many local history projects and preservation projects" (p. 73). Two examples of such collections include the American Memory project, sponsored by the Library of Congress (http://memory.loc.gov/ammem/index.html) and the University of Maryland Libraries Digital Collections (http://digital.lib.umd.edu/). However, there is one digitization project that has gained far more press and attention than any other—the Google Books Project (http://books.google.com, discussed later in this chapter). In addition, many libraries provide links to Websites through OPACs or library Webpages. E-books, serials, music, video, and institutional repositories are also covered in the following sections.

E-Books

Today, publishers find the Web world something of a challenge and many are still struggling to find a satisfactory method to employ it and generate an adequate income stream to remain profitable. Some have tried issuing "born digital" titles with less than great success. Most can offer other firms, such as Amazon and Barnes & Noble, e-versions of titles they released in paper. Finding the proper pricing structure for this approach is still very much up in the air. Perhaps the type of e-readers on market in 2011 and beyond (such as Kindle, Sony Reader, and Nook) will overcome the proprietary issues that caused earlier e-readers to fail.

Something to Watch

In late September 2011, Amazon announced a program in which its Kindle books would become available at over 11,000 public libraries nationwide via the local library catalog. As noted in Amazon's press release announcing the service, "Libraries are a critical part of our communities and we're excited to be making Kindle books available at more than 11,000 local libraries around the country. We're even doing a little extra here—normally, making margin notes in library books is a big no-no. But we're fixing this by extending our Whispersync technology to library books, so your notes, highlights and bookmarks are always backed up and available the next time you check out the book or if you decide to buy the book" (Jay Marine, director, Amazon Kindle, September 21, 2011, http://tinyurl.com/65leta6). Early adopters of this service include Newport Beach (California) Public Library (http://www.newportbeachca.gov/nbpl/), Phoenix Public Libraries (Edythe Jensen, October 1, 2011, "E-Books Push Phoenix-Area Libraries Into A New Era," *Arizona Republic* http://tinyurl.com/3pbkg5n), and the Indianapolis Marion County Public Library (http://www.imcpl.org/). How popular this service becomes over time remains to be seen and is worth watching.

E-book readers present something of a conundrum for both publishers and libraries. As Emile Algenio and Alexia Thompson-Young (2005) noted, "Publishers want to sell books to customers and libraries want to lend books to users. E-books challenge both of these goals, since one e-book could be accessed by multiple library users at a time or could be protected by software that requires payment per view" (p. 114). Just how e-readers and library service will play out is impossible to accurately predict; however, libraries have effectively dealt with a variety of information delivery systems in the past and we expect they will do so again in this case.

E-Readers

Personal e-readers are extremely popular, even among individuals who are not technologically inclined. It appears likely that the current generation of e-readers will have greater staying power than their predecessors. This is in part because there will continue to be a steady and varied supply of titles available to download. There is also a strong probability that the current single function units will morph in some manner with the existing multifunction cell phones, iPods, MP3 players, and other handheld devices.

For libraries, the readers present challenges for creating new service models as well as acquisition budgets. First, there is a question of just how many individuals will be willing to pay the current cost for an electronic device that is a single function proprietary device? Which e-reader to start with? In Chapter 8, we reviewed the battle between VHS and Beta, with Beta declared the loser. Although the situation is somewhat different today, there is still the memory of both the cassette and DVD video format battles as well as what happened to libraries that jumped on the e-reader bandwagon after the first readers appeared on the market.

Assuming a library does decide to provide services for e-readers, there are still questions regarding which platforms to support, how much money to commit to the service, and whether users should pay some or all of the costs. And, perhaps most important, how should the library handle the increased workload that current readers would create for the staff? It should be kept in mind that there are digitized e-books that libraries can provide access to online and there are titles intended for downloading onto a reader. In 2007, Lynn Connaway and Heather Wicht reported that e-books only represented 5 percent of academic library collections, just over 2 percent of public library collections, and between 15 and 60 percent of special library collections. Most of the holdings were for e-titles made available online rather than download to a reader. Connaway and Wicht also identified four barriers to widespread library adaptation of e-books. Those barriers remain in place in 2011:

- Lack of standards for software and hardware;
- Usage rights (single user) tend to go against the operating philosophy of libraries (open access);
- Pricing models that are rather unrealistic for library budgets, especially during lean economic times; and
- Lack of a library-based "discovery" system (titles are currently available only through OPACs, which do not match the ease of use of Google and Yahoo when searching for titles).

Presently, efforts to get e-readers into the education market have been more or less a research and development activity rather than for market

---

Something to Ponder

In late 2009, the *Boston Globe* (Allis, 2010) carried an article reporting that the Cushing Academy (Ashburnham, Massachusetts), a college preparatory school, was discarding all 20,000 print books from its library. In their place, the school purchased e-readers—18 Amazon and Sony readers—and the plan was to download books for student use. You have to wonder how well served the 450 students will be with just 18 e-reader devices. Several questions seem reasonable to raise. First, and foremost, how many of those 20,000 books are actually available for downloading? Second, with the limited capacity of e-readers—only a tiny fraction could be available even if each of the 18 devices had unique titles loaded—who will decide what titles to have on the readers? Then there is the question of the added workload for the library staff as the readers will require appropriate logins, passwords, alias accounts, and so forth each time new titles are loaded and different students want access to the devices.

Our question then is, how well served do you think students will be in the short term (three to five years)? Do you think they will be as prepared for their higher education experience as they might be had the print material been retained?

---

penetration. Anne Behler (2009) reported on a joint project between Sony and the Pennsylvania State University Libraries to test 100 of Sony's E-Book Readers for general-use lending and in-classroom settings. One issue the libraries had to contend with during the pilot was that the Sony Reader is designed for a single user, or at best a family (the usage terms are for no more than five readers for a single download), which represents serious costs as well as workload considerations. The project's major finding, in terms of library usage, was that "Unfortunately, the current hardware dependent-technology model is not scalable to a larger academic setting, particularly a library-supported one" (p. 57). One of the significant factors in reaching that conclusion, and one that seems applicable to any size library, was the considerable staff time that was required—in order to create numerous separate logins, passwords, alias e-mail accounts, and to load books onto readers. The readers did not fare much better in the classroom setting.

Google Books Project

We are reasonably certain that anyone with more than passing interest in the Web and reading has some knowledge of the Google Books Project (GBP). To say GBP has mixed reviews from many people and diverse groups is an understatement. Probably the only people completely happy with the concept are the attorneys who represent the various parties currently involved in the litigation over Google's idea. By the time you read this, at least eight years will have passed since Google began the effort, and five of those years have been devoted to lawsuits. Many more years are likely to pass before everything is sorted out by the courts. What the ultimate arrangement will be is impossible to predict. While it seems highly likely to be different than what is now (2011) proposed, it appears that it will exist in one form or another.

Other countries have put forward strong objections as well. In September 2009, Google, at a hearing convened by the European Commission, attempted to answer some of the European concerns. They were not all that successful, and in May 2011, three French publishers filed a lawsuit against Google for what they termed illegal scanning of thousands of their titles without permission (*CILIP Update*, 2011, p. 10). Thus, the Google Books Project's global expansion was encountering very real challenges at the time this volume was prepared. Despite this action, in July 2011, Google announced a partnership with the British Library to digitize their materials (Kelley and Warburton, 2011, p. 14).

The goal of the GBP, in a nutshell, is to digitize all the books in major U.S. and foreign libraries and make them available to anyone, with some advertisements associated with what a person views. At some point, only limited access would be provided unless a subscription fee is paid. As noted by Google, end users who search the system "see basic bibliographic information about the book, and in many cases, a few snippets—a few sentences showing your search term in context. If the book is out of copyright, you'll be able to view and download the entire book. In all cases, you'll see links directing you to online bookstores where you can buy the book and libraries where you can borrow it" (http://books.google.com/googlebooks/library.html).

Currently, the project scans all items in a participating library's collection, not just those in the public domain—and does so without gaining permission from copyright holders. Despite the fact that currently only selected portions of copyrighted texts are visible in search results, that approach, as you might imagine, upset a number of authors and publishers, thus the legal wrangles.

The notion that some company would be allowed to make digital copies of copyrighted works got the attention of many rights holders who sued Google in 2005. The case was complex and took until October 28, 2008, before a proposed settlement was reached. The settlement was revised and submitted to the federal judge hearing the case in 2010; in March 2011, the judge rejected the proposed settlement indicating that it would give Google "a significant advantage over competitors, rewarding it for engaging in wholesale copying of copyrighted works without permission, while releasing claims well beyond those presented in the case" (*Authors Guild et al. v. Google Inc.*, p. 2). As noted by Band (2011), the options available to the parties in the suit after the ruling included:

> 1) they could abandon negotiations and litigate the original issue; 2) they could submit a revised (presumably opt-in) settlement; 3) they could appeal Judge Chin's rejection; or 4) the plaintiffs could abandon the suit. All parties have been committed to orphan works legislation, and may return to Congress for a solution. It is too early to say which of these outcomes is most likely. (pp. 1–2)

An article in the September 5, 2009, issue of *The Economist* (2009b) reported: "Now Google and its former antagonists are seeking judicial

---

Check These Out

An overview of the entire GBS legal history is available from the ALA Washington Office Website: http://wo.ala.org/gbs/. Google's report on the settlement may be viewed at http://books.google.com/googlebooks/agreement/.

In addition, Charles W. Bailey has created a "Google Books Bibliography," which is regularly updated, and will help keep you informed about the current state of GBS affairs (http://www.digital-scholarship.org/gbsb/gbsb.htm).

approval for the deal they reached last year to settle the class-action suit. Among other things, this would allow the company to scan millions of out-of-print books, including orphan works, without seeking permission from individual copyright holders" (p. 72). As part of the settlement, Google would set aside funds from sales of digitized works in a special fund (a "book-rights registry") to presumably pay copyright holders a share of the sales income. One impact of the Google/research libraries agreement would be to "in effect create a legally sanctioned cartel for digital-book rights that could artificially inflate the price of library subscriptions" (*The Economist*, 2009a, p. 18).

How does, or will, GBP impact libraries in the long term? There were several components to the service side in the 2010 proposal (all users—free service, all users—fee-based service, free public access service [PAS] for public libraries and not-for-profit academic institutions, and institutional subscriptions). The "current proposal" aspect is particularly noteworthy as clearly Google expected to generate a revenue stream from more than just posting advertisements on the displayed pages. Assuming a settlement is ever reached and implemented, the PAS component would be available to public and nonprofit academic libraries and institutions upon request on a one-"terminal" basis. A public library system would be allowed one such terminal in each building in its system. Academic libraries would be eligible for terminals based on institutional full-time equivalents. Although the settlement mentions the possibility of free or fee-based expansion beyond one terminal, it does not address the when and at what cost such expansion might occur. (Note: K–12 schools and special libraries are not mentioned in the settlement.)

What could a person do at a free library-based Google terminal? All the books in the Institutional Subscription Database would be viewable. The Institutional Subscription Database would include all public domain titles as well as all copyrighted but "not commercially available" titles. Users could print pages from the title at a "reasonable per page charge," the rate to be set by Google in conjunction with its partners. Users could not cut-and-paste text from the material. With an institutional subscription, the user could do the above and cut-and-paste up to four pages at a time and could, using multiple cut-and-paste operations, copy the entire title. Similarly a person could, using multiple commands, print the entire text. However, as noted by Band (2011), with the 2011 court rejection, "access to a relatively comprehensive institutional subscription, had already been reduced significantly compared to the original proposed settlement, and is barred by this decision unless reversed if appealed" (p. 3).

It is unclear what the drafters of the agreement had in mind by the phrase "not commercially available." Are books for sale by out-of-print dealers "commercially available"? It seems likely that the dealers would say so as much of their stock are titles not yet in the public domain and are available for purchase. There is no indication there was anyone from that field at the table when the proposed settlement was reached in 2005. Today, the future is still unclear. The bottom line is we will have to await the "next steps" undertaken by Google, publishers, and libraries before we can realistically assess the impact of the project on library services, library budgets, and collection management activities.

Alternatives to Google Books Project

Alternatives to the GBP include Project Gutenberg (http://www.guten berg.org/ebooks/) and the HathiTrust (mentioned in Chapter 7). Project

---

Check This Out

For a step-by-step discussion of how titles are added to Project Gutenberg, see Nicholasa Tomaiuolo's 2009 article, "U-Content Project Gutenberg, Me, and You," in *Searcher* (17, no. 1: 26–34).

Gutenberg was founded in 1971, with a mission "to encourage the creation and distribution of eBooks" (http://www.gutenberg.org/wiki/Gutenberg:About). Since its inception, Project Gutenberg has grown to include over 36,000 titles—a majority of which are in the public domain. Project Gutenberg is unique in that it is based on the premise of user-generated content (UGC), where individuals are free to contribute content to the project. An outgrowth of the original Project Gutenberg is the Project Gutenberg Consortia Center (PGCC), intended for e-books that are public domain under the U.S. copyright laws (*Searcher*, 2009, p. 32). The goal of PGCC is "to open a Project Gutenberg Consortia Center for each of the major copyright terms throughout the world, starting with 'life +50 and life +70'" (http://www.gutenberg.cc/). Unlike Project Gutenberg, the focus of the PGCC is on the distribution of currently existing e-titles. Over 75,000 titles were available on the site as of mid-2011.

HathiTrust (http://www.hathitrust.org/), on the other hand, is a membership-based organization. Titles in the project come from member libraries who also participated in the GBP but also includes content scanned by participating libraries themselves. The level of access granted to view individual titles is based on the copyright of the work itself (http://www.hathitrust.org/access_use). HathiTrust currently includes digitized books, although in the future, it may evolve to include other archival material. Although speaking on the concept of Institutional Repositories (IR, discussed later in this chapter), Furlough (2009) made the following observation that can be applied to the HathiTrust model: "Commercial agents, such as Google, can outperform existing library systems on speed and breadth of basic searches, but the preservation and scholarly use of digital assets are still fertile ground for libraries, technologists, and library users" (p. 20).

Serials

Everyone, on a general level, loves e-serials. They are frequently the go-to source for articles by many users. They are much more searchable than their print cousins, and they are generally available through libraries 24/7. Those of us who know e-serials in greater depth recognize that the foregoing statements are more or less correct. However, we are also aware that there are a number of "warts" associated with e-serials, which users either do not know about or ignore. Most users have a belief that print and e-journals are identical. They also believe that e-journals are superior to print titles. Funding authorities did, and some still do, believe e-journals will save money in comparison to print subscriptions. Funding authorities also had, and may still harbor, the hope that e-resources will render the library obsolete, thus saving significant amounts of money. Both users and funding agencies probably rarely, if ever, think about long-term access; they believe the information will always be there. CM personnel understand e-serial shortcomings and do their best to address the issues whenever they can.

Of all the beliefs about e-resources, and journals in particular, held by the general public, one that is 100 percent true is that e-journals are much more searchable. Journal database search engines generate more useful information in a shorter time than was ever possible for a single user in a print-only environment.

Even the notion that e-resources are available 24/7 is not completely accurate. Certainly their availability is far superior to print journals given few libraries are open 24/7. However, anyone who engages in almost daily searching of journal databases has occasionally seen the "server not found" error message. Such messages are generally the result of overloaded server demands somewhere in the system. Another "service disruption" is that all servers require some maintenance, which means eventually there must be some downtime. A few vendors, such as *ebrary*, do their maintenance on a regular schedule, which allows the library to post that information for users. (As of early 2011, *ebrary*'s scheduled maintenance period was two hours the first Tuesday of each month.) Lack of availability is a minor problem for most users; however, CM officers ought to monitor the lack of access situation, especially when the library pays for access on the basis of number of simultaneous users. Increasing that number is usually a modest cost consideration, which in return generates greater user satisfaction.

We have mentioned several times that for e-journals, "full text" has different meanings for different e-vendors. Regular users of an e-journal database may be aware, on some level, that it might be necessary to download the text portion of an article in one particular database and do another download(s) for any graphic material (or locate them via another means, such as a print or microform copy). *LexisNexis Academic* is such an example. Users interested in letters to the editor, editorials, advertising, photographs, or tables often find that the e-version lacks one or more of those features. They begin to realize there are differences between the print and e-version of a journal issue. Finally, there is the fact that full-text HTML and PDF files are very different. Anyone with the requirement of providing page citations is not too happy when only an HTML version of an article is accessible.

The notion that e-journals are superior to the paper format, in addition to the full-text issue, is also flawed. E-journals are not always more, or even as, current as the hard copy publication. Today it is less of a problem than when almost all of the hard copies had to be scanned before becoming available for database access. The major issue with currency today is the "embargoes" that some publishers place on digital access to their material. An embargo is a predetermined time that must pass after a paper issue appears and before that material will be made available digitally. Embargoes range in length from a few weeks to a number of months. Why the embargo? The answer is some publishers see it as a means of maintaining paper subscriptions as well as benefiting from online access.

As for saving money, that was and is a vain hope. If anything, the costs have escalated as libraries cannot always cancel the paper subscription when it acquires digital access to the material. In terms of e-serials costs, the picture is murky. How do vendors set their prices? Some of the factors that complicate the pricing situation are:

- Pricing that links paper and digital versions of a title (dropping a paper subscription may raise the price of the e-version),

- Pricing based on the concept of "site" (frequently, branches of a library each count as an independent unit rather than as part of a single system),
- Pricing based on the number of simultaneous users (maximum number of readers allowed at one time),
- Pricing based on a license for a single library versus one obtained through a consortium, and
- Pricing based on only receiving current issues of a title or having access to both the current issues and back files.

Publishers employed a dual pricing model for some time for print titles, offering one price for individual subscribers and another for institutions and libraries. The rationale behind the model was that the institutional subscription provided access for many readers, some of whom might be individual subscribers if it were not for the institutional subscription. For electronic serials, some publishers and vendors employ a somewhat similar tiered model. This model is based on a range of factors, such as the size of the library's acquisition budget or the number of potential readers or users. Most of the tiered schedules have multiple tiers available, using such factors as an acquisitions budget (under $100,000, $100,001 to $250,000, and so forth) as price points. Tiered pricing is rather common for consortia purchases, and the final cost for a library becomes a function of how many libraries decide to participate in the deal.

Some publishers allow free online access when a library or individual places an order for a print subscription. An example is *The Economist*, which allows for online access to back issues, additional material for a story in the print issue, and access to additional news stories. (As of mid-2011, *The Economist* also offered a mobile version of its Website, free mobile device apps for subscribers to access content online, with its full-print version also available for downloading on Kindle and Nook devices. Free iPod audio was also available, with professional newscasters reading the articles.) One reason for providing the access for libraries is that it appears to maintain a subscriber base, which is a factor in how the publication is able to charge advertisers—more subscribers equals a higher advertising fee. The extra material available online becomes a bonus for the library users.

Some libraries have a hope that going e-only would cut costs. The December 2010 issue of *College & Research Library News* carried an article related to such hopes. Michael Hanson and Teresa Heidenwolf (2010) wrote about a small college library's experience with employing a pay-for-view service for some journal articles. The authors indicated the library's goals for the project were twofold. It had hoped "not only to [increase] users' access to journals and [reduce] costs, but also to [get] a better picture of what our faculty and students would use if they had access to all of a publisher's titles" (p. 586). After a year of use, the library found there was little match between what was used and what it had subscribed to in the past. Previous subscriptions were used, but not as much as new titles. Hanson and Heidenwolf concluded their article by noting, "we expect that when we have a year's worth of use data from other publishers' packages they will similarly revel that our selections were not as on-target as we had presumed" (p. 588). Although the article did not explore the cost side of the project, you might expect, given the usage data for both old and new titles, the prospect of cutting costs were dim at best.

Online Music/Audio

Selecting music resources, be it print scores, CD recordings, or digital files, calls for an understanding of the subject in more depth than most other format and subject areas. Daniel Zager (2007) identified eleven elements in the selection decision:

- Composer
- Instrumentation
- Editor and reputation
- Series
- Score type (full, study, vocal/piano)
- Competing versions by other editors/publishers (p. 568).

- Genre and work
- Edition/Arrangement
- Publisher and reputation
- Date (new or reprint)
- Cost

Although the focus in the above is slanted toward classical music, these elements are applicable to almost all other music genres. They are also not all that different from the general selection elements we covered in Chapter 4.

Music was one of the first nonprint formats that libraries added to their collections more than 100 years ago. It remained a mainstay in many academic and public libraries until the start of the 21st century. Libraries with such collections today find them aging and not the most current, as issues within the recording industry and the digital world have made developing an e-music collection a challenge. As is true of so many e-information resources, music has been entangled with legal issues.

A few years ago, D. J. Hoek (2009) wrote:

> I am not an expert on current or future technologies, and I certainly am no authority on copyright or licensing, but I do have a particular interest in building, preserving, and providing access to music collections. It appears that recent changes in the distribution of sound recordings are challenging our ability to continue this most foundational aspect of our profession. (p. 55)

The changes Hoek referred to were, and remain, the growing use of download-only music files, especially from major record labels. One of his examples of the challenges for libraries trying to acquire such recordings was Deutsche Grammophon's decision to release a 2008 prize-winning recording of Berlioz's *Symphonie Fantastique* by the Los Angeles Philharmonic Orchestra only as a digital download file. Why is this problematic? The issue is that such files are only legally available from the company or from iTunes, both of which have a license agreement stating the file is only for sale to end users. The sticking point is that libraries are, and always have been, distributors of information, not the end users.

To a degree, the problem now facing library music collections arose during the first few years of this century as the music industry attempted to address the digital world. Peer-to-peer file sharing technologies and services, such as Kazaa and Napster, led to widespread sharing of music files without permission, much less payment to, copyright holders. For the recording industry (Recording Industry Association of America [RIAA]), the issue was significant in that a very high percentage of those engaged in this activity were young people who had previously been a mainstay component in the sales of recordings. RIAA started actively pursuing those who downloaded files illegally. The RIAA was able to add language to a digital copyright bill (Digital Millennium Copyright Act, DMCA—P.L. 105-304; http://www.copy right.gov/legislation/pl105-304.pdf) that made any Internet service provider (ISP) also liable for illegal downloads unless it actively assisted in enforcing copyright laws. (That addition made any organization providing its staff or members with Internet access an ISP, including academic, public, and school libraries.) By 2005, legal actions against individuals and the firms that provided the peer-to-peer services had slowed the downloading activity. Both Kazaa and Napster still exist—but as subscription-based services (Kazaa charging $9.99 a month, and Napster offering several options based on the type of access—computer only or computer and mobile bundled—ranging from $4 to $10 a month). Both have extensive language in their "terms and conditions" documents outlining activities prohibited by copyright (Kazaa: http://www.kazaa.com/#/terms, Napster: http://home.napster.com/info/terms .html). During and since that time the industry has also changed its distribution practices, as Hoek identified, which has had an impact on music access through libraries.

So, what are the options for libraries wishing to provide access to digital music files for their users? As of 2011, there are only a few choices available beyond securing downloads from recording companies that do not have end-user-only licenses. Essentially, the only other option is through aggregator services, something that some music librarians believe does away with one of CM's basic functions—selecting individual items. One of the firms offering such packages is Alexander Street Press, mentioned earlier in this chapter. Alexander Street Press started online music access in 2010. As of mid-2011, its collections covered classical, jazz, contemporary world music, the *Smithsonian Global Sound*® package, and a product called "American Song" that covers a variety of American music genres. The files are fully accessible on iPhones and iPad Touch devices, and users can create personal playlists. Subscriptions also include access to scores (Nesting, 2010, p. 54). The vendor hopes to have over 1 million recordings available. Libraries subscribing to all of the collections will also get access to a collection of 140,000 popular music files (http://alexanderstreet.typepad.com/music/2010/02/music-online-to-triple-in-size.html).

Another music aggregator is Naxos Music Library (http://www.naxos musiclibrary.com). It is a service specifically designed for music education and libraries. By mid-2011, its Website indicated it had over 54,000 CD-length recordings consisting of over 785,000 individual files, including classical, jazz, classic rock, nostalgia, and world music. In addition to the files themselves, Naxos provides access to liner notes, original cover artwork, and other production data. Other features include a pronunciation guide for composer and artist names, a glossary and guide to musical terms and work analyses, interactive music courses for Australia, Canada, South Korea, the United Kingdom, and the United States, graded music-exam playlists, and a "junior" section. Subscriber fees are based on the number of simultaneous users the library requires.

A not-for-profit "aggregator" is DRAM, which focuses on the educational community's interest in streaming music (http://www.dramonline.org/). Its focus is on U.S. music. The service is available to member libraries (academic and public) and allows in-library and remote access to its files through an authorized institution. The maximum fee, in 2011, was less than $2,000 for the largest academic libraries and $800 for the largest public libraries.

A major online resource for print reference material about music is *Oxford Music Online* (http://www.oxfordmusiconline.com/). Included in the

---

Check These Out

A good article on using an "aggregator" for library music collection building is Stephanie Krueger and Philip Ponella's 2008 essay "DRAM/Variations3: A Music Resource Case Study," in *Library Hi Tech* (26, no. 1: 68–79).

A sound summary of the history of joint efforts in creating music collections in libraries is Karl Madden's 2010 article "Cooperative Collection Management in Music: Past and Present," in *New Library World* (111, nos. 7/8: 333–346).

An interesting article by a nonlibrarian that deals with collecting musical recordings is Carlos R. Abril's 2006 piece "Music that Represents Culture: Selecting Music with Integrity," in *Music Educators Journal* (93, no. 1: 38–45).

Another article worth reviewing is Kate Pritchard's (2010) "Let's Get This Party Started," which provides insight into how a library might use streaming music with teenagers (*School Library Journal* 56, no. 3: 34–37).

---

package is *Grove Music Online*, which itself contains *The New Grove Dictionary of Music and Musicians* (2nd edition), *The New Grove Dictionary of Opera*, and *The New Grove Dictionary of Jazz* (2nd edition), and updates to these titles. *Oxford Music Online* also includes access to *The Oxford Companion to Music*, *The Oxford Dictionary of Music*, and the *Encyclopedia of Popular Music*.

We end this section about online audio with a brief note regarding audio books. Audiobooks on EBSCO*host*® (formerly Netlibrary) offers iPod compatible e-books for libraries to make available to users either through direct purchase, short-term lease, or as part of a subscription package (http://www.ebscohost.com/audiobooks/home). Three other resources are OverDrive (http://www.overdrive.com/), Ingram Digital (http://www.ingram digital.com/), and Recorded Books (http://www.recordedbooks.com/). Over-Drive is a relatively recent supplier to libraries and focuses on digital material; Ingram is a long-standing supplier of books to bookstores and libraries, while Recorded Books has a K–12 focus.

Video

You may have seen, and perhaps read, an article or two regarding possible changes to the concept of "net neutrality." If so, you, like many others of us, probably gave only a passing thought, if any, to what implementations there might be for libraries if such changes were to take place. In the past, any data packet on the Internet was and, as of the time we prepared this section, still is treated the same (net neutrality). That is, no packet had a higher or lower priority for transmission. What some bandwidth service providers (telephone and cable companies, for example) propose is a system of preferential service for those who pay a fee. What that would mean, if it happens, is any organization paying a fee could deliver faster, better quality material (especially image-rich files such as video) than those not paying the fee. Those proposing the change argue that packets that take up more bandwidth should pay a higher fee and the current system penalizes everyone with, if nothing more, having slower service. Opponents suggest such a system would allow those with "deep pockets" to dominate service. In late 2010, the Federal Communications Commission (FCC) voted in favor of the net neutrality order (Terry, 2011, p. 108). However, as of early 2011, "two bills seeking to prohibit the FCC from regulating the Internet have already been introduced, H.R. 96 and H.R. 166" (p. 112). The outcome of the proposed bills and their ultimate impact is uncertain as we prepared this volume. It probably will be something in between the opposing views, with some type of prioritization of data with an associated cost, but at a much lower level than bandwidth companies want.

Our point in discussing the above is that libraries must carefully consider how capable their technological infrastructure is before moving into online video activities. Available bandwidth matters for both the sending and receiving parties.

There are two aspects to online video and libraries—access to content produced by others and access to library generated content. Both are likely to increase in importance over time as it is obvious people like visual materials. Just looking at the growth of YouTube makes it clear how attractive video material is for many people.

Library-generated content is a topic beyond the scope of this book, but something CM officers should keep in mind. This area is likely to grow quickly and become enmeshed with collection management activities. Although commercial video production company quality may be desirable, it is clear that anything slightly above the average YouTube quality is acceptable to most people. Thus, with even modest equipment with some planning, time, and effort on the library's part, a library can produce acceptable online video content. What are some of the possibilities?

- On demand "how-to-use" instruction for library services/databases.

- On demand information literacy sessions.

- On demand library tours.

- On demand reviews of collection resources by staff and/or users.

- On demand staff training sessions.

- On demand "how-to-do" pieces on some activity (not necessarily library related—fixing a leaky faucet—with perhaps a connection to existing library resources).

- Public relations material, coverage of library events, storytelling, and so forth.

The list is only limited by your imagination and, of course, the time to do it.

Providing access to video content from other sources has been a long-standing CM activity. We discussed traditional video formats and their limitations in the previous chapter.

On the academic library side, the Arizona Universities Library Consortium (AULC) started an on-demand service for accessing streaming video that may prove to be a workable model for groups of educational libraries (Farrelly, 2008). In 2008, the group partnered with Films Media Group, an outgrowth of a long-standing film organization Films for the Humanities, allowing students and faculty members access to all 5,500 educational videos available from the company. (The service, Films On Demand, is available at http://ffh.films.com/digitallanding.aspx.) Through this program, members of the AULC—including the University of Arizona, Arizona State University, and Northern Arizona University libraries—provide on- and off-campus students with access to the films; when any title has been accessed three times, AULC purchases the perpetual streaming rights for that title. The AULC

Check These Out

Public Libraries has a regular section about Internet/technology news, ideas, and services. Michael Porter and David Lee King are often contributors to that section. One of their essays related to library-generated online video worth reviewing is "Hi-Fi, Sci-Fi Libraries" (47, no. 5: 35–37, 2008).

Another article on the same topic is Kathy Fredrick's 2008 article titled "Streaming Consciousness: Online Video Sharing," in *School Library Media Activities Monthly* (24, no. 10: 44–46).

Jason Paul Michel, Susan Hurst, and Andrew Revelle (2009) wrote about "Vodcasting, iTunes U, and Faculty Collaboration" in the *Electronic Journal of Academic and Special Librarianship* (10, no. 1, http://southernlibrarianship.icaap.org/), while Angela Jowitt (2007) explored the reactions of users to a library's podcasting activities, not all of which were favorable in "Perceptions and Usage of Library Instructional Podcasts by Staff and Students at New Zealand's Universal College of Learning" (*References Services Review* 36, no. 3: 312–336).

Other examples of how library-generated video can be employed are Wei Fang's "Online Law School Video Repository: The Flash Way" (*Computers in Libraries* 29, no. 6: 20–24, 2009); Scott Nicholson's "Inviting the World into the Online Classroom" (*Journal of Education for Library and Information Science* 51, no. 4: 233–240, 2010); and Jennifer Wooten's "Want to Get Teens Excited About Summer Reading? Just Add Video. Flipped!" in *School Library Journal* (55, no. 5: 38–40, 2009).

---

hosts the files on its server (Farrelly, 2008, p. 67). As noted by Farrelly, "the AULC/FMG On Demand agreement is believed to be the first and a unique attempt at a patron-driven acquisition model for streaming video" (p. 68).

We have already mentioned three sources of online video—Alexander Street Press, Films Media Group, and OverDrive. OverDrive is the only one of these three vendors that offers popular movies, television series, and children's programs. We also mentioned Naxos in the section on online music; that firm also provides online video of musical performances and is strong in the area of ballet. Once the major motion picture studios work out a pricing system for libraries and educational institutions in general, we expect there will be a growing number of library vendors (Baker & Taylor and Brodart, for example) that currently offer DVDs that will also offer online video services.

Web Resources

As information professionals know all too well, there is "stuff" and "good stuff" on the Web. Serious efforts are made to help others learn how to assess Websites and other e-resources through programs such as information literacy sessions or courses. Another approach is to post links to the "good stuff" that are believed to be accurate, informative, and useful on library Websites.

Is posting such links part of CM's activities? We most certainly believe so. Selecting appropriate sites is not that different from selecting other library resources, although it is a little more time consuming. Unlike other resources, Websites have a habit of changing over time. One great advantage of Webpages is they are relatively easy to update, delete material on, and even take down. They also have a habit of changing URLs with no notice. Thus, unlike other resources that once they are in the collection do not change in character and content, Websites are moving targets. That in turn means someone should monitor the sites on a regular schedule.

Surfing the Internet can be enjoyable, but is not all that efficient for identifying potential appropriate sites for linking from the library's Web-pages. Seeking out online Webliographies is a quicker approach. Another method is to look at links other libraries have in place. Most libraries have a formal or informal list of libraries they consider their peers which they employ from time to time for comparative purposes. Starting with those libraries' Webpages is a good way to monitor what may be appropriate for your users. Discussion lists are yet another source for identifying possible additions for your links.

One concern with Web material is there is no vetting of the type you come to depend on with other collection formats. Anyone can post anything, claim credentials not held, and so forth, as no one is responsible for verifying any of the sites' content. Thus, when surfing for potential sites, you are on your own. Some of the more obvious issues are out-of-date information, opinions stated as facts, biases, and more and more often just plain old-fashioned fraud. None of us are experts on all the topics we may be responsible for when wearing our CM hats. Having some input from other information professionals is useful, if not essential.

One long-standing online, at least in Internet terms, resource for learning about Websites that have been "reviewed" by information professionals is the Internet Scout Project (http://scout.wisc.edu). The service has been operational since 1994 with the goal to develop "better tools and services for finding, filtering, and presenting online information and metadata. . . . Our turnkey portal software, for example, allows digital collection developers to share their unique online materials with colleagues and students throughout the world" (http://scout.wisc.edu/about). The *Scout Report* appears online each Friday providing a current awareness service regarding Web resources. Another resource that can be particularly useful in school and public library settings is "Great Web Sites for Kids," updated by the American Library Associations' Association for Library Service for Children (http://www.ala.org/greatsites).

Needless to say, there are books listing Websites; however, they are of limited value except in the first year or two after publication as Web addresses and content change quickly. Professional journals that review library materials generally also review potential Web resources—for example, *Booklist*'s "Reference on the Web" section. *College & Research Library News* has an "Internet Resources" section in most of its issues that are topical in character. Although many of the topics are oriented toward higher education, many others are not. A few examples of subjects that could be of interest to any type of library are:

- Human rights (May 2011)
- Alternative news and information (January 2011)
- Preparing for retirement (December 2010)
- Grant writing on the Web (October 2010)
- Health care management resources (September 2009)
- Alternative energy (2005)

A subscription to *College & Research Library News* is not required in order to access the "Internet Resources" archives. They are available online at http://crln.acrl.org/content/by/year. Search "Internet Resources."

Keeping links current and reevaluating the Webpage content takes time. Someone should have the responsibility to check all the links on a regular basis. When there is a change, the person(s) who selected the sites should review the pages to check on the changes. Broken links and poor quality changes are not minor matters. Too many of such problems will quickly lead to doubts about the quality of other library services, especially among younger users who spend large amounts of time online.

Institutional Repositories (IR)

There is no doubt that scholars and researchers, regardless of their discipline, have added new approaches to their collaborative activities over the past 10 to 15 years as the Internet became ever more available. It took a long time, more than 100 years, for librarians to begin to get a handle on what has been called the "invisible college" and associated "gray literature." New methods of communication and the ease of collaborating with scholars around the world have made the challenge for information professionals greater than ever.

What are the invisible college and gray literature? As you may guess, the "college" is a label for what is more popularly known as social networking. One desired outcome of scholarly work is to "advance humankind's knowledge" and perhaps improve life. One result of that objective, as we noted earlier in the text, is fewer and fewer individuals knowing more and more about less and less. In some fields of research and scholarship, there may only be a dozen or so people in the world with identical research interests. Getting to know and interacting with those individuals are important activities for a researcher. They share ideas, data, and insights in order to advance all their work. In the days of snail mail, land-line telephones, and travel grants, it was difficult to know all those in the world who shared one's research interests. International conferences were very important to the networking process. Today, E-mail, wikis, collaborative software, and so forth have changed the picture dramatically.

"Gray literature" was and is the material, text, and data that result from the sharing between scholars. Only a small proportion of a researcher's work ever appears in the "open" or published literature (books and journals). Close colleagues often share drafts of potential open literature material. Feedback often leads to changes and deletions, with the published version being very different from the early drafts. It was and is a vetting process prior to that of the traditional prepublication vetting. Some of the material that does not make "the final cut" can provide useful clues to further work for others, if they learn about the material. Conference papers and presentations were and still are of value to people long after the program is concluded. Only a small percentage of such papers ever appear in the open literature. In the past, exchanging copies of such presentations was common. Today such exchanges still take place, but in electronic form. For a library serving researchers, tracking down hard copies of such presentations was difficult at best. That difficulty is compounded today.

IRs are an effort to capture and make available as much of the gray literature as possible. The IR concept itself is relatively new, with the term first being introduced post-2000. Clifford Lynch (2003), a proponent of information technology and expanding its scope in libraries, defined institutional repositories as a set of services that a university offers to the members of its community for the management and dissemination of digital materials created by the institution and its community members. It is most essentially an organizational commitment to the stewardship of these digital materials, including long-term preservation where appropriate, as well as organization and access or distribution. (p. 328)

By 2005, there were 815 universities in 13 countries offering IR programs (van Westrienen and Lynch, 2005). Certainly that number has grown since then.

Like the concept of the information commons, the idea of such repositories has a variety of meanings and functions depending on the institution. To some degree, the term repository suggests one of the less positive views about academic libraries—as a storehouse of little used, dusty materials. This is unfortunate as such programs are active in nature rather than a static image of a storehouse. Most scholars know little about IR services at present and, for a majority of those who do, find the word repository less than positive. Perhaps as they become aware of and use services such as OAIster® they will have a different view of the concept. We discuss OAIster® below.

The purpose of a repository program is to encourage the campus community (students and faculty especially) to deposit or contribute material they create as part of their teaching, learning, and scholarly activities that may have broader interest than the original purpose that led to its creation. Further, the program makes this material available, normally through open access, to anyone worldwide who has an interest in the topic.

A major open source repository software program is DSpace (http://www.dspace.org), first created in 1991 through a partnership by MIT and Hewlett-Packard. Government, research, commercial, and academic institutions throughout the world currently use DSpace technology to manage their repository activities (http://www.dspace.org/whos-using-dspace). Other possibilities include the "Digital Commons" from Berkeley Electronic Press™ (http://digitalcommons.bepress.com/), Eprints' (http://www.eprints .org) Open Access and IR services, and ExLibris's (http://www.exlibrisgroup .com) SFX® OpenURL Link resolver and "MetaLib" products. A library must decide which option will work best for its planned application.

What is included in many of the existing IRs? The most common elements are data sets, draft documents, other gray literature, theses and dissertations, grant proposals, conference presentations, and a variety of institutional digital material. In many ways, the IR concept is a variation of what the profit sector calls knowledge management. That is, IRs are an effort to gain some control over and provide structure and access to the many varieties of digital material every organization produces every day.

Access to the content of IRs is the key to success for library IR programs and services. Open access material is searchable through a Google search; however, those materials are lumped together with hundreds, if not millions, of other hits. Users, if they read or use some IR items, are unlikely to realize that fact. To employ a marketing term, the material is not "branded." Thus the material will do little to improve the scholars' perception of IR programs. Earlier we mentioned OAIster®, which is a free search tool designed just for IR materials. The program is accessible through its own URL (http://oaister .worldcat.org/). The program was developed by the University of Michigan Library's Digital Library Production Service and is now a joint program with OCLC. As of mid-2011, there were over 23 million records in the database from more than 1,100 institutions (http://www.oclc.org/oaister/sup port/OAIster.htm). It employs what is called the Open Archives Initiative Protocol for Metadata Harvesting (OAI-PMH) program.

Gaining the support from the campus community to contribute material to the IR can be challenging. As noted by Connell (2011), "All institutional repositories face the issue of content recruitment" (p. 253). One method employed at some institutions in order to ensure materials are contributed is to require that all thesis and dissertations be submitted in a digital format that is compatible with the IR software. A few institutions have expanded this concept to include undergraduate capstone or honors papers.

With regard to establishing IRs, Mike Furlough (2009) cautioned that "No library should implement a digital repository program without examining the role it will play in its broader strategy for collection development, stewardship, and providing access to its primary constituencies. The strategy should be based on a clear understanding of the community's needs and the requirement for long-term stewardship of the data collected" (p. 22).

Creating an IR is not easy. There are three big issues involved: technology, staff time, and getting people to provide e-materials. Soo Young Rieh and Kevin Smith (2009) argued against widespread use of IRs, indicating "The Open Archives Initiative Protocol for Metadata Harvesting (OAI-PMH) provides a structure for creating repositories searchable through Google and made interpretable with other repositories and search tools, but its application requires a degree of sophistication that may not be available at every university" (pp. 12–13).

One final thought on IRs. Currently they are more likely to be found in a research university environment. However, as seen with DSpace, IRs

---

Check These Out

The fall 2008 (vol. 57, no. 2) issue of *Library Trends* has the theme "Introduction: Institutional Repositories: Current State and Future," with several interesting articles, including "Perceptions and Experiences of Staff in the Planning and Implementation of Institutional Repositories" by Soo Young Rieh, Beth St. Jean, Elizabeth Yakel, Karen Markey, and Kim Jihyun (pp. 168–190), and Dorothea Salo's "Innkeeper at the Roach Motel" (pp. 98–123), which provides an argument for providing adequate resources for repository activities.

Charles Bailey maintains an extensive "Institutional Repository Bibliography," which is updated periodically (http://digital-scholarship.org/irb/irb.html).

Mark P. Newton, C.C. Miller, and Marianne Stowell Bracke explored the efforts of the e-Data Task Force to create a data repository at Purdue Libraries in their 2011 article titled "Librarian Roles in Institutional Repository Data Set Collecting: Outcomes of a Research Library Task Force" (*Collection Management* 36, no. 1: 53–67). The repository itself is accessible at http://www4.lib.purdue.edu/lcris/edata/.

Two additional articles worth reviewing are Ronald C. Jantz and Myoung C. Wilson's "Institutional Repositories: Faculty Deposits, Marketing, and the Reform of Scholarly Communication," in *Journal of Academic Librarianship* (34, no. 3: 186–195, 2008), and Mary Piorun and Lisa A. Palmer's "Digitizing Dissertations for an Institutional Repository: A Process and Cost Analysis," in *Journal of the Medical Library Association* (96, no. 3: 223–229, 2008).

In addition, an in-depth overview of the scholarly communication landscape is provided by Nancy L. Marin and K. Kirby Smith in *Current Models of Digital Scholarly Communication* (Washington, DC: Association of Research Libraries, 2008).

can be created for virtually any organizational type. Given this, we think they will become more widespread as the technology becomes less complex to use. Perhaps the label for the concept will change as well. School district libraries and programs might consider using an IR approach for teaching materials created by their faculty. Exemplary student work might also be included in such a program. Public libraries might become key components in local government's efforts to make better use of staff digitally generated materials. Will it happen? Probably not in the short term, as the technology is presently too complex for most libraries. In time, that is very likely to change.

Managing Electronic Resources

E-resources are wonderful, especially from the end user's perspective. They also create a number of challenges for CM personnel, their libraries, as well as consortia. For the individual, there is a virtual alphabet soup of technical concepts with implications for e-materials to understand— some of which are DC®/DCMI, DLF, DMCA, DOI®, DRM, EAD, ERMI, OAI, PURL, SFX®, and XML. All of these, and more, relate to managing library e-resources in one way or another. Because you are likely to run across these concepts in your CM work, we briefly review them below.

Dublin Core® (DC, http://dublincore.org/) is outside the scope of this text, but will likely be encountered elsewhere in your degree program. The Dublin Core Metadata Initiative (DCMI) focuses on providing standards to assist in finding, sharing, and managing digital information. Many of the standards underlay a majority of the e-products a library provides access to and the manner in which the library provides that access.

The Digital Library Federation (DLF, http://www.diglib.org) is a program managed under the umbrella of the Council on Library and Information Resources. Although research libraries are the primary members of DLF, its initiatives benefit any library engaged in creating and maintaining e-resources. One such effort is ERMI (Electronic Resource Management Initiative, http://www.diglib.org/standards/dlf-erm02.htm), which addresses the process of managing licensed products.

DMCA (Digital Millennium Copyright Act, P.L. 105-304, http://www.copyright.gov/legislation/dmca.pdf) is a law we mentioned in the section on e-music. Its scope is broad and has implications for how all e-resources are handled. We cover this law and other copyright issues in Chapter 11.

A Digital Object Identifier (DOI®) is somewhat like an ISBN or ISSN. A DOI® is designed to be a permanent indicator of an item's location on the Web, thus making the management of "intellectual property in a networked environment much easier and more convenient, and [allowing for] the construction of automated services and transactions" (http://www.doi.org). Some libraries use the DOI®, when available, rather than a URL as it provides a more stable link to the material. A listing of publications on the DOI® concept is available at http://www.doi.org/publications.html.

DRM (Digital Rights Management) is a set of "technologies" that e-producers (books, games, music, serials, and video) may employ to control access to and use of their copyrighted material, especially copying, by third parties. From a library resource point of view, the use of DRM technologies can and may prevent legal fair use activities by end users. Knowing what, if any, DRM technologies are embedded in a product or service is important during the selection process. The ALA Digital Rights Management Webpage (http://www.ala.org/ala/issuesadvocacy/copyright/digitalrights/index.cfm) provides a glossary of terms as well as links to DRM resources and legislation. This is a legal issue that we will explore in more depth in Chapter 11.

EAD (Encoded Archival Description, http://www.loc.gov/ead/index.html) is now part of the Library of Congress's service program, in partnership with the Society of American Archivists. It is a standard for machine readable finding aids for e-materials created by archives, libraries, museums, and repositories. The standard employs SGML (Standard Generalized Markup Language) and XML (see below) as the base for encoding information.

The OAI (Open Archives Initiative) is a group that

> develops and promotes interoperability standards that aim to facilitate the efficient dissemination of content. OAI has its roots in the open access and institutional repository movements.... Over time, however, the work of OAI has expanded to promote broad access to digital resources for eScholarship, eLearning, and eScience. (http://www.openarchives.org/)

One of the accomplishments of this group was the development of a metadata harvesting program we mentioned in the repository section of this chapter—OAI-PMH.

OpenURL is the standardized (and very familiar) "Web address." It was developed by the National Information Standards Organization (NISO), a component of the American National Standards Institute (ANSI) as standard Z39.88. OCLC (http://www.oclc.org/research/activities/openurl/default .htm) is the body currently responsible for maintaining the standard.

A Persistent Uniform Resource Locator (PURL) helps address the problem we noted in the Web resources section of this chapter—disappearing URLs. PURLs, also developed at OCLC, enable individuals to locate items even if the original Web address has changed. In this way, PURLs provide a "continuity of references to network resources that may migrate from machine to machine for business, social or technical reasons" (http://purl .oclc.org/docs/index.html).

As mentioned in the IR section of this chapter, SFX® (http://www .exlibrisgroup.com/category/SFXOverview) is an Open URL link resolver. SFX® is a proprietary program developed by ExLibris. Many libraries use SFX® as it provides extra benefits such as e-usage data. Having sound e-usage data is critical when it comes to evaluating collection resources.

XML (eXtensible Markup Language, http://www.xml.com/) is one of many document markup languages in existence. With any full-text material, whether book or serial, one issue to consider is the way the text was digitized: ASCII, Adobe, HTML, or SGML. ASCII is the oldest and in many ways, the easiest approach to digitization. However, with ASCII, one loses most of the formatting of the original document, as well as any images. Adobe Acrobat PDF (Portable Document Format) is an approach that retains formatting and images and is frequently encountered on the Internet. HTML (Hypertext Markup Language) is probably the most common method used on the World Wide Web. It is in fact a sublanguage of SGML (Standard Generalized Markup Language). Many organizations used SGML to digitize their internal documents; however, the currently favored standard is XML. There are several advantages to using XML: it is an international standard, and it is device and system independent. Having documents in a standard markup language makes it easier to change systems without incurring significant document conversion costs.

The above is just a sample of the variety of terms encountered by CM personnel and their libraries when they become involved with e-resources. End users don't really care about the technology side of e-resources, they just want them available 24/7; how that takes place is the library's concern. By the time you read this chapter, it is highly likely the soup will be even thicker. One source that can be helpful in deciphering other terms encountered is Joan M. Reitz's *ODLIS: Online Dictionary for Library and Information Science* (http://www.abc-clio.com/ODLIS/odlis_A.aspx).

Points to Keep in Mind

- Both traditional and e-formats will likely coexist for some time to come. Each has something to offer libraries and their users.

- Selecting e-resources, although employing many of the same criteria as traditional formats, is a more complex process. There are more factors to take into account, especially technological factors, and it is often a group process with participants inside and outside your library.

- Technological considerations are central to making the final decision, with the library's technological infrastructure and the vendor technological requirements carrying equal weight in the final decision.

- E-books are likely to be increasingly popular. For libraries, the proprietary aspect of the current devices creates substantial challenges and cost considerations.

- A shift to e-serials is an ongoing process in most libraries, as they secure the necessary funding or are able to leverage the price advantages of consortia pricing of publishers' or aggregators' packages.

- E-serials are likely to remain the largest percentage of a library's e-resources during the lifetime of this edition.

- E-music has become a challenge for libraries due to producer concerns regarding who may have access to what and on what terms.

- Streaming video is likely to become a major source of video content for libraries.

- Institutional repositories, while currently used to increase access to and use of scholarly information, have long-term potential for all libraries as technologies become easier to implement and maintain.

- Electronic resources management has several elements; two of the more significant components are how the library provides access to its e-resources and how it handles the maintenance of such materials.

- Managing e-resources is challenging as you need to understand current information technologies as well as monitor new developments.

Works Cited

Algenio, Emilie, and Alexia Thompson-Young. 2005. "Licensing E-Books: The Good, the Bad, and the Ugly." *Journal of Library Administration* 42, nos. 3/4: 113–128.

Allis, Sam. 2010. "Cushing Academy's Bookless Library a Popular Spot." *Boston Globe* November 6: G13.

Authors Guild et al. v. Google, 05 Civ. 8136 (DC 2011). http://www.nysd.uscourts .gov/cases/show.php?db=special&id=115.

Band, Jonathan. 2011. "A Guide for the Perplexed Part IV: The Rejection of the Google Books Settlement." ALA Washington Office. http://www.district dispatch.org/wp-content/uploads/2011/04/GuideIV-FINALV3.pdf.

Behler, Anne. 2009. "E-readers In Action." *American Libraries* 40, no. 10: 56–59.

Bertot, John Carlo, Charles McClure, and Joe Ryan. 2001. *Statistics and Performance Measures for Public Library Networked Services*. Chicago: American Library Association.

CILIP Update. 2011. "French Publishers Sue Google for $14 Billion." *CILIP Update* 10, no. 6: 10.

Connaway, Lynn Silipigni, and Heather L. Wicht. 2007. "What Happened to the E-Book Revolution: The Gradual Integration of E-Books into Academic Libraries. *Journal of Electronic Publishing* 10, no. 3. http://hdl.handle .net/2027/spo.3336451.0010.302.

Connell, Tschera Harkness. 2011. "The Use of Institutional Repositories: The Ohio State University Experience." *College & Research Libraries* 72, no. 3: 253–274.

Doering, William, and Galadriel Chilton. 2009. "ERMes: Open Source Simplicity for Your E-Resource Management." *Computers in Libraries* 29, no. 8: 20–24.

The Economist. 2009a. "Google's Big Books Case." 392, no. 8647, September 5: 18–21.

The Economist. 2009b. "Tome Raider." 392, no. 8647, September 5: 72–73.

Farrelly, Deg. 2008. "Use-Determined Streaming Video Acquisition: The Arizona Model for FMG On Demand." *College and University Media Review* 14, no. 1: 65–78.

Furlough, Mike. 2009. "What We Talk About When We Talk About Repositories." *Reference and User Services Quarterly* 49, no. 1: 18–32.

Hanson, Michael, and Teresa Heidenwolf. 2010. "Making the Right Choices: Pay-Per View Use Data and Selection Decisions." *College & Research Libraries News* 71, no. 11: 586–588.

Hoek, D.J. 2009. "The Download Dilemma." *American Libraries* 40, nos. 8/9: 54–57.

Holden, Jesse. 2010. *Acquisitions in the New Information Universe*. New York: Neal-Schuman.

Jewell, Timothy D. 2001. *Selection and Presentation of Commercially Available Electronic Resources*. Washington, DC: Digital Library Federation and Council on Library and Information Resources. http://www.clir.org/pubs/ reports/pub99/pub99.pdf.

Jewell, Timothy D., Ivy Anderson, Adam Chandler, Sharon E. Farb, Kimberly Parker, Angela Riggio, and Nathan D.M. Robertson. 2004. *Electronic Resource Management: Report of the DLF ERM Initiative*. Washington, DC: Digital Library Foundation. http://www.diglib.org/pubs/dlf102/.

Kelley, Michael, and Bob Warburton. 2011. "British Library, Google Plan Digitization Project." *Library Journal* 136, no. 12: 14.

Koehn, Shona L., and Suliman Hawamdeh. 2010. "The Acquisition and Management of Electronic Resources: Can Use Justify Cost?" *Library Quarterly* 80, no. 2: 161–174.

Kovacs, Diane K. 2007. *The Kovacs Guide to Electronic Library Collection Development*. 2nd ed. New York: Neal-Schumann.

Lynch, Clifford. 2003. "Institutional Repositories: Essential Information for Scholarship in the Digital Age." *ARL Monthly Report*, no. 226. Washington, DC: Association of Research Libraries.

Miller, William. 2008. "Moving into the World of E-Books." *Acquisitions Librarian* 19, nos. 3/4: 161–163.

Murray, Adam. 2008. "Electronic Resource Management 2.0: Using Web 2.0 Technologies as Cost-Effective Alternatives to an Electronic Resource Management System." *Journal of Electronic Resources Librarianship* 20, no. 3: 156–168.

Nesting, Vicki. 2010. "New Product News: Alexander Street Streaming Music and Video Content to Go Mobile in 2010." *Public Libraries* 49, no. 2: 54–55.

Peters, Tom. 2010. "As the Book Changes Form the Library Must Champion Its Own Power Base: Readers." *APLIS* 23, no. 1: 16–21.

Pritchard, Sarah. 2008. "Deconstructing the Library: Reconceptualizing Collections, Space, and Services." *Journal of Library Administration* 48, no. 2: 219–233.

Rieh, Soo Young, and Kevin Smith. 2009. "Institutional Repositories: The Great Debate." *Bulletin of the American Society for Information Science and Technology* 35, no. 4: 12–16.

Searcher. 2009. "Interview with Michael Hart." 17, no. 1: 32–33.

Stemper, Jim, and Susan Barribeau. 2006. "Perpetual Access to Electronic Journals: A Survey of One Academic Library's Licenses." *Library Resources and Technical Services* 50, no. 2: 91–109.

Terry, Jenni. 2011. "Net Neutrality." *College & Research Libraries News* 72, no. 2: 108, 112.

van Westrienen, Gerard, and Clifford Lynch. 2005. "Academic Institutional Repositories: Deployment Status in 13 Nations as of Mid 2005." *D-Lib Magazine* 11, no. 9. http://www.dlib.org/dlib/september05/westrienen/09westrienen.html.

Whittaker, Martha. 2008. "The Challenge of Acquisitions in the Digital Age." *Portal: Libraries and the Academy* 8, no. 4: 439–445.

Wilson, Lizabeth A. 2008. "Local to Global: The Emerging Research Library." *Journal of Library Administration* 48, no. 2: 127–139.

Wolf, Robert. 2009. "Budget Crisis: A Review of Perpetual Access." *North Carolina Libraries* 67, no. 1: 34.

Zager, Daniel. 2007. "Essential Partners in Collection Development: Vendors and Music Librarians." *Notes* 63, no. 3: 565–575.

Suggested Readings

Best, Rickey D. 2009. "Is the 'Big Deal' Dead?" *Serials Librarian* 57, no. 4: 353–363.

Bobay, Julie. 2008. "Institutional Repositories: Why Go There?" *Indiana Libraries* 27, no. 1: 7–9.

Clobridge, Abby. 2010. *Building a Digital Repository Program with Limited Resources*. Oxford, UK: Chandos.

Colvin, Jenny. 2010. "For Your Consideration: Models for Digital Music Distribution in Libraries." *Music Reference Services Quarterly* 13, nos. 1/2: 35–38.

Davis, Denise. 2010. "E-Books: Collection Vortex or Black Hole?" *Public Libraries* 49, no. 4: 10–13, 53.

Donlan, Rebecca. 2007. "Decision Points for Going E-Only: Beware the Fallacy of the Single Solution." *Reference Librarian* 47, no. 1: 121–124.

Dougherty, William C. 2010. "The Google Books Project: Will It Make Libraries Obsolete?" *Journal of Academic Librarianship* 36, no. 1: 86-89.

Feick, Tina, and Gary Ives. 2006. "Big E-Package Deals: Smoothing the Way Through Subscription Agents." *Serials Librarian* 50, nos. 3/4: 267–270.

Griscom, Richard. 2003. "Distant Music: Delivering Audio Over the Internet." *Notes* 59, no. 3: 521–541.

Jones, Edgar. 2010. "Google Books as a General Research Collection." *Library Resources and Technical Services* 54, no. 2: 77–89.

Kenney, Brain, 2009. "The Trouble with Google: Why Have School Libraries Been Left Out in the Cold?" *School Library Journal* 55, no. 4: 11.

Koehn, Shona L., and Suliman Hawamdeh. 2010. "The Acquisition and Management of Electronic Resources: Can Use Justify Cost?" *Library Quarterly* 80, no. 2: 161–174.

Mihlrad, Leigh. 2010. "A Brief Introduction to ERMS." *Journal of Electronic Resources in Medical Libraries* 7, no. 2: 151–158.

Miller, Rachel. 2007. "Acts of Vision: The Practice of Licensing." *Collection Management* 32, nos. 1/2: 173–190.

Morris, Carolyn. 2008. "Issues in Vendor/Library Relations—Buying eBooks: Does Workflow Work? Part I." *Against the Grain* 20, no. 4: 85–87.

Morris, Carolyn. 2009. "Issues in Vendor/Library Relations—Buying eBooks: Does Workflow Work? Part II." *Against the Grain* 20, no. 6: 76–77.

Morrison, Heather, and Andrew Waller. 2008. "Open Access and Evolving Scholarly Communication." *College & Research Library News* 69, no. 8: 486–490.

Nichols, Jane. 2011. "Perusing Google eBookstore." *Collection Management* 36, no. 2: 131–136.

Pogue, David. 2010. "The Trouble with E-Readers: Electronic Books Are Still Too Crude to Replace Ink and Paper." *Scientific American* 303, no. 5: 36.

Polanka, Sue. 2011. *No Shelf Required: E-Books in Libraries*. Chicago: American Library Association.

Porter, Michael, and David Lee King. 2010. "E-Books, E-readers, and Next Steps." *Public Libraries* 49, no. 6: 20–23.

Price, Kate, and Virginia Havergal, eds. 2011. *E-Books in Libraries: A Practical Guide*. London: Facet.

Raab, Ralph. 2010. "Books and Literacy in the Digital Age." *American Libraries* 41, no. 8: 34–37.

Redden, Linda. 2005. "Video Streaming in K–12 Classrooms." *Media and Methods* 42, no. 1: 14–15.

Sale, Arthur. 2010. "Advice on Filling Your Repository." *Serials* 23, no. 3: 207–211.

Schmidt, Karen, Wendy Allen Shelburne, and David Steven Vess. 2008. "Approaches to Selection, Access, and Collection Development in the Web World: A Case Study With Fugitive Literature." *Library Resources and Technical Services* 52, no. 3: 184–191.

Shelburne, Wendy Allen. 2009. "E-Book Usage in an Academic Library: User Attitudes and Behaviors." *Library Collections, Acquisitions, and Technical Services* 33, nos. 2/3: 59–72.

Slater, Robert. 2009. "E-Books or Print Books, 'Big Deals' or Local Selections—What Gets More Use?" *Library Collections, Acquisitions, and Technical Services* 33, no. 1: 31–41.

Slater, Robert. 2010. "Why Aren't E-Books Gaining More Ground in Academic Libraries? E-Book Use and Perceptions: A Review of Published Literature and Research." *Journal of Web Librarianship* 4, no. 4: 305–331.

Stamison, Christine M. 2011. "Developing a Sound E-Book Strategy." *Information Outlook* 15, no. 5: 10–12.

Stewart, Christopher. 2011. "Keeping Track of It All: The Challenge of Measuring Digital Resource Usage." *Journal of Academic Librarianship* 37, no. 2: 174–176.

Walker, Mary. 2009. "E-Resource Statistics: What to Do When You Have No Money." *Journal of Electronic Resources Librarianship* 21, no. 3: 237–250.

Waller, Andrew, and Gwen Bird. 2006. "'We Own It': Dealing With 'Perpetual Access' in Big Deals." *Serials Librarian* 50, nos. 1/2: 179–196.

White, Marilyn, and Susan Sanders. 2009. "E-Resources Management: How We Positioned Our Organization to Implement an Electronic Resources Management System." *Journal of Electronic Resources Librarianship* 21, nos. 3/4: 183–191.

Williams, Greg. 2011. "EPUB: Primer, Preview, and Prognostications." *Collection Management* 36, no. 3: 182–191.

10
Preservation Issues

Preservation, a hallmark of great libraries, plays an important role in maintaining quality collections by requiring libraries to "think outside the book" both literally and physically with regards to environment, storage, and handling.
—Michael A. Arthur and Lee Dotson, 2009

Technological and economic developments have caused us to look at preservation in new ways and to change our approach to its management. To a large extent, the field has gone from single item conservation, which focuses on the treatment of one object at a time, to preventive conservation, which endeavors to make the most effective use of new technologies to preserve not just single items but entire collections.
—Sherelyn Ogden, 2007

New developments [in technology] suggest fascinating implications for the cultural heritage community involved in the work of image preservation and access.
—Karen F. Gracy, 2007

Though electronic information surrounds children today from their preschool years on, books will still be central in imparting the written record of civilization. Sitting cross-legged on the floor at story time, children are read to from a book. When they are tucked in at bedtime, Mom reads to them from a book.
—Nancy Kalikow Maxwell, 2006

Libraries have and continue to invest millions of dollars in their collections. People often forget that investment is substantially greater than the cost of the items acquired and any needed license fees. Whether it is a physical or virtual item, the library also invests staff time and equipment in acquiring, processing, and maintaining each one. Those costs generally equal or exceed the item's initial purchase price. Achieving the maximum return on those investments over time is an essential part of the library's stewardship responsibility. It is the long-term aspect of that stewardship that is the focus of this chapter.

Preserving and conserving resources is an essential element in achieving long-term usage and value for monies spent. Some of the components of preservation and conservation are active, while others are passive. Many of the passive elements are a matter of thinking and planning for possible eventualities. With luck, those plans never require implementation.

Successfully accomplishing long-term use and value of collections requires total staff involvement, not just by CM personnel. Certainly the CM officers will play a lead role in the process as well as carrying out some of the requisite activities. However, some of the activities that allow for the long-term success in this area are the responsibility of others. Preservation is an area where success is dependent on true teamwork on the part of the entire staff. Conservation is usually handled by one or two of the staff or by outside specialists.

People often use the terms preservation and conservation interchangeably. Doing so causes no great misunderstanding; however, the terms do have different meanings in the world of archives, libraries, and museums. We follow the definitions of the terms developed by the Society of American Archivists (SAA). SAA's first two definitions of preservation are:

> 1. The professional discipline of protecting materials by minimizing chemical and physical deterioration and damage to minimize the loss of information and to extend the life of cultural property.
> 2. The act of keeping from harm, injury, decay, or destruction, especially through noninvasive treatment. (http://www.archivists .org/glossary/term_details.asp?DefinitionKey=78)

The society's definition of conservation is:

> The repair or stabilization of materials through chemical or physical treatment to ensure that they survive in their original form as long as possible. (http://www.archivists.org/glossary/ term_details.asp?DefinitionKey=79)

Our focus in this chapter is primarily on preservation rather than conservation. That is, the maintaining of collections for as long as possible in their original state.

Libraries and Cultural Patrimony

Archives, libraries, and museums are the primary guardians of society's heritage. Each has a role to play in attempting to ensure that knowledge, beliefs, values, and so forth are available generation after generation. T.J. Swanson (2008) suggested how museums, archives, and libraries assist people today to better understand the past. He observed that "Since their first appearance in Boston in 1791, American historical societies have served as repositories for unique collections of locally significant books, archives and artifacts . . . historical society libraries remain invaluable resources for history researchers" (p. 31). Michael Gorman (2007) made a clear case for preservation when he wrote, "The term 'cultural heritage' contains within it a clear implication—that of onward transmission. The word 'heritage' means something transmitted by or acquired from a predecessor. In order for that generational transfer to take place, the item of cultural heritage must be recorded and preserved" (p. 95).

If they ever think about the matter, most people assume that once a library, archive, or museum acquires an item it will be there forever. Information professionals in these fields know this is not the case for all items. In Chapter 6, we covered the concept of deselection (withdrawing items from the collection). Museums use the term deaccession for their withdrawal or transfer process. Some archives have, as part of their responsibilities, housing the operational documents or records of its parent organization. Many of those records are only retained for a specified time (retention schedule is the term archivists/record managers use for the process), after which the material is usually destroyed. Clearly not every item has long-term value for cultural heritage purposes.

It is also reasonably clear that some person or group of persons must make decisions regarding what to or not to preserve. Preserving an item is no small decision, as there is a daily cost, if very small in size, associated with its retention. It is a little like the story of the foolish businessman who agrees to hire a person for a penny for the first day's work and then to double that amount each succeeding workday. The first week's cost is still only a few cents; however, the amount becomes overwhelming a few weeks later. The cost of preserving some items may far outweigh any cultural heritage benefit or value. Many of the items retained are not actually assessed but simply occupy space until a space problem or other issue forces thoughtful consideration. Information professionals play a significant role in transmitting cultural heritage and one many do not think about as they carry on their daily work duties. Michèle Cloonan (2007) noted, "It is clear that preservation decisions may be multifaceted. In selecting items to preserve, the curator must be cognizant of the sensitivities that may ensue and the other

Something to Ponder

Advisory Board member Virginia Walter addressed the cultural patrimony issue from the point of view of a researcher, noting:

As somebody who does research on children's literature that often requires looking at out-of-print books, I am frequently frustrated by collection development policies that favor weeding to create a user-friendly contemporary collection over the archiving of materials needed by scholars. Social historians, as well as children's literature specialists, find much that is useful in children's books of the past. Where are we going to find all of those books about the planet Pluto or the brontosaurus when scientists determined that those entities no longer exist? Children's librarians rightfully removed the misleading books from their shelves so as to not give children inaccurate information—but isn't it important to know that those books once proclaimed the "truth"?

What are your thoughts on the matter? What priority should be given to preserving information or items that, although outdated, was considered "current knowledge" at a certain point in time?

issues they may face" (p. 141). She went on to observe that "We can preserve some things some of the time, but not everything all of the time" (p. 145).

Preserving the Investment in the Collection

Neither size nor type of library has much to do with a library's need to think about and act on the issue of preservation. As Swanson (2008) stated, even small libraries can and do have items of value from a heritage point of view. Even the smallest school library must get the "maximum mileage" out of the items it acquires. Thus, the first few sections of what follows has relevance for all libraries.

There is a small percentage of materials that have a short useful (shelf) life (such as annual telephone directories and the like). However, the vast majority of library acquisitions have a substantial, if not indefinite, expected shelf life. To realize a long-term shelf life, the staff must take steps to preserve the material.

There are several aspects to preserving a collection. Some are relatively simple to carry out, such as proper handling and storage of materials, environmental control (temperature and humidity), security (to protect against theft and mutilation), disaster preparedness planning, basic conservation (binding and repair), and insurance. Most of these issues are broad concerns, and detailed discussion of them is beyond the scope of this book; however, we do briefly touch on each topic. All these factors work together to prolong the useful life of the materials in the collection. Even insurance fulfills this function, because claims payments will help the library replace damaged items.

Other issues, such as acidic paper, have been preservation problems for many years. Acidic paper is one that is, or was, an issue for the largest libraries with long-term preservation responsibilities. Today, there is hope that scanning such material will reduce the costs as well as ensure long-term preservation. The hope may be a vain one, at least in terms of reducing costs; more about digital preservation later in this chapter.

Proper Handling

"Housekeeping" may appear to be part of the fussy librarian stereotype that some of the general public holds about libraries and librarians. If people understood that some of the "fussy practices," such as keeping volumes upright on the shelf, are part of an effort to maximize usage of materials acquired with their money, the image might change a little. Storage and handling are the two fundamental steps in preserving a collection. Neither step requires extra expenditures on the part of the library, but both require the participation of all staff. Libraries purchase storage units from time to time; some thought is necessary regarding what is the most appropriate type of storage unit available for the particular format. (This does not necessarily translate into the most expensive unit.)

Too narrow or shallow a shelf (particularly for oversized/folio items) will result in items being knocked off and damaged, or worse—falling off and injuring someone. Filling shelves or drawers too tightly is a poor practice. Equally harmful is allowing the material to fall over on the shelf (because proper supports are lacking) or slide around in a drawer, because either practice will lead to damage in time. Buying adjustable shelving units provides the library a measure of flexibility.

Check This Out

One interesting article on the merits of proper shelving practices is Anthony F. Verdesca Jr.'s 2010 article "On Sherpas and Shelving Books," in *Journal of Access Services* (7, no. 3: 191–194).

Anyone with some experience in shelving books (except a conservation specialist) probably has found a way to squeeze "just one more book" onto a shelf when good practice calls for shifting the material to provide proper space. This often happens when shelvers are under pressure to finish shelving a book truck within a certain time period. Having sound performance standards is proper management; however, libraries must be certain that the reshelving standard includes time for shifting materials. Failure to do so leads to cracked book spines, as well as torn headbands resulting from users or staff attempting to pull an item from a tightly packed shelf. Books should be vertical or horizontal on the shelf, not leaning this way or that. Fore-edge shelving should be avoided because it places undue strain on the binding (bindings are designed for horizontal or vertical storage). Proper supports and bookends help to keep materials in good order.

Part of CM's responsibility is to ensure the staff understands the reason for housekeeping practices that appear arcane. Efforts to train the users are not likely to have much payoff when considering the time and effort required. (Although it is possible this tactic would be effective in a school library setting.)

Environmental Control

Climate control (temperature and humidity) is a key component of a preservation program. Few libraries are able to follow the example of the Newberry Library in Chicago, where 10 stories of stacks are double-shelled, windowless, and monitored by a computerized environmental system. Something much less complex will still help extend the useful life of most materials. The major concerns for environmental control are humidity, temperature, and light. Architects and librarians attempt to take these issues into account when planning a library building. This is often easier said than done, because the ideal environmental conditions for humans and those for preserving materials don't match. For example, the book stacks for the Newberry Library storage facility call for a constant temperature of 60°F +/–5°F.

Few people are happy engaging in sedentary work all day in a room with a 60-degree temperature. Most library designs place human comfort ahead of material preservation. The only time designers can effectively meet both sets of requirements is in situations like the Newberry, where the stacks are closed to the public and even employees are in the stacks for only short periods. Still, this arrangement does not answer all concerns about the environment for preserving materials. There also are differences in the ideal conditions for preserving various types of materials. Thus, building design characteristics are almost always a compromise with the people factor carrying the most weight.

Parent institutional energy conservation requirements also lead to cooler winter temperatures and warmer summer temperatures. Cooler winter temperatures are better for materials, but normally the temperature is still well above 65 degrees. The greatest damage occurs in summer, when reducing air conditioning costs becomes an institutional priority. (A related problem is that changes in air temperature affect relative humidity.) One way to reduce air conditioning costs is to turn off the system when the library is closed, but overnight shutdowns are damaging to materials. When the system is off for some time, such as the weekend, the temperature can rise dramatically. When the air conditioning is turned back on, the temperature falls fairly quickly. This roller coaster of temperature and humidity swings is more damaging to materials than storing them at a steady, somewhat higher temperature. Temperature cycling is damaging (it ages paper prematurely), but so are high temperatures. For every rise of 10 °C, book paper deteriorates twice as fast. With rapid fluctuations in temperature, the primary problem is the humidity level, which causes damage to the materials.

Why is a swing in temperature and humidity damaging to collections? Almost every item in the collection is a composite of materials. Hard-bound volumes are the most complex in their composition. Certainly the bulk of material is paper of more or less standard weight; however, even that is inconsistent across a collection. For example, art books with high-quality color illustrations will have a coated paper for the illustrations, while the text, more often than not, is on an uncoated paper. The different papers will expand and contract at different rates as the temperature and humidity varies, which stresses the volume. The reality is there is more than a difference in paper quality involved in a typical volume. Volumes also contain one or more types of cardboard in the binding, a cloth backing for the binding, thread used to sew the binding, and various adhesives. Each of these materials reacts to temperature and humidity at different rates. Media formats also consist of several types of material with different expansion and contraction rates. The amount of stress from one cycle of temperature and humidity fluctuation is very small. However, this issue is similar to the low daily cost of an item's long-term retention; over time the small increments add up to very real problems.

From the Authors' Experience

At one point, Evans was head of a three-story branch library and archive at a large university. The library had been collecting print and manuscript material for over 147 years. Needless to say, the collections had and continue to have value to researchers worldwide.

The library's ventilating system was under the centralized control of the university's facilities department. There was no local control over the environment. One of the facilities department's priorities was keeping energy costs as low as possible. Because the library was not open weekends, facilities would turn the temperature down to 45 degrees during the winter, turned off the air conditioning in summer for the weekend, and would adjust the temperature on week nights. The result was wild temperature swings in the collections of 35 to 40 degrees on an ongoing basis.

When Evans supplied the senior managers of the library system with data about the great variations in temperature and humidity, a major confrontation took place between the library system and the facilities department. It took the university president to step in and resolve the matter. The good news was that the libraries gained local control of their environments. In this case, long-term preservation of collections thankfully overrode the issue of short-term energy savings.

The Library of Congress Preservation Leaflet no. 2 (1983) recommends a temperature of 55°F in book storage areas and a maximum of 75°F (below 70°F, if possible) in reading areas, all with a 50 percent relative humidity. Paul Banks, a well-known preservation specialist who set the standards for the Newberry storage area, also recommended 50 percent relative humidity.

Other materials (microfilms, videotapes, photographs, and so forth) have somewhat different ideal temperature and humidity storage requirements. The ideal range for microforms is 70°F +/–5° with humidity at 40 percent plus or minus 5 percent. The same ranges apply to still photographs and safety motion picture film. In contrast, nitrate-based motion picture film must be stored below 55°F but can tolerate humidity up to 45 percent. Videotapes do best at 65°F +/–5° and no more than 45 percent humidity. Audiodiscs (LPs, 45s, and so forth) can handle temperatures up to 75°F and 50 percent humidity. However, the upper limits for audiotapes are 70°F and 45 percent humidity.

The National Archives set even higher standards when it established its facility in College Park, Maryland. Text and map storage areas called for 70°F and 45 percent relative humidity. Black-and-white film, audiotapes, and sound recordings have a 65°F and 30 percent relative humidity limit. Glass negatives, black-and-white photographs and negatives, slides, posters, and electronic materials are in areas with 65°F temperature and 35 percent relative humidity. Storage areas for color photography film, slides, and photographs are still cooler—38°F and 35 percent relative humidity. Coldest of all is the storage areas for color motion picture film and color serial film, at 25°F and 30 percent relative humidity.

Recalling basic chemistry, we know that increasing the temperature also increases chemical activity. Roughly, chemical reactions double with each 10 °C increase in temperature. Freezing books would be the best way to preserve them; however, it is not likely that readers would be willing to sit about in earmuffs, overcoats, and mittens. Libraries are fortunate to achieve a controlled temperature below 70°F in areas where people work for extended periods. One reason for wanting the lower temperatures is to slow down the chemical decomposition of wood pulp paper, which many books and journals contain. However, lower temperatures only slow the process, but they do not stop it.

Light, both natural and artificial, negatively influences preservation in two ways. First, it contributes to the heat buildup in a building. Naturally, designers take this into account when specifying the building's heating, ventilating, and air conditioning system. Fluorescent lighting is not a major heat contributor, but in older libraries where incandescent fixtures exist, the heat generated by the fixtures can be a problem. If the light fixtures are close to materials (i.e., in exhibit cases), there can be significant temperature differentials from the bottom to the top shelf in a storage unit. Sunlight can generate miniclimates, hotter near windows than the rest of the space. The Newberry Library's windowless storage unit eliminates the sunlight problem. Many libraries have designs featuring numerous windows to provide natural lighting (thus reducing electric costs) and to satisfy users' desire to see outside. The cost of these designs has been high in terms of money spent after a few years to reduce the sunlight problem and to repair damaged materials.

A second concern with light is ultraviolet radiation, a result of sunlight, fluorescent, and tungsten lights. Ultraviolet light is the most damaging form of light because it quickly causes materials to fade, turn yellow, and become brittle. Windows and fluorescent light fixtures should have ultraviolet

---

Check This Out

Mold can be a serious problem for paper-based collections and people as well. For example, *Aspergillus fumigatus* can be toxic, in sufficient quantities, and many molds can cause serious (even debilitating) allergy problems for some people. A good source of information about controlling mold is the Northeast Document Conservation Center's (2007) "Emergency Salvage of Moldy Books and Paper" (http://www.nedcc.org/resources/leaflets/3Emergency_Management/08SalvageMoldyBooks.php).

---

screens or filters built in or installed. Tungsten lighting has the lowest levels of ultraviolet radiation, but even these lights should have filters. The longer one exposes materials to unfiltered light, the more quickly damage occurs. Nonprint materials are even more sensitive and they require greater protective measures than do print materials.

Air filters that reduce the gases in the air inside the library are useful, if expensive. Urban activities pump a variety of harmful gases into the air every day. Some enter the building as people come and go. Few buildings have airlocks and ventilating systems that remove all harmful gases. Whenever it is economical, the ventilation system should remove the most harmful substances. Sulfur dioxide is a major air pollutant and a concern for preservation programs, because it combines with water vapor to form sulfuric acid. Hydrogen sulfide, another common pollutant, also forms an acid that is harmful to both organic and inorganic materials. In addition to gases, air filters can also reduce the amount of solid particles in the building's air. Dust and dirt include mold spores, which can cause problems if the air conditioning fails in warm, humid weather. Solid particles act as abrasives, contributing to materials wearing out. Dusty, gritty shelves wear away the edges of bindings—and, all too often, dusting books and their shelves is not in anyone's job description (or included as part of the regular custodial/maintenance contract).

Finally, insects contribute to the destruction of books and other items in the collection. Silverfish enjoy nothing more than a feast of wood pulp paper, flour paste, and glue. Cockroaches seem to eat anything, but have a particular taste for book glue. Termites prefer wood, but wood pulp paper is a good second choice. Larder beetle larvae (book worms), though lacking intellectual curiosity, can devour *War and Peace* in a short time. Finally, book lice enjoy the starch and gelatin sizing on paper. Other less destructive insects can infest collections in the temperate zones; in a tropical setting, the numbers and varieties increase dramatically.

Control of insects presents a few challenges, because pesticides create pollution problems. Naturally, the best control is to keep the insects out. One way to control insects, especially cockroaches, is to keep food and drink out of the library. A second step is to keep the temperature and humidity as low as possible, because insects multiply faster and are more active at higher temperatures and humidity levels. If the library faces a significant insect infestation, it is better to call on a commercial service rather than attempt to handle the problem with library staff.

What are the signs of insect infestation? Most of the insects that cause damage prefer the dark and to stay out of sight. When one sees them, it is a signal that the population may be so large that there is nowhere to hide. Obviously, if one finds "remains" of insects on shelves, windowsills, or the floor, it is a sign of potential trouble. Unusual dust, "sawdust," or colored

---

Check These Out

An older, but still good source of information about pest management in libraries and archives is Chicora Foundation, Inc.'s (1994) *Managing: Pests in Your Collection* (http://palimpsest.stanford.edu/byorg/chicora/chicpest.html). This is one of many resources available on COnservation OnLine (COOL's) "Pest Management" Webpage (http://cool.conservation-us.org/bytopic/pest/).

More recent entries on the topic are Jacqueline E. Shalberg's (2008) "An Introduction to Integrated Pest Management for Libraries, Museums and Archives" (*Indiana Libraries* 27, no. 3: 84–88), and Bruce E. Massis and Angel Gondek's (2011) "Bedbugs in our US Libraries" (*New Library World* 112, nos. 7/8: 377–381).

---

powder on bookshelves is likely to be "frass" (insect droppings) and is a clear indication of a problem. Other ways pests can enter the collection are through items returned by patrons. In one 2009 case, a patron was barred from the Denver Public Library because of repeatedly returning loaned items (including titles borrowed through ILL) that were infested with bedbugs. Over 30 titles returned by the patron had to be destroyed ("Bedbugs Lead to PL Ban," 2009, p. 14).

Gifts to the library require careful examination before being stored in any area where insects could get into the general collection. Shipments that arrive from overseas also need careful study. As the concern for the environment increases, many in-library fumigation units have ceased to operate or been extensively (and expensively) modified. This may mean using commercial systems, with additional costs and delays in getting and keeping material on the shelf.

Security

We include physical security of the collection in our discussion of preservation because some of the issues are conservation issues—for example, mutilation and water or smoke damage.

A full-scale library security program involves several elements. Broadly, the program's goals are to ensure the well-being of people and to protect the collections and equipment from damage or theft. What follows emphasizes the collections, with only passing mention of the people and equipment issues; topics covered include theft, mutilation, and disaster preparedness. For a fuller discussion of security programs, see chapter 14 of Evans and Carter's *Introduction to Library Public Services* (7th edition, 2009).

We tell people, only half in jest, that if a library wishes to identify its true core collection, all it has to do is prepare a list of all the lost and missing books and mutilated journal titles. Normally, these are the items that, for one reason or another, are (or were) under pressure from users, including high-use materials.

Every library loses books each year to individuals who, if caught by the security system, say they forgot to check the material out. Journals and other noncirculating material are subject to some degree of mutilation. Each incident of theft and mutilation means some small financial loss for the library, if nothing more than the cost of the material and the labor expended getting the item ready to circulate. Other costs include staff time in searching for the item, deciding how or whether to replace it, and acquisitions processing. Though a single incident seldom represents a significant cost, the total annual cost may be surprising, even if one calculates only the amount paid for replacement materials. Many academic libraries spend more than $20,000 per year on replacement materials, and few of those replacements are for items too worn to remain in circulation. This rate of loss occurs despite a high-quality electronic security exit system and targeting every book and every issue of every journal that goes into the collection. Needless to say, time and money expended to prevent theft or replace materials is time and money not spent on expanding user resources.

There are several givens for an exit control or security program. First, there will be some level of loss no matter what the library does. Second, the systems help basically honest people stay honest. A professional thief will circumvent almost any library security system, as Stephen Blumberg and David Siegelman demonstrated a few years ago (Allen, 1991). Therefore, the library must decide how important the problem is and how much loss it can tolerate. The goal is to balance the cost of the security program against the losses. The less loss the library will accept, the higher the security costs, so finding the proper balance is important.

Most libraries employ some mix of people-based elements and electronic systems for security. Door guards or monitors who check every item taken from the library are the most effective and most costly option. This method works well only when the person doing the checking is not a peer of the people being checked. That is, using students to check fellow students, much less their teachers, does not work well. Retired individuals are very effective. They interact well with users but also do the job without favoring anyone. The major drawback to exit monitors, after the cost, is, when there are peaks and valleys in the exit flow, there can be long queues during the peaks.

Electronic exit control systems are common and often give a false sense of security. Every system has a weakness that the person who regularly "forgets to check out books" eventually discovers and the professional thief knows. Also, some materials (for example, magnetic tape and videotape) cannot have the "target" deactivated without damaging the content, and some materials simply do not have a place for a target. Some systems are susceptible to electronic interference, such as frequencies generated by computers or even fluorescent light ballasts. Finally, the inventive thief can jam the operating frequency and no one on the staff would know the difference.

From the Authors' Experience

Saponaro worked at a university library that was plagued one summer with what seemed to be frequent fire system "false alarms." What was originally thought to be a faulty alarm system actually turned out to be the work of a thief who would pull the fire alarm as they were getting ready to exit the building with titles they had removed from the business and economics collection. Once they left the library, they would then proceed to strip the items of their property markings and attempt to sell them to an off-campus book buyback facility. The facility then alerted campus police. Through the combined efforts of campus police and library staff, one of whom saw the individual exit the library during one of the alarm incidents, the individual was arrested and later tried and convicted. It was later revealed the individual was a graduate of the university, and this individual had indeed been pulling the alarms to "cover" for the thefts, as that enabled the person to exit through one of the library's emergency exits undetected.

Mutilation is another ongoing problem, which, during a year, can generate a surprisingly large loss for the library. There are few cost-effective options for handling this problem. Having copy services available and at competitive prices will help. Monitors walking through the building will reduce many security problems but will not stop mutilation. Studies suggest that even users who see someone mutilating library materials will not report the activity. One option that customers do not like, but that does stop the mutilation of journals, is to supply only microform back files of journals that are subject to high mutilation. This option does not safeguard the current issues, and it requires providing microform reader-printers, which are more expensive than microform readers. Another option is to keep current issues of titles prone to theft or mutilation in a staff-only area and make them available for in-house use only. This option requires staff time and effort in terms of retrieving and refiling the titles, but can be an alternative to theft or mutilation concerns. Web-based services are a partial answer to some of the problems, assuming the library can afford the digital back files. Theft and mutilation are a part of doing business. How much they cost the library depends on the local situation. Those costs come at the expense of adding greater variety to the collections and, in the long run, they hurt the user.

Disaster Preparedness

Disaster preparedness planning is vital for the protection of people, collections, and equipment. Planners must think in terms of both natural and man-made disasters. Earthquakes, hurricanes, tornadoes, heavy rains, and floods are the most common natural disasters for which one should plan. (In 2011, Japan suffered a devastating 9.0 earthquake, combined with a tsunami, showing that in extreme situations, multiple disasters can occur at once.) The most common man-made disaster is water damage, which can be caused by a broken water pipe or sprinkler head, a faulty air conditioning system, or broken windows and the result of not having adequate funding for preventive maintenance. In the case of a fire, water may cause more damage than the flames.

The following are the basic steps to take in preparing a disaster plan:

1. Study the library for potential problems. Often, the institution's risk management officer (insurance) is more than willing to help in that assessment.

2. Meet with local fire and safety officers for the same purpose.

3. Establish a planning team to develop a plan. This team may become the disaster handling team.

4. Establish procedures for handling each type of disaster and, if appropriate, form different teams to handle each situation.

5. Establish a telephone calling tree, or other fast notification system, for each disaster. A *telephone tree* is a plan for who calls whom in what order.

6. Develop a salvage priority list for the collections. If necessary, mark a set of floor plans and include them in the disaster planning and response manual. Most plans do not have more than three levels of priority: first priority is irreplaceable or costly materials, second priority is materials that are expensive or difficult to replace, and

third priority is the rest of the collection. Some plans include a category of "hand-carry" one or two items from the immediate work area, if the disaster strikes during normal working hours. Establishing priorities can be a challenge for planners, because everyone has some vested interest in the subject areas with which they work.

7. Develop a list of recovery supplies the library will maintain on site (for example, plastic sheeting and butcher paper).

8. Include a list of resources—people and companies—who could assist in the recovery work.

After the planners finish a disaster response plan, the library should make it available to all staff on site, as well as to those off site so that disaster team members may access it easily via a staff Website or intranet. Others who may want copies are the group within the parent organization that plans for disaster response efforts and the local fire station. Practicing some of the response efforts is critical to achieve a successful outcome when a problem does strike.

Locating water, gas, and electrical system shutoffs is a good starting point for training the disaster team. Next, the team should check fire extinguisher locations to determine whether the units are operational and are inspected regularly. The team also should implement a program to train staff in use of the extinguishers. Usually, the local fire department will do this at no charge. There are three types of fire extinguishers: "A" for wood and paper fires, "B" for oil and electrical fires, and "C" for either type of fire. Match the type to a location and anticipated problems. Floor plans should clearly identify locations of shutoffs and extinguishers.

Salvage operations require careful planning and adequate personnel and materials. It is a good idea to develop a list of potential volunteers if the situation is too large for the staff to handle within a reasonable time. Keep in mind that the library can count on only about 72 hours of assistance from volunteers—that is, 72 hours from the time the first request for assistance goes out. Thus, there should be a plan for what to do after 72 hours, if the disaster is major.

Water damage is a potentially destructive problem, as is the development of mold and mildew. Mold can develop in as little as 48 hours, depending on the temperature. What basic steps should one follow in a water emergency? The best way to handle large quantities of water-soaked paper is to freeze it and process the material as time and money allow. Planners should identify companies with large freezer facilities and discuss with them the possibility of using or renting their freezers in case of emergency. Often, such companies are willing to do this at no cost, because of the good publicity they gain from such generosity. Large grocery store chains and meat packing plants are possible participants. Refrigerated trucks can be most useful, if costly to rent. Getting wet materials to the freezing units is a problem: milk crates, open plastic boxes, or clothes baskets work well, because they allow water to drain. Plastic interlocking milk crates are ideal, because they are about the right size for a person to handle when three-fourths full of wet material. Sometimes, local dairies are willing to assist by supplying free crates for the duration of the emergency.

Freezer or butcher paper is best for separating the materials. Never use newsprint, because it tends to stick to wet paper and the ink comes off. Finally, find some drying facilities. There are three primary methods of drying wet

---

Check These Out

A variety of disaster-related online information is available at the Conservation OnLine (COOL) "Disaster Preparedness and Response" Webpage (http://cool.conservation-us.org/bytopic/disasters/). This includes Peter Waters's 1993 *Procedures for Salvage of Water-Damaged Library Materials* (http://cool.conservation-us.org/bytopic/disasters/primer/waters.html).

Another source of information is ALA's "Disaster Preparedness and Recovery" Webpage (http://www.ala.org/ala/issuesadvocacy/advocacy/federallegislation/govinfo/disasterpreparedness/index.cfm).

---

books: (1) freezing/freeze-drying, (2) vacuum drying, and (3) vacuum freeze-drying. Vacuum freeze-drying is the best way to handle wet items. Often, vacuum drying facilities are difficult to locate and can handle only a small volume of material at a time, so materials may be in the freezer for a long time while a small quantity is done whenever the source and funding permit.

Two other steps are important when designing a disaster preparedness plan. One is to identify the nearest conservation specialist(s). Most are willing to serve as a telephone resource, and often they will come to the scene. A second important step is to arrange for special purchasing power. Although some groups, organizations, and companies may be willing to assist free of charge, many will not, and the library may need to commit quickly to a specific expense. Having to wait even a few hours for approval may cause irreversible damage.

Although most disasters are minor—a few hundred water-damaged items—a large disaster is always possible. One example was the April 1986 fire that struck the Los Angeles Public Library. For more than 10 years, there had been concern about the fire danger, but the hope that a new building would be constructed forestalled major modifications in the existing building. According to *Library Hotline* (1986, p. 2), it took 1,700 volunteers working around the clock to shrink-wrap and freeze the 400,000 water-soaked books (about 20 percent of the Central Library's collection). In addition, the city paid a salvage contractor $500,000 for the firm's services (p. 2). One can only speculate what the costs and problems might have been with no disaster preparedness plan.

Another major water damage event took place in 1997 at Colorado State University. After an unusually heavy rainstorm, major flooding occurred on the campus, with much of the water damming up against the wall of the lower level of the library. The wall collapsed as a result of the water pressure and a huge wave of water poured into the building. More than 500,000 items, with an estimated value of more than $100 million on the lower level, became water soaked (Kniffel, 1997, p. 16). Recovery took several years to fully realize. Although insurance helped cover some of the costs, the final recovery was assisted by donations of materials from libraries and publishers (Delaney, 1998, pp. 59–70).

The above suggests that library insurance may assist in the recovery after a major disaster. Like personal home fire or renters insurance, there is almost always a deductible as well as issues of what the insurance actually will cover. Most standard policies do not include flood damage except at an extra cost and other water damage (such as a break in a sprinkler system pipe) may be a topic of debate with the insurance company.

It is essential to have face-to-face discussions, prior to purchasing insurance coverage, to have a clear understanding of what is and is not covered and on what basis payments are made. Discussions regarding the collection valuation can be interesting, especially when it comes to what to do about coverage for special collections and archives materials. If a Shakespeare folio is stolen or destroyed by fire, it is highly unlikely the library could ever replace it, even if the library insured the folio for several million dollars. Risk managers and insurance agents rarely see the point of covering something that is irreplaceable.

Anyone who has dealt with homeowners' or renters' insurance representatives and policies can understand the complexities involved. The usual payment is based on replacement value, based on depreciated value from time of purchase to time of claim, which often is much less than the actual replacement cost. An interesting CM question is, "Does the collection valuation increase or decrease over time?" What does *replacement* mean? Will there be funds to process the material, or merely to acquire it? What damage is covered? For example, in 1989, 12 ranges of shelving containing 20,000 volumes collapsed at the Columbia University library annex. Many, if not most, of the volumes were brittle, so the fall was very damaging. However, the embrittlement was a preexisting condition. After some long negotiations, the insurer agreed to pay for volumes with damage to the cover or text block attachments, but not for volumes with broken pages. There were questions about serial runs as well; this was finally resolved with the insurer paying for the entire run of back files, if more than one-third of the run was damaged (Gertz, 1992, p. 2).

For a good discussion about replacement, actual cash value, average replacement cost, valuable papers, and records coverage, as well as other basic insurance topics and libraries, see Judith Fortson's (1993) "Disaster Planning: Managing the Financial Risk." Having insurance is a sound practice, because almost every library at some time will have a disaster of some type and size; but do not expect insurance coverage to make the collection "whole" again (to return it to its before claim status), to use an insurance term. Having insurance is one more step in protecting the library's and institution's investment.

All of the above applies to all library types to a greater or lesser degree. Preservation starts with the purchase decision (which ought to include consideration of how well the material will stand up to the expected use) and should end with the question of what to do about worn or damaged materials and items identified in the weeding process.

Check These Out

The following books are excellent resources for thinking about disaster management in general as well as in terms of collections:

Alire, Camila A. 2000. *Library Disaster Planning and Recovery Handbook*. New York: Neal-Schuman Publishers.

Wilkinson, Frances K., Linda K. Lewis, and Nancy K. Dennis. 2009. *Comprehensive Guide to Emergency and Disaster Preparedness and Recovery*. Chicago: American Library Association.

Digital Preservation

Preserving digital resources is a very complex issue and is, at present, in the purview of large libraries. Why is it complex? There are a number of technical issues for starters. There are ownership issues that are no longer straightforward (for example, freelance writers may retain all rights beyond first publication; when their material is part of a package with publisher/aggregator rights, the problems mount). Finally, there are issues relating to who realistically has an interest in and the resources available to preserve the material in the long term. Ingrid Mason (2007) made the point that "Technological innovation per se is unpredictable and volatile, and, in itself, poses feasibility issues for collecting organizations and their fitness to respond proactively to develop the means to acquire and preserve digital material" (p. 200).

Let's start with the technology aspect of long-term preservation. One way to approach the challenges is to split them into two broad categories—storage and access. How and where digital material is stored is a factor (for example, floppy disks, zip drives, tape drives, CDs, etc.). Some readers may not know much about, or even know of, some of these formats. That is our point. Digital storage devices change rapidly, as does the rest of technology. How long the stored data will last and remain error free long term is unknown. Tangley (1998) reported on an example from NASA in her article titled "Whoops, There Goes Another CD-ROM." She noted that despite NASA's following best practices, up to 20 percent of the data they had from the 1976 Viking mission to Mars was gone or unreadable (p. 67). Twenty years does not seem long term to us, and just how soon had the data corruption started? Scholars today can read the Dead Sea Scrolls written thousands of years ago as well as provide interpretations of their meaning. Yet it is difficult—and at times impossible—to read digital data we stored not all that long ago. Danny Bradbury (2007) related the story of how the BBC in the early 2000s decided to try to reissue a 1950s television series for which they had discarded the original tapes. BBC eventually recovered all of the episodes primarily from private individuals who had taped the show off the air. A major challenge was that most of the tapes came from the United States, which employs a different television standard than the United Kingdom. As Bradbury noted, "the BBC did a lot of work building hardware that would intelligently convert NTSC [National Television Standards Committee—U.S. broadcast system] recording back into PAL [Phase Alternating Line system—used in Europe]" (p. 42).

Access is the second technological issue that relates to hardware, operating systems, and software capable of retrieving the stored information or data. All of these elements change over time, and not an insignificant number disappear from the marketplace. The storage device may have uncorrupted data, but is the hardware, operating system, and application available as functional entities? Where do you find, in 2011 and beyond, XyWrite or WordStar applications? You can, for a fee, get XyWrite files converted by companies such as Advanced Computer Innovation (http://www.file-convert.com), which is devoted to creating "Accurate, easy-to-use and cost-effective File Conversion" of applications such as XyWrite. WordStar, a competitor to Microsoft Word, had a longer history of use, but also failed to survive. These are just two examples of how both storage and access become complex challenges for preserving digital materials.

Libraries have serious concerns around these issues. Many academic libraries house a special collections department and perhaps also the

---

Check This Out

An interesting assessment of digital longevity is Roger Pogue's 2011 commentary "Seeing Forever: Digital Photos and Videos Are Great, but Don't Expect Your Grandkids to See Them," located in *Scientific American* (304, no. 4: 34).

---

archives for their institution. In addition, libraries have to wonder about the long-term commitment of commercial vendors of databases after the older materials cease to provide an adequate income stream. Who will indefinitely archive such material and at what cost? As more academic libraries create institutional repositories, thoughtful consideration needs to be given to long-term preservation and how to maintain document integrity. Yaniv Levi (2008) stated:

> While many libraries and information centers have digital asset management systems or digital repositories for managing and storing digital objects, these systems are not designed with the preservation of the digital knowledge in mind. Rather they focus on access management, or facilitating the day-to-day use of digital content by users. On the other hand, digital preservation is about guaranteeing the future usability of accessibility to digital content. (p. 22)

Answering the question about who should be responsible for digital preservation is not easy. Four main players have an interest in doing so as well as some responsibility. The originators (authors) of the content have a vested interest, but few of them have resources to do much beyond making backup copies of their work and rarely have time to migrate the material from platform to platform.

Publishers and the vendors who package and sell access to the information have the greatest resources, both technologically and financially, to address the preservation issue. However, given that most of them are for-profit entities, their focus is on revenue generation (and even not-for-profits generally have to break even financially), and they have little incentive to retain material that fails to produce income. The reality is that long-term storage of very low-use material will do almost nothing positive for the bottom line of such organizations.

Individual libraries and cooperative library efforts are the other two groups with a strong interest in long-term preservation. In the past, these two groups handled preservation activities and neither originators nor sellers took much notice; but today, information and intellectual property have taken on a significant financial value. As a result, publishers and vendors generally no longer sell the material, but rather lease it to libraries and place limits on what a library can and cannot do with material—including long-term preservation.

For digital serials that are purchased via individual subscriptions—that is, not as a part of a publisher or vendor package of serial titles—a library might be allowed to create a "dim" or "dark" archive on its server for material for which it paid the subscription price. (A digital dark archive is one that allows no public access to the stored information except under the most exceptional circumstance—a trigger event—such as the publisher going out of business. A dim archive allows some limited public access under less

---

From the Authors' Experience

Another of the many hats Evans wore at Loyola Marymount University was that of campus archaeologist and liaison with the local Native American group (Tongva nation). In the early 1980s, the university acquired property for a campus expansion that contained two archaeological sites. A firm was hired to excavate portions of the sites and prepare a report for the university (1984 and 1986).

Between 1994 and 1997, the university expansion took place. In 1998, the Tongvas requested that the university create a campus memorial for the two village sites that were destroyed by the expansion activities. The university president asked Evans to handle the matter. As a starting point, Evans read the report about the 1980s field-work that was in the library archives department. Much to Evans' surprise, the second chapter of the report indicated that it was a two-volume document; however, no one at the university indicated they had ever seen volume 2. Volume 2 would be essential for any further analysis of the literally tons of excavated material housed at the university. Without that information, the material was just so much junk. The plan was to rebury the material under the memorial site, if the provenance information (volume 2) was not recovered.

The archaeological firm did not have a paper copy. All it had from all of its work in the 1980s were floppy disks for a Tandy (RadioShack) computer. Archaeologists did not want the material reburied, especially by the firm that did the work. It took the company 29 months and a considerable amount of money to recover the data. (They also started converting all their old Tandy disks to the then current standards.)

The above makes the clear point that both storage and access are linked in ways that present long-term preservation of information a challenge.

---

drastic circumstances—such as an extended period where online access is otherwise unavailable.) As noted by Kenney and her colleagues (2006), "what librarians really want, in short, is at least a dim archive—though the level of dimness can vary" (p. 55). If the activity falls to individual libraries, there will likely be costly duplication and probably great holes in the coverage.

As was true when large libraries worked to resolve acidic paper challenges (see below), collaboration is the best hope for achieving long-term preservation. In writing about large-scale library preservation efforts, Paula De Stefano and Tyler Walters (2007) wrote, "Collaboration and partnerships have allowed [research libraries] to pool resources, collect cooperatively, manage collections efficiently, achieve long-term preservation goals more effectively, and adapt to new technology" (p. 230). The following are four of the more established cooperative efforts:

JSTOR: Today, over 6,000 organizations worldwide participate in JSTOR, which was founded in 1995 and archives scholarly high-quality academic journals in the humanities, social sciences, and sciences, as well as monographs and other materials valuable for academic work. The archives are expanded continuously to add international publications. In 2009, JSTOR merged with and became a service of ITHAKA (http://www.ithaka.org/), a not-for-profit organization to help the academic community use digital technologies to preserve the scholarly record and to advance scholarship and teaching in sustainable ways. Libraries pay a rather substantial annual fee—tens of thousands of dollars—to participate in the program. See http://about.jstor.org/about-us/organization for more details.

LOCKSS (Lots Of Copies Keep Stuff Safe): Based at Stanford University Libraries, LOCKSS is an international community initiative that provides libraries with digital preservation tools and support so they can easily and inexpensively collect and preserve their own copies of authorized e-content (http://www.lockss.org/lockss/How_It_Works). In addition to numerous libraries participating in the program, as of mid-2011, over 450 publishers had elected to use LOCKSS as their digital preservation and postcancellation partner.

OCLC Digital Archive™: The OCLC Digital Archive™ is one of many services and products offered by OCLC. It is also a local library digital preservation system with an integrated monitoring and reporting mechanism (http://www.oclc.org/digitalarchive/default.htm).

PubMed Central (PMC): The National Library of Medicine/National Institutes of Health provides a free digital archive of biomedical and life science journal literature through PubMed (http://www.ncbi.nlm.nih.gov/pmc/).

As we enter the second decade of the 21st century, there are two relatively new collaborations emerging: HathiTrust (mentioned in Chapters 7 and 9) and the Library of Congress's National Digital Stewardship Alliance.

In late 2010, the Library of Congress announced the formation of the Stewardship Alliance as a "partnership of institutions and organizations dedicated to preserving and providing access to selected databases, web pages, video, and audio and other digital content with enduring value" (http://www.loc.gov/today/pr/2010/10-178.html). Partners as of mid-2011 ranged from vendors (OCLC, Thomson Reuters) to consortia (CRL) to individual institutions (Harvard University, University of Maryland). The goal of the initiative is to develop standards for digital preservation. Members

---

Something to Watch

One unique collaborative activity that has recently emerged is the Lyrasis Mass Digitization Collaborative (MDC). The MDC was created in 2008 by Lyrasis with grants from the Alfred P. Sloan Foundation to assist members with digitization projects. The current focus on the MDC is on print materials, and items must be either in the public domain or have permission from the copyright holder in order to be included (http://www.lyrasis.org/Products-and-Services/Digital-Services/Mass-Digitization-Collaborative/FAQs.aspx). The process of including an item is relatively simple, as noted by Anderson and Gemmill (2011):

Libraries place an order; select items for digitization; prepare metadata; and ship or deliver to the scanning center. The collaborative shares the new digital resources on the web through its partnership with the Internet Archive and the archive's involvement in the Open Content Alliance. (p. 37)

Yearbooks, course catalogs, student handbooks, and similar materials are among the items that have been digitized by participating institutions such as the University of Maryland–College Park (http://www.lib.umd.edu/univarchives/catalogs.html), the College of William and Mary (https://digitalarchive.wm.edu/handle/10288/2112), and the New Jersey State Library (http://www.archive.org/details/njstatelibrary).

agree to participate in one or more of five working groups, created by the alliance to focus on various elements of digital preservation, including "Content; Standards and Practices; Infrastructure; Innovation; and Outreach" (http://www.digitalpreservation.gov/ndsa/working_groups/index.html).

Librarians do have some recommended guidelines for checking digital and other media formats. Staff should inspect and rewind motion picture film once every three years, inspect and rewind videotapes and audiotapes every two years, and inspect still photographs every three years. Peter Graham's (1994) paper dealing with electronic preservation is an excellent source of information about the issues related to preserving intellectual content in an electronic environment. The Commission on Preservation and Access (1994) published a mission and goals statement for digital consortia that have helped resolve some of the unanswered questions about digitized data and long-term retention. The goals are:

1. Verify and monitor the usefulness of digital imagery for preservation and access.

   a. Establish the convertibility of preservation media.

   b. Foster projects to capture special types of documents.

   c. Insure the longevity of digitized images.

   d. Cultivate research on the application of intelligent character recognition.

2. Define and promote shared methods and standards.

   a. Sponsor forums to define production quality standards.

   b. Promote the development and use of the document structure file.

   c. Create appropriate bibliographic control standards.

   d. Address copyright issues.

   e. Organize a document interchange project.

3. Enlarge the base of materials.

   a. Encourage the involvement of service bureaus.

   b. Focus on the conversion of thematically related materials.

   c. Mount a large inter-institutional collaborative project.

4. Develop and maintain reliable and affordable mechanisms to gain access to digital image documents.

   a. Involve a broad base of constituents in technology development.

   b. Forge effective support structures for end users.

   c. Determine the efficacy of access to digital materials in the context of traditional library collections. (pp. 2–5)

These goals are very similar to those developed for the paper preservation efforts that started almost 50 years ago. If these goals are achieved, there is reason to believe that the profession will resolve the digital preservation problems in time to save many valuable materials.

Check These Out

Gobina Chowdhury's 2010 article "From Digital Libraries to Digital Preservation Research: The Importance of Users and Context" in *Journal of Documentation* (66, no. 2: 207–223) provides a good overview of the issues surrounding digital preservation.

The Digital Library Federation (DLF) is one source of information on digitization, sharing of digital data, as well as the preservation of such materials. DLF is a consortium of libraries and other organizations that "are pioneering the use of electronic information technologies to extend library collections and services" (http://www.diglib .org), and their Website provides extensive information on the topic. One of its more broad-based reports is *Electronic Resource Management* (2004) by Timothy D. Jewell, et al. (http://www.diglib.org/pubs/dlf102/).

An excellent article on the subject of digital preservation is Trudi Bellardo Hahn's 2008 piece "Mass Digitization: Implications for Preserving the Scholarly Record," in *Library Resources and Technical Services* (52, no. 1: 18–26).

Conservation

One element in a library's conservation program is the basic binding and repair program. In-house repairs are fine as long as they employ good conservation methods and use materials that will not cause more harm. Repairers should do nothing that cannot be undone later, if necessary. For example, one should avoid using any adhesive tape other than a reversible adhesive, nonacidic tape to repair a torn page.

Most commercial binderies follow sound practices and employ materials that will not add to an already serious problem of decomposing books. An excellent overview of library binding practices, in a commercial setting, is Paul Parisi's (1993) "An Overview of Library Binding." Selecting a commercial binder should involve the chief collection officer, if the bindery operation is not under the supervision of that person. Most libraries spend thousands of dollars on bindery and repair work each year, and having a reliable and efficient binder, who uses the proper materials, benefits the library and its customers. Knowing something about bindery operations and the process the materials undergo can help the library staff responsible for selecting materials for binding to make better judgments about the type of binding to order, given the probable use of the material. Most commercial binders are pleased to explain their operations and give customers and new library employees tours of their plant.

One long-standing conservation issue for many libraries with large collections is acidic wood pulp paper. William J. Barrow is the person most often associated with identifying acid as the cause of the deterioration of wood pulp paper. For school and all but the largest public libraries, acidic paper is not a problem; collection items wear out or are deselected long before the paper quality is a concern. However, for libraries with long-term obligations, this was and remains a significant worry.

Estimates vary as to just how big the problem is. One project estimated that there were more than 600,000 brittle (brittleness is caused by the acidic paper) or moderately brittle books in a collection of 2 million books in the UCLA library system in 1979 (Evans, personal research). A *brittle book* is one in which a corner of a page breaks off when folded back and forth two or fewer times. The estimate was based on a random sample of books in the collection. An estimated 1 million volumes in the Widener Library (Harvard University) were once identified to be in a similar condition (*Harvard Crimson*, 1986, p. 1). In the early 1980s, the Library of Congress estimated that it had 6 million brittle volumes (*Brittle Books*, 1986, p. 8). According to Richard Dougherty (1992), the Commission on Preservation and Access once estimated that "more than 25 percent of the world's greatest monographic collections are already embrittled beyond redemption" (p. 1). The problem grows with each passing day and nothing is done to stop the process. Unfortunately, few libraries have sufficient funding to do more than address a small percentage of the items needing attention as the cost of doing conservation work with these items is very high.

Embrittlement is the result of the short fibers and chemical residues from the paper manufacturing process. The longer the fibers in the paper, the stronger the paper is. When ground wood pulp replaced cloth and rags as the standard base for paper manufacturing, the long-term strength of paper dropped sharply. A weak paper combined with the acidic residue from sizing and bleaching, as well as lignin (a component of the wood used for paper), creates self-destructing material. At one end of the scale is newsprint, which is very acidic (the rapid darkening of a newspaper left in the sun occurs because of the acid in the newsprint); at the other end is the nonacidic paper that more and more publishers are using in books.

Each year, the number of brittle items (titles published after about 1850 and until the early 1990s) already in the collection increases. What can be done about materials that are self-destructing in the stacks? Maintaining environmental factors (temperature, humidity, and light) at the recommended levels slows the chemical processes; thus, this is a first step to take. For the already-brittle materials in the collection, the two concerns are permanence (shelf life) and durability (use). Permanence is the first issue, and there are several ways to stop the acidic activity. After the acidic action is under control, several options exist to enhance durability. Several mass deacidification systems are designed to process large numbers of books at one time. A good review of the history of deacidification systems is found in an article by John W. Baty and his colleagues (2010), "Deacidification for the Conservation and Preservation of Paper-Based Works: A Review."

Given the magnitude of the acid paper problem, almost every large library faces decisions on what to do and how to approach the challenge. CM personnel play a key role in those decisions. When an item in the collection deteriorates to the point that it cannot be rebound, what should one do? Ten options exist, each with an increase in institutional costs:

- Ignore the problem and return the item to storage (lowest cost).
- Withdraw the item from the collection and do not replace it.
- Seek a reprint edition on alkaline paper.
- Convert the material to microfilm and decide what to do with the original.
- Convert the material to an electronic format.
- Photocopy the material on alkaline paper and decide what to do with the original.
- Seek a replacement copy through the out-of-print trade.
- Place the item in an alkaline protective enclosure made for the item and return it to the collection.

- Withdraw the item from the main collection and place it in a controlled access storage facility.

- Deacidify and strengthen the item and return it to use (very, very expensive).

Ignoring the problem is the most reasonable alternative for materials about which you are confident that long-term retention is unnecessary or undesirable and only a limited amount of use is probable. If there is little or no probability of use in the near future, withdrawing the item is probably the most effective option.

Points to Keep in Mind

- Preservation and conservation of cultural heritage are essential for a society's ongoing success.

- Archives, libraries, and museums are three of the key players in the preservation of cultural heritage.

- Every type of library has, or should have, some interest in achieving the longest possible value and use of the items in its collection whether or not there is a cultural heritage value associated with the items.

- Basic library "housekeeping" practices are the foundation of preservation efforts.

- Activities such as proper shelving and storage methods, not packing storage units too tight, and so forth all extend the useful life of collection items.

- Temperature and humidity control is a balancing act between people and collection needs. The closer you come to collection needs, the longer the items will last.

- Roller coaster variations in temperature and humidity are more damaging to collections than keeping them at a constant, but higher than desirable, level.

- Different formats have different ideal storage environments that add to the challenge of proper library environmental control.

- Light, both natural and artificial, can also be damaging to collections unless preventive measures are taken.

- Insect and mold are yet two additional threats to collection longevity.

- Risk management is an element in a good preservation program.

- Disaster preparedness is also part of a sound program.

- Collection insurance will assist in rebuilding a damaged collection but is unlikely to cover the full cost of recovery.

- During the last half of the 20th century, acidic wood pulp paper was the biggest preservation and conservation concern. While this still remains an issue, it has been far surpassed by 21st-century worries about the longevity of digital resources.

- Long-term digital preservation has several components.

- How data and information are stored and the availability of the requisite hardware and software to access the material are two underlying factors for future use of the material.

- Speed of technological change is a contributing factor for libraries and others hoping to keep digital material accessible and understandable.

- Who can and should undertake the preservation of digital resources is rather murky due to legal and commercial interests in the content.

- It seems likely that libraries, archives, and museums will have to take the lead and do so in large-scale joint efforts if we are to succeed in long-term preservation efforts.

Works Cited

Allen, Susan. 1991. "The Blumberg Case: A Costly Lesson for Librarians." *AB Bookman's Weekly* 88, September 2: 769–773.

Anderson, Kathy, and Laurie Gemmill. 2011. "Step Easily into the Digital Future." *American Libraries* 42, nos. 7/8: 36–39.

Arthur, Michael A., and Lee Dotson. 2009. "Bringing Preservation to the Forefront: Preservation Initiatives at the University of Central Florida Libraries." *Florida Libraries* 52, no. 2: 16–18.

Baty, John W., Crystal L. Maitland, William Minter, Martin A. Hubbe, and Sonya K. Jordan-Mowery. 2010. "Deacidification for the Conservation and Preservation of Paper-Based Works: A Review." *BioResources* 5, no. 3: 1955–2023.

"Bedbugs Lead to PL Ban." 2009. *Library Journal* 134, no. 18, November 1: 14.

Bradbury, Danny. 2007. "See You in 2050." *Engineering and Technology* 2, no. 11: 42–44.

Brittle Books: Reports of the Committee on Preservation and Access. Washington, DC: Council on Library Resources, 1986.

Cloonan, Michèle V. 2007. "The Paradox of Preservation." *Library Trends* 56, no. 1: 133–147.

Commission on Preservation and Access. 1994. *Digital Preservation Consortium: Mission and Goals*. Washington, DC: Commission on Preservation and Access. http://www.clir.org/pubs/reports/dpcmiss/dpcmiss.html.

De Stefano, Paula, and Tyler Walters. 2007. "A Natural Collaboration: Preservation for Archival Collections in ARL Libraries." *Library Trends* 56, no. 1: 230–258.

Delaney, Thomas. 1998. "The Day It Rained in Fort Collins, Colorado." *Journal of Interlibrary Loan, Document Delivery and Information Supply* 8, no. 4: 59–70.

Dougherty, Richard. 1992. "Redefining Preservation and Reconceptualizing Information Service." *Library Issues* 13, November: 1.

Evans, G. Edward, and Thomas L. Carter. 2009. *Introduction to Library Public Services*, 7th ed. Westport, CT: Libraries Unlimited.

Fortson, Judith. 1993. "Disaster Planning: Managing the Financial Risk." *Bottom Line: Managing Library Finances* 6, no. 1: 26–33.

Gertz, Janet. 1992. "Columbia Libraries Annex Disaster." *Archival Products News* 1, no. 2: 2.

Gorman, Michael. 2007. "The Wrong Path and the Right Path: The Role of Libraries in Access to, and Preservation of, Cultural Heritage." *Progressive Librarian* no. 28: 87–99.

Gracy, Karen F. 2007. "Moving Image Preservation and Cultural Capital." *Library Trends* 26, no. 1: 183–197.

Graham, Peter. 1994. *Intellectual Preservation: Electronic Preservation of the Third Kind.* Washington, DC: Commission on Preservation and Access.

Harvard Crimson. October 23, 1986: 1.

Kenney, Anne R., Richard Entlich, Peter B. Hirtle, Nancy Y. McGovern, and Ellie L. Buckley. 2006. *E-Journal Archiving Metes and Bounds: A Survey of the Landscape.* Washington, DC: Council on Library and Information Resources. http://www.clir.org/pubs/reports/pub138/pub138.pdf.

Kniffel, Leonard. 1997. "Flood Toll at Colorado State Could Reach $100 Million." *American Libraries* 28, no. 8: 16.

Levi, Yani. 2008. "Digital Preservation: An Ever-Growing Challenge." *Information Today* 25, no. 11: 22.

Library Hotline. 1986. May 12: 2.

Library of Congress. Preservation Office. 1983. *Paper and Its Preservation: Environmental Controls.* Preservation Leaflet no. 2: A National Preservation Program Publication. Washington, DC: Library of Congress.

Mason, Ingrid. 2007. "Virtual Preservation: How Has Digital Culture Influenced Our Ideas about Permanence?" *Library Trends* 56, no. 1: 198–215.

Maxwell, Nancy Kalikow. 2006. *Sacred Stacks: The Higher Purpose of Libraries and Librarianship.* Chicago: American Library Association.

Ogden, Sherelyn. 2007. "Understanding, Respect, and Collaboration in Cultural Heritage Preservation: A Conservator's Developing Perspective." *Library Trends* 56, no. 1: 275–287.

Parisi, Paul A. 1993. "An Overview of Library Binding: Where We Are, How We Got Here, What We Do." *New Library Scene* 11, no. 6: 17–18.

Swanson, T. John. 2008. "Condition Survey Methodology Applied to a Small Historical Society Library." *Rural Libraries* 28, no. 1: 31–48.

Tangley, Laura. 1998. "Whoops There Goes Another CD-ROM." *U.S. News & World Report* 124, no. 6: 67–68.

Selected Internet Resources

American Library Association Preservation Week Activities and Resources: http://www.ala.org/ala/mgrps/divs/alcts/confevents/preswk/index.cfm

Conservation OnLine (COOL)—Resources for Conservation Professionals: http://cool.conservation-us.org/

Library of Congress Preservation Directorate: http://www.loc.gov/preservation/

Northeast Document Conservation Center Resources Page: http://www.nedcc.org/resources/introduction.php

Parks Library Preservation—Blog from the Preservation Department at the University of Iowa's Parks Library: http://parkslibrarypreservation.word press.com/about/

Preservation Beat—Blog from the University of Iowa Libraries: http://blog.lib.uiowa.edu/preservation/

Preservation and Conservation Administration News Blog: http://prescan
.wordpress.com/about/

Preservation Underground—Blog from the Duke University Libraries Preservation
and Conservation Departments: http://blogs.library.duke.edu/preservation/

Suggested Readings

Adams, Wright R. 2009. "Archiving Digital Materials: An Overview of the Issues."
Journal of Interlibrary Loan, Document Delivery 19, no. 4: 325–335.

Baird, Brian J. 1995. "Motivating Student Employees: Examples from Collections
Conservation." *Library Resources and Technical Services* 39, no. 4: 410–416.

Brawner, Lee B. 1993. "Insurance and Risk Management for Libraries." *Public
Library Quarterly* 13, no. 2: 29–34.

Calzonetti, Jo Ann, and Victor Fleischer. 2011. "Don't Count on Luck, Be Prepared."
College & Research Libraries News 72, no. 2: 82–85.

Carr, Patrick L. 2011. "The Commitment to Securing Perpetual Journal Access: A
Survey of Academic Research Libraries." *Library Resources and Technical
Services* 55, no. 1: 4–16.

Choudury, Sayeed. 2010. "Data Curation: An Ecological Perspective." *College &
Research Library News* 71, no. 4: 194–196.

Cloonan, Michèle V. 2007. "The Moral Imperative to Preserve." *Library Trends* 55,
no. 3: 746–755.

Cloonan, Michèle V. 2011. "The Boundaries of Preservation and Conservation
Research." *Libraries and the Cultural Record* 46, no. 2: 220–229.

De Lusenet, Yola. 2007. "Tending the Garden or Harvesting the Fields: Digital
Preservation and the UNESCO Charter on the Preservation of the Digital
Heritage." *Library Trends* 56, no. 1: 164–182.

Eggert, Paul. 2007. "The Conservator's Gaze and the Nature of the Work." *Library
Trends* 56, no. 1: 80–106.

Fineberg, Gail. 2009. "Preserving Fragile Books: Embrittled Books Find New Life in
Digital Form." *Library of Congress Information Bulletin* 698, no. 3: 51–52.

Foot, Mirjam M. 1996. "Housing Our Collections: Environment and Storage for
Libraries and Archives." *IFLA Journal* 22, no. 2: 110–114.

Hamilton, Rebecca. 2011. "The State Library of Louisiana and Public Libraries'
Response to Hurricanes: Issues, Strategies, and Lessons." *Public Library
Quarterly* 30, no. 1: 40–53.

Harvey, Ross. 2007. "UNESCO's Memory of the World Programme." *Library Trends*
56, no. 1: 159–274.

Kesse, Erich. 2008. "Identification of Infested Paper, Book and Textile Formats."
University of Florida Libraries Preservation Bulletin 7.2. http://cool
.conservation-us.org/byauth/kesse/kesseid.html.

Kuzyk, Raya. 2007. "Serving Through Disaster." *Library Journal* 132, no. 5: 26–28.

Lampert, Cory, and Jason Vaughan. 2009. "Success Factors and Strategic Planning:
Rebuilding an Academic Library Digitization Program." *Information Technology and Libraries* 28, no. 3: 116–136.

Library Trends. 2009. "Library of Congress National Information Infrastructure
and Preservation Program." 57, no. 3: entire issue.

Lunde, Diane B., and Patricia A. Smith. 2009. "Disaster and Security: Colorado State Style." *Library and Archival Security* 22, no. 2: 99–114.

McCormick, Paul. 2008. "Preserving Canada's Cultural Heritage: University of Toronto Libraries." *Feliciter* 54, no. 4:178–181.

Mullen, Katie. 2011. "After the Deluge: Tips on Dealing Successfully with a Disaster Salvage Vendor." *MAC Newsletter* 38, no. 4: 17–20.

Newman, John, and Chris Wolf. 1997. "The Security Audit." *Colorado Libraries* 23, Spring: 19–21.

Pedersen-Summey, Terri L. 1990. "Theft and Mutilation of Library Materials." *College & Research Libraries* 51, no. 2: 120–128.

Phillips, Margaret E. 2005. "What Should We Preserve? The Question for Heritage Libraries in a Digital World." *Library Trends* 54, no. 1: 57–71.

Schiller, Kurt. 2011. "Disaster Response: Technology Makes a Difference." *Information Today* 28, no. 5: 1, 39–40.

Teper, Jennifer Hain, and Emily F. Shaw. 2011. "Planning for Preservation During Mass Digitization Projects." *Portal: Libraries and the Academy* 11, no. 2: 717–739.

Yakel, Elizabeth. 2007. "Archives and Manuscripts: Digital Curation." *OCLC Systems and Services* 23, no. 4: 335–340.

Yi, Myongho. 2011. "Balanced Security Controls for 21st Century Libraries." *Library and Archival Security* 24, no. 1: 39–45.

11
Legal Issues

Digital content is changing both the face of research and the ways in which libraries provide materials and services to their users. One noteworthy manifestation of this trend is libraries taking advantage of digital technologies to preserve printed and analog works, which operate in different ways.

—Laura N. Gasaway, 2010

You have just signed a license agreement to access an electronic database. You know that the use of the database is subject to certain terms and conditions as set out in the license agreement. What are your obligations, however in informing others—the end users—about those terms and conditions? Are you now the copyright police . . . ?

—Lesley Ellen Harris, 2009

Why is the Library Copyright Alliance (LCA) interested in a legal battle between watch manufacturer Omega and big box retailer Costco? Because a pending Supreme Court case may threaten the "first sale doctrine" in the copyright Act, which allows libraries to lend freely copies of all the books it has bought.

—*Library Journal*, 2010

Ah, for the days when CM officers only needed to know the basics of one copyright law and keep up to date regarding the Internal Revenue Service's (IRS) regulations regarding gifts in kind (generally books and magazines). Both of those issues are still with us; however, things have become ever-more complicated as time has passed. Today, CM officers must become familiar with the legalese in electronic resource contracts and licenses. Yes, the library's legal counsel, assuming there is one in place, can be consulted.

273

However, doing so is expensive, especially if that is done each time the library thinks about adding a new electronic product or service.

There are a number of technical issues that are also legal in nature such as digital rights management (DRM) and how and to whom the library may provide access to e-resources (proxy servers, passwords, accounts, and the like).

Accessibility is another legal issue, and something many of us do not think much about as we go about our business of building and maintaining our collections. The Americans with Disabilities Act (1990, ADA) is fairly well known due to the many physical changes in our environment that occurred as a result of the ADA. Wheelchair ramps at buildings and the small "ramps" cut into the curbing at most street corners are two of the most commonly seen changes that resulted from ADA's passage. What, if anything, does ADA have to do with CM? Actually, rather a lot. Title III of the ADA states that it is a violation to discriminate "on the basis of disability in the full and equal enjoyment of the goods, services, facilities, privileges, advantages, or accommodations of any place of public accommodation" (42 U.S.C. § 12182(a) 2000). A question to ponder from time to time is, what percentage of your library's collections is accessible to the visually impaired users? Does collection access meet the "full and equal" provision of the ADA? Large print books are one way to meet this need; however, only a small fraction of the total publishing output is available in that format. What accommodation has the library made for access to the balance of its resources? Have the visual challenges of the available e-resources and the library's Website been addressed? These are some of the questions to think about and legal issues to consider with regard to collections. There are solutions available, but you must think about the issues on an ongoing basis. The authors know from firsthand experience that failure to address these issues for just one user can lead to at least a visit from the user's lawyer and perhaps even a lawsuit.

There are two law-related issues we will mention here but will explore in more depth in the next chapter. The first issue is the Children's Internet Protection Act (CIPA, 20 U.S.C. §6801, 6778, 9134, 2003), which impacts school and public libraries in particular and academic libraries to a lesser extent. CIPA deals with the need to protect children from certain types of Internet material through the use of filtering software.

The second issue relates to what can or does occur when there has been a settlement or court decision regarding some information product, company, or even an author. Barbara M. Jones (2009) explored defamation cases and their impact on library collections. As she noted, "The global exchange and purchase of information via the Internet has undoubtedly enhanced scholarly communication and library collections. But all sorts of legal and cultural barriers confront information crossing national borders" (p. 41). Her article describes several recent defamations cases against authors and their publishers and the fallout of losing the case somewhere in the world.

Check This Out

Diane Murley provides some sound advice regarding improving accessibility for Websites in her 2008 article "Web Site Accessibility" (*Law Library Journal* 100, no. 2: 401–406).

From the Advisory Board

Virginia Walter notes that one recent piece of legislation that would potentially have affected libraries with collections of children's books is the Consumer Product Safety Improvement Act (CPSIA), passed in 2008. The specific issue was the requirement for lead testing of children's books before they could be circulated to the public.

In mid-2011, an article on the *Publisher's Weekly* Website ("Good News for Libraries, Bad News for Publishers in Proposed CPSIA Amendment" by Karen Raugust, http://tinyurl.com/4xkazqn) reported that a proposed bill, Enhancing CPSC Authority and Discretion Act (ECADA), would limit lead-testing requirements to children's books printed after 1985. This is considered a small victory for libraries and booksellers, although some burden remains to prove "safe" levels of lead. On August 1, 2011, Representative Mary Bono Mack introduced a bill (H.R. 2715) designed to provide the Consumer Product Safety Commission (CPSC) with greater authority and discretion in enforcing the consumer product safety laws, including date exemptions and exempting books from testing. This bill passed both the House and Senate in two days.

For more background on CPSIA, see the *Publisher's Weekly* CPSIA Timeline at http://tinyurl.com/3nus9bt, and Laura Speer's 2009 article, "What's All This Talk about Lead and Children's Books?" (*Arkansas Libraries* 66, no. 2: 23–24).

Finally, you will need to hone your negotiating skills, a skill that is also valuable in other areas of your personal and work life. We mentioned this need in Chapter 9 and will explore it further in this chapter.

We wish to make it clear from the outset of this chapter we *are not* giving legal advice. We are only providing a framework or background to assist in your thinking about some of the legal issues related to CM work. Our advice is, when in doubt about legal issues consult the library's legal counsel.

One thing to keep in mind is not all legal issues are major concerns and some come and go. Some new issues may or may not turn out to be significant for CM and library operations, only time will tell. We start with the lesser issues and then address the larger concerns.

Gifts and the IRS

We noted in earlier chapters that libraries of all types receive gifts from time to time. Some gifts are useful and occasionally even very valuable; however, much of the time they are of little interest to the library. Nevertheless, the individuals giving the material generally believe that it is very valuable. People often expect, want, or request a document from the library indicating the value of their gift.

One of the IRS regulations relevant to libraries has to do with gifts and donations to a library or not-for-profit information center. Any library, or its parent institution, that receives a gift-in-kind (books, journals, manuscripts, and so forth) with an appraised value of $5,000 or more must report the gift to the IRS. A second regulation forbids the receiving party (in this case the library) to provide an estimated value for a gift-in-kind. A third disinterested party or organization must make the valuation. The latter requirement grew out of concern that recipients were placing unrealistically high values on gifts. The donor received a larger tax deduction than was warranted, and it did not cost the receiving organization anything to place a high value on the gift. Normally, an appraiser charges a fee for valuing gifts,

---

From the Authors' Experience

While at Loyola Marymount University Library, Evans received a gift of 483 books about Japanese art, architecture, and landscape design. The donor merely wanted a letter listing the items. A check of what appeared to be special or unique books using Abebooks' Website indicated that the collection was probably worth a substantial amount of money. After some negotiation with the university's development staff, the collection's appraised value was $39,743. The donor might well have accepted a letter simply stating the number of books given and thus would have lost a substantial tax deduction.

As a result of that positive experience, the donor became a major supporter of library projects that would not have been possible without the donor's financial commitments to the projects.

---

and the donor is supposed to pay the fee. Most often, the appraisers are antiquarian dealers who charge a flat fee for the service unless the collection is large or complex. If the appraisal is complex, the appraiser charges either a percentage of the appraised value or an hourly fee.

Typically, with gifts thought to be less than $500 in value, the library may write a letter of acknowledgment indicating the number and type of items received. (The IRS requires its Form 8283—Noncash Charitable Contributions—for all gifts of $500 or more.) For gifts of less than $250, the IRS does not require a letter; however, a letter from the library thanking the donor for a gift is also a good idea regardless of the assumed value. The donor can set a value on the gift for tax purposes.

If asked, the library can provide some Websites such as Abebooks (http://www.abebooks.com/) and BookFinder (http://www.bookfinder.com/) so that donors can review retail prices for items similar to their donation. However, the final value of the gift is established by the donor and her or his tax accountant. (Note: CM staff have a major role to play in the acceptance of gifts and must have a sound knowledge of material prices. Just because the gift is small in terms of number of items does not mean that the fair market value is below $5,000.)

To meet IRS requirements, an acknowledgment letter must contain the library's name, the date of the contribution, and the location or place of the gift. At a minimum, that description should state the number and kind of gift (for example, 100 mass-market paperbacks, 40 hardcover books, 6 complete and 20 unbound volumes *of National Geographic*). Gifts can be a challenge at times; however, they can fill gaps in the collection from time to time, accepting (with the understanding the library may use the material as it deems necessary) them can generate goodwill, and they may generate some income for collection building through local and online book sales.

Inventory Control

Another IRS regulation that indirectly did impact CM is known as the *Thor Power Tool* decision from 1979 (439 U.S. 522). The ruling overturned a long-standing practice common in business (including the publishing industry), which was writing down the value of inventories to a low level each year. The practice produced a paper loss that the firm deducted from its income, thus reducing tax liability. The U.S. Supreme Court, deciding that this was taking a current deduction for an estimated future loss, said the practice was inappropriate. Only if the inventory is defective or if there is objective evidence that the firm offered the inventory for sale below cost could it employ the write down.

What does the *Thor* decision have to do with collection development? Publishers who followed the write-down practice claimed it was the only way they could afford to publish small runs of books expected to sell slowly (four to five years to sell out the first printing). Publishers talked about destroying some of their stock, and some did. In 1981 and 1982, jobbers indicated that they had received increased out-of-print and out-of-stock reports from publishers. Blackwell North America stated in a promotional flyer in mid-1981, "[We] are receiving more o.p., o.s. and generally non-reports, than ever before. In fact, our reports to libraries on unavailable titles have increased 47 percent over a year ago."

What probably helped resolve the concern was the 1987 Tax Reform Act. Though it did not address the question of inventories, the act did reduce corporate tax rates, thus reducing the need to find deductions. Concern has decreased, but publishers appear to declare items out of print more quickly now than before the *Thor* decision. No one is certain whether there was a decline in short-run titles published or whether such a decline, if it existed, was the result of the *Thor* decision or of a changing economy. The decision did mean that librarians could not count on finding this year's imprints available in two or three years. Previously, a library might well have decided not to buy some current items, thinking that they could be ordered in a year or two, when funding would be better. After the *Thor* decision, it was probably best to buy materials immediately rather than wait, if they met a significant need or filled a gap. An article by Margaret McKinley (1990), "The *Thor* Inventory Ruling," provided a good review of the issue. It left the impression that while there was an impact, it was not all that great. The primary reason for that was that library print acquisitions budgets had not grown much due to the rise in e-resources as well as the significant role consortia play in resource sharing, thus there was less concern about books being declared out of print.

Today, with e-book and POD options, publishers no longer have the inventory issues they once had. Thus, they tend to keep books in print indefinitely, depending on the "long tail" of book sales to accrue a little more profit.

Lending Rights and the First Sale Doctrine

The lending of books from U.S. libraries goes back to the early 19th century and remains a significant factor in their service programs. This is despite the fact that under U.S. copyright law (17 U.S.C.), a rights holder has the exclusive right "(3) to distribute copies or phonorecords of the copyrighted work to the public by sale or other transfer of ownership, or by rental, lease, or lending" (Chapter 1 § 106, http://www.copyright.gov/title17/92chap1.html#106). Copyright holders of items in a library's collection have the right to control the lending of their materials as a condition of the item's sale. In the absence of such a condition, the first sale doctrine applies. That concept essentially means that after the first sale the rights holder has no say in the later resale or loaning of the item. The vast majority of items in library collections are purchased through a jobber who makes the first purchase and then resells the item. So long as there is no prior lending condition as a part of the first sale, libraries are free to lend the item.

The first sale doctrine seems fairly straightforward in terms of print books, but how it is and will be applied in the world of e-books is another matter. In 2001, Blaise Cronin wrote an essay on the future of first sale for e-books that was eerily prophetic. He invited readers to "Imagine an e-book future in which use, both personal and institutional, is tracked at the transaction level, where publishers monitor and model consumer behavior and retain the ability to revoke access. This is fundamentally different from the world of p-books" (p. 42). Today, with the popularity of e-books and readers, such a future may be coming to pass, as seen in the early 2011 decision by HarperCollins to restrict the number of checkouts for its e-book products (discussed in Chapter 9). How these issues will be resolved in the courts remains to be seen. Michael Seringhaus (2010), when speaking of Amazon and Kindle e-books in particular, noted, "It is not clear whether courts will uphold Amazon's characterization of Kindle e-book transactions as mere licenses, or instead reclassify them as sales. If the transaction is deemed a sale, Kindle e-books would trigger the protection of the copyright 'first sale' doctrine, allowing e-book owners to lend, trade, and resell them" (p. 5). This appears to be the crux of the matter. Another unresolved issue is how the Google Books Project, discussed in Chapter 9, and containing elements of the first sale doctrine will ultimately be resolved.

Why do we bring this up? The reason is that in October 2010 the U.S. Supreme Court reached a split decision in the case of *Costco v. Omega* (four to four, as the newest justice recused herself due to prior involvement in the case), which meant that the Circuit Court's decision (541 F.3d 382) stood. In the case, Omega watches sued Costco Wholesale alleging copyright infringement over the way in which Costco obtained the watches it sold in its warehouses. The decision essentially changed the first sale doctrine. One of our opening quotations for this chapter raised the question of what would happen if the courts supported the Omega position, which they did.

Will this decision impact library lending? It does not seem too likely for items produced in the United States, as Omega's position was its watches are produced outside the United States and thus, Omega had the right to set a U.S. price (higher than elsewhere in the world). Further, Costco could not purchase watches elsewhere in the world (first sale) and resell them in the United States at the lower cost. Certainly, there is much more to be resolved before the true impact will be felt from this case. The worst case scenario is that U.S. publishers will use the decision to move all of their production activities offshore in order to retain greater control of the use of their products after the first sale. Even the publisher of this book lists an overseas office on the title page, which could become the hub of the production activities. If that were all that is involved, then there would be little to worry about. However, that is not the entire picture.

Another element in the picture also comes from outside the United States. Some countries (Australia, Canada, and the United Kingdom, for example) employ the concept of public lending right (PLR) for authors and libraries. This is a system that allows an author to be compensated for the circulated use of his or her copyrighted work from libraries. Many Americans, including librarians, are not fully aware of this right. It is better known elsewhere in the world, and in most countries where it exists, it operates successfully. In view of copyright owners' increasing attempts to charge a fee for types of usage that were free in the past, it may not be too long before the

PLR will come to the United States. Certainly the Omega decisions remove one of the issues that clouded the efforts to get a U.S. PLR program in place.

Under PLR, authors are compensated in some manner for the circulated use or presence of their works in a library. Where does the money come from? There are only three logical sources: the user, the library, or the funding authority. In most countries, the money comes from a separate fund established for that purpose by the national government. Does the presence of a PLR program have any negative impact on library budgets? No one really knows, but it seems likely that there is some spillover that ultimately reduces library funding. There is nothing in the literature that indicates PLR has adverse effects on library budgets. However, collections built using the demand principle increase the pressure on the PLR fund, and a self-feeding cycle may begin, which makes less money available to buy low-use titles.

The PLR system started in the Scandinavian countries after World War II. Initially, it was considered a way to encourage writers to write in languages that had a small number of native speakers (for example, Danish, Finnish, Icelandic, Norwegian, and Swedish). For more than 20 years, the concept did not spread beyond Scandinavia. Starting in the early 1970s, the idea spread to the Netherlands (1972), the Federal Republic of Germany (1972), New Zealand (1973), Australia (1974), the United Kingdom (1983), and Canada (1986). Although some legislation contains the provision that all libraries are to be included, in most countries only public libraries are involved in data collection. Details of the systems vary, but some form of sampling is used to collect the data, unless there is a single source from which the public libraries buy their books. A detailed review of various programs is the solid, if dated, information about PLR in a special issue of *Library Trends*, edited by Perry D. Morrison and Dennis Hyatt (1981). A more recent look at the concept in terms of the United States is Richard LeComte's (2009) article; his notes section provides a thorough list of items on the topic. LeComte concluded his article with the following, "Finally, the structure of American copyright and the first-sale doctrine made for a legal atmosphere inhospitable to PLR" (p. 412). (As mentioned previously, the first sale doctrine was modified as of 2010.)

In 1985, the Council of Writers Organizations was able to get U.S. Senator Charles Matthias of Maryland to submit PLR-enabling legislation. Nothing has happened in the intervening years. Does such legislation have much chance of becoming law? Assuming that the plan would copy other countries' practice of a national funding system, and as long as the federal deficit and budget cutting remain congressional priorities, establishment of a PLR system appears unlikely. However, this assumption may not be valid, for several reasons. First, two other sources of funding are possible: the user and the library. Second, § 106 of the copyright law lists lending as an exclusive right of the copyright owner. Third is the attitude exemplified by Leonard Wood, who once noted, "The fate of a book after it is sold is an important one for the book industry, reflecting as it does the possibility of lost sales; passalong readership of a book, unlike that of a magazine, does not translate into potential revenue" (1983, p. 20). If publishers, authors, and others, such as music producers (audio collections) and motion picture producers (video collections), join forces, we might well see another cost imposed on libraries and their users. And finally, the 2010 *Omega* decision modified a significant barrier to revisiting the issue, and perhaps this time publishers will join in the effort in order to enhance their bottom lines.

Copyright Laws and Libraries

We turn now to a major legal factor that does have an influence on CM work—copyright. Before looking at the impact of copyright on libraries and their services, we believe there is a need to have some general understanding of such laws and information.

Copyright grants the creators of works certain rights that protect their interest in the work, such as realizing some income or benefit from the effort to create the item in the first place. (A few very creative as well as fortunate individuals can actually make a living wage or income from their works; these are few in number compared to the number of individuals who create copyrightable works.) The term copyright originated from the law's first purpose, which was to protect against unauthorized printing and selling of a work. It was a straightforward and seemingly reasonable method of encouraging individuals or businesses to take a financial risk to produce and distribute information. Over time, the concept has grown and has become ever more complex, going far beyond someone copying someone else's work and selling it. Today it is thought of in terms of protecting "intellectual property"—a concept that relates to almost all types of works created by individuals as well as organizations. In addition, most countries have such laws, with varying definitions of issues. International conventions further complicate matters.

England was the first country to legalize creative ownership in 1710 with the Statute of Anne. That law did two things: it gave parliamentary recognition to a royal decree of 1556, and gave legal recognition that an author was the ultimate holder of the copyright of a work. The first component of the law, the 1556 decree, had a less noble purpose: the repression of religious freedom, in this case, limiting the Protestant Reformation. Censorship, rather than free public dissemination of information and thought, was the goal.

The Statute of Anne was a notable piece of legislation that did more than merely give legal sanction to censorship and an author's right to control his or her creative efforts. Although by 1710 authors and publishers were allies in the fight to retain or gain more control over the use of their creations, it was an uneasy alliance. As the creators of a work, authors thought they should have a greater share and say in the distribution of their works, as well as thinking they should have a larger portion of the profits. (Not much has changed in that regard over the past 300 years.) With the enactment of the Statute of Anne, authors received a 14-year monopoly on the publication of their works. An additional 14-year monopoly was possible, if the author was still alive at the end of the first term.

Starting in 1790 and ending in 1891, the U.S. Congress passed a series of laws granting exclusive rights to American authors and their representatives, but not to nonresident foreign authors. In 1831, Congress passed an act extending the copyright term: the new first term was for 28 years, though the second term remained 14 years. The term of copyright is a factor in when the material becomes "public domain" and when others, such as a library, may, for example, legally digitize a work without permission. By 1870, U.S. copyright expanded coverage to art prints, musical compositions, photographs, "works of fine arts," translation rights, and the right to dramatize nondramatic works. In 1887, performance rights for plays and musical compositions received coverage. Performance rights are a library issue, as we noted in the media section of Chapter 8.

In 1909, Congress passed a new copyright act that was a matter of extended debate from 1905 to 1909. (Each time a revision in copyright law has been put forward, the length of debate time has increased, as has the number of groups wanting to have their voices heard.) Several important issues remained unresolved in 1909, including libraries' rights to import books printed in foreign countries and the use of copyrighted music on mechanical instruments, such as phonograph records and piano rolls. After considerable debate, libraries and musicians received the desired rights. Libraries could import a limited number of copies of a foreign work, and copyright owners were to receive payment for the use of their music in mechanical devices. Composers worried about technological developments in 1909; in the 1970s, authors and publishers worried about copying technology. Today, everyone worries about technology and copyright.

Other provisions of the 1909 law included coverage of motion pictures; allowance to the owner of a nondramatic literary work to control public renditions of the work for profit and to control the making of transcriptions or sound recordings of the work; and granting of full copyright protection to foreign authors.

Several of the U.S. copyright provisions created barriers for the United States to be an effective member of international copyright conventions. The three major stumbling blocks were the term of protection, the renewal requirements, and the manufacturing clause (i.e., the requirement that works of foreign authors be printed in the United States in order to be protected).

At the international level, there are two important copyright conventions: the Berne Convention (1886) and the Universal Copyright Convention (1952). The conventions attempted to "rationalize" copyright worldwide. That was and continues to be a challenge. When it was just a print and analog world, it was difficult enough with countries having and insisting on various definitions of issues such as the fair use concept. The arrival of the Internet has made matters just that much more difficult.

Today, the major international body trying to bring some standardization to the field is the World Intellectual Property Organization (WIPO). WIPO is an agency of the United Nations, "dedicated to developing a balanced and accessible international intellectual property (IP) system, which rewards creativity, stimulates innovation and contributes to economic development while safeguarding the public interest" (http://www.wipo.int/about-wipo/en/what_is_wipo.html). It consists of 184 member countries as of mid-2011. Earlier, we mentioned that IP was a very broad concept in today's digital world. WIPO's definition of IP is comprehensive, referring to "creations of the mind: inventions, literary and artistic works, and symbols, names, images, and designs used in commerce" (http://www.wipo.int/about-ip/en/). WIPO further divides the concept into two categories:

> Industrial property, which includes inventions (patents), trademarks, industrial designs, and geographic indications of source; and Copyright, which includes literary and artistic works such as novels, poems and plays, films, musical works, artistic works such as drawings, paintings, photographs and sculptures, and architectural designs. Rights related to copyright include those of performing artists in their performances, producers of phonograms in their recordings, and those of broadcasters in their radio and television programs. (http://www.wipo.int/about-ip/en/)

The WIPO Website contains a number of useful explanations of how copyright laws vary around the world, as well as a detailed discussion of copyright. The Digital Millennium Copyright Act (DMCA) is the most recent U.S. copyright legislation, and is discussed later in this chapter.

Libraries and the Law

How is copyright an issue in collection development? There are at least five significant areas where the law and library services intersect: fair use (§ 107), photocopying/scanning (§ 107 and 108), interlibrary loan (§ 108(d)), performance (§ 107), and out-of-print status (§ 108). These provisions have implications for such areas as resource sharing, number of copies needed to legally meet demand, and maintaining collection integrity. As is true of most legal issues, copyright is not cut and dried. "It depends" is the all too common beginning to answers to the question, "Is this legal?," especially when it relates to the library.

The following list of resources libraries collect and that are covered in the U.S. law provides a sense of how copyright may impact CM activities:

Audiovisuals (news broadcasts) § 108(f)(3)

Other Audiovisuals § 107, 108(h)

Books § 107, 108

Graphic works § 107, 108(h)

Importing copies § 602(a)(3)

Instructional transmission § 107, 110

Motion pictures § 107, 108(h)

Musical works § 107, 108(h)

Periodical article § 107, 108

Pictorial work § 107, 108(h)

Public broadcasting programs § 107, 108(d)(3)

Sound recordings § 107, 108, 114

As you can see from the above, the two major sections of the law are 107 and 108. However, other sections of the law may also come into play, especially for educational libraries supporting instructional activities.

Perhaps the two most vexing copyright issues for both the library and users are copying and fair use. The two concerns are interlinked both for individuals needing information and for teachers wishing to use copyrighted material(s) in their courses. There is no question that some people copy materials for commercial purposes, especially music and video products. However, much of the "improper" usage is a function of not understanding the nature of copyright and what fair usage may be in various circumstances. There are many misconceptions about copyright and we can only touch on a few of them.

One common misconception is that if one does not charge for or gain financially from the usage, there is no violation of copyright. We noted earlier that libraries should also purchase performance rights for the films and videos they purchase, if they are to be used in library programming. Even a free "public performance" during a children's program requires permission, if one did not pay for performance rights. Use in face-to-face instruction has been thought to be "fair use," but even that idea is questioned by many copyright holders.

Yet another common misunderstanding relates to the notice of copyright (the presence of either the word copyright or the © symbol on the item).

"It did not indicate that it was copyrighted, so it must be public domain" is a common response to an alleged violation. One factor in the confusion about the need to have a notice of copyright is because, in the United States, it *was* necessary until April 1, 1989. After that date, the United States joined most of the rest of the world as a signatory to the Berne copyright convention, which grants copyright with or without notice. Thus, the only safe assumption now is that everything is copyrighted, unless one has definite knowledge that it is public domain.

There is a perception, especially among younger people who grew up with the Internet and its philosophy of openness, that anything accessible on the Internet is unconditionally available for their use. Further, the notion that the contents of a Website may be copyrighted does not enter into their thinking until they face an allegation of violating someone's copyright. In Chapter 9, we discussed the current problems libraries face in trying to maintain digital music collections that have come about in part by too many people thinking Internet material was free of use limitations.

Although not a misconception as such, and reflected in the view that Web material is free, is people's attitudes. There appears to be a sense that infringing copyright is not really a crime. In addition, there is a belief that copyright holders are greedy and that the cost to purchase or ask for permission to use copyrighted material is much too high. Therefore, using the material without permission is reasonable. Certainly that was a refrain Evans often heard from students caught up in the Recording Industry Association of America (RIAA) charges of illegal downloading of music. The attitude is rather like drivers who know that the speed limit is 65 miles per hour, but think that it really is okay to drive 70 miles per hour. Legally, it is not okay either to exceed the speed limit or to infringe on copyright, even if no one is looking.

Fair Use and Copying

Fair use is an area full of "yes, you can/no, you can't." Now that the United States has passed the DMCA (P.L. 105-304), which is discussed below in more detail, the issue of what will and will not be deemed fair use is even murkier. Older guidelines seem to be under scrutiny, and the goal appears to be a further lessening of fair use rights. The public still does have some rights to gain access to and use copyrighted material. Where to draw the line between creators' and users' rights is a complicated problem and has become more so with digitization of material and scanning devices.

In the past, copying printed matter for personal use was no problem. Word-for-word hand copying of extensive sections of books or complete magazine articles was uncommon—people took notes. Today, quick, inexpensive copy services, as well as the ability to download digitized copyrighted material, exist everywhere. All of us have made photocopies of complete journal articles or have printed many pages of Internet material rather than take notes; some of those items were from current issues of periodicals that we could have purchased for not much more than the cost of the copied item. All of us have done it and, if we thought about it at all, we thought that just one copy isn't going to hurt anyone. Unfortunately, as the number of such copies and printing increases, so too does the problem. Audio and video items present additional problems as institutions and individuals who own the hardware to play these materials often have copying capabilities.

Much of the controversy regarding fair use and copying centered on educational and library involvement in alleged activities. Today, readily available computer technology has amplified rights holders' concerns about their rights being violated. These concerns go beyond educational institutions and libraries. It is one of the factors behind rights holders employing DRM software to control how their copyrighted material is used; we touch on DRM again later in this chapter. Copyright disputes deeply divide authors, publishers, and producers from libraries, schools, and users, almost destroying what were once friendly working relationships. The relationship has not yet deteriorated to the point of open hostility, but unless true compromises emerge, hostility may be the result.

Libraries are caught in the middle of these issues. Librarians may agree that prices are high, but they also know that if there was no income and profit for the producers there would be no information. They believe in free access to information, especially for educational purposes, once the library acquires the material or information. Finding the balance is the challenge. In many ways, the only organized voice for users is library and educational associations.

Digital Millennium Copyright Act (DMCA)

The purpose of the DMCA was to update existing U.S. copyright law in terms of the digital world, as well as to conform to the 1996 WIPO treaties. Congress also passed a Copyright Term Extension Act in 1998 (P.L. 105-298, also referred to as the "Sonny Bono Copyright Term Extension Act"), which added 20 years to the protection term for both individuals and corporate bodies. The old protection terms were life plus 50 years for individuals and 75 years for corporate entities. (There was an exception for libraries, archives, and nonprofit educational institutions during the last 20 years of protection. Essentially, these groups would have greater fair usage during the last 20 years, if the work was not commercially available. One must wonder just how often that will be necessary. How many requests do libraries receive for special fair usage of material that is 70 years old?)

The 1978 copyright law is still in force, but changed dramatically as a result of amendments and the DMCA. The fair use doctrine is given statutory recognition for the first time in the 1978 law. Traditionally, fair use has been a judicially created limitation on the exclusive rights of copyright owners, developed by the courts because the 1909 copyright law made no provision for any copying. In the law, fair use allows copying of a limited amount of material without permission from, or payment to, the copyright owner, when the use is reasonable and not harmful to the rights of the copyright owner (§ 107).

The law extends copyright protection to unpublished works. Instead of the old dual system of protecting works under common law before publication and under federal law after publication, the law establishes a single system of statutory protection for all works, whether published or unpublished (§ 301).

A five-member Copyright Royalty Tribunal exists to review royalty rates and to settle disputes among parties entitled to several specified types of statutory royalties in areas not directly affecting libraries (§ 801).

A worrisome statement regarding DMCA and fair use was made by Marybeth Peters, U.S. Register of Copyrights, in a 1998 interview with *Library Journal* staff. She was asked if ALA's concern regarding proposed changes in DMCA that would dramatically change fair use was valid. Her response was, "I disagree. What the library community is arguing is that if a copyright owner employs technological protection measures to safeguard his work, they may never be able to get around that protection to exercise their fair use rights. My point is you can't argue fair use to get access to a work" (quote in St. Lifer, 1998, p. 43). Later in the interview she said, "Fair use is a defense to copyright infringement: to the unauthorized exercise of any of the exclusive rights of a copyright owner" (p. 43). We are not clear how exercising the permission given in § 107 for fair use is a defense against infringement, but then we are not lawyers. She went on to say, in relation to what became DMCA, "That is why the act of circumventing a technological protection measure that prevents unauthorized exercise of any of the copyright owners' rights *is not* prohibited. For example, if a librarian obtained legal access to a work" (p. 43).

If all of that seems confusing, it is because the matter is confusing. It is also the reason there are ongoing discussions about the concept. Attempts have been made to help define what really constitutes fair use. After passage of the 1976 law, the Conference on Technological Use, drawing on the House Judiciary Committee report, developed some guidelines. Though helpful, neither users nor owners have been pleased with its results as technology evolved. Another effort, in 1994, by the Conference on Fair Use (CONFU), attempted to resolve some of the technological concerns. (Several groups— for example, the American Association of University Professors and Association of American Law Schools—had opposed the existing guidelines as not representing the needs of higher education well.) CONFU negotiators spent two years developing the report they issued in 1996. The proposed guidelines generated expressions of concern from a substantial number of educational organizations, unlike the earlier guidelines. Perhaps the most important point to keep in mind is that the fair use guidelines do *not* have the force of law. They are only interpretations of the law and they are not the only possible interpretation.

Fair use doctrine is codified in general terms in § 107. That section refers to such purposes as criticism, commentary, news reporting, teaching, scholarship, or research, and it specifies four criteria to use in determining whether a particular instance of copying or other reproduction is fair. The statutory criteria in § 107 are:

1. The purpose and character of the use, including whether such use is of a commercial nature or is for nonprofit educational purposes.

2. The nature of the copyrighted work.

3. The amount and substantiality of the portion used in relation to the copyrighted work as a whole.

4. The effect of the use upon the potential market for or value of the copyrighted work.

Depending on the circumstances, fair use might cover making a single copy or multiple copies. For example, multiple copying for classroom use may be considered fair use under certain circumstances. In deciding whether any particular instance of copying is fair use, you must always consider the statutory fair use criteria.

In addition to copying that would fall within the fair use section of the statute, certain types of library copying that may not be considered fair use are authorized by § 108. Section 108 in no way limits the library's fair use right (§ 108(f)(4)). Section 108(a) contains general conditions and limitations that apply to the authorized copying outlined in the rest of the section. These general conditions apply:

1. The copy is made without any purpose of direct or indirect commercial advantage.

2. The collections of the library are open to the public or available not only to researchers affiliated with the library but also to other persons doing research in a specialized field.

3. The copy includes a notice of copyright.

The House Judiciary Committee's report clarified the status of special libraries in for-profit institutions with respect to the criterion "without direct or indirect commercial advantage" (§ 108(a)(1)). It is the library or archives within the institution that must meet the criteria, not the institution itself.

In addition to the general conditions of § 108(a), it is possible for contractual obligations between a publisher or distributor and a library to limit copying that would otherwise be permissible under § 108. Furthermore, the limited types of copying authorized by § 108 can be augmented by written agreement at the time of purchase (§ 108(f)(4)). Section 108(f)(4) states that the rights of reproduction granted to libraries do not override any contractual obligations assumed by the library when it obtained a work for its collection. In view of this provision, librarians must be especially sensitive to the conditions under which they purchase materials. Before executing an agreement that would limit their rights under the copyright law, they should consult with legal counsel. *This is the key section with regard to licensing agreements*.

Section 108(d) authorizes the making of a single copy of a single article or a copy of a small part of a copyrighted work in the library's collections, provided that (1) the copy becomes the property of the user; (2) the library has no notice that the use of the copy would be for any purpose other than private study, scholarship, or research; and (3) the library both includes on its order form and displays prominently at the place where users submit copying requests a warning about copyright in accordance with requirements prescribed by the Register of Copyrights. On November 16, 1977, the *Federal Register* published the new regulation and provided the form for the warning signs that the library must post near all library copy machines (Figure 11.1).

The *Federal Register* (February 26, 1991) printed the text for a second warning sign for computer software. The warning is similar to the first warning, but the wording differs (Figure 11.2).

Section 108(d) authorizes the making of a single copy of a single article or a copy of a small part of a copyrighted work for purposes of interlibrary loan, provided that it meets all the conditions previously listed regarding a single copy of a single article from the library's own collections. It further provided (§ 108(g)(2)) that requests for interlibrary loan photocopies are not in such aggregate quantities as to substitute for purchases or subscriptions. The wording of the statute places responsibility for compliance on the library requesting the photocopy, not on the library fulfilling the request. A library or archive may receive no more than five photocopies per year of articles published in the restricted issues of a periodical. (They may be five copies of one article or single copies of five different articles.) The restriction

NOTICE: WARNING CONCERNING COPYRIGHT RESTRICTIONS

The copyright law of the United States (Title 17, United States Code) governs the making of photocopies or other reproductions of copyrighted material.

Under certain conditions specified in the law, libraries and archives are authorized to furnish a photocopy or other reproduction. One of these specified conditions is that the photocopy or reproduction is not to be "used for any purpose other than private study, scholarship, or research." If a user makes a request for, or later uses, a photocopy or reproduction for purposes in excess of "fair use," that user may be liable for copyright infringement.

This institution reserves the right to refuse to accept a copying order if, in its judgment, fulfillment of the order would involve violation of copyright law.

Source: *Federal Register* (November 16, 1977).

Figure 11.1.   Official Text of the Required Copyright Warning Sign

NOTICE: WARNING CONCERNING COPYRIGHT RESTRICTIONS

The copyright law of the United States (Title 17, United States Code) governs the reproduction, distribution, adaptation, public performance, and public display of copyrighted material.

Under certain conditions specified in law, nonprofit libraries are authorized to lend, lease or rent copies of computer programs to patrons on a nonprofit basis and for nonprofit purposes. Any person who makes an unauthorized copy or adaptation of the computer program, or redistributes the loan copy, or publicly performs or displays the computer program, except as permitted by Title 17 of the United States Code, may be liable for copyright infringement. This institution reserves the right to refuse to fulfill a loan request if, in its judgment, fulfillment of the request would lead to violation of the copyright law.

Source: *Federal Register* (February 26, 1991).

Figure 11.2.   Official Wording of the Required Copyright Notice for Computer Software

applies only to issues published within the past five years. Duplication of older issues is limited only by the broad provisions of § 108(g)(2), which prohibit copying that by its nature would substitute for a subscription.

DMCA and Technology Issues

DMCA amended U.S. law to comply with WIPO treaties on such matters as term of coverage. It did more than that; it also addressed a great many of the technology aspects of copyright. One of the education/library community's concerns about the decline of fair use rights relates to § 1201. This section prohibits gaining unauthorized access to material by circumventing any technological protection measures a copyright holder may have put in place. The implementation of this section began in 2000. Section 1201 is not intended to limit fair use, but fair use is *not* a defense for circumventing technological protection measures. These other elements in the section have limited implication for collection development, at least at the time we wrote this chapter.

Section 1202 prohibits tampering with copyright management information (CMI). The DMCA identified the following as constituting CMI:

- Information that identifies the copyrighted work, including title of the work, the author, and the copyright owner.

- Information that identifies a performer whose performance is fixed in a work, with certain exceptions.

- In the case of an audiovisual work, information that identifies the writer, performers, or director, with certain exceptions.

- Terms and conditions for use of the work.

- Identifying numbers or symbols that accompany the above information or links to such information; for example, embedded pointers and hypertext links.

- Such other information as the Register of Copyrights may prescribe by regulation, with an exception to protect the privacy of users.

One aspect of the DMCA that will probably be very important to libraries is Title II: Online Service Provider Liability (§ 512(c)). The reason for this is that the DMCA defines "online service provider" (OSP) very broadly, and libraries that offer electronic resources or Internet access could be considered OSPs. The law creates some "safe harbors" for certain specified OSP activities. When an activity is within the safe harbor, the OSP qualifies for an exemption from liability. One should read the most current material available about this title, as it is complex and legal interpretation of it is likely to evolve.

Title IV provides some clarification about library and archival digitization activity for preservation purposes. It allows the creation of up to three digital preservation copies of an eligible copyrighted work and the electronic loan of those copies to qualifying institutions. An additional feature is that it permits preservation, including in a digital form, of an item in a format that has become obsolete.

Distance education activities are also addressed in Title IV. The Register of Copyright provided a report on "how to promote distance education through digital technologies" (Library of Congress, 1999, p. 1). Part of the report was intended to address the value of having licenses available for use of copyrighted works in distance education programs.

Check This Out

Bobby Glushko provides suggestions for libraries to consider when planning digitization projects in his 2011 article "Keeping Library Digitization Legal" (*American Libraries* 42, nos. 5/6: 28–29).

Enforcement

Copyright holders are quick to enforce their rights. One of the earliest lawsuits was instituted just four years after the 1976 legislation became law. A group of book publishers filed a complaint against the Gnomon Corporation (*Basic Books v. Gnomon*) for alleged copyright infringements. Gnomon operated a number of photocopy stores in the eastern United States, many located near academic institutions. The publishers claimed that the company encouraged copyright violations by promoting its Micro-Publishing service with university and college teachers. By May 1980, publishers had their first favorable ruling and announced that their next target would be large for-profit corporations with libraries that did not use the Copyright Clearance Center (CCC, http://www.copyright.com/). By the early 1990s, publishers and commercial copy services had worked out a system for providing academic institutions with custom readers. The system uses an electronic copyright approval procedure that permits a copying service or other company to quickly secure the requisite permissions and legally produce the reader in the needed quantities. Many academic campus bookstores offer similar services, and most of them use the services of the CCC.

Contractual Compliance

Following the various guidelines is one obvious way to achieve a limited form of compliance. For some libraries, the guidelines are too narrow and the cost of acquiring, processing, and housing the needed copyrighted material is high. Are these libraries and information centers cut off from needed information?

The CCC is a not-for-profit service designed to serve rights holders, libraries, and other users of copyrighted material by providing a central source from which to secure necessary permissions and to pay the required fee. It is, in a sense, a licensing system; CCC does not copy documents, but functions as a clearinghouse for both print and online content. Several thousand organizations are members. There are millions of titles and individual images registered with the CCC. Although it handles mostly U.S. publications, some publications from other countries are included as well. Its Website indicated that CCC's purpose is to serve:

> the interests of those who supply content as well as those who
> use it. Businesses, academic institutions and other organizations
> rely on our solutions for the rights to use and share copyrighted
> material. Publishers, authors and other rightsholders trust CCC
> to help them drive new bottom-line revenue from global and
> hard-to-reach markets, while reducing overhead costs and
> improving customer satisfaction. (http://www.copyright.com/
> viewPage.do?pageCode=au1-n)

CCC's services include pay per item and an annual license for print and online materials, pay per image (ReadyImages®), and educational material related to copyright and IP issues. An annual subscription covers both single copy and multiple copy needs for course packs and classroom handouts as well as for electronic courses and reserve purposes. The primary advantage of the subscription is that it provides access to the search interface to CCC's database. Such access greatly speeds up the process of having permission. Also, for academic institutions that hold an annual license, CCC offers the

"Get It Now" service, designed to work with existing ILL services by "providing library patrons with the immediate fulfillment of full-text articles from unsubscribed journals—24 hours a day, 7 days a week—through a cost-effective, and easy-to-use application integrated into your ILL workflow and/or OpenURL Link Resolver" (http://www.copyright.com/content/cc3/en/toolbar/productsAndSolutions/getitnow.html.html). (Very often faculty requests for course packs, class use, and course reserves arrive at the last moment and faculty want the material made available immediately.)

Although CCC does have material from other countries, it is a small fraction of the content users may want. Most countries have an organization similar to CCC; such as the Canadian Copyright Licensing Agency (http://www.accesscopyright.ca) and the United Kingdom's Copyright Licensing Agency (http://www.cla.co.uk). Both of these agencies offer educational institution licensing programs.

As you might expect, you need permission of one type or another for other collection formats. Perhaps the most common are video formats, including theatrical motion pictures. We have mentioned a number of times the necessity of securing performance rights for video formats. Most of the educational video vendors include the cost of performance rights in their advertised prices; however, you should insist on getting a written confirmation for each title acquired and keep the document as long as the item is in the collection. Nonspecialized vendors rarely include performance rights costs in their offerings; you must ask for that cost and be sure to get confirmation that the final price in fact covers the additional expense for the rights. Should you not get the rights at the time of purchase, you can contact the producer and pay for that right at a later date. The underlying message is that it is unwise for a library to use a video for which it is not certain it has performance rights.

For theatrical motion pictures, there are several options. One such option is the Motion Picture Licensing Corporation (MPLC, http://www.mplc.org), which states the case for having a license, recognizing the reality that "who has the time or the budget to track down the copyright owner of each title, and report the dates and times for each exhibition?" As a way of addressing this situation, the MPLC has created the Umbrella License®. This product allows subscribers to have unlimited exhibitions of a title for the cost of an annual license fee. For public and school libraries, there is also the option of using the services of Movie Licensing USA® (http://www.movlic.com/), which has agreements with most of the major Hollywood movie studios, including Disney and MGM (http://www.movlic.com/studios.html). The fees for such services can be substantial; however, the cost of a lawsuit would be higher, and if the organization lost, it could be forced to pay at least $50,000 plus other costs and fees. When in doubt, ask for permission or pay the requisite fee upfront.

One other difference between print materials and media relates to archiving. Under existing law, a library does not have the right to make a backup/archival copy of the item unless it has written permission to do so.

Libraries that provide classroom media support face significant copyright questions. Teachers and professors may want to use a personal tape they made in class using the school's equipment. Is that legal? The answer depends on many factors. A key issue is, when did the taping occur? Few tapes the teachers want to use are home videos; most are copies of a broadcast program the teacher made using a personal video recorder. Such off-air recordings may be legally used if they are 45 days old or less and played in the classroom with a teacher present. The tapes must be erased after 45 days to comply with the guidelines.

From the Advisory Board

Carol Sinwell recalls two unexpected issues that she encountered regarding the use of media technology in the classroom:

First, we encountered a conflict when our technology manager made a decision to replace classroom instructional station video equipment with DVD-only players. He did this without any forewarning to faculty—or to librarians. When the news crossed our paths, I immediately confronted the manager about this decision. He informed me that it was time to move to DVD format as video was a dying platform and he wouldn't support it. Second, he told faculty that he/they could transform the videos to DVD format.

I explained to him that you cannot change classroom equipment without informing faculty ahead of time. (I went through this in the early 1990s when we were moving from 16 mm films to video formats—faculty did not want to change—thus, librarians worked hard to enlighten faculty that we could help in finding the 16 mm titles in video format—or even better, newer versions/films on their content area—as we worked with them to create a newer collection, we were able to phase out the 16 mm films/projectors.) [I also explained] you cannot tell people that [they] can blithely copy videos over into DVD format—[due to] copyright issues—and I said—even if you received copying rights from the owner, who was going to do this copying?—the answer was a bit muddled—it sounded like he had indicated his staff would do it and then it sounded like he told the faculty they would have to do it.

Once the information technology [IT] director heard of the scenario, he explained to faculty that video players would be phased out over the next few years, but the players would stay in classrooms for the time being. Meanwhile, the librarians have been weeding unused videos—which has been significant and they have been buying primarily DVDs.

The other lesson learned by librarians was—buying Blu-ray DVDs before the classrooms had Blu-ray DVD players—so when an instructor was all set to play his "reserved" DVD in the classroom, it didn't work. Library staff and IT staff quickly scrambled to move a Blu-ray DVD player from the library to the classroom so the instructor could successfully complete his class as planned.

Thus, communication between the library and IT is critical and needs to be nurtured and finessed.

Disappearance of Material

There are occasions when yesterday's e-content was there and then—poof—it's gone today. Such disappearances arise most often from a court decision or legal settlement. One major example, which is still not fully resolved, started in 2001 (*New York Times v. Tasini*, 533 U.S. 483). The original Supreme Court decision revolved around the question of when "revised collective work" is actually a revision or a new work and, in the case of freelance writers, who owns the copyright. What the court ruled was, when a user of a digital version of the material sees an independent article and perceives it to be independent (i.e., it is not in the original context of the publication, including advertisements), such material is not a revised work and the author retains all rights. The result was that database vendors and publishers either had to locate the author and negotiate a new contract or

---

Check This Out

For a further discussion of the impact of the *Tasini* decision, see Barbara Quint's 2009 article "Where Have All the Archives Gone?" in *Information Today* (26, no. 7: 1–2, 38–39).

---

remove the digital material. As a result, thousands of articles disappeared from databases.

The court also suggested the parties attempt to reach a settlement to resolve matters. In 2009, the court rejected a proposed settlement that would have created a method for handling material for which the publisher could not locate the author. Once again thousands of digital articles were in jeopardy of disappearing. Adam Liptak (2009) noted that without a comprehensive settlement in place, "publishers and databases will have no choice but to search for and delete whole swaths of freelance works from their digital archives, or risk repetitive litigation over the same dispute the parties sought to settle in this case" (p. B2).

Digital Rights Management (DRM)

In Chapter 9, we described the concept behind digital rights management (DRM). DRM is not itself based in law; rather it is part of a business model that focuses on controlling the rights that are based on law. Piracy, misuse, and misunderstandings have been a part of the copyright scene since the Statute of Anne became law. In today's digital world, the possibilities for piracy and misuses abound and are very easy to accomplish if the IP is left unprotected. Many rights holders worry, with cause, that they may lose all control over their IP work(s). DMCA's passage with the anticircumvention clause links DRM and copyright.

U.S. Code 17 Sec. 1201(a)(1) (DMCA) indicates that "No person shall circumvent a technological measure that effectively controls access to a work protected under this title." Section 1201(a)(3) defines circumventions as "(A) to circumvent a technological measure means to descramble a scrambled work, to decrypt an encrypted work, or otherwise to avoid, bypass, remove, deactivate, or impair a technological measure, without the authority of the copyright owner; and (B) a technological measure effectively controls access to a work if the measure, in the ordinary course of its operation, requires the application of information, or a process or a treatment, with the authority of the copyright owner, to gain access to the work."

Certainly in the past the question of what constitutes reasonable or fair use has been contentious. DRM and, in general, the digital world have only magnified the division between producers, be they individual creators or companies, and end users. The opening sentences of Sarah Houghton-Jan's (2007) article on the topic convey the feelings of many who dislike DRM: "Digital Rights Management, aka DRM. Also known as 'Digital Restrictions Management,' 'Despicable Rights Meddling,' or even 'Delirious Righteous Morons' by some, the technology and its controversial application of controlling digital content has sparked an escalating battle over copyright protection and fair use. The stakes are huge for content producers and consumers and, yes, libraries too" (p. 53). A view in favor of DRM comes from Shri C. V Bhatt (2008), who concluded his article on the topic by noting, "For creators and all sorts of content communities, DRM is likely to enable the growth and success of e-market and finally will be the key point in e-commerce system for marketing of the digital content, and will enable a smooth, safe, secure movement of the digital work from the creator and producer to retailers and consumers at a cost" (p. 42).

What are some of the typical "uses" a person, and a library, makes of digital content that may be controlled by DRM technology? The most obvious uses are to read, listen, and view such material. Others that may not come to mind as quickly are copying, pasting, printing, and E-mailing. All of these uses can be interfered with by DRM to a lesser or greater extent, even when that use would clearly be considered fair use in the analog or print world. These are especially significant factors in the educational library setting. Kristin Eschenfelder (2008) explored what she labeled soft and hard restrictions in the area of scholarly digital resources. Although her focus was on academic libraries, many of her points apply to almost any library environment where e-database access is available. To Eschenfelder, "soft restrictions" are impediments to easily using the material, while "hard restrictions" are forbidden uses (p. 208). Some of the soft restrictions are a function of DRM technology, while others are license issues. An example of a license soft restriction she gave was that some vendors indicate they block suspicious or "excessive" use without clearly stating what constitutes either usage (p. 209). Statements such as "if a suspicious usage pattern indicates excessive copying, the activity is logged and you are sent a copyright warning message" (p. 209) leaves a person in the dark as to what specific actions would cause such a message to be generated.

Other library concerns regarding DRM include device compatibility (Microsoft, Apple, for example) and e-readers, archival or long-term preservation challenges, and access to digital material in compliance with ADA. Many of the DRM-protected materials keep "assistive technologies" from working, essentially denying a visually impaired person from having access even when the material is legally acquired. A good article by Guy Whitehouse (2009) describes the challenges for the visually impaired and DRM.

There is some hope that over time the above issues will be resolved, at least for libraries and archives. The U.S. Copyright Office is mandated to review the impact of the noncircumvention clause of DMCA every three years. At the time we prepared this chapter, four such reviews had occurred—2000, 2003, 2006, and 2009. The final exceptions to the clause for 2009 appeared in July 2010 in the *Federal Register* (vol. 75, no. 143: 43825–43835). Five exceptions were approved, while many others were denied. One interesting pattern in the exceptions allowed is that some exemptions do not get renewed in the next review cycle. Thus, even if you are pleased that the review panel allows for an exception for something you wanted in one cycle, that means you can only count on about three years to take advantage of the opportunity. It may or may not be allowed in the next review cycle. So, the five exceptions allowable between 2009 and 2012 may or may not still exist in 2013.

Barry Sookman and Dan Glover (2010) summed up the nature of copyright, use, and licenses when they wrote, "In the digital space, however, rights that once seemed crisp and clear are blurred. Digital acquisition and lending invariably involves the act of making new copies. It also tends to involve agreements (licenses) between libraries and publishers that define the scope of the permitted copying" (p. 14). What is the relationship between

---

Check These Out

The following are very useful guides to the complex issues of copyright and its compliance:

Behrnd-Klodt, Menzi L. 2008. *Navigating Legal Issues in Archives*. Chicago: Society of American Archivists.

Butler, Rebecca P. 2011. *Copyright for Teachers and Librarians in the 21st Century*. New York: Neal-Schuman.

The Copyright & New Media Law Newsletter. Edited by Lesley Ellen Harris. Quarterly. Chicago: ALA Editions.

Crews, Kenneth D. 2011. *Copyright Law for Librarians and Educators: Creative Strategies and Practical Solutions*, 3rd ed. Chicago: ALA Editions.

Gathegi, John N. 2011. *The Digital Librarian's Legal Handbook*. New York: Neal-Schuman.

Lipinski, Tomas A. 2008. *The Librarian's Legal Companion for Buying and Licensing Information Resources*. New York: Neal-Schuman.

Padfield, Tim. 2010. *Copyright for Archivists and Records Managers*, 4th ed. New York: Neal-Schuman.

Russell, Carrie. 2011. *Complete Copyright for K–12 Librarians and Educators*. Chicago: ALA Editions.

---

copyright and licenses? Perhaps the best short description of the similarities and differences was written by Ann Okerson (1997), who noted:

- Copyright represents a set of general regulations negotiated through statutory enactment.

- Licenses or contracts . . . represent a market-driven approach to such regulation. Each license is arranged between a willing surveyor and willing licensee, resource by resource. The owner of a piece of property is free to ask whatever price and set whatever conditions the market will bear. (p. 137)

More and more producers and libraries are turning to contracts or licenses to handle access and use.

Licenses and Contracts

What is the difference, if any, between a contract and license? They are certainly related; however, there are differences, and understanding the differences can help the library avoid legal entanglements. A contract is a "voluntary, deliberate, and legally binding [enforceable] agreement between two or more competent parties. . . . Each party to a contract acquires rights and duties relative to the rights and duties of the other parties" (http://www .businessdictionary.com/definition/contract.html). A license, on the other hand, is a "revocable written (formal) or implied agreement by an authority or proprietor (the licensor) not to assert his or her right (for a specific period and under specified conditions) to prevent another party (the licensor) from engaging in certain activity that is normally forbidden (such as selling liquor or making copies of a copyrighted work)" (http://www.business dictionary.com/definition/license.html). Essentially, a license is the privilege to use something under certain conditions.

Typical library licensing agreements outline the lessee's (library) responsibility for such things as security, customer service, payment and delivery, limitations and warranties, termination, indemnification, and assignment. All of these factors can affect the expected use allowable. Though having to add attorney fees to the cost of building a collection is unappealing, the fact is that most of the producers will negotiate changes, and librarians should demand changes that benefit or at least do not create unreasonable demands on libraries and end users.

The library should maintain a master file of copies of all the licensing agreements. There should be a staff member who is responsible for knowing the terms of these documents as well as for being able to answer or secure answers to questions about the agreements. Compliance is a key issue, and the library must do what it can to ensure compliance. However, some licensing agreements contain language that places responsibility on the library (subscriber) to monitor what users do with material after they leave the premises. Such clauses are beyond any library's ability to handle, and librarians should insist that they be deleted from the agreement.

The key is knowing what is in the agreement before purchasing the item or resource in question. As with computer software, the licensing agreement often comes with the product, that is, after the purchase. It is sealed in a package with a warning message to the effect that opening the package constitutes accepting the terms of the agreement inside the package. When considering a product from a new vendor, ask for a copy of the licensing agreement before making a final decision to purchase. This gives the staff an opportunity to review the document. It also provides an opportunity to request changes that the vendor may or may not be willing to make. In any event, it will give the library a chance to consider whether it can live with the conditions of the licensing agreement before committing to the purchase.

Because licensing has become a major issue for libraries, a number of library associations (including ARL, ALA, the American Association of Law Libraries, the Medical Library Association, and the Special Libraries Association) worked together and proposed a set of 15 "Principles for Licensing Electronic Resources" (ARL, 1997). These principles included suggested elements for all aspects of the licensing process as well as enforcement and

---

Check These Out

Lesley Ellen Harris (the author of one of the opening quotations for this chapter), provides a comprehensive overview of the licensing process in her work *Licensing Digital Content: A Practical Guide for Librarians* (2nd ed., Chicago: American Library Association, 2009). Also of interest is the companion blog, which is frequently updated http://www.licensingdigitalcontent.blogspot.com/.

Another interesting article that discusses the challenges of licensing digital materials in particular is D.J. Hoek's (2011) piece "Licenses and Acquisitions: The Case of Digital Downloads," in *College & Research Libraries News* (72, no. 3: 155–157).

termination of rights. Although these principles were formulated some years ago, they remain just as valid today as they did when they were introduced and are well worth reviewing.

The Art of Negotiation

The concept of negotiating a license may seem daunting. However, it is important to remember that everyone negotiates every day, even if they do not realize they are doing so. If nothing else, one interacts with family members and coworkers and functions to bring about an agreement over everything from who waters the office plants to who prepares dinner. This is negotiation in action, and as Jill Grogg (2008) noted, for many librarians, negotiations fall into the category of those business activities in which they would rather not have to engage. However, she observed, "If librarians felt more comfortable with the specifics of contract law, copyright, and intellectual property as well as with negotiation in general, we would be better stewards for our resources and better representatives for our users" (p. 211).

Negotiation is about resolving a matter in such a way that all parties involved achieve some gain rather than all or nothing. The "I Win! You Lose!" approach (also known as "zero sum" outcomes) is not what is needed if libraries and vendors are to succeed in achieving their long-term goals. A few of the most common goals for libraries and vendors to achieve in the negotiation process include:

Library Goals:

- Secure the highest quality content appropriate for its service community,
- Ensure reliable/stable electronic access,
- Expend available funds as prudently as possible,
- Provide maximum usage rights for the service population,
- Reduce staffing costs associated with the product's usage as much as possible, and
- Avoid any limitations on existing/traditional services (such as interlibrary loan).

Vendor Goals:

- Realize a maximum profit from its product(s),
- Improve/expand its product(s),
- Protect its intellectual property rights/content,
- Offer products that customers want and need,
- Retain a satisfied customer base, and
- Secure positive customer recommendations through quality customer service and support.

In order to have a mutually beneficial negotiation, certain elements must be present on both sides of the negotiation table. First and foremost, there should be no hidden agendas. There must be open and honest exchanges of information regarding the positions of both parties. Everyone must be willing to listen and learn what the other side's views are and make serious efforts to understand those positions. If everyone can maintain control of what they know are their "hot button" statements or words, the prospect for a good resolution is greatly improved. Finally, and most important, there must be a willingness to compromise; having a set of "never change" positions may well lead to an impasse.

There is a Native American saying that you should not criticize someone else "until you have walked in his moccasins." Indeed, the ability to see, think, and feel the issues as though you are on the other side is as valuable to negotiation as knowing all of the necessary facts and figures. Getting all relevant emotions out in the open is essential, as unexpressed feelings become barriers to the process. The goal is to defeat the problem, not one another.

What are the skills and characteristics of an effective negotiator?

- *Patience*: Take your time. Negotiations involve an element of conflict as well as uncertainty, and many people try to deal with these factors quickly because they are uncomfortable with them. A patient negotiator has an advantage.

- *Preparation and knowledge*: Work to understand your needs and issues and those of the other side.

- *Tolerance for conflict, uncertainty, and ambiguity*: Be willing to leave an issue unresolved and move on to another issue when necessary, and remember that resolutions you make will affect those unresolved issues. The negotiator who is best able to handle these factors has an advantage.

- *Willingness to take some reasonable risks*: Know that every negotiation/agreement involves a greater or lesser degree of risk. Being unwilling to take some risk almost always results in a failed negotiation.

- *Ability to relate* to the people "on the other side of the table."

- *Good listening skills*.

- *High self-esteem*: Possess a sure sense of your abilities and be able to take on personal responsibilities without allowing the other side to gain something your side did not want to concede. Wanting everyone to like you is not a good trait for an effective negotiator.

- *A sense of humor*.

- *Integrity*.

- *Physical and mental stamina*: Have the mental and physical stamina to handle long negotiations and avoid making mistakes. Dealing with labor contracts or the purchase of new software can take 15 to 18 hours.

- *Persistence*: Know when to continue and when to walk away. Many people are not persistent enough in negotiations, either taking the first rejection as final or conceding something too soon.

Having the appropriate skills and characteristics is important, but of equal importance is the preparation and understanding of the negotiation process. The process consists of:

- Developing knowledge of the other side;
- Setting the goals for your side;
- Developing alternatives (what is negotiable);
- Identifying and testing your assumptions;
- Developing a strategy and set of tactics;
- Rehearsing;
- Identifying your "take or leave it" point; and
- Establishing a time line for reaching an agreement.

A successful negotiator should differentiate between wants and needs for both sides; ask high and offer low, but be realistic; make it clear that the other side was not "giving in," but that the object conceded was of value; and strive for a profitable agreement for both sides.

Points to Keep in Mind

- There are several legal issues that impact CM activities.
- Accepting donations of material for the collection may have legal consequences for both the donor and the library.
- Providing equal access to library resources for all people, even the visually impaired, is both a legal and ethical issue.
- Public lending rights, which exist in many other countries, *may* become an issue in the United States as a result of a 2010 Supreme Court decision.
- Copyright laws are complex and impact CM work in various ways—fair use, copying activities, and "performance" activities in particular.
- Resource sharing programs may run afoul of copyright laws if the laws are not carefully thought through at the outset.
- DRM, although not a law, does have its basis in law and presents challenges to some CM efforts, especially fair use and copying that would not be questioned in an analog situation.
- Licenses are revocable agreements to allow certain uses, granted by licensor, to another party under certain conditions.
- Licensing access to collection resources is now a standard activity for libraries, not fully understanding the terms and conditions of the license can be detrimental to people's effective use of the resource.
- Libraries should do their best to negotiate the best possible license terms for their end users.
- Negotiating appropriate terms and conditions requires practice and skill.

Works Cited

Association of Research Libraries. 1997. "Principles for Licensing Electronic Resources." July 15. http://www.arl.org/sc/marketplace/license/licprinciples.shtml.

Bhatt, Shri C.V. 2008. "Is Digital Rights Management an IPR?" *Journal of Library and Information Technology* 28, no. 5: 39–42.

Cronin, B. 2001. "The End of First Sale." *Library Journal* 126, no. 19: 42.

Eschenfelder, Kristin R. 2008. "Every Library's Nightmare? Digital Rights Management, Use Restrictions, and Licensed Scholarly Digital Resources." *College & Research Libraries* 69, no. 3: 205–226.

Gasaway, Laura N. 2010. "Libraries, Digital Content, and Copyright." *Vanderbilt Journal of Entertainment and Technology Law* 12, no. 4: 755–778.

Grogg, Jill E. 2008. "Negotiation for the Librarian." *Journal of Electronic Resources Librarianship* 20, no. 4: 210–212.

Harris, Lesley Ellen. 2009. "Licenses and Legalities." *American Libraries* 40, nos. 6/7: 58–60.

Houghton-Jan, Sarah. 2007. "Imagine No Restrictions." *School Library Journal* 53, no. 6: 52–54.

Jones, Barbara M. 2009. "Libel Tourism: Why Libraries Should Care." *American Libraries* 40, no. 11: 40–43.

LeComte, Richard. 2009. "Writers Blocked: The Debate Over Public Lending Right in the United States During the 1980s." *Libraries and the Cultural Record* 44, no. 4: 395–417.

Library Journal. 2010. "Copyright Case Could Threaten Library Lending." 135, no. 13: 13.

Library of Congress. 1999. *Report on Copyright and Digital Distance Education*. Washington, DC: United States Copyright Office. http://www.copyright.gov/reports/de_rprt.pdf.

Liptak, Adam. 2009. "Supreme Court to Revisit a Case on Breach of Copyright." *New York Times*, March 3, Late Edition, sec. B: 2.

McKinley, Margaret. 1990. "The *Thor* Inventory Ruling: Fact or Fiction." *Serials Librarian* 17, nos. 3/4: 191–194.

Morrison, Perry D., and Dennis Hyatt, eds. 1981. "Public Lending Right." *Library Trends* 29, no. 4: 565–719. [Entire issue devoted to the topic.]

Okerson, Ann. 1997. "Copyright or Contract?" *Library Journal* 122, no. 14: 136–139.

Seringhaus, Michael. 2010. "E-Book Transactions: Amazon 'Kindles' the Copy Ownership Debate." *Student Prize Papers*. Paper 60. http://digitalcommons.law.yale.edu/ylsspps_papers/60.

St. Lifer, Evan. 1998. "Inching Toward Copyright Détente." *Library Journal* 123, no. 13: 42–43.

Sookman, Barry, and Dan Glover. 2010. "Digital Copying and Libraries: Copyright and Licensing Considerations." *Feliciter* 56, no. 1: 14–16.

Thor Power Tool Co. v. Commissioner of Internal Revenue. 439 U.S. 522 (1979).

Whitehouse, Guy. 2009. "A New Clash Between Human Rights and Copyright: The Push for Enhanced Exceptions for the Print-Disabled." *Publishing Research Quarterly* 25, no. 4: 219–231.

Wood, Leonard A. 1983. "The Pass-Along Market for Books: Something to Ponder for Publishers." *Publishers Weekly* 224, no. 3: 20.

Suggested Readings

Block, Carson. 2007. "DRM-It! I Want DRM-Free, Downloadable Audio Books for Our Patrons." *Colorado Libraries* 33, no. 4: 43–44.

Böhner, Dörte. 2008. "Digital Rights Description as Part of Digital Rights Management: A Challenge for Libraries." *Library Hi Tech* 26, no. 4: 598–605.

Butler, Brandon. 2010. "Challenges in Employing Fair Use in Academic and Research Libraries." *Research Library Issues* no. 273: 17–25.

Cameron, Jamie. 1993. "The Changing Scene in Journal Publishing." *Publishers Weekly* 240, no. 22: 24.

Carrico, Steven, Jason Fleming, and Betsey Simpson. 2010. "Virtual Bookplates: Enhancing Donor Recognition and Library Development." *College & Research Libraries News* 71, no. 8: 419–423.

Cichocki, Kristen M. 2008. "Unlocking the Future of Public Libraries: Digital Licensing that Preserves Access." *University of Baltimore Intellectual Property Law Journal* 16, nos. 1/2: 29–59.

Conference on Fair Use. 1996. *An Interim Report to the Commissioner.* Washington, DC: U.S. Patent and Trademark Office.

Culler, David. 2010. "'Getting to Yes' Through Negotiation." *Quill* 98, no. 1: 37.

Dockens, Elaine B. 2010. "Vendor Pitfalls in Negotiating Large Multi-Year Contracts." *AALL Spectrum* 14, no. 4: 8–12.

Dougherty, William C. 2010. "The Copyright Quagmire." *Journal of Academic Librarianship* 36, no. 4: 351–353.

Dye, Jessica. 2006. "Scanning the Stacks: The Digital Rights Issues Behind Book Digitization Projects." *EContent* 29, no. 1: 32–37.

Grogg, Jill E., and Beth Ashmore. 2009. "The Art of the Deal: Negotiating in Times of Economic Stress." *Searcher* 17, no. 6: 42–49.

Harris, Christopher. 2010. "A Whole New Mind-Set." *School Library Journal* 56, no. 12: 14.

Kieft, Robert H., and Lizanne Payne. 2010. "A Nation-Wide Planning Framework for Large-Scale Collaboration on Legacy Print Monograph Collections." *Collaborative Librarianship* 2, no. 4: 229–233.

Knutson, Alyssa. 2009. "Proceed With Caution: How Digital Archives Have Been Left in the Dark." *Berkeley Technology Law Journal* 24, no. 1: 437–473.

Liberman, Varda, Nicholas R. Anderson, and Lee Ross. 2010. "Achieving Difficult Agreements: Effects of Positive Expectations on Negotiation Process and Outcomes." *Journal of Experimental Social Psychology* 48, no. 4: 494–504.

McMenemy, David, and Paul F. Burton. 2005. "Managing Access: Legal and Policy Issues of ICT Use." In *Delivering Digital Services*, ed. Alan Paultez, 19–34. London: Facet.

Pike, George H. 2008. "Revisiting Tasini." *Information Today* 25, no. 1: 17, 20.

Pike, George H. 2009. "Copyright Office to Consider DMCA Exemptions." *Information Today* 26, no. 3: 13, 17.

Puckett, Jason. 2009. "Digital Rights Management as Information Access Barrier." *Progressive Librarian* nos. 34/35: 11–24.

Russell, Carrie. 2005. "Singing a Different Tune: Kids Are Downloading More and More Music—But Is It Legal?" *School Library Journal* 51, no. 3: 35.

Smith, Brendan L. 2010. "Un-Google That." *American Bar Association Journal* 96, no. 9: 18–19.

Stemper, Jim, and Susan Barribeau. 2006. "Perpetual Access to Electronic Journals." *Library Resources and Technical Services* 50, no. 2: 91–109.

Terry, Jenni. 2010. "Access to Copyrighted Works for Those With Disabilities." *College & Research Libraries News* 71, no. 1: 38.

Valenza, Joyce Kasman. 2011. "Opening Gates: On Celebrating Creative Commons and Flexing the Fair Use Muscle." *Library Media Connection* 29, no. 4: 30, 32.

Waller, Andrew, and Gwen Bird. 2006. "'We Own It': Dealing With 'Perpetual Access' in Big Deals." *Serials Librarian* 50, no.1: 179–196.

12
Access, Ethics, and Intellectual Freedom

What does Intellectual Freedom really mean? It means buying books that we may not personally agree with for our library. It means keeping books that not all of our patrons will like on the shelf. And keeping circulation records private, so people can feel free to explore topics without fear of retribution.

—Wendy Cornelisen, 2010

Too often, we think of intellectual freedom as an issue solely related to public and school libraries. . . . While academic libraries do need to address censorship attempts from time to time, perhaps the most frequent intellectual freedom issue on most college and university campuses is privacy.

—Joe Dahlstrom, 2010

Self-censorship. It's a dirty secret that no one in the profession wants to talk about or admit practicing. Yet everyone knows some librarians bypass good books—those with literary merit or that fill a need in their collections. The reasons range from a book's sexual content and gay themes to its language and violence—and it happens in more public and K–12 libraries than you think.

—Debra Lau Whelan, 2009

Whelen [2009], for example, reported that in a recent *School Library Journal* study, 70 percent of the school media specialists said they would not purchase certain controversial titles because they wanted to avoid censorship conflicts.

—Susan K. Burke, 2010

Without the above quotations, you might well wonder what access, ethics, and intellectual freedom had to do with collection management work. The topics are interrelated with CM activities. Jean Preer (2008) once noted, "Ethics is about choices" (p. 1). We might reword her definition to say "Selection is about choices." What we elect to add, or not to add, to our collections has an impact on our users' access to information as well as on their freedom to explore ideas, topics, and even recreational enjoyment without restriction. Collection managers are, in a very real sense, "gatekeepers" to knowledge for our clientele; yes, users may be able to find the desired material elsewhere, especially in today's digital world, but through our choices we make that access easy or hard. There are few hard and fast "rules" for how to handle these complex interrelated issues. In what follows, we attempt to outline some of the issues involved and how CM officers and libraries have from time to time addressed them.

One convenient approach to thinking about the issues is to view intellectual freedom (IF) as the overarching concept with the other topics as subdivisions—ethics, access, privacy, and censorship. In predigital days, these concepts seemed highly complex; little did we know how complicated they would become with the arrival of the Internet and developments in technology. We do indeed live in interesting times; especially in the area of this chapter's topics.

There is a tendency to think of IF solely in terms of libraries, their users, and censorship. That is not unreasonable; however, while most censorship issues are IF related, not all IF issues are censorship related. Given the link between IF and the First Amendment rights, there have been several legal battles over library services, such as using library meeting rooms for religious services and Internet access (more about this one later in the chapter). Two additional examples of noncensorship IF come from journalism and education or developmental psychology. IF is also about people's right to know, which underlies effective democratic decision making. Journalists use the concept of the public's right to know in their work and base their position on the First Amendment, just as libraries do with the right to read. As David O'Brien (1981) wrote, "The political ideal of the public's right to know has been enhanced by the Supreme Court's broad interpretation of the First Amendment as securing the conditions for an informed people and electorate" (p. 166).

David Moshman (2003) made a case for IF being an essential element in the intellectual development of people who are capable of assessing, processing, discussing, refining, and defending concepts and ideas. He delineated a set of IFs that are necessary for the type of intellectual development he put forward: freedom of belief and identity, expression and discussion, inquiry, freedom from indoctrination, quality, privacy, and due process (p. 36). As you will see as you read this chapter, several of these freedoms are related to libraries and their collections.

Libraries, the First Amendment, and Intellectual Freedom

The ALA and its many divisions, sections, and interest groups have issued a number of documents related to the topics in this chapter. Among the most relevant are:

"Library Bill of Rights"—1939; revised 1944, 1948, 1961, 1967, 1980, 1996
(http://www.ala.org/ala/issuesadvocacy/intfreedom/librarybill/lbor.pdf),

"Labeling and Rating Systems"—1951; amended 1971, 1981, 1990, 2009 (http://www.ala.org/ala/issuesadvocacy/intfreedom/librarybill/inter pretations/Labeling_and_Rating_.pdf),

"Freedom to Read Statement"—1953; revised 1972, 1991, 2000, 2004 (http:// www.ala.org/ala/aboutala/offices/oif/statementspols/ftrstatement/ freedomtoreadstatement.pdf),

"Policy on Confidentiality of Library Records"—1971; revised 1975, 1986 (http://www.ala.org/ala/aboutala/offices/oif/statementspols/otherpoli cies/confidentialitylibraryrecords.pdf),

"Diversity in Collection Development"—1982; amended 1990, 2008 (http:// www.ala.org/ala/issuesadvocacy/intfreedom/librarybill/interpreta tions/Diversity%20in%20Collect.pdf),

"Access to Resources and Services in the School Library Media Program"—1986; amended 1990, 2000, 2005, 2008 (http://www.ala.org/ala/ issuesadvocacy/intfreedom/librarybill/interpretations/accessresources .cfm),

"Code of Ethics of the American Library Association"—1997; amended 2008 (http://www.ala.org/advocacy/proethics/codeofethics/codeethics),

"Schools and the Children's Internet Protection Act"—2001 (http://www.ala .org/offices/oif/ifissues/schoolschildrens),

"Privacy: An Interpretation of the Library Bill of Rights"—2002 (http://www .ala.org/ala/issuesadvocacy/intfreedom/librarybill/interpretations/ privacyinterpretation.pdf),

"Guidelines for Librarians on the U.S.A. Patriot Act"—2002 (http://www.ala .org/advocacy/files/advleg/federallegislation/theusapatriotact/patstep .pdf).

"Minors' Rights to Receive Information Under the First Amendment"—2004 (http://www.ala.org/ala/mgrps/affiliates/relatedgroups/freedomtoread foundation/ftrfinaction/jennerblockmemo/MinorsRightsMemo.pdf),

"Resolution on Radio Frequency Identification (RFID) Technology and Privacy Principles"—2005 (http://www.ala.org/ala/aboutala/offices/oif/ statementspols/ifresolutions/rfidresolution.cfm).

The Library Bill of Rights (LBR) states among other topics that library resources should provide for the interests of the entire service community and that the materials reflect all points of view on controversial topics. Further, libraries must not restrict anyone's access to these resources on

---

Check These Out

A number of other resources related to the topics in this chapter are available from ALA and are well worth a look. These include: "The Children's Internet Protection Act (CIPA)" resource page: http://www.ala.org/advocacy/advleg/federallegislation/ cipa, and "Libraries and the Internet Toolkit": http://www.ala.org/ala/aboutala/offices/ oif/iftoolkits/litoolkit/default.cfm.

the basis of national origin, age, background, and so forth. The statement "Diversity in Collection Development" goes into more detail on the subject of allowing all people full access. Several of the other documents listed above also relate to access issues, especially for children and young adults. LBR also states libraries should resist efforts to censor materials or restrict access to resources.

The Freedom to Read Statement (FR) links the concept of unfettered reading to the U.S. Constitution, particularly the First Amendment. As a result, you will see IF and FR linked to the First Amendment without any additional reference to the U.S. Constitution. FR contains seven "propositions" calling for libraries, publishers, and booksellers to collaborate in ensuring that both the freedom of expression and the freedom to access those expressions are protected. Most, if not all, censorship challenges related to FR and its link to the First Amendment.

The Code of Ethics of the American Library Association acknowledges that "Ethical dilemmas occur when values conflict." Nevertheless, it delineates eight guiding principles for the ethical behavior of librarians. The first three on the list and the seventh are all related to CM activities to a greater or lesser degree. Many of the documents listed above have ethical issues built into them, although they do not always employ the words "ethics" or "ethical."

The ALA's organizational structure for dealing with intellectual freedom concerns is somewhat confusing. The Intellectual Freedom Committee (IFC) is responsible for making recommendations to the association regarding matters of intellectual freedom. The Office for Intellectual Freedom (OIF), which has a full-time staff, has the charge of educating librarians and others about intellectual freedom and censorship matters. It also is the support service for the IFC, and it implements the association's policies related to intellectual freedom. As part of its educational function, the OIF produces several publications: *Newsletter on Intellectual Freedom* (news and current developments relating to intellectual freedom), *OIF Memorandum* (addressed to local library association intellectual freedom committees), and the *Intellectual Freedom Manual*.

Although the OIF does not provide legal assistance when a library faces a complaint, it does provide telephone consultation (occasionally with the addition of written statements or names of persons who might be able to testify in support of intellectual freedom). Very rarely does the OIF staff come to the library to provide moral and professional support.

Often, librarians are surprised to learn that the OIF does not provide legal aid. Instead, legal assistance might be available from the Freedom to Read Foundation (FRF). The FRF is not part of the ALA (it is a separate legal entity), but the two are so closely affiliated that many people have difficulty drawing the line between the two. The executive director of the FRF is also the director of the OIF; with such an arrangement, it is not surprising

---

Check This Out

While OIF exists at the national level, some state-level organizations may also provide support. For example, the Children's Cooperative Book Center assists Wisconsin librarians and teachers when dealing with challenges to materials. Like OIF, they do not provide legal assistance, but they will provide background information on the title being challenged (http://www.education.wisc.edu/ccbc/freedom/ifservices.asp).

Check This Out

IF is a complex concept in the real world. Confronting an IF situation for the first time can be intimidating, worrisome, stressful, and perhaps a little scary. One way to prepare yourself for that time, and it is likely to occur at some time in your career, is to think about what you will do when it does happen. Case studies, in the safety of the classroom or workshop, are one method for thinking about what to do and how to handle such an event where you can hear from others about how they would approach the matter.

Joyce Brooks and Jody Howard (2002) provide four "scenes" in which IF is in play in their article "What Would You Do? School Library Media Centers and Intellectual Freedom" (*Colorado Libraries* 28, no. 3: 17–19). School library media centers serve as the setting for the scenarios; however, it is easy to see how these cases could just as well happen in the academic or public library environment. (Most special libraries do not face very many IF issues as they are rarely open to the public and have a rather narrow focus in terms of CM work.)

Two titles published by ALA Editions (Chicago, 2009) and well worth a review are *Protecting Intellectual Freedom in Your School Library* by Pat R. Scales for the OIF and *Protecting Intellectual Freedom in Your Academic Library* by Barbara M. Jones for the OIF. The Scales title includes a chapter on "Materials Selection" (pp. 1–34), that contains a series of case studies on selection issues, ranging from electronic database selection to curriculum demands. The Jones title contains a similar chapter on "Collection Development" (pp. 63–100), which includes case studies as well as a checklist of intellectual freedom tools for CM librarians. A third volume, *Protecting Intellectual Freedom in Your Public Library* by June Pinnell-Stephens, was expected to be released in late 2012.

---

that people think the FRF is part of the ALA. Be aware that there is no assurance of receiving financial or legal aid from the FRF; there are too many cases and insufficient funds to assist everyone. Anyone interested in becoming involved in intellectual freedom activities should consider joining ALA's Intellectual Freedom Round Table, which is the general membership unit related to intellectual freedom. Although the ALA offers a variety of support services for handling censors' complaints, the best support is local preparation before the need arises.

Obviously all the "position papers" or documents issued by the ALA must be broad brushstrokes in order to include the variations in libraries and their environments. They must be general in content and are rarely, if ever, prescriptive in nature. Thus, they are the starting point for thinking about the issues in terms of your library's environment. Real-world situations rarely lend themselves to general principle or position statements. They are almost always highly nuanced. Your best option is to think seriously about the issues and your beliefs regarding them, prior to encountering a situation that will require ethical choices.

Anne Klinefelter (2010), in discussing CM and the First Amendment, noted that "Selectivity in library collections, though, is unavoidable given scarcity of resources for collections, staff, facilities, and technology. . . . Given this selectivity, and given the general societal consensus that libraries are an overall benefit, courts are wary of applying standard First Amendment analysis in library cases for fear the entire library system could be found in violation of the First Amendment" (pp. 347–348).

What is the "standard First Amendment analysis"? Usually, the courts require that there be total neutrality (*no* abridgement of freedom of speech) for there to be First Amendment protection. (Note: generally any library receiving government funds could look for First Amendment protection as a government agent/agency.) Selectivity is clearly not neutral. For example, in a public library setting, selecting on the basis of quality would mean items of lesser quality would have little chance of being in the collection—that could translate into an abridgement of free speech case against a government agency. Under a strict constitutional interpretation/standard analysis of the First Amendment, quality selection would be unconstitutional. Fortunately, at least to date, no court has applied the strict interpretation to library cases. Klinefelter's article is one we believe anyone going into librarianship should read as it examines a variety of library-related court cases and goes beyond just CM issues. With that background on IF and the First Amendment in mind, we turn to questions of choices.

Ethics, Personal Beliefs, Biases, and Collection Management

In writing about ethics, integrity, and leadership Ann M. Martin (2009) stated, "social behavior adapts to the times, resulting in new dilemmas for school library media specialists. As a result, ethics adapt to social change, while the concept of integrity remains constant. . . . Library media specialists are obliged to know, understand, and adhere to the ethical principles that are the foundation of our profession" (p. 6). Although her statement addressed school library media specialists, we believe it applies to anyone in the profession, regardless of the library environment.

CM is always a matter of choices, some easy, some not so easy, some of an ethical nature, and many that are not. The ALA Code of Ethics is a starting rather than an ending point in CM choice making. We are, in theory, supposed to build collections that reflect the needs and interests of our service community. We are supposed to reflect all points of view in terms of controversial topics. We are supposed to be thoughtful and careful stewards of the monies we have available to create such collections. With just those three points in mind you can probably imagine where some dilemmas (ethical, personal integrity, personal values, for example) might arise. Just one example, what would you do if just one person—user or not—held a view contrary to everyone else in the service community and asked that her or his view be reflected in the collection? That would be easy to answer in a world of infinite financial resources—in our experience a nonexistent world—it is not so easy in the real world. You might think just one person is an unlikely situation, and we agree, but does it matter, from an ethical perspective, if it is just one, 100, or 1,000 out of a great many more?

In Chapter 4 we said we would explore the "affective" side of collection building, to use Brian Quinn's (2007) term. He made the point that selection is not just a rational process: "The psychological literature indicates that decision making is not simply a cognitive process. . . . Making a decision about whether to purchase a book, cancel a journal, or add a database or aggregated package is fraught with uncertainly and ambiguity" (pp. 5, 7). How we go about our CM work activities reflects a variety of factors, some of which are psychological in nature. Looking at the management and psychology literature, you find ample evidence that those involved in decision-making processes are almost never 100 percent certain of what the outcome will be. Almost every decision carries with it some degree of uncertainty. The greater the level of uncertainty, the more stresses the decision maker(s) is likely to experience.

Certainly the vast majority of library selection decisions are straightforward and the degree of uncertainty is almost nonexistent. However, even the most apparently simple selection decision may well carry some unacknowledged baggage with it and have nothing to do with stress. Everyone has a belief system, biases, and a set of values. All of these may color our choices, but most are not always at the forefront of our cognitive behaviors. Can we really shut these out when doing our selection work? Do we even think about them from time to time and perhaps reflect on the collection choices we have made? The answer is probably somewhere between once or twice (when someone has brought the matter up) to never. The fact is, we cannot shut our beliefs on and off like a light bulb. Thus, keeping in mind we may, unconsciously, be building a collection that matches our values and beliefs is important in building a balanced collection.

One potential bias, and one that gets media attention from time to time, is political beliefs. Questions about the political bias of library collections are raised occasionally by those with conservative views. Will Manley (2010) did an opinion piece in which he wrote: "Despite our core value of intellectual freedom, librarians are not very tolerant of listening to points of view that stray from the basic liberal agenda. That is why conservative librarians are afraid to speak out: They fear professional ostracism" (p. 56). He went on to suggest there are several values that both the political left and the right have in common and the importance of using these commonalities to benefit everyone.

John Budd (2006/07) commented, "The collections of public libraries are sometimes used as evidence for political stances of librarians who select materials for the collections" (p. 78). In the article, Budd looked at a set of political titles that had over 900 circulations between 2003 and 2005. His data set was from the SirsiDynix ILS database that the company maintains for all the libraries (416) using its system, thus his study pool was large. Thirty titles met the 900 circulation threshold. Of that number, 10 were "right leaning," 7 "left leaning," and the balance fell somewhere in the middle (p. 86). For the group, those numbers would suggest there is a balance nationwide, at least for libraries with SirsiDynix systems. What the article did not or could not answer was, how balanced is an individual library's collection? It is likely there was a mixed pattern—some rights, some lefts, and some in between—just like the overall sample results. It also seems likely that those on the right or left of the center point were, to some degree, a function of selector beliefs or values. Some may have been the result of the service communities' primary reading interest—which is not inappropriate in itself. The question would be, from an ALA Code of Ethics point of view, were contrary views reasonably well represented?

The point of the above discussion is not to illustrate a right or wrong issue, but rather to highlight the fact that not all selection work is based on cognitive factors alone. We could have just as easily chosen topics such as religious beliefs, attitudes regarding gender issues, or rights of illegal immigrants—all of which have been debated by librarians in terms of services and collections.

Factors other than our beliefs, values, and philosophy of life can and do influence our selection decisions. Psychological and management literature on decision making shows that something as simple as our mood at the time

---

Check This Out

Questioning Library Neutrality, edited by Alison Lewis (Duluth, MN: Library Juice Press, 2008) contains 12 essays that address various aspects of attempts by libraries to maintain balanced collections and services. Topics range across the spectrum of concerns, such as policy issues, myths about library neutrality, and librarian activism. It is worth the effort to track down a copy.

---

can play a role in what we decide. Very happy or unhappy moods reduce our focus on the task at hand. When the work environment is unsettled or stressful, we also have a tendency not to focus as sharply on the decision-making activity. Anything that distracts us from our selection has the potential to make our choices a little less sound than might otherwise be.

We turn now to another affective issue that is widely acknowledged, at least by public and school librarians, when selecting collection items. Our opening quotations from Debra Lau Whelan and Susan Burke make the point there can be a moderately high amount of self-censorship in the field. Whether it arises from discomfort with confrontation, economic fear (job loss), fear of physical violence (yes, it has happened), or some other reason, the result is the same—IF rights of one or more people may be impacted.

Is librarian censorship something new? Not at all. You may recall in Chapter 2 we briefly discussed Arthur Bostwick's 1908 speech to the ALA convention "Librarian as Censor" in which he makes the case that librarians should *not* select certain materials. There are still a few librarians who long ago in their youth encountered a public or school librarian who believed that quality was *the* basis for having an item in the collection. Often they went further, as "reader advisers," to get children and young people to read only quality items (quality based on their value system) and occasionally not allow the individual to check out an item.

Starting after World War II, government and patriotic group efforts to control library materials related to "un-American" topics led many librarians to engage in self-censorship. One of the first major studies of self-censorship was Marjorie Fiske's 1959 book, *Book Selection and Censorship*. At that time, laws existed in California that required state employees to sign loyalty oaths. (That practice lasted into the 1960s.) Pressure was felt to only have "patriotic" materials in library collections. One issue focused on schools teaching the principles of the United Nations, as well as having materials in the library supporting those principles. There was great pressure not to have such material in school libraries. The California Library Association became so concerned about the situation and its commitment to IF that it commissioned a study of the matter, administered by Fiske. One of the oldest favorite test questions in a collection development class was some version of: "Is selection a form of censorship?" Librarians often waffle or weasel-word their view about such a question, as Fiske illustrated in a quotation from a librarian in her study: "We haven't been censoring but we have been 'conservative'. After all, this is a conservative community and that is how parents want it to be" (Fiske, 1959, p. 62).

Fiske's overall findings were, among other things, that two-thirds of the librarians admitted they self-censored some of the time, and 20 percent did so regularly (p. 68). A good article about the events and the study is Cindy Mediavilla's (1997) "The War on Books and Ideas: The California Library

---

Something to Ponder

A question for you: didn't the statement quoted from Fiske's report reflect the view that collections reflect local interests? Another question: how far should you go to provide materials that do not appear to reflect local interests in the name of balance and IF?

Association and Anti-Communist Censorship in the 1940s and 1950s." Ethics, integrity, professional positions, and the real world do not always come together neatly or easily, at least not in terms of CM activities.

How warranted is the concern about being challenged on a selection? In an academic or special library environment the chances are small to almost nonexistent. However, in public and school settings, there is a reasonably high probability that some time during your career one of your choices will be challenged. Some sense of the frequency of reported challenges appeared in a 2002 article by Nicolle Steffen regarding challenges to material in Colorado public libraries. For 2001, 11 percent (13 libraries) of the public libraries reported one or more challenges (50 challenges for the year). The challenges were a mix of materials and activities—50 percent were for books, 30.6 percent were for videos, and the balance were for Internet, music, periodicals, and exhibits/events (p. 9). She also looked at data from 1998 to 2001 and reported that 43.9 percent of the challenges were for adult materials and 42.7 percent were for children's items (p. 10).

A recent review (mid-2011) of the Colorado State Library's Website for more recent material shows the latest complete analysis was for 2009. Although a higher percentage of libraries reported having a challenge (16.5 percent) during this more recent time period, only 48 items were challenged—the lowest number in a decade according to the report. The types of material challenged did not change very much—52 percent books, 27 percent video, 8 percent for both computer/Internet concerns and periodicals, and 2 percent each for audio books and music. The four highest reasons for the challenges, in 2009, were sexuality explicit material, offensive language, unsuited for the age group, and nudity, which were all between 10 and 19 percent of the total reasons. Violence, "other," and antifamily were between 5 and 8 percent. The full list, as well as the entire report, is available at http://www.lrs.org/documents/fastfacts/289_Challenges_Public_Libraries_2009.pdf. Interestingly, 2010 preliminary data showed 98 materials challenges were made, much higher than the previous report (http://www.lrs.org/public/statsresults.php?year=2010&all=on&allchall=on&canned=on). However, these are preliminary data, and a full report may "edit out" some of these challenges as duplicates.

Although school media center data are not as easily located, one source of information is the ALA's OIF, which tracks challenges to library materials. OIF reported that from 2001 to 2009, there were 4,659 such challenges reported. (Although it is noted that not all challenges or incidents are reported to OIF.) Of these challenges, "1,720 of these challenges (approximately 37%) were in classrooms; 30% (or 1,432) were in school libraries; 24% (or 1,119) took place in public libraries. . . . The majority of challenges were initiated by parents (almost exactly 48%), while patrons and administrators followed behind (10% each)" (http://www.ala.org/ala/issuesadvocacy/banned/frequentlychallenged/21stcenturychallenged/index.cfm).

Although very much related, challenges and censorship are not identical. ALA's OIF has five categories for the complaint/challenge process. An "expression of concern" is the lowest level; this happens when a person asks about an item and the person's comments/question is judgmental in tone, but the matter goes no further. An "oral complaint" is the second stage, but again there is no follow-up by the person complaining. The third level is "written complaint." The fourth level is "public attack" in which there are efforts to get press attention, as well as gaining other people's support. This is a tactic most often employed by an organized group rather than a single person. "Censorship," the end of the process, is where there is a successful effort to remove or change the access status of the item challenged (http://www.ala .org/ala/issuesadvocacy/banned/challengeslibrarymaterials/index.cfm).

Just because an item is challenged does not mean that censorship will necessarily be the outcome. For example, using the 2009 Colorado State Library data, of the 48 challenged materials, 6 percent were dropped for some reason, 71 percent resulted in no change of the item's status, 10 percent were "moved"—reclassified say from YA to the adult collection or access changed (some form of controlled access), and 13 percent were removed from the collection. Where you place "moved" on the scale of successful censorship efforts does not change the fact that, at least for that year, such efforts succeeded no more than 20 percent of the time.

The failure to succeed more often than not does not lessen the concern, pressure, or stress of going through such a challenge. There will be meetings, reports, and so forth that will be required in order to even resolve oral and written complaints, and if there are public attacks, the stress level will increase. In all but the smallest public libraries, the person that selected an item will not be alone—senior managers will carry much, but not all, of the burden of addressing the concern. In a school setting, there are rarely other professionals to share the load. Handling a challenge takes time, effort, and willingness to work extra time—the other duties do not go away just because of a challenge. Is it any wonder school media specialists think about and admit they sometimes don't select something they think has the potential for generating a challenge?

There are some steps to take to prepare for and, to some degree, reduce the chances of a full-blown challenge. Knowing the dangers of censorship and having a commitment to avoid it is not enough in today's world. Librarians must prepare for challenges long before there is a compliant. The first step in preparing for the eventual challenge is to prepare a policy statement about how to handle complaints, and have the policy approved by all the appropriate authorities. There is nothing worse than having no idea of what to do when facing an angry person who is complaining about library materials. Even with policies and procedures, the situation may escalate into physical violence (there have been cases of bruises all the way up to broken bones); without procedures, the odds of violence occurring increase.

A typical procedure is to have the individual(s) file a formal complaint by filling out a form that specifies what is at issue. For some individuals, just filling out the form reduces their concern(s), and the prospect of going through a formal process causes them not to go any further. Several organizations, such as the ALA and the National Council of Teachers of English, have recommended forms that are somewhat effective in defusing the immediate anger.

After the library develops the policies and procedures and they are approved, everyone working in public services needs to understand the procedure(s) and receive training in implementing the system. Sometimes role playing is helpful in reinforcing the training. ALA's OIF has a series of

---

From the Advisory Board

Carol Sinwell notes several challenges to the Fairfax County Public Library (FCPL) Collection Policy. For example, in the mid-1990s, objections were raised about the *Washington Blade*, a weekly newspaper focused on the homosexual community, being available as a handout in the libraries. Although the objection required FCPL to perform a complete examination of its collections, nothing was changed. The decision withstood highly publicized public participation by 200 to 300 people and was upheld by the county attorney. FCPL offered the compromise of placing the newspaper out of the reach of young children.

When FCPL receives challenges from users, such as a recent one by a Muslim group to a specific work of fiction, the challenger is asked if they have read the book; to define what is objectionable about the book; and to state what they wish to have done about the book. These concerns are then addressed through an established book reconsideration process. During this process, the challenged title is evaluated by FCPL librarians, who read the book and any published reviews. The librarians individually submit their written evaluations and their opinions as to how they think the request for reconsideration should be handled to the director of collection development. This input is evaluated and forms a basis for deciding the fate of the book. The complainant is notified in writing of the decision. After completing this process, the book, which the Muslim group had challenged, remained in the library collection. The collection is consistently evaluated and books are removed when they are inaccurate or are no longer current or in poor condition. The library receives 40,000 to 50,000 suggestions (in all forms) each year and averages five or six book challenges a year.

Sam Clay, director of the FCPL once stated: "If the Library is doing its job of representing all points of view, we have something in our collection to offend everyone" (http://www.lwv-fairfax.org/files/libraryprogram.pdf, p. R-7).

---

materials available with suggestions for what to do before a potential censor arrives (http://www.ala.org/ala/issuesadvocacy/banned/challengeslibrary materials/essentialpreparation/index.cfm). Another good source is Frances Jones's (1983) *Defusing Censorship: The Librarian's Guide to Handling Censorship Conflicts*; unlike many other topics, challenges to library materials is neither new nor has it changed much over time.

Major confrontations usually involve an organized group as well as intellectual freedom and free speech issues, which in turn revolve around interpretations of points of law and possible violations of existing law. Therefore, a challenge that gets to the attack level normally involves attorneys and judges rather than librarians and the community. We hear about the cases that reach the courts, but seldom about daily local problems. All cases start as local problems between the library and an individual or group from the community and are usually settled quickly. Depending on the nature of the material, the level of emotional involvement, and the prior administrative actions (that is, policies), the library may be able to quickly resolve the issue, or the problem may escalate until it reaches the courtroom.

Privacy

Why include a discussion of privacy in a book about collection management? The answer is because it is part of the complex issue of IF and libraries may, unknowingly, be allowing outsiders to collect personal information

---

Something to Watch

One privacy issue that is not directly related to CM activities, but still bears watching, is the use of radio frequency identification (RFID) in libraries. With RFID, transponders located in library materials are "read" wirelessly by a remote antenna, and data are collected on the item(s). As noted by Deborah Caldwell-Stone (2010): "Because RFID tags do not require a clear line of sight and allow multiple items to be read in a stack, far less time and human effort are spent on processing materials. Patrons using RFID-enabled self-check stations and automated sorting equipment further free up library staff for essential work. Handheld RFID readers can be moved along the shelving units to read the tags attached to books on the shelves, allowing for more efficient and frequent inventory of the library's collection" (pp. 38–39). However, privacy concerns and security flaws in RFID led ALA to create a resolution and series of "privacy principles" related to RFID in 2005 (http://www.ala.org/ala/aboutala/offices/oif/statementspols/ifresolutions/rfidresolution.cfm).

Caldwell-Stone's review of RFID technology ("Chapter 6: RFID in Libraries," *Library Technology Reports* 46, no. 8: 38-44) is well worth reviewing. Additional information on RFID is available from ALA's OIF: http://www.ala.org/ala/aboutala/offices/oif/ifissues/rfid.cfm.

---

from those using our services. Many libraries have a confidentiality policy, and ALA's Policy on Confidentiality of Library Records offers guidance here. The policy in most libraries requires that staff eradicate past circulation data from the system in order to preserve user confidentiality. Libraries with automated circulation systems are in a good position to ensure confidentiality as today's systems are designed to break the link between the borrower and the items upon the material's return and any associated fees are paid. If the circulation system used in a library requires that the name of a borrower appear on a book card or some other record traceable to the book involved, staff should render the name illegible as part of the discharging process.

All library staff must be familiar with the concept of confidentiality because it is also certain someday a citizen or government official will approach the staff with a request for information regarding someone's reading habits or use of other services. A staff member receiving such a request should politely, but firmly, refuse to comply and immediately report the request to their supervisor and otherwise follow the library's confidentiality policy.

Angela Maycock (2010) noted: "Privacy, one of the foundations of intellectual freedom, is a compelling concern for school librarians. We live in an era when more and more personal information is available online" (p. 68). She was discussing the fact that many library database vendors, like almost all commercial Web organizations, collect data about people using their services. Certainly the concerns libraries have regarding user confidentiality go beyond online database usage. There are three major user privacy issues for libraries. One relates to personal information the library collects about a person as part of its normal business practices (such as basic contact information for borrowers and what they borrow). The second issue is what vendors may collect from library users. The third issue is most important, that being who may access that information and under what conditions.

At a minimum, libraries have the name, address, and telephone numbers for all of their registered borrowers. Many also ask for, but usually do not require, an E-mail address. Not too long ago, when ILS circulation systems first became available, social security numbers were employed as the

---

From the Advisory Board

Virginia Walter comments on privacy and access to library materials:

Access issues are problematic for many children's librarians who consider themselves to be advocates for children. Yes, the ALA "Bill of Rights" affirms that access should not be denied because of age. Yet they acknowledge that parents have the right to control their child's access to library materials, or even to the library itself. Children are both legally and in practice dependent on their parents. They are often dependent on their parents to bring them to the library in the first place. Their parents must sign before a child can get a library card (although more than one street-savvy kid has forged his parent's signature). They can determine what a child may or may not read. Many fundamentalist religious parents refuse to let their children check out books about the occult, including folk tales about witches or those popular books about the boy wizard, Harry Potter. Sex education books can be another delicate area. Children's librarians know that it is usually *not* in the child's best interest to exacerbate the conflict between a parent and child who wants the latest popular vampire book, but they usually wish there were some way to empower these children to read what they want.

Privacy is another interesting issue. Almost every public library I know allows parents to routinely check their children's library records, usually because they want to know if everything has been returned. However, a few libraries—Santa Clara City, for one—require that the *child* approve a parent's access to the child's records. One rationale for this, aside from the legal opinion of some city attorneys that the right to privacy is not abrogated by age, is that the information on a child's library record has been used to determine a child's address and acquire access to a child that had been blocked legally, usually in a court case involving custody.

---

borrower's identification number in the system. That is no longer the case; however, the information may still be in the system unless there was a proactive effort to delete the data. Although today's circulation modules break the link between borrower and item upon return, the data may be on one or more system backup tapes. This information is something a library can control; further it has a legal obligation to do so—all the states and the District of Columbia have regulations or laws relating to library patron confidentiality. Libraries are also ethically bound not to reveal the reading habits of borrowers. This is consistent with ALA's Library Bill of Rights principles, intellectual freedom (the right to read and think whatever one wishes), as well as ALA's Code of Ethics, which states "we protect each library user's right to privacy and confidentiality with respect to information sought or received, and resources consulted, borrowed, acquired or transmitted" (http://www.ala.org/advocacy/proethics/codeofethics/codeethics). Only the reader and library staff, in the legitimate performance of their duties, have a right to know what resources a user consulted or checked out.

One area where the library does not have much control over is what vendors may be collecting about our users' interests as reflected in their interactions with the vendors' online databases. Trina Magi (2010) noted that the current "Web 2.0 environment . . . poses new challenges for librarians in their commitment to protect user privacy as vendors of online databases incorporate personalization features into their search-retrieval

---

Something to Watch

In spring 2011, the Reader Privacy Act of 2011 (SB 602) was introduced in the California State Legislature. The bill was sponsored by the Electronic Frontier Foundation (EFF) and the California affiliates of the American Civil Liberties Union (ALCU), in recognition of the amount of patron use data that electronic book vendors, such as Amazon, have at their disposal. If successful, the bill would "prevent a commercial provider of a book service from disclosing data without a warrant in a criminal case or a court order in a civil case" (Michael Kelley and Lynn Blumenstein, 2011, "California Moves to Safeguard Reader Privacy," *Library Journal* 136, no. 9: 15). Background information on the bill is available from EFF (http://www.eff.org/cases/sb-602-californias-reader-privacy-act-2011). The bill unanimously passed the Senate in May and was in committee at the time this volume was being prepared. Its outcome bears watching.

---

interfaces, thereby collecting personally identifiable user information not subject to library oversight" (p. 254). Most of the major online library product vendors have a prominently placed button on their opening search page that allows users to personalize their search—some examples are EBSCO's "MyEBSCOhost" and Emerald's "Your Profile."

What might vendors collect and do with such data? Even without personalization, many vendors have the option for E-mailing the requested file(s) to the person. That alone provides a vendor with two pieces of marketable information: what the person may be interested in and a means of contacting the person. The personalized profile can generate more marketable data. Magi (2010) reported that LexisNexis sells marketing lists such as "Homeowner" and "Relatives and Room Mates" (p. 268). Even without selling the information to third parties, a vendor may have potential income-generating data. Did you know that EBSCO is part of EBSCO Industries, which includes, among other operations, a fishing tackle manufacturer, a real estate firm, an office and technology furniture retailer, and rifle manufacturing company?

Magi's (2010) analysis covered 27 library vendor privacy policies—they all had such a policy. However, most were vague about what data they gather as a result of using their services and how they, or third parties, might use that information. Only a few had "opt out" features when it came to personalization. Overall, her assessment of vendor policies suggested that none would fully meet ALA's view of user confidentiality. She suggests that it is more a matter of vendors' lack of knowledge of the field's position on privacy and IF rather than some sinister profit-making effort. Essentially, the vendors are merely following the practices of most commercial Web companies (p. 267). She, and we, strongly suggest CM personnel, at the time of assessing the possible purchase of an online product, ask for and evaluate the vendor's privacy policy and, if necessary, negotiate changes that more closely reflect the profession's IF concerns.

Who may have access to information about what a person uses has become complicated since 9/11. As long as libraries have existed, police, government officials, ministers, parents, spouses, and others have asked libraries about the reading habits of borrowers. Only during the past 70 years, however, has the profession expressed a desire to keep circulation records confidential. In 1938, the ALA's Code of Ethics specified the confidentiality of

---

Check These Out

The following items explore the issues of privacy, libraries, and digital environment in more detail:

Barnes, Susan B. 2006. "A Privacy Paradox: Social Networking in the United States." *First Monday* 11, no. 9.

(http://firstmonday.org/htbin/cgiwrap/bin/ojs/index.php/fm/article/view/1394/1312)

Hsu, Julia (Chiung-wen). 2006. "Privacy Concerns, Privacy Practices, and Web Site Categories: Toward a Situational Paradigm." *Online Information Review* 30, no. 5: 569–586.

Litwin, Rory. 2003. "The Central Problem of Library 2.0: Privacy." In *Library Juice Concentrate*, ed. Rory Litwin, 71–74. Duluth, MN: Library Juice Press.

Magi, Trina J. 2011. "Fourteen Reasons Privacy Matters: A Multidisciplinary Review of Scholarly Literature." *Library Quarterly* 81, no. 2: 187–209.

Sturges, Paul, Eric Davies, James Dearnley, Ursula Iliffe, Charles Oppenheim, and Rachel Hardy. 2003. "User Privacy in the Digital Library Environment: An Investigation of the Policies and Preparedness." *Library Management* 24, no. 1: 44–50.

Woodward, Jennette. 2007. *What Every Librarian Should Know About Electronic Privacy*. Westport, CT: Libraries Unlimited.

---

library records, the first formal acknowledgment of this issue in the United States. Since 1970, the profession's stand on confidentiality has become stronger. Law enforcement officers, with a warrant or subpoena, may have access, others may not, except with a court order.

After 9/11, there was a change regarding access to library records, at least for federal law enforcement officers. The USA Patriot Act (P.L. 107-56) authorized warrantless searches as well as including a requirement that the library not communicate to anyone that such search occurred or was under way.

What data might be available from library records for law enforcement officials that they might more easily access elsewhere? Actually, not all that much. What a suspect might have been interested in, that relates to law enforcement's concerns, may well be available in more detail from those who know the person. Karl Gruben (2006) wrote, "In actuality, the Department of Justice does not have as much interest in what Johnny is reading as it does what he is looking at or emailing or Instant Messaging on the Internet, particularly since there is suspicion that the 9/11 hijackers communicated through Internet terminals available in public libraries" (p. 303).

First enacted in October 2001, the USA Patriot Act has been an ongoing concern for libraries. The full title of the act is Uniting and Strengthening America by Providing Appropriate Tools Required to Intercept and Obstruct Terrorism Act of 2001. Section 215 of the act allows the government to secure secret warrants to obtain "business records"—this includes library records and those from library database vendors for named individuals. The act also authorizes the issuance of National Security Letters (NSLs), which do not require a judge's review, that require organizations to secretly provide information. At least one library has been on the receiving end of such a letter. Between 2003 and 2005, the FBI issued over 140,000 NSLs (Pike, 2007, p. 18). If you are on duty when the FBI arrives, direct the person to the administrative office and let that office handle the situation. Do not offer assistance, even if the administrative office is closed and you are pressed to assist. One should not provide information until directed to do so by the senior library administrator or the library's legal counsel.

Access—Filtering

Filtering access to the Internet has been a recent hot topic for the general public, government officials, and libraries. Public and school libraries appear to be caught between the proverbial rock and a hard place on this issue, as long as they offer Internet access to the public and are short of funds for providing that access. Some of the general public, governing boards, and elected government officials want libraries to use filtering software that will deny access to certain types of sites. Others, believing in free speech (First Amendment), do not want filtering. The primary reason given for filtering is to keep children from having access to "unacceptable" sites.

The Children's Internet Protection Act (CIPA), enacted in 2000 as part of the FY2001 Consolidated Appropriations Act (P.L. 106-554), requires libraries and schools to install filters on their Internet computers and have an "Internet Safety" (acceptable use policy) in place if they want to receive federal funds for Internet connectivity (E-Rate funds). The penalty for not doing so is loss of federal funding. The intent of the law is to protect minors from pornography; however, implementing the law challenges the principle of intellectual freedom and hampers the effectiveness of the Web as a reference source. Public and school libraries have developed various policies on implementing CIPA, from installing filters on all public stations, installing filters on some stations designated for children, and declining to install filters at all. Some public libraries take a middle ground, either designating certain stations without filters as "adults only" or disabling filters upon the request of an adult (allowed by CIPA). A rather large number have chosen to forgo E-Rate funds in the name of IF and professional ethics.

Some of the cases involving libraries and filtering around the time CIPA was enacted reflected the problems that arise no matter which option is chosen (filter or no filter). For example, in Loudoun County, Virginia, the public library board of trustees adopted a policy in 1997 calling for the installation of filtering software on all public access computers that connected to the Internet. A citizens group (Mainstream Loudoun) filed a suit against the board in 1998. Their basic argument was that first, filters on all computers reduced everyone to the status of children, and second, filters cannot block access just to sites deemed inappropriate for children. (As an example of

---

Check These Out

Two excellent pieces that describe how filtering software works are Paul Resnick's 1997 *Scientific American* article "Filtering Information on the Internet" (276, no. 3: 62–64) and Steven J. Murdoch and Ross Anderson's chapter, "Tools and Technology of Internet Filtering," in *Access Denied: The Practice and Policy of Global Internet Filtering*, edited by Ronald Deibert, John Palfrey, Rafal Rohozinski, and Jonathan Zittrain (Cambridge: MIT Press, 2008, 57–73).

the limits on filtering, some filters would deny a person access to sites relating to breast cancer, because the word *breast* is considered a "stop" word.) Although the court held in favor of the plaintiffs, the board appealed the decision. Virginia later revised a section of its code (VA Code § 42.1–36.1) to include regulations requiring Internet filters in public libraries, as well as public and private school libraries (VA Code § 22.1-70.2).

At the same time as the Loudoun case was being heard, the other side of the issue was also in court on the other side of the country. The Pacific Justice Institute, an "organization specializing in the defense of religious freedom" (http://www.pacificjustice.org), filed a lawsuit in 1998 against the city of Livermore, California, and its public library on behalf of a mother, because it did not have filtering software in place (Minow, 1998, p. 1). According to the complaint, the woman's son had, on at least 10 occasions, downloaded images of nude women using library computers connected to the Internet. The suit was dismissed in January 1999, for the second time in a few months, on the basis that filtering was too restrictive of free speech and the right to receive free speech. Michael Millen, the attorney for the plaintiff, announced that he was appealing the decision (cited in Minow, 1998, p. 13).

The ALA prepared a Statement on Library Use of Filtering Software in 1997 (http://www.ala.org/ala/aboutala/offices/oif/statementspols/ifresolu tions/statementlibrary.cfm). Not everyone in the ALA agreed with this statement, and it was revised in November 2000.

What is the filtering environment like today? Essentially the dilemmas related to IF, filtering, and public libraries still bedevil both librarians and some members of their service community. A good article that covers the history of CIPA is by Paul Jaeger and Zhang Yan (2009). In their article, the authors made the point that public libraries and schools were singled out in CIPA in part because they provide children with Internet access. More important, earlier efforts to regulate Internet content (COPA, Child Internet Online Protection Act) were ruled unconstitutional, a violation of the First Amendment, which only left controlling Internet access by children (pp. 8–9).

Jaeger and Yan indicated that by 2005, 100 percent of the U.S. public schools had implemented CIPA filtering and "safety policies." In terms of public libraries, by 2008 only 38.2 percent had implemented filtering (pp. 9–10). The level of filtering is determined by the individual library or system, so not all filtering is equal. It is not "all or nothing" as some people believe. As mentioned previously, adults in public libraries that do use filtering software may request the staff disable the filter while the person uses the computer. That option for adults appears to be a good one; however, as Jaeger and Yan noted, there are problems in its implementation "including librarians not allowing the filter to be turned off, librarians not knowing how to turn the filter off, the filtering software being too complicated to turn off without injuring the performance of the workstation in other applications, or the filtering software being unable to be turned off in a reasonable amount of time" (p. 12). You have to wonder just how many librarians actually refuse

---

Check This Out

Helen R. Adams (2009) provided "Reflections on Ethics in Practice" (*Knowledge Quest* 37, no. 3: 66–69), giving some additional "how would you handle this" scenarios, most of which relate to privacy and access.

From the Advisory Board

Sandra Hughes-Hassell notes that another access issue that impacts school and public libraries is the practice of labeling or assigning a rating to books and other forms of media developed for children and teens. Pat Scales, a former school librarian and a member of the National Coalition Against Censorship's (http://www.ncac.org/) council of advisers, has provided a thoughtful piece on this practice titled "Weighing In: Three Bombs, Two Lips, and a Martini Glass," which was published in the August 2010 issue of *Booklist* (106, no. 22: 46).

---

to turn off a filter on the basis of personal values, or is it they are aware of how complicated and time consuming the process is and they don't communicate those facts? Also, once the person is finished working on the machine, the process must be reversed, taking yet more staff time. Other unanswered questions are, for libraries that do filter, do users know when they sit down to use a machine that it has filtering software and that, if it does, they have the right to request that it be turned off?

In between children and adults is a large group of library users—young adults. What about their IF rights in CIPA environment? As Barbara A. Jansen (2010) wrote, "the landscape of Web 2.0 offers various viewpoints, original information from many sources, and means to express ideas and share results with a wide audience" (p. 49). She also noted that, "In addition to blocking access to educationally viable resources . . . restricting access to social media sites in schools also calls into question the erosion of the principles of intellectual freedom for youth" (p. 48).

Bibliotherapy—Readers Advisory Activities

We now give you one last concept to ponder. It is not actually an IF issue, but it does have elements of ethics, privacy, and access associated with it and thus it is at least marginally related to what we do or do not select for the collection. The concept is bibliotherapy. A standard definition of the term is the "use of literature to bring about a therapeutic interaction between participant and facilitator" (Hynes and Hynes-Berry, 1986, p. 10).

Libraries frequently take the position in censorship challenges that reading or viewing something from a library collection does no harm. Yet there is evidence that reading can have a therapeutic impact on people and their behavior. The issue is complicated. To a degree, both positions have some merit. Some years ago John Berry (1992) explored the question of the impact of reading on people in a *Library Journal* editorial, noting:

> If words don't incite action, I'm in the wrong line of work. . . . If they don't motivate people to act, antisocially or otherwise, then our First Amendment is of little value and less importance. This is a tough contradiction for those of us who must argue the case against censorship. . . . We can't support free expression by saying it won't do any harm. It is obvious that the action triggered by words and pictures can do harm and often does. (p. 6)

The profession should devote more time to learning about the circumstances in which reading or viewing may cause someone to harm themselves, others, or property. Perhaps a course or two in bibliotherapy should be required of any professional working in public service areas and especially CM personnel.

Bibliotherapy is not a new concept; it is almost 100 years old in terms of its acknowledged application. Certainly almost all children's books written prior to the 1850s were didactic and written to teach certain values and behaviors. Perhaps such material should not be considered therapeutic; however, the intent was to achieve a desired behavior or value system. Perhaps the first use of the term bibliotherapy was by Samuel Crothers (1916) in an article about using books to help "troubled" individuals. In the early 1920s, Sadie Peterson Delaney, chief librarian at the Tuskegee Veterans Administration Hospital, was using books to help World War I veterans regain mental and physical abilities. For more than 34 years she was a leading spokesperson for and teacher of bibliotherapy (Gubert, 1993).

There is a link between bibliotherapy and readers advisory activities in libraries, best books lists, and selection. For example, Edwin Starbuck published two guides to literature for children and young people that would provide moral guidance—*A Guide to Literature for Character Training* (vol. 1, *Fairy Tale, Myth and Legend*, 1928, Norwood; and vol. 2, *Fiction*, 1930, Macmillan). A similar title was Clara J. Kircher's work *Character Formation Through Books* (Washington, DC: Catholic University of America Press, 1945). Another related title is Jim Trelease's *Read Aloud Handbook* (6th ed., New York: Penguin, 2006). Such books were designed to help parents and librarians in selecting the right books for a given purpose or age group.

In the late 1930s, W.C. Menninger, founder of the Menninger Psychiatric Clinic, incorporated bibliotherapy into his therapeutic treatment program. Until the post–World War II period, the therapy was focused on adults (Jones, 2006). Mental health professionals have established that in certain circumstances bibliotherapy is an effective treatment option in conjunction with other treatments (for example, see Timothy Apodoca and William R. Miller, 2003; Pieter Cuijpers, 1997; and Mark Floyd, 2003). Most bibliotherapists operate on the basis of several assumptions:

- The process is interactive; it involves both participant and facilitator.

- Literature encompasses all forms of communication—not just books.

- The process is both clinical and developmental.

- The process can be one-on-one or group based.

- The outcome is improved self-esteem and better assimilation of appropriate psychological or social values for the participant(s).

- The process is a therapy but draws heavily on the healthy aspects of the mind.

- The process depends on the facilitator's ability to select the appropriate material for the participant to read and consider.

The important key to the concept is to know the medical diagnosis and the content of useful materials. It is *not* thinking you know what is amiss and recommending something; that is tempting for all of us, but especially for librarians working with children and youth. It is about working with mental health professionals. Jami L. Jones (2006) gave some sound advice to librarians regarding mixing developmental reading, reader advisory/"coping" activities, and bibliotherapy: "Even recommending a book as part of reader's

From the Authors' Experience

Evans was a library intern in a Veterans Administration hospital while in library school. At that time, he had not heard of bibliotherapy. As part of his duties he took books and magazines to the locked psychiatric ward for patients.

The procedure required he call the ward and let them know that he was on his way. The elevator lobby for the psychiatric floor barely allowed for the book truck and two people. There were two locked doors between the lobby and the actual ward. A buzzer called a ward staff person to lock the doors and move the book truck into the locked area between the elevator and the ward. Here a psychiatrist examined every item on the book truck, often removing items. Any items requested by a patient had to be reviewed by the doctor assigned to that person.

About halfway through his internship he was given some background by the ward staff in what to put on the truck prior to going to the ward. He became a marginal team member in the sense that doctors and nurses asked him to inform them of any patient requests for specific items, and he was frequently asked to provide a detailed description of the titles' content. That assistance reduced the number of items the staff removed, but it never reduced the incorrect items to zero for any visit. The issue was, of course, there was always patient progress, or lack of, as well as patient turnover, which, in the absence of being involved on a day-to-day basis with the ward, meant he had incomplete information about what to bring on a given day.

That experience has always made Evans reluctant to suggest an item to people with the idea the material will help the person.

advisory may touch on bibliotherapy if the book is used to heal. . . . Concern kicks in when giving someone a book who has mental health issues morphs into therapy. . . . Perhaps one role for librarians in the science of bibliotherapy is to partner with mental health specialists to provide the names of books as well as specific passages that could be useful in therapy" (p. 26).

There is much we do not know about the relationship between reading or viewing something and later behavior. Perhaps when we know more, our freedom-to-read statements may need revision. In many ways, the issues of filtering are rather like this as well. If we need to protect children from Internet materials, is it not also likely that we need to protect them from other materials as well? Determining the effect or lack of effect of reading, viewing, and listening on behavior should be a high priority. The field makes the case for free and open access to all material for anyone at any time, yet there is evidence that reading, viewing, and listening to certain material by certain people at certain times does affect behavior in a positive or negative way.

Points to Keep in Mind

- Intellectual freedom is an important concept to think about and understand when you become engaged in CM activities.

- The ALA has a number of position documents that relate to IF, ethics, privacy, and access that provide sound starting points for your thinking.

- Selection decisions are a combination of both cognitive and affective factors.

- Ethical dilemmas are not uncommon in selection activities as you must try to balance personal beliefs and values with those of your profession.

- Privacy, in terms of library usage, is related to IF.

- Online library database vendors do collect personal data about users of their product(s) and do sell that information to third parties. That practice goes against the notion of library user privacy.

- CM staff should review a vendor's privacy policy during the selection process and negotiate terms that better protect user confidentiality, if necessary.

- The USA Patriot Act can have serious consequences for libraries, their staff, and their users.

- Because of CIPA, filtering is a given for school media centers.

- CIPA and public libraries are uncomfortable bedfellows. The number of public libraries that forgo federal funds for Internet connectivity is greater than those that accept the CIPA terms. However, it seems likely there will be ongoing issues between libraries that do not filter and some of its service community constituents to engage in filtering Internet access.

- Bibliotherapy does work in certain circumstances and the library profession does not have a sound understanding of the relationship between reading or viewing something and later behavior.

- Librarians should be cautious about recommending materials that will "help" a person as there is little certainty the results will be positive. Working with mental health specialists is the key to successful bibliotherapy.

A Closing Thought

A final thought about collection management: it is complex, challenging, and, at times, confusing. However, it is also personally highly rewarding and enriching. Enjoy the challenges, they are worth experiencing!

Works Cited

Apodaca, Timothy R., and William R. Miller. 2003. "A Meta-Analysis of the Effectiveness of Bibliotherapy for Alcohol Problems." *Journal of Clinical Psychology* 59, no. 3: 289–304.

Berry III, John N. 1992. "If Words Will Never Hurt Me, Then. . . . ." *Library Journal* 117, no. 1: 6.

Budd, John M. 2006/07. "Politics and Public Library Collections." *Progressive Librarian* no. 28 (Winter): 78–86.

Burke, Susan K. 2010. "Social Tolerance and Racist Materials in Public Libraries." *Reference and User Services Quarterly* 49, no. 4: 369–379.

Colorado State Library. 2009. "Challenged Materials in Colorado Public Libraries." http://www.lrs.org/documents/fastfacts/289_Challenges_Public_Libraries_2009.pdf.

Cornelisen, Wendy. 2010. "In My Opinion! Defining Intellectual Freedom." *Tennessee Libraries* 60, no. 1: 11. http://www.tnla.org/displaycommon.cfm?an=1& subarticlenbr=346.

Crothers, Samuel M. 1916. "A Literary Clinic." *Atlantic Monthly* 118, no. 3: 291–301.

Cuijpers, Pieter. 1997. "Bibliotherapy in Unipolar Depression: A Meta-Analysis." *Journal of Behavior Therapy and Experimental Psychiatry* 28, no. 2: 139–147.

Dahlstrom, Joe. 2010. "Intellectual Freedom—An Academic Responsibility." *Texas Library Journal* 86, no. 1: 28–29.

Fiske, Marjorie. 1959. *Book Selection and Censorship*. Berkeley, CA: University of California Press.

Floyd, Mark. 2003. "Bibliotherapy as an Adjunct to Psychotherapy for Depression in Older Adults." *Journal of Clinical Psychology* 59, no. 2: 187–195.

Gruben, Karl T. 2006. "What Is Johnny Doing in the Library? Libraries, the U.S.A. Patriot Act, and Its Amendments." *St. Thomas Law Review* 19, no. 2: 297–328.

Gubert, Betty K. 1993. "Sadie Peterson Delaney: Pioneer Bibliotherapist." *American Libraries* 24, no. 2: 124–125, 127, 129–130.

Hynes, Arleen M., and Mary Hynes-Berry. 1986. *Bibliotherapy—The Interactive Process: A Handbook*. Boulder, CO: Westview.

Jaeger, Paul, and Zhang Yan. 2009. "One Law With Two Outcomes: Comparing the Implementation of CIPA in Public Libraries and Schools." *Information Technology and Libraries* 25, no. 1: 6–14.

Jansen, Barbara A. 2010. "Internet Filtering 2.0: Checking Intellectual Freedom and Participative Practices at the Schoolhouse Door." *Knowledge Quest* 39, no. 1: 46–53.

Jones, Frances M. 1983. *Defusing Censorship: The Librarian's Guide to Handling Censorship Conflicts*. Phoenix, AZ: Oryx.

Jones, Jami L. 2006. "A Closer Look at Bibliotherapy." *Young Adult Library Services* 5, no. 1: 24–27.

Klinefelter, Anne. 2010. "First Amendment Limits on Library Collection Management." *Law Library Journal* 102, no. 3: 343–374.

Magi, Trina. 2010. "A Content Analysis of Library Vendor Policies: Do They Meet Our Standards?" *College & Research Libraries* 71, no. 3: 254–272.

Manley Will. 2010. "Conservatives Among Us." *American Libraries* 41, no. 10: 56.

Martin, Ann M. 2009. "Leadership: Integrity and the ALA Code of Ethics." *Knowledge Quest* 37, no. 3: 6–11.

Maycock, Angela. 2010. "Choose Privacy Week and School Libraries." *Knowledge Quest* 39, no. 1: 68–72.

Mediavilla, Cindy. 1997. "The War on Books and Ideas: The California Library Association and Anti-Communist Censorship in the 1940s and 1950s." *Library Trends* 46, no. 2: 331–347.

Minow, Mary. 1998. "Internet Lawsuits." *California Libraries* 8, no. 3: 1, 12–13.

Moshman, David. 2003. "Intellectual Freedom for Intellectual Development." *Liberal Education* 89, no. 3: 30–37.

O'Brien, David. 1981. *The Public's Right to Know: The Supreme Court and First Amendment*. New York: Praeger.

Pike, George H. 2007. "The PATRIOT Act Illuminated." *Information Today* 24, no. 5: 17–18.

Preer, Jean. 2008. *Library Ethics*. Westport, CT: Libraries Unlimited.

Quinn, Brian. 2007. "Cognitive and Affective Process in Collection Development." *Library Resources and Technical Services* 51, no. 1: 5–15.

Steffen, Nicolle O. 2002. "Challenging Times: Challenged Materials in Colorado Public Libraries." *Colorado Libraries* 28, no. 3: 9–12.

Whelan, Debra Lau. 2009. "A Dirty Little Secret: Self-Censorship: Self-Censorship Is Rampant and Lethal." *School Library Journal* 55, no. 2: 26–30.

Suggested Readings

Adams, Helen R. 2008. "The Code of Ethics and Intellectual Freedom." *School Library Media Activities Monthly* 24, no. 9: 31.

Adams, Helen R. 2010. "Intellectual Freedom Online: The New Battleground for Minors' First Amendment Rights." *Knowledge Quest* 39, no. 1: 10–15.

Alexander, Linda B., and Sarah D. Miselis. 2007. "Barriers to GLBTQ Collection Development and Strategies for Overcoming Them." *Young Adult Library Services* 5, no. 3: 43–49.

American Libraries. 2001. "Conference Call: Should Sect Meet State in the Stacks?" 32, no. 3: 37–40.

Bary, Karen, and Martin Garnar. 2002. "How to Handle Harry: When Mr. Potter Becomes a Problem." *Colorado Libraries* 28, no. 3: 13–16.

Best, Ricky. 2010. "Censorship or Selection? Academic Library Holdings of the Top Ten Most Challenged Books of 2007." *Education Libraries* 33, no. 2: 18–35.

Brewster, Liz. 2008. "The Reading Remedy: Bibliotherapy in Practice." *APLIS* 21, no. 4: 172–177.

Brewster, Liz. 2009. "Reader Development and Mental Wellbeing: The Accidental Bibliothrapist." *APLIS* 22, no. 1: 13–16.

Burke, Susan K. 2008. "Removal of Gay-Themed Materials from Public Libraries: Public Opinion Trends, 1973–2006." *Public Library Quarterly* 27, no. 3: 247–264.

Chaffee, Gary J. 2008. "Effects of the USA Patriot Act on Wyoming Libraries, Library Professionals, and Nonprofessionals." *Library Administration and Management* 22, no. 4: 183–198.

Chamra, Theresa. 2010. "Minors' First Amendment Rights: CIPA and School Libraries." *Knowledge Quest* 39, no. 1: 16–21.

Christensen, Peter G. 1999. "Justifying the Freedom to Read: From Democratic Right to Human Right." *Public Library Quarterly* 17, no. 2: 15–32.

Clay, Edwin S. 2001. "Collection Development: Getting the Point." *Public Libraries* 40, no. 5: 265.

Doyle, Robert P. 2010. *Banned Books: Challenging Our Freedom to Read*. Chicago: American Library Association.

Everhart, Nancy. 2010. "Intellectual Freedom and You." *Knowledge Quest* 39, no. 1: 6–8.

Farmer, Lesley S. J. 2005. "Ethics." *Education Libraries* 28, no. 1: 3.

Fernandez, Peter. 2009. "Online Social Networking Sites and Privacy: Revisiting Ethical Considerations for a New Generation Technology." *Library Philosophy and Practice* 11, no. 1: 1–9.

Fredrick, Kathy. 2009. "Privacy Please!" *School Library Media Activities Monthly* 25, no. 6: 43–45.

Gilbert, Ellen D. 2005. "Confidentially Speaking: American Libraries and the USA Patriot Act." *Library Philosophy and Practice* 8, no. 1: 1–7.

Harris, Frances Jacobson. 2009. "Ethics from Web 1.0 to Web 2.0." *Knowledge Quest* 37, no. 3: 56–61.

Hill, Susan N. 2005. "A View From the Right." *American Libraries* 36, no. 1: 45.

Jaeger, Paul T., John Carlo Bertot, Charles R. McClure, and Lesley A. Langa. 2005. "CIPA Decisions, Implementation and Impacts." *Public Libraries* 44, no. 2: 105–109.

Jaeger, Paul T., John Carlo Bertot, Charles R. McClure, and Lesley A. Langa. 2006. "The Policy Implication of Internet Connectivity in Public Libraries." *Government Information Quarterly* 23, no. 1: 123–141.

Jones, Barbara M. 2009. "Librarians Shushed No More: The USA Patriot Act, the Connecticut Four, and Professional Ethics." *Newsletter on Intellectual Freedom* 58, no. 6: 195, 221–223.

Kelsey, Marie. 2007. "Are We Lucky for the First Amendment? A Brief History of Students' Right to Read." *Knowledge Quest* 36, no. 2: 26–29.

Koehler, Wallace. 2006. "National Library Associations as Reflected in Their Codes of Ethics." *Library Management* 27, nos. 1/2: 83–100.

Kolencik, Patricia Liotta, and Carianne Bernadowski. 2007. *Teaching with Books that Heal: Authentic Literature and Literacy Strategies to Help Children Cope with Everyday Problems.* Columbus, OH: Linworth.

LaRue, James. 2002. "Cooking the Books: Is Book Burning Protected Speech?" *Colorado Libraries* 28, no. 3: 6–8.

LaRue, James. 2007. *The New Inquisition: Understanding and Managing Intellectual Freedom Challenges.* Westport, CT: Libraries Unlimited.

Lord, Catherine. 2003. "An Access Challenge Is a Customer Service Opportunity." *ALKI* 19, no. 2: 18–21.

Lu, Ya-ling. 2008. "Helping Children Cope: What Is Bibliotherapy?" *Children and Libraries* 6, no. 1: 47–49.

Meeler, David. 2008. "Is Information All We Need to Protect?" *Monist* 91, no. 1: 151–169.

O'Dell, Judith. 2009. "Libraries and the Future of Search." *Library Philosophy and Practice* 11, no. 1: 1–13.

Perrault, Anne Marie. 2011. "Rethinking School Libraries: Beyond Access to Empowerment." *Knowledge Quest* 39, no. 3: 6–7.

Reid, Michele M. 2009. "The USA Patriot Act and Academic Libraries." *College & Research Library News* 70, no. 11: 646–650.

Ryan, Mary L. 2010. "Does It Really Matter Who's Paying for Dinner?" *Journal of the Medical Library Association* 98, no. 1: 1–3. [Librarian ethics and vendors.]

Schrader, Alvin M. 1997. "Why You Can't 'Censorproof' Your Public Library: What Research Tells Us." *Public Library Quarterly* 16, no. 1: 3–30.

Sens, Jean-Mark. 2010. "'Not I Said the Pig: Who Defends Intellectual Freedom for Librarians?" *Library Philosophy and Practice* 12, no. 2: 1–4.

Spackman, Andy. 2010. "Our Conservative Ideals: The Profession's Values Are Not Solely Liberal Ones." *American Libraries* 41, no. 4: 25.

Spurlin, Candice J., and Patrick M. Garry. 2009. "Does Filtering Stop the Flow of Valuable Information? A Case Study of the Children's Internet Protection Act (CIPA) in South Dakota." *South Dakota Law Review* 54, no. 1: 89–96.

Stripling, Barbara, Connie Williams, Melissa Johnston, and Holly Anderson. 2010. "Minors and Internet Interactivity." *Knowledge Quest* 39, no. 1: 38–45.

Woolwine, David E. 2007. "Libraries and the Balance of Liberty and Security." *Library Philosophy and Practice* 9, no. 2: 1–17.

Woolwine, David E. 2009. "The Patriot Act and Early ALA Action: Habermas, Strauss, or Derrida?" *Library Philosophy and Practice* 11, no. 2: 1–11.

Index

About the Authors

G. EDWARD EVANS is an administrator, researcher, teacher, and writer. He holds several graduate degrees in anthropology and library and information science. As a researcher he has published in both fields and held a Fulbright (librarianship) and National Science Foundation (anthropology) Fellowship. His teaching experience has also been in both fields in the United States and the Nordic countries, in particular UCLA's Graduate School of Librarianship and Information Science. Most of his administrative experience has been in private academic libraries—Harvard and Loyola Marymount universities. He has retired from full-time work as Associate Academic Vice President for Libraries and Information Resources at Loyola Marymount University. In terms of his writing, he currently has eight titles in print, several of which have been translated into one or more of eight languages. Semiretired, he consulates for and volunteers at the Museum of Northern Arizona library and archives and the Flagstaff City–Coconino Country Library System.

MARGARET (MAGGIE) ZARNOSKY SAPONARO is currently Librarian for Journalism and Hearing and Speech Sciences at the University Libraries, University of Maryland, where she is responsible for collection management, reference, and instruction for these disciplines. Her prior work experience includes serving as Manager, Staff Learning and Development at the University of Maryland, as Associate Director of Learning Resources at the Alexandria Campus of Northern Virginia Community College, and as Librarian for the College of Human Resources at Virginia Polytechnic Institute and State University. She has also served as an adjunct faculty member for the University of Virginia. She is a member of the American Library Association, ACRL, and the Special Libraries Association. She holds an MLS from UCLA, with postgraduate work in the areas of personnel programs and public administration. Her research interests are in the areas of collection management, instruction, and emerging technologies in libraries.